Core Statistical Concepts
With Excel®

Sara Miller McCune founded SAGE Publishing in 1965 to support the dissemination of usable knowledge and educate a global community. SAGE publishes more than 1000 journals and over 800 new books each year, spanning a wide range of subject areas. Our growing selection of library products includes archives, data, case studies and video. SAGE remains majority owned by our founder and after her lifetime will become owned by a charitable trust that secures the company's continued independence.

Los Angeles | London | New Delhi | Singapore | Washington DC | Melbourne

Core Statistical Concepts With Excel®

An Interactive Modular Approach

Gregory J. Privitera

St. Bonaventure University

Darryl J. Mayeaux

St. Bonaventure University

Los Angeles | London | New Delhi
Singapore | Washington DC | Melbourne

FOR INFORMATION:

SAGE Publications, Inc.
2455 Teller Road
Thousand Oaks, California 91320
E-mail: order@sagepub.com

SAGE Publications Ltd.
1 Oliver's Yard
55 City Road
London EC1Y 1SP
United Kingdom

SAGE Publications India Pvt. Ltd.
B 1/I 1 Mohan Cooperative Industrial Area
Mathura Road, New Delhi 110 044
India

SAGE Publications Asia-Pacific Pte. Ltd.
18 Cross Street #10-10/11/12
China Square Central
Singapore 048423

Acquisitions Editor: Abbie Rickard
Editorial Assistant: Elizabeth Cruz
Production Editor: Kelly DeRosa
Copy Editor: Cate Huisman
Typesetter: C&M Digitals (P) Ltd.
Proofreader: Susan Schon
Indexer: Sheila Bodell
Cover Designer: Candice Harman
Marketing Manager: Katherine Hepburn

Printed in the United States of America

Library of Congress Cataloging-in-Publication Data

Names: Privitera, Gregory J., author. | Mayeaux, Darryl J., author.

Title: Core statistical concepts with Excel : an interactive modular approach / Gregory J.Privitera, St. Bonaventure University, Darryl J.Mayeaux, St. Bonaventure University.

Description: Thousand Oaks : SAGE Publications, [2018] | Includes bibliographical references and index.

Identifiers: LCCN 2018052435 | ISBN 9781544309040 (pbk. : alk. paper)

Subjects: LCSH: Microsoft Excel (Computer file) | Social sciences—Statistical methods.

Classification: LCC HF5548.4.M523 .P759 2018 | DDC 519.50285/554—dc23 LC record available at https://lccn.loc.gov/2018052435

This book is printed on acid-free paper.

19 20 21 22 23 10 9 8 7 6 5 4 3 2 1

• Contents •

• Detailed Contents •

• Preface to the Instructor •

Philosophical Approach

Proficiency with using Excel®* is a key skill set students need when going to most graduate schools in the behavioral sciences. There is a need for resources that can "bring to life" statistical concepts in an interactive way. Excel is an excellent platform from which to create interactive exercises that "show" core statistical concepts to students. From this viewpoint, and on the basis of years of experience and student feedback, we were inspired to write a book that professors could truly teach from—one that connects statistical concepts to applications with Excel using current, practical research examples in a way that is approachable for students. This book is designed not only to engage students in using statistics to summarize data and make decisions about behavior, but also to emphasize the ongoing spirit of discovery that emerges when using today's technologies to understand the application of statistics to modern-day research problems. How does the text achieve this goal? It exposes students to statistical applications in current research and gives them step-by-step instruction for using Excel software as a useful tool not only to manage but also analyze data—all through the use of the following key themes, features, and pedagogy.

Themes, Features, and Pedagogy

Emphasis on Student Learning

- **Organization that builds upon skills and concepts.** The book is organized so that the learning units follow a logical flow both in terms of technical skills (from more basic skills in Excel to more complex) and conceptually (from descriptive to inferential statistics). This organization will make the book accessible regardless of whether a student is using it in a class to understand the concepts of statistics or to sharpen his or her technical skills in Excel. For professors, this book will essentially provide lesson plans with learning tools.

- **Section-opening vignettes.** We open each new section with an introductory vignette that connects students to the material using everyday language. These vignettes make accessible the information that will be introduced and help students to see "the bigger picture" for the content being taught.

---

*Microsoft® Excel® is the registered trademark of Microsoft Corporation.

- **Modular approach in each learning unit.** Each learning unit is created to largely stand alone such that students can pull out any given learning unit and be able to navigate the examples in it without requiring reading of previous learning units.

- **Definitional formulas for inferential statistics.** We illustrate the meaning of what inferential statistics reveal by using definitional formulas. The computational complexity of definitional formulas as compared to computational formulas is neutralized by the computational power of Excel.

- **Core statistical concepts appendix.** To help the learning units stand alone, we pull out core statistical concepts, such as *degrees of freedom, normal distributions,* and *scales of measurement,* into stand-alone lessons in an appendix. This appendix allows students to review each learning unit, and then, as concepts come up that are relevant across multiple learning units, they can readily find the information they need to brush up or simply check their progress as they move through each learning unit.

- **Additional features.** Additional features in each learning unit are aimed at helping students pull out key concepts and recall important material. For example, key terms are bolded, boxed, and defined as they are introduced to make it easier for students to find these terms when reviewing the material and to grab their attention as they read the learning units. At the end of the book, each key term is summarized in a glossary, and templates for all Excel files used in the book are provided for students; answer keys are provided for instructors.

Focus on Current Research

- **Current research examples.** Many of the statistics computed in this book are based on or use data from published research. This allows students to see the types of questions that behavioral researchers ask while the students are learning about the statistics researchers use to answer research questions. Students do not need a background in research methods to read through the research examples, which is important, because most students have not taken a course in research methods prior to taking a statistics course.

- **Balanced coverage to reflect the field of statistics today.** We take into account recent developments in the area of statistics. With concerns for null hypothesis significance testing, we highlight and emphasize the importance of testing assumptions for hypothesis testing and further explore alternatives to include confidence intervals. Throughout the book, students are taught to manage and analyze data responsibly.

Integration of Excel to Introduce Statistical Concepts

- **Step-by-step exercises.** In most learning units, we include a stepwise approach for each exercise. This makes the book more user-friendly and makes it easier for students to follow along with the exercise provided. The steps also promote a stronger understanding of the concepts being illustrated and make it easier for students to see which Excel skills are needed as they work through each exercise.

- **Skill set toolbox.** In each learning unit, we include a section labeled the "Toolbox," which outlines the skills in Excel that students will master in the unit. It makes the book more student-friendly by providing students with one place they can go to find the Excel skills that they can master in each learning unit.

- **Global Excel skills appendix.** Likewise, there are global skills in Excel students will need across the learning units, such as formatting cells, anchoring cell references, and distinguishing between formulas and functions. This appendix allows students to review these globally necessary skills for each learning unit in one place, instead of having to find where such concepts were initially introduced in other learning units.

In addition, there is one more overarching feature that we refer to as *teachability*. This book was written not only with the student in mind; it was also written with the instructor in mind. Here are some brief highlights of what you will find in each learning unit:

Learning Unit Overviews

Learning Unit 1. Mean, Median, and Mode

This learning unit explores measures of central tendency, how they are computed, and when they are used. An emphasis is placed on interpreting and utilizing Excel to compute the mean, the median, and the mode. Students learn to appropriately use these measures to describe data for many different types of distributions.

Learning Unit 2. Variability

This learning unit explores variability. We illustrate to students what variability is actually measuring and provide simple explanations to connect variability with central tendency. An emphasis is placed on interpretation and utilizing Excel to compute the range, the variance, and the standard deviation for populations and samples.

Learning Unit 3. Shapes of Distributions

This learning unit explores the normal distribution and skewed distributions. Particular focus is given to the normal distribution given the importance of this distribution for parametric statistics. To illustrate these distributions, Excel is utilized to show how shapes of distributions change side-by-side with the data being distributed.

Learning Unit 4. Probability and the Normal Distribution

This learning unit explores the calculation of probability of an event's occurrence and the relationship of that probability to the normal distribution. We integrate central tendency and variability to promote an understanding of the characteristics of a normal distribution and how to identify probabilities using the normal distribution. We connect the theoretical features of a normal distribution with an empirical demonstration in Excel.

Learning Unit 5. The Standard Normal Distribution: *z* Scores

This learning unit explores calculation of standardized scores. We emphasize understanding the relationship of one score to other scores in a normal distribution. We use Excel to illustrate these relationships with a large data set.

Learning Unit 6. Sampling Distributions

This learning unit explores the characteristics of samples taken from populations. Particular focus is on sampling strategies and the relationships of mean and variance in a sample with the mean and variance in a population. We use Excel to illustrate the characteristics of the distributions of sample means and sample variances from a population of scores.

Learning Unit 7. Hypothesis Testing: Significance, Effect Size, and Confidence Intervals

This learning unit explores steps in the formulation and evaluation of hypotheses. We emphasize multiple ways of evaluating hypotheses: probabilities of being correct and incorrect, shifts in the population, variance explained, and point and interval estimates. This provides the foundations for data analysis in each subsequent learning unit on inferential statistics.

Learning Unit 8. Power

This learning unit explores the relationship between effect size and power and between sample size and power. We focus on simple numerical examples to illustrate how increases in either effect size or sample size increase power.

Learning Unit 9. *t* Tests: One-Sample, Two-Independent-Sample, and Related-Samples Designs

This learning unit explores the evaluation of one or two means. In Excel we use three data sets to focus on how *t* tests use the mean and variance of the sample to evaluate the sample's relationship to the characteristics of the hypothesized population. We then turn to data analysis using functions built into Excel and using the Analysis ToolPak.

Learning Unit 10. One-Way Analysis of Variance: Between-Subjects and Repeated-Measures Designs

This learning unit explores the evaluation of more than two means of groups formed by the manipulation of one factor. In Excel we use two data sets to illustrate with definitional formulas how total variance is partitioned into two sources (between-subjects) or three sources (within-subjects). Those sources of variance are used to calculate ratios of variance obtained and interpreted in light of the ratios hypothesized for the population. We then turn to data analysis using the Analysis ToolPak.

Learning Unit 11. Two-Way Analysis of Variance: Between-Subjects Factorial Design

This learning unit explores the evaluation of four means from groups formed by the manipulation of two factors. In Excel we use one data set to illustrate with definitional formulas how total variance is partitioned into four sources. Those sources of variance are used to calculate ratios of variance obtained and interpreted in light of the ratios hypothesized for the population. We then turn to data analysis using the Analysis ToolPak.

Learning Unit 12. Correlation

This learning unit explores how one variable is used to explain the variance in another variable. In Excel we use definitional formulas and two data sets to illustrate the calculation and meaning of correlation coefficients. We also illustrate how to reduce the impact of an outlier by transforming raw scores into ranks. We then turn to data analysis using functions built into Excel.

Learning Unit 13. Linear Regression

This learning unit explores how one variable is used to predict the score on another variable. In Excel we use one data set to illustrate the calculation of a formula for a regression line. We evaluate the variance predicted by that line relative to the residual variance. We then turn to data analysis using functions built into Excel and using the Analysis ToolPak.

Appendix A. Core Statistical Concepts

This appendix reveals in small installments many core theoretical concepts in statistics. Those segments are referenced as needed throughout the learning units.

Appendix B. Global Excel Skills

This appendix reveals in small installments many technical skills needed in using Excel. Those specific skills described in different segments are referenced as needed throughout the learning units.

Appendix C. Statistical Tables

This appendix gives the tables needed to find critical values for the test statistics taught in this book.

Supplements and digital resources for this book include the following:

SAGE Instructor Resource Site
Includes data that can be provided to students.

- Excel workbooks with only the data included in the text for student use.

Also includes instructor resources, from sample syllabi for quarter and semester courses.

- For each Learning Unit, PowerPoint files with definitions of bolded terms, editable formulas, tables, and figures that are not Excel screen captures.

- Excel workbooks with data and solutions included in the text. For instructor use and distribution one spreadsheet of the workbook displays the formulas and functions used in the calculations. A second spreadsheet in the workbook displays the results of the calculations. This parallels the presentation figures with a panel containing formulas and functions and a panel containing the results of the calculations.

- For each Learning Unit, test bank of questions and multiple-choice answers for practice or assessment.

- For each exercise in each Learning Unit, supplemental data exercises, not appearing in the text, for practice or assessment. Instructors can provide a data-only workbook to the students and retain the solutions workbook for themselves.

- Instructor's manual providing overview of the resources.

Thank you for choosing *Core Statistical Concepts With Excel: An Interactive Modular Approach,* and best wishes for a successful semester!

Gregory J. Privitera
Darryl J. Mayeaux
St. Bonaventure, New York

• To the Student •

Microsoft Excel is a widely used tool for managing and analyzing data across the behavioral sciences. Proficiency with Excel benefits scientists and students, quite simply because they are surrounded by data. In applied and scientific fields of the behavioral sciences, you find terms like *data-driven, data-based,* or even *big data* increasingly used to identify the criteria for decision making by professionals. In your classes, you may be expected to create and report tables or figures for a research paper, or to summarize and describe a set of data. Even in your everyday life, Excel can be useful, such as for creating a file to manage bills, bank accounts, or household budgets.

In this book, we will assume that you know very little about using Excel, although you should be generally familiar with computer files and how to manipulate letters or numbers in them. For example, we assume that you are familiar with the following operations that are common across a variety of computer applications:

- launching an application

- opening a blank document

- opening an existing file

- downloading a file from a web page

- saving a file

- scrolling

- moving the cursor using either a mouse or keyboard keys

- selecting or highlighting using either a mouse or keyboard keys

- copying

- cutting

- pasting

- closing a file

- quitting an application

In this book, we created 13 *learning units*—many of which can stand alone. Where they do not stand alone, we connect you to the learning units where core knowledge is needed to master the learning unit material.

Each learning unit provides one or more exercises that illustrate key statistical concepts in behavioral statistics. A "toolbox" of skills in Excel and step-by-step exercises using those tools let you "see" interactive examples of core statistical concepts to promote a deeper understanding. Thus, you learn about Excel incidentally as you work through exercises that "bring light to" or make sense of the core statistical concepts in most introductory statistics courses in the behavioral sciences. We hope that you get as much out of engaging with this book as we did in writing it.

• Orientation to Excel •

Navigating through Excel can seem complicated. There are multiple ways to achieve some of the same ends, such as formatting cells. Rather than provide a comprehensive overview of Excel, the basic orientation presented here highlights aspects of the user interface that recur in many learning units of this text. We focus on methods that are common to Microsoft Excel for Mac (16.14.1) and Windows (16.0.8431.2270). Within the learning units, we occasionally refer the user to Appendix B: Global Excel Skills for a more detailed explanation of the functionality of Excel. All screen captures are from Excel for Mac OS. We note in the text or in a figure any differences between the Mac OS and Windows versions.

Workbooks, Worksheets, Cells

A workbook, shown in Figure 0.1, is composed of worksheets, encircled at the bottom of Figures 0.1a and 0.1b.

- Double click a worksheet's current name to rename it.
- Click the + to add a worksheet.
- Right click the name of the worksheet for the option to delete it.

A matrix of cells composes every worksheet. Every cell has a unique name to identify its location. That name consists of one or more letters designating a column and a number designating a row. In Figure 0.1, the active cell, the one in which you can work, is B7, as indicated by the arrows pointing to "B" and "7."

If a cell is not blank or empty, it can

- have one or more of its four sides with a darker line for a border,
- be shaded with a color, and
- contain letters, numbers, and other symbols.

When a cell is selected, the name of the selected cell and its contents are displayed in the formula bar, circled in gray above the arrows in Figures 0.1a and 0.1b.

Formulas and Functions

As mentioned above, cells can contain numbers, letters, and other symbols. In the simplest use, we can type words that act as labels for numbers or columns of numbers, such as "Participant ID", "Control Group", or "Mean". We can also keep track of numbers, such as IQ scores, household income, percentages, and proportions.

We will show you that Excel is far more powerful than simply keeping track of words and numbers. The power comes from the speed and accuracy of its calculations.

FIGURE 0.1 ● **Major features of a blank workbook in Excel. (a) Excel for Mac. (b) Excel for Windows.**

(a)

(b)

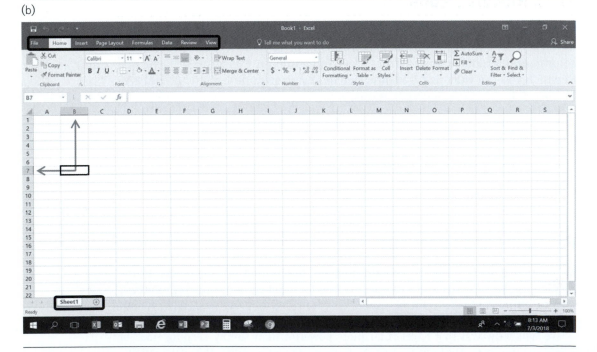

Cells that perform calculations start with an equal sign, =. What follows can be *formulas*, numbers with mathematical operators, such as =1+2, which will yield the answer 3.

Alternatively, what follows the = can be *functions*, which are predetermined commands for simple or complex computations. For example, we can add numbers with the function called SUM. Open and close parentheses, ( ), always follow the name of the function. Within the parentheses can be a series of *arguments* separated by commas. Functions can specify simple mathematical operations, such as =SUM(1,2), which will also yield the same answer as the formula above: 3. As we will see in the learning units contained in this text, there are functions to accomplish either simple or very sophisticated calculations. Those functions can be used in combination with mathematical operators. For example, the function specified above followed by a forward slash, / (the mathematical operator for dividing), can yield an average. For example, =SUM(1,2)/2 will yield the answer 1.5. We describe formulas and functions here to make you aware of the difference between the two.

Notice that when you type in the name of a function, an option to obtain help appears in a gray box hovering over an adjacent cell. It has a brief prompt of what is expected given the function that you named, SUM in this case. If you click on the name of the function, it will launch an Excel Help window. You will probably find this useful as we dive deeper into the use of functions.

Often through this text, we will introduce a mathematical concept with a formula. We may also use a formula in combination with a function. Once you have mastered the statistical concept, we introduce very powerful functions within Excel, where they are available, that vastly simplify calculations.

Tabs, Ribbons, Icons

To work with the cells in a worksheet, tabs are associated with different ribbons of icons. The names of the tabs are encircled at the top of Figure 0.1a and 0.1b. Figures 0.2 through 0.8 highlight many of the primary tabs that we will use in this text. Encircled on each ribbon are some of the icons frequently used in this book. If you are unable to find an icon or a caption, be sure to open the spreadsheet's window as wide as possible.

FIGURE 0.2 ● The Home tab contains icons for formatting text and numbers, aligning the content of cells, merging cells, filling content across cells, and sorting data. (a) Excel for Mac. (b) Excel for Windows.

(a)

(b)

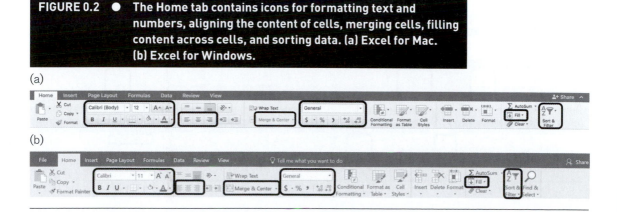

FIGURE 0.3 ●   The Insert tab contains icons for creating pivot tables, charts, and equations. (a) Excel for Mac. (b) Excel for Windows.

(a)

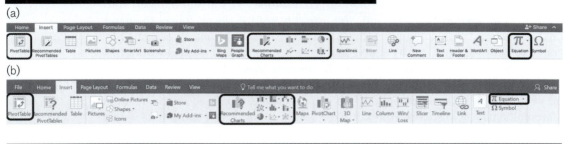

(b)

FIGURE 0.4 ●   The Formulas tab contains an icon for help for learning about and selecting formulas to use in cells. (a) Excel for Mac. (b) Excel for Windows.

(a)

(b)

FIGURE 0.5 ●   The Data tab contains icons for refreshing data, sorting data, and analyzing data. (a) Excel for Mac. (b) Excel for Windows.

(a)

(b)

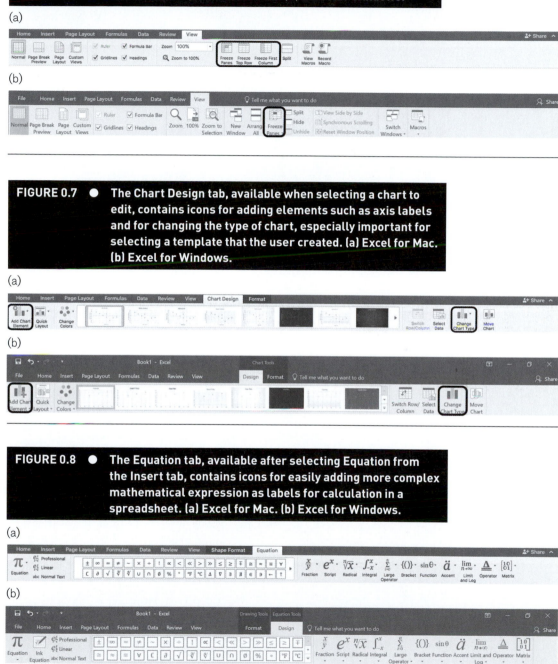

FIGURE 0.6 ● The View tab contains icons for freezing the display of rows and columns. (a) Excel for Mac. (b) Excel for Windows.

(a)

(b)

FIGURE 0.7 ● The Chart Design tab, available when selecting a chart to edit, contains icons for adding elements such as axis labels and for changing the type of chart, especially important for selecting a template that the user created. (a) Excel for Mac. (b) Excel for Windows.

(a)

(b)

FIGURE 0.8 ● The Equation tab, available after selecting Equation from the Insert tab, contains icons for easily adding more complex mathematical expression as labels for calculation in a spreadsheet. (a) Excel for Mac. (b) Excel for Windows.

(a)

(b)

• About the Authors •

Gregory J. Privitera is a professor and chair of the Department of Psychology at St. Bonaventure University, where he is a recipient of their highest teaching honor, the Award for Professional Excellence in Teaching, and their highest honor for scholarship, the Award for Professional Excellence in Research and Publication. Dr. Privitera received his PhD in behavioral neuroscience in the field of psychology at the State University of New York at Buffalo and continued to complete postdoctoral research at Arizona State University. He is an author of multiple books on statistics, research methods, and health psychology, as well as more than three dozen peer-reviewed scientific articles aimed at advancing our understanding of health and well-being. He oversees a variety of undergraduate research projects at St. Bonaventure University, where dozens of undergraduate students, many of whom are now earning graduate degrees at various institutions, have coauthored research in his laboratories. For his work with students and fruitful record of academic and research advisement, Dr. Privitera was honored as Advisor of the Year by St. Bonaventure University in 2013. He is also the award-winning author of *Research Methods for the Behavioral Sciences*, for which he received the Most Promising New Textbook Award from the Text and Academic Authors Association in 2014. In addition to his teaching, research, and advisement, Dr. Privitera is a veteran of the U.S. Marine Corps and is married with two children: a daughter, Grace Ann, and a son, Aiden Andrew.

Darryl J. Mayeaux is a professor of psychology and honors program director at St. Bonaventure University, where he was a recipient of their Junior Faculty Award for Professional Excellence. Dr. Mayeaux received his PhD in psychology at the University of California, Davis, and continued to complete postdoctoral research in the Department of Animal Science at UC Davis and the Department of Psychology at Cornell University as an NIH postdoctoral fellow. He is an author of peer-reviewed scientific articles on development in primates and on learning in laboratory rodent models. He oversees research projects in the biological psychology laboratory, where he has coauthored research with dozens of undergraduate students, many of whom have gone on to earn graduate degrees at various institutions. In addition to teaching, research, and advisement, Dr. Mayeaux is an enthusiastic participant in marathons and long-course triathlons. He is married to Gail Mayeaux.

Central Tendency and Variability

Words like *typically, usually,* or *often* describe what we think should happen. A basketball player *typically* makes her free throws. An employee *usually* meets a deadline. Airline flights *often* arrive on time. Describing central tendencies provides snapshots of behaviors and events in life. We often see sensational claims related to central tendency, such as a weight loss supplement where "on average, people lose 10 pounds in 7 days," or an insurance company claiming that "people who switch typically save about $300 per year." For everyday decisions, people typically like to know what will happen, or at least, to get a good sense of what should happen. What is *usual*, however, is not what always occurs. Occasionally, a player misses, and employees and airlines may be early or late. Not everyone loses weight at the same rate or saves the same amount of money. Borrowing a disclaimer from advertising, your mileage may vary.

In the behavioral sciences, the main trend and the variability around it are vitally important for the decisions that researchers make. Researchers studying mental disorders, for example, may count the types of symptoms expressed most often by patients to decide how to improve diagnosis; employee wellness programs may reduce employer healthcare costs. In each example, researchers use central tendency as a way to gauge decision making about those behaviors. We do expect, however, that events and behaviors will vary in their occurrence. For example, patients may express five symptoms of their disorder on average, but not all patients express exactly five symptoms; employee wellness programs may reduce employer healthcare costs by 15% on average, but not all wellness programs show this outcome. Whereas measures of central tendency take a snapshot of what the center of a distribution looks like, variability widens the lens to capture an image of the entire distribution.

Statistics provides a useful way to measure central tendency and variability. In this section, we introduce several measures that help researchers understand the center of a distribution and how observations on either side of that center. These measures provide easy to use summaries of many observations.

LEARNING UNIT 1

Mean, Median, and Mode

Excel Toolbox

Mathematical operators and symbols

- +
- /
- ( )

Functions

- SUM
- AVERAGE
- MEDIAN
- COUNTIF
- MODE

Other tools

- format cells
- sort
- fill down or paste
- freeze panes
- anchor cell reference

Statistics play a fundamental role in understanding phenomena every day, from weather forecasts to sports analysis to our own health (e.g., risks of disease, calories in our food). Likewise, you may read articles or even news reports asking questions such as,

"At what age do children say their first word?"

"How many children graduate college?"

"At what age do most people get married?"

"How many food calories do people eat?"

"What is the best price for purchasing a car?"

"How much time do people spend on social media?"

To answer these questions, we use tools that help describe or summarize representative values that can help us answer these questions. One representation describes what the center of the data looks like. Measures of **central tendency** are single values that have a "tendency" to be near the "center" of a distribution. Although we lose some meaning any time we reduce a set of data to a single score, statistical measures of central tendency ensure that the single score meaningfully represents a set of data. In this unit, we will use three measures of central tendency to describe samples and populations of data: the mean, the median, and the mode.

Measures of **central tendency** are statistical measures for locating a single score that is most representative or descriptive of scores near the center of a distribution.

The **mean**, also called an **arithmetic mean** or **average**, is the sum of a set of scores in a distribution, divided by the total number of scores summed.

The mean for a set of scores in an entire population is referred to as a **population mean**; the mean for a sample (or subset of scores from a population) is referred to as a **sample mean**.

Mean

The most commonly reported measure of central tendency is the mean. The **mean**, also called an **arithmetic mean** or **average**, is the sum of (Σ) a set of scores (x) divided by the number of scores summed, in either a population (N) or a sample (n). The formulas for the population mean and the sample mean are as follows.

The **population mean** (μ) is the sum of N scores (x) divided by N:

$$\mu = \frac{\sum x}{N}$$

The **sample mean** is the sum of n scores (x) divided by n:

$$M = \frac{\sum x}{n}$$

The Greek letter sigma, Σ, means "sum of," and the numbers or expression to the right of Σ are the items summed. In this formula, x represents each score in a data set. The Greek letter *mu*, μ (pronounced "mew"), identifies the population mean; the italicized M identifies the sample mean. You may sometimes see the sample mean identified with $\bar{x}$ (read "x-bar"). Although both notations are acceptable, M is the more common notation used to represent a sample mean in published research and thus is the notation used in this book.

You have probably calculated a mean, or at least seen one, such as your average grades on several exams in a class. With just a few scores, you can probably do this in your head. For example, take our question from the opening vignette about how much time people spend on social media. Suppose you have five people who spent 90, 180, 95, 125, and 110 minutes per day on social media; then the mean number of minutes per day is 120 (600 min per day ÷ 5 people). In the behavioral sciences, data sets typically consist of many more than five values; often, hundreds or thousands of values are measured. In these cases, it would be much more difficult to compute the mean without the aid of a technology. Excel facilitates such calculations.

To practice computing a mean, suppose the mean times that five consumers spend on social media per day are 90, 180, 95, 125, and 110 minutes per day. To make this calculation, launch or open Microsoft Excel as a blank document, a workbook. Save that workbook, with the name "Mean_Median_Mode.xlsx."

Type the word "Mean" in cells A2 and A3. To perform a simple calculation in cell B2, enter this formula: =(90+180+95+125+110)/5, as shown in Figure 1.1a. Hitting Enter (Return) displays the answer to this formula in cell B2; the mean number of minutes that people spend on social media in a day is 120, as shown in Figure 1.1b. This value, 120, is actually approximately how many minutes per day the average consumer is believed to spend on social media, according to estimates reported by Mediakix (2016).

FIGURE 1.1 ● (a) The formula or function in a cell that calculate means. (b) The result of the calculation specified by the formula or function in a cell.

(a)

	A	B	C	D	E
1					Raw Scores
2	Mean	=(90+180+95+125+110)/5		90	90
3	Mean	=SUM(90,180,95,125,110)/5		180	180
4				95	95
5				125	125
6				110	110
7					
8			Mean	=SUM(D2:D6)/5	=AVERAGE(E2:E6)

(b)

	A	B	C	D	E
1				Raw Scores	
2	Mean	120.0		90	90
3	Mean	120.0		180	180
4				95	95
5				125	125
6				110	110
7					
8			Mean	120.0	120.0

Appendix B

See **Appendix B1**, p. 301, for how to switch between displaying and hiding formulas in cells.

See **Appendix B2**, p. 301, for how to adjust the number of decimal places displayed and align cell contents.

Calculating an average can also be done with the help of functions. One such function, SUM, adds a series of numbers. So now, let us use the function called SUM. For our example of social media use, type the following function and its argument into cell B3: =SUM(90,180,95,125,110)/5, as shown in Figure 1.1a. Here was have a function (the SUM function) with its argument (the numbers separated by commas) and a formula (we entered "/" to divide the SUM by 5). We can enter more or fewer values, as required, although for our example, we had five values. If we stopped typing after the ")" and hit Enter, we would have obtained the total or sum of the five values. To find the mean, we create a formula by dividing the result of the SUM function by 5, that is, the total number of scores that were summed. Hitting Enter (Return) displays the answer to this formula. We again obtain the mean number of minutes that consumers spend on social media is 120 minutes per day. For cell B3, the combination of function and formula are shown in Figure 1.1a, and the result obtained is shown in Figure 1.1b. We present a mix of viewing contents of a cell and the results of the calculation to facilitate your learning of Excel as you practice computing statistical concepts.

Appendix B

See **Appendix B2**, p. 301, for how to adjust and merge cells and align cell contents.

There is still a better way to utilize functions in Excel. Instead of typing individual values all in a single cell as we did, we can instead list them individually in separate cells. This may be the kind of data format in which we have numbers that have been downloaded from a source or have been entered manually during data collection. Let us label cell D1 "Raw Scores" and merge and center it with cell E1.

In cells D2 through D6, enter the individual values, one in each cell, as shown in Figure 1.1. In cell C8, type "Mean" to keep track of our calculations. In cell D8, enter =SUM(D2:D6)/5. Notice that the arguments in this function refer to cells that contain the data. We don't have to list every cell. Separate the addresses of the first and last cells in a consecutive range with a colon, :, as in cell D8 in Figure 1.1a. When you hit Enter, you obtain the same answer as we computed previously, 120 minutes per day, as shown in Figure 1.1b.

Appendix B

See **Appendix B4**, p. 304, for how to highlight cells and for pasting or filling cell content.

We can simplify this even further. Excel has a function specifically for calculating a mean, called AVERAGE. To use this function, select cells D2 to D6. Then fill right or copy and paste to cells E2 to E6. In E8, type =AVERAGE(E2:E6), as shown in Figure 1.1a. Hit Enter. Same answer, 120 minutes per day, as shown in Figure 1.1b. Note that in Excel, the function AVERAGE calculates a mean, the term more commonly used in behavioral statistics.

Now we are ready to apply your knowledge to examples that are more representative of what you will encounter for statistical analysis in which much larger data sets are typically observed in the behavioral sciences.

Download Social_Media_Use.xlsx from the student study site: http://study.sagepub. com/priviteraexcel1e.

The spreadsheet that you downloaded contains minutes per day of social media use for 120 consumers. The consumer ID numbers appear in column A. The data are in column B. The data are labeled in the first three rows of columns A and B. (It is always a good idea label your numbers!) Scroll down to the bottom of the data set, which ends in cell B123. Label cell A125 "Mean".

Appendix B

See **Appendix B3**, p. 303, for how to freeze the display of a limited number of rows and columns in a spreadsheet.

To calculate the mean, compute the AVERAGE function in cell B125, as shown in Figure 1.2a. As a shortcut if you do not know the cell addresses of the entire range: After you type "=AVERAGE(", move your cursor to click, drag, and highlight the cell range with your data. Then type ")", close parentheses, at the end of the argument. Hit Enter.

FIGURE 1.2 ● Functions to calculate central tendency for a large data set. (a) The function in a cell. (b)The results of the calculations by the function.

(a)

	A	B	C	D
1		Social Media		Social Media
2		Use (Minutes)		Use (Minutes)
3	Consumer ID	Scores		Ranked
122	119	114		193
123	120	134		213
124				
125	Mean	=AVERAGE(B4:B123)		
126	Median	=MEDIAN(B4:B123)		
127	Mode	=MODE(B4:B123)		

(b)

	A	B	C	D
1		Social Media		Social Media
2		Use (Minutes)		Use (Minutes)
3	Consumer ID	Scores		Ranked
122	119	114		193
123	120	134		213
124				
125	Mean	120.0		
126	Median	115		
127	Mode	106		

Median

Suppose you measure the following set of scores: 2, 3, 4, 5, 6, 6, and 100. The mean of these scores is 18 (add up the seven scores and divide by 7). Yet the score of 100 is an outlier in this data set, which causes the mean value to increase so much that it fails to reflect most of the data. The mean can be misleading when a data set has an outlier, because the mean will shift toward the value of that outlier. For this reason, we consider alternative measures of central tendency. One alternative measure is the **median**, which is the middle value or mid-point in a distribution. Thus, half the scores in a distribution fall above the median and half below. In this section, let us see how Excel can be used to compute the median.

Return to the spreadsheet of social media use of 120 consumers. To start, let us manipulate the data a bit. To preserve the original data in column B, highlight and copy B1:B123. Click on the first cell in another column, D1. Now paste.

Appendix B

See **Appendix B5**, p. 305, for more on sorting.

To find the score in the middle, we rearrange the order of the data. We place the smallest value at the top, then the next largest below that, and so on until the largest value is last. This makes it easier to see the value in the middle. Highlight D4 through D123. From the Home tab, click the Sort and Filter icon, which displays a menu with the option to Sort From Smallest to Largest.

With minutes per day of social media use now arranged from smallest to largest, 42 minutes is at the top in D4 and 213 minutes is at the bottom in D123. To remind ourselves of this, type "Ranked" in D3. If we want to find the score in the middle, we have to find the score that would be between the 60th and 61st scores in the distribution when it is listed in rank order. This would be score number: (120+1)/2 = 60.5; it lies between the scores in rows 63 and 64. The score is 115 minutes, as shown in cells D63 and D64 in Figure 1.3.

Seeking scores in the middle of a distribution would be increasingly laborious as the number of values increased. Instead, using a function for determining the

FIGURE 1.3 ● Finding the median.

	A	B	C	D
1		Social Media		Social Media
2		Use (Minutes)		Use (Minutes)
3	Consumer ID	Scores		Ranked
62	59	193		115
63	60	153		115
64	61	156		115
65	62	89		115

The **median** is the middle value in a distribution of data listed in numeric order.

median of a set of data makes it easy. In cell A126, type "Median". In cell B126 type =MEDIAN(B4:B123), as shown in Figure 1.2a. The cell range in parentheses contains the data. It will return a value of 115 minutes, as shown in cell B126 in Figure 1.2b. A value of 115 is the value that falls at the center of the distribution; it is exactly the value between the 60th and 61st scores in the data set when the minutes of use of social media are listed in numerical order. Note that when we employ this Excel function, it is not necessary to rank the scores as when we first explained the longer way in illustrating the concept of median.

Mode

In addition to the mean and median, a third common measure of central tendency is the **mode**. The mode is the score that occurs most often in a data set. One advantage of the mode is that it is simply a count; no calculations or formulas are necessary to compute a mode. To find the mode, list a set of scores in numeric order and count the score that occurs most often. The mode is generally reported in research journals with other measures of central tendency, such as the mean and median. It is rarely used as the sole way of describing data. In this section, let us see how Excel can be used to compute the mode.

Return to the spreadsheet with minutes of social media use by 120 people. In the section on calculating the median, we ranked the minutes of use in column D. No single score is obvious when we look at the numbers quickly. Is the most frequent score 106? 114? 115? If we were doing this by hand, we would list each occurrence of a score and then count the number of times that it occurs. We'll do something similar with Excel to illustrate the concept of mode.

First, we can have Excel list each possible value for minutes of use in the range from lowest to highest. Then we can have Excel count the occurrence of each score. Scrolling in column D from row 4 to row 123, we see that the fewest minutes of social media use is 42, and the most is 213 minutes. In B130, type the low score, 42. In B131, type =B130+1, as shown in Figure 1.4a. This yields a value

> **Appendix B**
>
> See **Appendix B4**, p. 304, for pasting or filling cell content.

of 43, as shown in B131 in Figure 1.4b. We have the smallest two scores of the 172 possible unique scores from 42 to 213 minutes, inclusive. Select B131 and fill down to B301, or copy and paste through B301 for the remaining 170 scores.

Now for the counting. In cell C3, type "Frequency". From the individual scores listed from B4 to B123, Excel can count the frequency of occurrence of each unique time listed from B130 to B240. In C130, type =COUNTIF(B4:B123,B130), as shown in Figure 1.4a. This function expects two arguments; one is the range of cells to examine, B4:B123, and the other is the criterion for counting, the value listed in cell B130, which is 42. C130 now has the value of 1, the number of times that the score of 42 minutes occurred, as shown in Figure 1.4b.

Finding the frequencies of each number of minutes of social media use is *almost* as simple as filling down. Almost. Previously when we used the fill down feature, Excel automatically adjusted the cell addresses in each newly filled cell by one row. The formula in B131 refers to cell B130. When we filled down, the formula in B132

The **mode** is the value in a data set that occurs most often or most frequently.

FIGURE 1.4 ● Cells tabulating frequency of scores. (a) The formula or function in a cell. (b)The result of the calculations by the formulas or functions.

(a)

	B	C
1	Social Media	
2	Use (Minutes)	
3	Scores	Frequency
130	42	=COUNTIF(B$4:B$123,B130)
131	=B130+1	=COUNTIF(B$4:B$123,B131)
132	=B131+1	=COUNTIF(B$4:B$123,B132)
133	=B132+1	=COUNTIF(B$4:B$123,B133)
134	=B133+1	=COUNTIF(B$4:B$123,B134)

(b)

	B	C
1	Social Media	
2	Use (Minutes)	
3	Scores	Frequency
130	42	1
131	43	0
132	44	0
133	45	0
134	46	0

refers to B131. Excel automatically added one to the row number. If we look all the way down at B240, it refers to the value in B239. We refer to this result as a relative cell reference. The formula in each filled cell refers to the same relative position: one cell above.

A *point of caution*: If we did fill down from C130, it would correctly increase the cell reference from B130 to B131. The problem is that it would also increase the cell reference from B4:B123 to B5:B124, thereby failing to refer to the correct range of cells that contain data. To anchor the reference to the cell range for the data, we use a $ in front of the parts of the cell address that we want to hold constant. In this case, those would be the number 4 and the number 123: =COUNTIF(B$4:B$123,B130). Select cell C130 and fill down to C301. Each cell from C131 to C301 has just been filled and refers to the same data range above in column B. Cells C131 through C301, however, do have a different criterion for counting, which is specified in the cell immediately to the left in column B. Look closely at the rows of references in the arguments of the functions shown in column C of Figure 1.4a. The cell reference for the data range B4:B123 stays the same, but the cell reference for the criterion for counting frequency increases by one each row going down.

Appendix B

See **Appendix B6**, p. 306, for anchoring cell references in Excel.

We now have the frequency of each score in the range of minutes of use. Scroll through to find the largest frequency. Notice many of the large frequencies are toward the middle of the range of minutes of social media use per day. The most frequent score of minutes of use is 106 minutes; its frequency is 6. Small frequencies of extreme scores at the top and bottom flank the more common scores in the middle.

We asked you to copy the social media use data into column D and rank order them to facilitate understanding of median and mode. Again, it's not necessary to do that for the functions that we describe here. Type the label "Mode" in A127 so we don't lose track of what the number in B127 represents. In cell B127, type =MODE(B4:B123), as shown in Figure 1.2a. It returns the value of 106 minutes, as shown in Figure 1.2b, but it does not reveal how often it occurred. Of course, as we just saw, we can have Excel count the frequency of the occurrence of 106 minutes. In later learning units, we will show more powerful tools for displaying more informative summaries of data.

Choosing an Appropriate Measure of Central Tendency

In this learning unit we discussed three measures of central tendency: the mean, median, and mode. Note that each measure of central tendency informs us about a set of data in a different way. Each is informative. Choosing which measure of central tendency to use to describe a set of data depends largely on

> **Appendix A**
>
> See **Appendix A1**, p. 279, for a review of normal and skewed distributions.
>
> See **Appendix A2**, p. 282, for a review of scales of measurement.

- the type of distribution and

- the scale of measurement of the data.

In this section, we close our learning unit by evaluating the decision-making process for choosing an appropriate measure of central tendency.

The mean is typically used to describe data that are approximately normally distributed and are measured on an interval or ratio scale. The normal distribution is a symmetrical distribution in which scores are similarly distributed on either side of the mean. In a normal distribution, the median and mode have the same value as the mean. Because the mean is more informative (i.e., all values in a data set are included in its calculation), the mean is the most appropriate measure of central tendency for these types of distributions.

The mean is also appropriate for data that are measured on an interval or a ratio scale. The mean is used for data that can be described in terms of the *distance* that scores deviate from the mean. After all, one of the characteristics of the mean (described in Appendix A1) is that the mean balances a set of scores—in other words, it is the fulcrum of a distribution: It is located at exactly the point where the sum of the differences of scores from their mean is 0. For this reason, data that are described by the mean should meaningfully convey differences (or deviations) from the mean. Differences between two scores are meaningfully conveyed for data on an interval or ratio scale only. Hence, the mean is an appropriate measure of central tendency used to describe interval and ratio scale data.

The median is typically used to describe data distributions that are skewed and measures on an ordinal scale. A skewed distribution (described in Appendix A1) occurs whenever a data set includes a score or group of scores that fall substantially above (positively skewed distribution) or substantially below (negatively skewed distribution) most other scores in a distribution.

Scores that fall substantially above or below most other scores in a distribution will distort the value of the mean, making it a less meaningful measure for describing all data in a distribution. The value of the median, on the other hand, is not influenced by the value of these unusually high or low scores. For this reason, the median is more representative of all data in a skewed distribution and is therefore the most appropriate measure of central tendency to describe these types of distributions.

The median is also used to describe ranked or ordinal data that convey *direction* only. For example, the fifth person to finish a task took longer than the first person to finish a task; a child in first grade is in a lower grade than a child in fourth grade. In both examples, the ordinal data convey direction (greater than or less than) only. Because the *distance* (or deviation) of ordinal scale scores from their mean is not meaningful, the median is an appropriate measure used to describe ordinal scale data.

The mode is typically used to describe data with modal distributions and measures on a nominal scale. The mode can be used to describe most data that are measured. Sometimes it can complement other measures of central tendency. For example, to choose between two professors teaching the same class, it would be informative to know the average or mean grade students earned in each class. In addition to knowing the mean grade that students earned in each class, it would be informative to know the grade that most students earned in each class (the mode). Both measures—the mean and mode—would be informative. Thus the mode can be used to describe any distribution that has a mode; although it is typically reported with the mean for a normal distribution and with a median for a skewed distribution.

The mode is also used to describe nominal data that identify something or someone, nothing more. Because a nominal scale value is not a *quantity*, it does not make

TABLE 1.1 ● A Summary for When It Is Appropriate to Use Each Measure of Central Tendency to Describe Data

Measure of Central Tendency	Shape of Distribution	Measurement Scale
Mean	Normal	Interval, ratio
Median	Skewed	Ordinal
Mode	Modal	Nominal

sense to use the mean or median to describe these data. The mode is used instead. For example, the mean or median season of birth for patients with schizophrenia is not very meaningful or sensible. But describing these nominal data with the mode is meaningful when it is said, for example, that most patients with schizophrenia are born in winter months. Anytime you see phrases such as *most often*, *typical*, or *common*, the mode is being used to describe these data. Table 1.1 summarizes when it is appropriate to use each measure of central tendency.

LEARNING UNIT 2

Variability

Excel Toolbox

Mathematical operators and symbols

- –
- /
- ^2 [square]
- ^.5 [square root]

Functions

- MAX
- MIN
- MEDIAN
- QUARTILE
- QUARTILE.INC
- QUARTILE.EXC
- COUNT
- AVERAGE
- VAR
- VAR.P
- VAR.S

(Continued)

(Continued)

- STDEV
- STDEV.P
- STDEV.S

Other tools

- format cells
- sort
- fill down or paste
- freeze panes
- anchor cell reference

Suppose you learn that the average math SAT score for incoming college freshmen is about a 500 (out of 800). Knowing this can be helpful in terms of determining whether you scored better or worse than your peers. However, what about the scores for all other incoming college freshmen? Scores can vary across the country and across different schools. What is the highest score incoming college freshmen earn? What is the lowest score? What percentage of incoming college freshmen earn above or below a certain SAT score? The idea here is that the mean, like the median and mode, informs you only of scores at or near the center of the distribution, but tells you little to nothing of the remaining scores in the data set.

To better understand a data set, we need to determine where all the other scores are in relation to the mean. We need a measure of **variability**—that is, a way to measure the dispersion or spread of scores around the mean. By definition, the variability of scores can never be negative; variability ranges from 0 to ∞ (positive infinity). If four students receive the same scores of 8, 8, 8, and 8 on some assessment, then their scores do not vary, because they are all the same value—the variability is 0. However, if the scores are 8, 8, 8, and 9, then they do vary, because at least one of the scores differs from the others. Thus, scores can either not vary (variability is 0) or vary (variability is greater than 0). A negative variability is meaningless.

Measures of **variability** are measures of the dispersion or spread of scores in a distribution.

The focus of this learning unit is measures of variability: range, quartiles, interquartiles, variance, and standard deviation. As with central tendency, we explain how measures of variability are informative, descriptive, and useful for making sense of data.

Range

The simplest way to describe how dispersed scores are is to identify the range of scores in a distribution. The **range** is the difference between the largest value (*L*) and smallest value (*S*) in a data set. The formula for the range can be stated as follows:

$$\text{Range} = L - S$$

The range is most informative for data sets without outliers. For example, suppose you measure five scores: 1, 2, 3, 4, and 5. The range of these data is 5 – 1 = 4. In this example, the range gives a fair description of the variability of these data. Now suppose your friend also measures five scores: 2, 4, 6, 8, and 100. The range is now 100 – 2 = 98, because the outlier is the largest value in the data set. In this example, a range of 98 is misleading, because only one value is greater than 8.

Appendix A

See **Appendix A3**, p. 284, for a discussion on outliers in data distributions.

To perform a simple demonstration of range with IQ scores, launch or open Excel as a blank document. In column B, type in the numbers shown in cells B4 to B13 of Figure 2.1. By simply looking at the small set of numbers, you can see that the largest IQ score is 129 and the smallest IQ score is 73, a difference of 56 (i.e., 129 – 73 = 56).

Although Excel does not provide a function for calculating range, we can create a formula with two functions. In cell A15, type the word "Range" to keep track of what we calculate. The function MAX returns the largest value from a set of scores; the function MIN returns the smallest value from a set of scores. In cell B15, type: =MAX(B4:B13) – MIN(B4:B13), as shown in Figure 2.1a. Hit Enter. The value that returned when Excel subtracts the minimum IQ score from the maximum IQ score is 56.

Appendix B

See **Appendix B2**, p. 301, for formatting cells.

See **Appendix B5**, p. 305, for more on sorting.

Now you are ready to apply your knowledge to examples that are more representative of what you will encounter for statistical analysis, in which much larger data sets are typically observed in the behavioral sciences.

Download IQ_Scores_Variability.xlsx from the student study site: http://study.sagepub.com/priviteraexcel1e. This workbook contains two worksheets identified by names on the tabs at the bottom of the window. Use the worksheet titled "Range and Quartiles."

Column B contains 600 IQ scores from children in a long-term study of cognitive development. For this example, copy all 600 scores and paste them into column C. At the top, label column C "Sorted IQ Scores". Now sort just those scores in column C from smallest to largest. Although sorting is not necessary, it helps illustrate the concept of range and the concept of quartiles in the next section.

Range is the difference between the largest value (*L*) and smallest value (*S*) in a data set.

**FIGURE 2.1 ●   (a) The formula and functions for determining range.
(b) The result of the calculation of range.**

(a)

	A	B
1		
2		IQ
3		Scores
4	116	
5	89	
6	73	
7	88	
8	91	
9	102	
10	95	
11	120	
12	97	
13	129	
14		
15	**Range**	=MAX(B4:B13)-MIN(B4:B13)

(b)

	A	B
1		
2		IQ
3		Scores
4		116
5		89
6		73
7		88
8		91
9		102
10		95
11		120
12		97
13		129
14		
15	**Range**	56

**FIGURE 2.2 ●   (a) The formulas and functions for calculating range.
(b) The results of the calculations of range.**

(a)

	A	B	C
1			ranked
2		IQ	IQ
3		scores	scores
601		87	137
602		112	138
603		94	140
604			
605	range		=MAX(C4:C603)-MIN(C4:C603)

(b)

	A	B	C
1			ranked
2		IQ	IQ
3		scores	scores
601		87	137
602		112	138
603		94	140
604			
605	range		77

We find at the top of the scores in column C the smallest score, 63, and at the bottom the largest score, 140. In cell A605, type the word "Range" to keep track of what we calculated, as shown in Figure 2.2. In cell C605, enter =MAX(C4:C603) – MIN(C4:C603), as shown in Figure 2.2a. This returns a value for range of 77 IQ points (Figure 2.2b).

Although the range provides a measure of variability, it accounts for only two values (the largest value and smallest value) in a distribution. Whether the data set has five scores or 5 million scores, calculations of the range consider only the largest value and smallest value in that distribution. The range in a data set of $n > 3$ may be very informative, but a typical data set for human participant research includes hundreds or even thousands of data points. For this reason, many researchers prefer other measures of variability to describe data sets.

Quartiles and Interquartiles

In this section, we will examine an alternative measure of variability that is more robust in terms of being informative with large data sets and handling outliers in a data set.

Quartiles are really one way in which data are divided into equal parts. When data sets are divided into two or more equal parts, the parts are called **fractiles**. The median is one example of a fractile, because the **median** splits data in half or into two equal parts. Other fractiles include **quartiles**, **deciles**, and **percentiles**, which split data into 4 parts, 10 parts, and 100 parts, respectively. In this section, we describe quartiles and interquartiles because these statistics can often be used to describe data sets in behavioral research.

When splitting data into quartiles, the four quartiles split a data set into four equal parts. Relating this to percentiles, the upper values of the four quartiles are the 25th percentile (Q1), the 50th percentile (Q2), the 75th percentile (Q3), and the 100th percentile (Q4) of a distribution. Thus, the quartiles split a data set into four equal parts, each containing 25% of the data. The 25th percentile is called the **lower quartile**, the 50th percentile is called the **median quartile**, and the 75th percentile is called the **upper quartile**.

By separating data into quartiles, we can organize the data by dividing a data set into four equal parts. If a child's IQ is above the median quartile, for example, then you know that the child's score is better than the scores of 50% of the child's peers. The quartiles essentially mark percentile boundaries in a distribution. To locate each quartile in a data set, we follow three steps:

Step 1: Locate the median for all data. This is the median quartile (Q2).

Step 2: Locate the median for scores below Q2. This is the lower quartile (Q1).

Step 3: Locate the median for scores above Q2. This is the upper quartile (Q3).

In this section, we will show you how Excel can be used to accomplish each step. Return to the "Range and Quartiles" worksheet of the workbook IQ_Scores_Variability.xlsx that you downloaded for use with range.

Fractiles are measures that divide a set of data into two or more equal parts. Fractiles include the **median**, **quartiles**, **deciles**, and **percentiles**, which split data into 2 parts, 4 parts, 10 parts, and 100 parts, respectively.

The **lower quartile** is the median value of the lower half of a data set at the 25th percentile of a distribution.

The **median quartile** is the median value of a data set at the 50th percentile of a distribution.

The **upper quartile** is the median value of the upper half of a data set at the 75th percentile of a distribution.

To find the quartiles in this data set, we return to column C, in which we sorted all the scores from smallest to largest. Scrolling through these ranked scores gives a sense of the relative location of each of the quartiles in the distribution. To do this visually, we can use the simple formula for finding the median position of a data set, where n is the number of scores in the sample:

$$\frac{n+1}{2}$$

Median quartile: We know that the data set has 600 scores. So we use the formula given to identify that the score in the middle of the distribution is between the 300th and the 301st scores when listed in numeric order. Scroll to the IQ score in the middle of the distribution, which is the median IQ score. This is the score between the 300th and 301st scores in cells D303 and D304, respectively. We find that the median quartile is 100, which is the average of the two values in cells D303 and D304.

Lower quartile: For the lower quartile, we consider only the 300 values below the median, then find the median position of those 300 scores using the formula given. In this example, the middle of the distribution for the smallest 300 scores is between the 150th and the 151st scores when listed in numeric order. Scroll to the IQ score in the middle of the distribution for the smallest 300 scores. This is the score between the 150th and 151st scores in cells D153 and D154, respectively. We find that the lower quartile is 89, which is the average of the two values in cells D153 and D154.

Upper quartile: For the upper quartile, we consider only the 300 values above the median, and then find the median position of those 300 scores using the formula given. In this example, the middle of the distribution for the largest 300 scores is between the 450th and the 451st scores when listed in numeric order. Scroll to the IQ score in the middle of the distribution for the largest 300 scores. This is the score between the 450th and 451st scores in cells D453 and D454, respectively. We find that the upper quartile is 111, which is the average of the two values in cells D453 and D454.

We can also use Excel functions to find these values without needing to make these calculations and search the document. There are several methods for determining quartiles. For this text, we will present the method most commonly taught for basic statistics in the behavioral sciences. For this reason, we will not use the QUARTILE functions in Excel and instead use functions and formulas that emulate the process we just used to identify the quartiles. (See below: A Note on Methods for Calculating Quartiles.)

Step 1: We first find the median quartile of the 600 IQ scores by typing in cell C608 =MEDIAN(C4:C603) (Figure 2.3a), which returns the value 100 for the median quartile, Q2 (Figure 2.3b).

Step 2: Second, we consider only the 300 values below the median, then find the median position of those 300 scores by typing in cell C607 =MEDIAN(C4:C303) (Figure 2.3a), which returns a value of 89 for the lower quartile, Q1 (Figure 2.3b).

Step 3: Third, we consider only the 300 values above the median, then find the median position of those 300 scores by typing in cell C609 =MEDIAN(C304:C603) (Figure 2.3a), which returns a value of 111 for the upper quartile, Q3 (Figure 2.3b).

The values given in the Excel spreadsheet are the same values we found when we sorted the data and looked for the quartiles by searching the document. In cells A607 through A609, type "Lower Quartile", "Median Quartile", and "Upper Quartile", respectively, to label the values calculated.

Using quartiles to describe data also allows us to compute an **interquartile range (IQR)**, which has the advantage of describing range, but without the outliers that often fall in the top or bottom 25% of data. An IQR is the range of scores in a distribution between Q1 and Q3. Hence, the IQR is the range of scores, minus the top and bottom 25% of scores, in a distribution. The top 25% of scores are above Q3 (the 75th percentile); the bottom 25% of scores are below Q1 (the 25th percentile). To compute an IQR, we therefore subtract the lower quartile (Q1) from the upper quartile (Q3):

$$IQR = Q3 - Q1$$

To use Excel to compute IQR, go to cell C611, where we can subtract the lower quartile from the upper quartile to find the IQR by typing =MEDIAN(C304:C603)–MEDIAN(C4:C303) (Figure 2.3a). It returns a value of 22 (Figure 2.3b).

Some statisticians also use the **semi-interquartile range (SIQR)**, also called the **quartile deviation**:

$$SIQR = \frac{Q_3 - Q_1}{2}, \text{ also represented as } SIQR = \frac{IQR}{2}$$

In cell C612 (Figure 2.3a) we divide the IQR by 2 to find the SIQR by typing =(MEDIAN(C304:C603) – MEDIAN(C4:C303))/2 (Figure 2.3a). It returns a value of 11 (Figure 2.3b). Note that the subtraction of the lower quartile from the upper quartile must be enclosed in parentheses for this operation to be performed before the division by 2.

A Note on Methods for Calculating Quartiles

Methods for calculating quartiles vary. We present the method used most commonly in the behavioral sciences. Other methods of calculating quartiles can give different results, especially in smaller data sets, as illustrated in this section.

Suppose a researcher recorded the time (in seconds) that 14 patrons waited to be served after ordering their meal. The times recorded were 62, 68, 74, 76, 80, 84, 85, 87, 87, 88, 92, 93, 96, and 98. Figure 2.4 shows these 14 scores and the quartiles that would be computed by researchers using the Excel MEDIAN function, as we did in the previous section. In this section, we will use a different method using Excel that will lead to a slightly different calculation of the lower and upper quartiles for this data set.

Using the Excel MEDIAN function, the median quartile is 86, the lower quartile is 76, and the upper quartile is 92. This method uses as the lower and upper quartiles the medians of the bottom half and top half, respectively, of the distribution, as shown in the row labeled "MEDIAN" in Figure 2.4.

Another method for calculating the lower and upper quartiles, using the Excel QUARTILE function, interpolates a numerical value and may either include or exclude the median. Using this new function, when the lower or upper quartile falls between scores, Excel interpolates a value rather than taking a midpoint between scores as we

The **interquartile range (IQR)** is the range of values between the upper (Q_3) and lower (Q_1) quartiles of a data set.

The **semi-interquartile range (SIQR)** or **quartile deviation** is a measure of half the distance between the upper quartile (Q_3) and lower quartile (Q_1) of a data set, and is computed by dividing the IQR in half.

FIGURE 2.3 ● **(a) The formula and functions for determining quartiles and interquartile ranges. (b) The results of the calculation of quartiles and interquartile ranges.**

(a)

	A	B	C
1			Sorted
2		IQ	IQ
3		Scores	Scores
601		87	137
602		112	138
603		94	140
604			
605	Range		=MAX(C4:C603)-MIN(C4:C603)
606			
607	Lower Quartile		=MEDIAN(C4:C303,)
608	Median Quartile		=MEDIAN(C4:C603)
609	Upper Quartile		=MEDIAN(C304:C603)
610			
611	Interquartile Range		=MEDIAN(C304:C603)-MEDIAN(C4:C303)
612	Semi-interquartile Range		=(MEDIAN(C304:C603)-MEDIAN(C4:C303))/2

(b)

	A	B	C
1			Sorted
2		IQ	IQ
3		Scores	Scores
601		87	137
602		112	138
603		94	140
604			
605	Range		77
606			
607	Lower Quartile		89
608	Median Quartile		100
609	Upper Quartile		111
610			
611	Interquartile Range		22
612	Semi-interquartile Range		11

demonstrated above. Here, we will use two versions of Excel functions that utilize this method.

One version of an Excel function is the QUARTILE.INC function, which will give the same result as when the Excel QUARTILE function is used. To visualize how QUARTILE.INC works, we follow three steps, starting with assigning a position index to each score. These results are show in the row labeled "QUARTILE & QUARTILE.INC" in Figure 2.4.

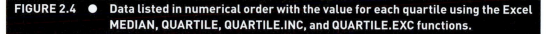

FIGURE 2.4 ● **Data listed in numerical order with the value for each quartile using the Excel MEDIAN, QUARTILE, QUARTILE.INC, and QUARTILE.EXC functions.**

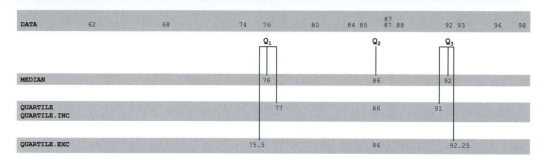

1. Assign a position index. The position index assigned to each score begins at 0 and ends with one less than the number of scores. Calculation of quartiles is based on $N - 1$ scores (14 scores – 1).

2. Find the lower quartile. The lower quartile is at the 25th percentile. Multiplying .25 by the 13 position indexes gives a position index of 3.25, one quarter of the way from the third position, 76, to the fourth position, 80. Because these two numbers are 4 apart, one quarter of the way is 1 second. We get a lower quartile of 77.

3. Find the upper quartile. The upper quartile is the 75th percentile. Multiplying .75 by the 13 position indexes gives a position index of 9.75, three quarters of the way from the ninth position, 88, to the tenth position, 92. Because these two are 4 seconds apart, three quarters of the way is 3 seconds. We get an upper quartile of 91.

Another version of an Excel function is the QUARTILE.EXC function, which will yield a different result. Here we follow the same three steps, but with a different method for assigning a position index to each score. These results are shown in the row labeled "QUARTILE.EXC" in Figure 2.4.

1. Assign a position index. The position index assigned to each score begins with 1 and ends with one more than the number of scores. Calculation of quartiles is thus based on $N + 1$ scores (14 scores + 1).

2. Find the lower quartile. The lower quartile is at the 25th percentile. Multiplying .25 by the 15 position indexes gives a position index of 3.75, three quarters of the way from the third position, 74, to the fourth position, 76. Because these two numbers are 2 apart, three quarters of the way is 1.5 seconds. We get a lower quartile of 75.5.

3. Find the upper quartile. The upper quartile is the 75th percentile. Multiplying .75 by the 15 position indexes gives a position index of 11.25, one quarter of

the way from the eleventh position, 92, to the twelfth position, 93. Because these two are 1 second apart, one quarter of the way is 0.25 seconds. We get an upper quartile of 92.25.

For the methods discussed, we can use the Excel MEDIAN function (results shown in Figure 2.4), or we can use two alternative functions: the Excel QUARTILE.INC function and the Excel QUARTILE.EXC function. Each function or method produces a slightly different estimate of the quartiles for the same data set. As a general rule, including the median yields a smaller semi-interquartile range; whereas excluding the median yields a larger semi-interquartile range.

Variance

A preferred estimate of variability is the variance, because it includes all scores, not just two extreme scores, to estimate variability. The **variance** measures the average squared distance that scores deviate from their mean. The value of the variance can be 0 (there is no variability) or greater than 0 (there is variability). A negative variance is meaningless.

There is a good reason that we square each deviation. The most straightforward way to measure variability is to subtract each score from its mean and to sum the deviations. The problem is that the sum will always be equal to zero. Table 2.1 shows an example of a small set of scores: 3, 5, and 7. Notice that the sum of the differences of scores from their mean is zero in the table. Here we would conclude that these scores do not vary from one another, but they do. To avoid this result, each deviation is squared to produce the smallest positive solution that is not zero.

Think of any solution to avoid this zero result as intentionally making an error. To minimize error, we need to ensure that the result we obtain is the smallest possible positive value—or the value with minimal error. It happens that squaring each deviation before summing the squared deviations will produce the smallest possible positive solution that is not zero. Thus, squaring deviations before summing provides a solution with minimal error.

Variance is the averaged squared distance that scores deviate from their mean.

TABLE 2.1 ● A List of Scores (Left Column) With a Mean of 5	
x	**x − Mean**
3	3 − 5 = −2
5	5 − 5 = 0
7	7 − 5 = 2
	Sum of deviations = 0

The sum of the differences of each score from their mean is 0 (right column). The sum of the differences of scores from their mean will always equal 0.

Another reason for squaring is that we can correct for this by taking the square root of the solution for variance (we will do this when we calculate *standard deviation* in the next section). This is not a perfect correction, but it is a simple and appropriate way to correct for squaring each deviation. Whether we have a sample or population of scores, these rules are the same: In both cases, squaring each deviation provides a solution with minimal error that can be corrected by taking the square root of the variance.

However, unlike calculations of the mean, the formula for variance does change for samples and populations, in terms of both notation and calculation.

The **population variance** is represented by the Greek symbol σ^2 (stated as "sigma squared"). Calculations of population variance are used to measure the dispersion of scores from their mean. A population variance, which is computed only for an entire population of scores, is defined by the following formula:

In this formula, the expression $x - \mu$ is a deviation; it is the difference of each score from its mean. This value is squared, then summed, in the numerator: $(x - \mu)^2$. The numerator for the variance formula is also called the **sum of squares (SS)** or the sum of the squared deviations of scores from their mean. The term N is the population size. To compute the population variance, split the steps into two parts:

Part 1: Calculate the *SS* (the numerator).

Part 2: Divide the *SS* by the population size (N).

If we compute variance without using a function in Excel, then this definitional formula for variance tells us exactly what we need to do in Excel; we will see it in action as we use Excel. To practice, return to the spreadsheet with 600 IQ scores. It is not necessary to sort the data. Use the worksheet called "Variance and Standard Deviation" in the workbook that you downloaded, IQ_Scores_Variability.xlsx. The data are in column B. We title column C "Deviation" (Score Minus the Mean) and column D "Square of Deviation". To keep track of what we calculate, in the following cells type these labels:

A605: Mean

A606: Sum

A607: Population Variance

A608: *df*

A609: Sample Variance

A610: Population Standard Deviation

A611: Sample Standard Deviation

We will follow these steps for the calculations shown in Figure 2.5. The functions and formulas are shown in Figure 2.5a and the resulting calculations are shown in Figure 2.5b.

Population variance is a measure of variability for the average squared distance that scores in a population deviate from the mean. It is computed only when all scores in a given population are recorded.

Sum of Squares (SS) is the sum of the squared deviations of scores from their mean.

- To calculate the mean in cell B605 enter =AVERAGE(B4:B603).

- In cell C4 (not shown in Figure 2.5), type =B4-B$605 to subtract the mean (cell B605) from the score in B4 and yield the deviation.

- In column D4 (not shown in Figure 2.5), square the deviation in C4 by typing =C4^2.

- Fill in the remaining 599 rows by selecting C4 and D4 and filling or pasting through cells C603 and D603.

- Enter into cell C606 =SUM(C4:C603).

- Enter into cell D606 =SUM(D4:D603). By squaring the deviations, we get nonnegative numbers. The result of summing the squared deviations in cell D606 is the *SS*.

Appendix B

See **Appendix B2**, p. 301, for how to adjust the number of decimal places that Excel displays.

See **Appendix B4**, p. 304, for how to highlight cells and for pasting or filling cell content.

See **Appendix B6**, p. 306, for anchoring cell references.

Notice in cell C606 that the sum of the deviations is 0. This will always be true, as introduced in Table 2.1. This is the reason we squared the deviations. Also, while the deviations in column C are a mix of values that are positive, negative, or zero, the squared deviations in column D are all positive or equal to zero. Again, the sum of the squared deviations of scores from the mean in cell D606 is the *SS*, which is the numerator for variance.

Our next step to finally get the population variance is to divide by the number of scores in the population, which is 600. To compute the population variance, follow this additional step, which is also shown in Figure 2.5:

- Enter into cell D607 =D606/COUNT(D4:D603). We obtain a population variance of 224.73.

- Excel offers several built-in functions for variance. There is one that will yield the same result that we just calculated. In cell B607 type =VAR.P(B4:603). We again obtain same value as in D607: 224.73.

To this point, we have treated the 600 IQ scores as a population of all scores. However, in the behavioral sciences, it is more common to analyze scores from a sample, which is a portion of all scores in a larger population. For this reason, let us now treat these 600 IQ scores as a sample of scores from a larger population and recalculate the variance for a sample.

Sample variance is a measure of variability for the average squared distance that scores in a sample deviate from the mean. It is computed when only a portion or sample of data is measured in a population.

The **sample variance** is used to measure how dispersed scores are from their mean when the data consist of less than an entire population of scores. The sample variance (denoted s^2) is defined by the following formula:

$$s^2 = \frac{\Sigma(x-M)^2}{n-1} \text{ or } \frac{SS}{n-1}$$

FIGURE 2.5 ● (a) The functions and formulas for calculating variance and standard deviation. (b) The results of the calculations of variance and standard deviation.

(a)

	A	B	C	D
1			Deviation	
2		IQ	(Score Minus	Square of
3		Scores	the Mean)	Deviation
601		87	=B601-B$605	=C601^2
602		112	=B602-B$605	=C602^2
603		94	=B603-B$605	=C603^2
604				
605	Mean	=AVERAGE(B4:B603)		
606	Sum		=SUM(C4:C603)	=SUM(D4:D603)
607	Population Variance	=VAR.P(B4:B603)		=D606/COUNT(D4:D603)
608	df			=COUNT(D4:D603)-1
609	Sample Variance	=VAR.S(B4:B603)		=D606/D608
610	Population Standard Deviation	=STDEV.P(B4:B603)		=D607^0.5
611	Sample Standard Deviation	=STDEV.S(B4:B603)		=D609^0.5

(b)

	A	B	C	D
1			Deviation	
2		IQ	(Score Minus	Square of
3		Scores	the Mean)	Deviation
601		87	-13	169
602		112	12	144
603		94	-6	36
604				
605	Mean	100.00		
606	Sum		0.00	134838.00
607	Population Variance	224.73		224.73
608	df			599
609	Sample Variance	225.11		225.11
610	Population Standard Deviation	14.99		14.99
611	Sample Standard Deviation	15.00		15.00

The numerator for sample variance is computed in the same way as that for the population variance: The numerator is the SS. It is the calculation in the denominator that differs for population and sample variance. To compute the sample variance, we divide the SS by the sample size (n) minus 1. The notations for the sample mean (M) and the sample size (n) have also changed to account for notation used with samples. To compute sample variance, we again split the steps into two parts:

Part 1: Calculate the *SS* (the numerator).

Part 2: Divide *SS* by (*n* – 1).

This calculation in Part 2, (*n* – 1), is also called **degrees of freedom (*df*)** for sample variance. Degrees of freedom are the number of scores that are free to vary in a sample. Basically, if you know the mean of a data set and the value of all scores in that data set except one, you can perfectly predict the last score (i.e., the last score is not free to vary). Suppose, for example, we have a sample of three participants with a mean score of 4 (*M* = 4). If we know the mean and we know that two of the scores are 3 and 4, then we know that the last score must be 5. Two of those three scores were free to vary. Thus, the $df = (n - 1) = 3 - 1 = 2$.

Appendix A

See **Appendix A12,** p. 298, for more on degrees of freedom for parametric tests.

We divide by (*n* – 1) in the denominator for sample variance because it happens to be the only way to ensure that the sample variance is an **unbiased estimator** of the population variance. Basically, we need to ensure that if we use the sample variance to estimate the population variance, then, on average, we hit the mark; meaning that, on average, the sample variance correctly estimates the population variance. Subtracting 1 in the denominator happens to be the only way to accomplish this.

To compute sample variance, we again compute the SS in the numerator and divide by the degrees of freedom, or (*n* – 1) in the denominator in Part 2. We will complete the following steps, which are shown in Figure 2.5:

The **degrees of freedom (*df*)** are the number of scores in a sample that are free to vary. All scores except one are free to vary in a sample: *n* – 1.

An **unbiased estimator** is any sample statistic, such as the sample variance when we divide *SS* by *n* – 1, obtained from a randomly selected sample that equals the value of its respective population parameter, such as a population variance, on average.

- Enter into cell D608 =COUNT(D4:D603)-1 to obtain the degrees of freedom.

- Enter into cell D609 =D606/D608 to obtain the sample variance: 225.11.

- Excel offers a function for sample variance as well. Enter into cell B609 =VAR.S(B4:B603). We obtain the same answer of 225.11.

The names of these two functions for population and sample variance differ in an obvious way. The function for population variance ends with a ".P", and the function for sample variance ends in ".S". Although a function called VAR calculates the sample variance, we recommend specifying whether your data set represents either the population or a sample by using VAR.P or VAR.S, respectively.

Standard Deviation

The **standard deviation**, also called the **root mean square deviation**, is the square root of the variance. Taking the square root of the variance basically "unsquares" the variance, and it is used as a measure for the average distance that scores deviate from their mean. The distance that scores deviate from their mean is measured as the number of standard deviations that scores deviate from their mean.

The **population standard deviation** is represented by the Greek letter for a lowercase *s*, called sigma: σ. The **sample standard deviation** is represented by a lowercase *s*. In research reports, you may also often see the sample standard deviation stated as *SD*. The notation for population standard deviation is as follows:

$$\sigma = \sqrt{\sigma^2} = \sqrt{\frac{SS}{N}}$$

The notation for sample standard deviation is as follows:

$$s = \sqrt{s^2} = \sqrt{\frac{SS}{n-1}}$$

Step 1: Compute the variance.

Step 2: Take the square root of the variance.

In Excel we can compute the population standard deviation for the 600 IQ scores by completing the following steps, which are shown in Figure 2.5:

- Enter into cell D610 =D607^.5 to obtain the population standard deviation of 14.99.

- Excel offers a function for the population standard deviation as well. Enter into cell B610 =STDEV.P(B4:B603) to obtain the population standard deviation. We obtain the same value of 14.99 as in cell D610.

In Excel we can compute the sample standard deviation for the 600 IQ scores by completing the following steps, which are also shown in Figure 2.5:

- Enter into cell D611 =D609^.5 to obtain the sample standard deviation of 15.00.

- Excel offers a function for the sample standard deviation as well. Enter into cell B611 =STDEV.S(B4:B603) to obtain the sample standard deviation. We obtain the same value of 15.00 as in cell D611.

As with variance, although a function called STDEV calculates the sample standard deviation, we recommend specifying either population or sample by using STDEV.P or STDEV.S, respectively.

Characteristics of the Standard Deviation

Although the standard deviation has many characteristics, we focus on four fundamental ones for samples and populations:

Standard deviation, also called the **root mean square** deviation, is a measure of variability for the average distance that scores deviate from their mean. It is calculated by taking the square root of the variance.

Population standard deviation(σ) is a measure of variability for the average distance that scores in a population deviate from their mean. It is calculated by taking the square root of the population variance.

Sample standard deviation (s) is a measure of variability for the average distance that scores in a sample deviate from their mean; it is calculated by taking the square root of the sample variance.

Appendix A

See **Appendix A4**, p. 285, for an explanation of the empirical rule for normal distributions.

See **Appendix A5**, p. 286, for an explanation of Chebyshev's theorem for any distribution (normal or not).

1. **The standard deviation is always positive**: $SD > 0$. The standard deviation is a measure of variability. Data sets can either vary (be greater than 0) or not vary (be equal to 0) from the mean. A negative variability is meaningless.

2. **The standard deviation is used to describe quantitative data**. The standard deviation is a numeric value—it is the square root of the variance. For this reason, the standard deviation is used to describe quantitative data, which can be continuous or discrete.

3. **The standard deviation is most informative when reported with the mean**. The standard deviation is the average distance that scores deviate from their mean. It is therefore most informative to report the mean and the standard deviation together. For normally distributed data, knowing just the mean and standard deviation can inform the reader of the distribution for close to all the recorded data. At least 99.7% of data fall within 3 SD of the mean for normal distributions (as described for the empirical rule in Appendix A4); at least 99% fall within 10 SD of the mean for any type of distribution (as described for Chebyshev's theorem in Appendix A5).

4. **The value for the standard deviation is affected by the value of each score in a distribution.** To change the standard deviation, you must change the distance of scores from the mean and from each other. Specifically, adding or subtracting the same constant to each score will not change the value of the standard deviation. However, multiplying or dividing each score using the same constant will cause the standard deviation to change by that constant.

The standard deviation is generally regarded as the most informative measure of variability. For this reason, you will come across the descriptive statistic throughout the published literature to describe variability in data sets.

LEARNING UNIT 3

Shapes of Distributions

Excel Toolbox

Mathematical operators and symbols

- –
- +
- /

Functions
- MIN
- MAX
- FREQUENCY [array function]

Other tools
- format cells
- anchor cell reference
- summarize with PivotTable
- create chart
- format chart

One way to make a data set more meaningful is to summarize how often scores occur using a *frequency distribution*. Frequency distributions summarize how often (or frequently) scores occur in a data set. To find the frequency of values, we must quite literally count the number of times that scores occur. In a **simple frequency distribution**, we can summarize how often each individual score occurs (**ungrouped data**) or how often scores occur in defined groups or intervals (**grouped data**). We often collect hundreds or even thousands of scores. With such large data sets with many different values recorded, it is generally clearer to summarize the frequency of scores in groups or **intervals**. When summarizing data this way, the data are called grouped data.

To construct a simple frequency distribution in Excel, follow three steps:

Step 1: Find the real range.

Step 2: Determine whether data will be ungrouped or grouped. If grouped, determine the width of the interval.

Step 3: Construct the frequency distribution with the array function FREQUENCY (or with a PivotTable as described in a subsequent section).

We will follow these three steps to construct frequency distributions for a normally distributed set of IQ scores and a skewed distribution of household incomes.

Normal Distribution Created With Frequency Array Function

Download IQ_Scores_Distribution.xlsx from the student study site: http://study.sagepub.com/priviteraexcel1e. This workbook contains a single spreadsheet with participant identification numbers in column A and IQ scores in column B.

Step 1: Find the real range. The **real range** is one more than the difference between the largest and smallest numbers in a list of data. For clarity, we will do this in several stages. We'll find the smallest (minimum) score and the largest (maximum) score, and then subtract the smallest score from the largest score and add one to that difference to find the real range.

First type into the following cells the labels to the right of the cell address, as shown in Figure 3.1:

D4: Smallest

D5: Largest

D6: Real Range

Next, enter into the following cells the function or formula to the right of the cell address, as shown in Figure 3.1a:

E4: =MIN(B4:B603)

E5: =MAX(B4:B603)

E6: =E5–E4+1

A **simple frequency distribution** is a summary display for (1) the frequency of each individual score or category (ungrouped data) in a distribution or (2) the frequency of scores falling within defined groups or intervals (grouped data) in a distribution.

Using **ungrouped data** means counting frequencies of each individual score.

Using **grouped data** means counting frequencies in defined groups of scores or intervals of scores.

An **interval** is a discrete range of values within which the frequency of a subset of scores is contained.

The **real range** is one more than the difference between the largest and smallest number in a list of data.

Step 2: Determine whether data will be ungrouped or grouped. If grouped, determine the width of the interval. Because the real range is so large, we will determine the interval width for grouping data. The **interval width** is the range of values contained in each interval of a grouped frequency distribution. To find this, we divide the real range by the number of intervals chosen. The recommended number of intervals is between 5 and 20. Anything less provides too little summary; anything more is often too confusing. Regardless, *you* choose the number of intervals. The computation for the interval width can be stated as follows:

Appendix B

See **Appendix B2**, p. 301, for formatting cells.

$$\text{Interval Width} = \frac{\text{Real Range}}{\text{Number of Intervals}}$$

The sample size of 600 is large enough that it will probably give us enough points in each of 13 intervals. Type into cell D7 "Interval Width". To calculate 13 interval widths that are equal in size, divide the real range by 13. Enter into E7 =E6/13, as

FIGURE 3.1 ● **Creating a frequency distribution. (a) Formulas, functions, and array functions. (b) Results of the calculations of formulas, functions, and array functions.**

(a)

	A	B	C	D	E	F
1						
2						
3	Child	IQ Score			IQ Score	
4	1	116		Smallest	=MIN(B4:B603)	
5	2	89		Largest	=MAX(B4:B603)	
6	3	73		Real Range	=E5-E4+1	
7	4	88		Interval Width	=E6/13	
8	5	91				
9	6	102		Upper Limit of Bin	IQ Score	Frequency
10	7	95		62	62 or smaller	=FREQUENCY(B4:B603,D10:D23)
11	8	120		=D10+E$7	63-68	=FREQUENCY(B4:B603,D10:D23)
12	9	97		=D11+E$7	69-74	=FREQUENCY(B4:B603,D10:D23)
13	10	129		=D12+E$7	74-80	=FREQUENCY(B4:B603,D10:D23)
14	11	95		=D13+E$7	81-86	=FREQUENCY(B4:B603,D10:D23)
15	12	103		=D14+E$7	87-92	=FREQUENCY(B4:B603,D10:D23)
16	13	117		=D15+E$7	93-98	=FREQUENCY(B4:B603,D10:D23)
17	14	66		=D16+E$7	99-104	=FREQUENCY(B4:B603,D10:D23)
18	15	133		=D17+E$7	105-110	=FREQUENCY(B4:B603,D10:D23)
19	16	124		=D18+E$7	111-116	=FREQUENCY(B4:B603,D10:D23)
20	17	108		=D19+E$7	117-122	=FREQUENCY(B4:B603,D10:D23)
21	18	127		=D20+E$7	123-128	=FREQUENCY(B4:B603,D10:D23)
22	19	92		=D21+E$7	129-134	=FREQUENCY(B4:B603,D10:D23)
23	20	94		=D22+E$7	135-140	=FREQUENCY(B4:B603,D10:D23)
24	21	78			141 or larger	=FREQUENCY(B4:B603,D10:D23)

An **interval width** is the range of values contained in each interval of a grouped frequency distribution.

(Continued)

FIGURE 3.1 ● (Continued)

(b)

	A	B	C	D	E	F
1						
2						
3	Child	IQ Score			IQ Score	
4	1	116		Smallest	63	
5	2	89		Largest	140	
6	3	73		Real Range	78	
7	4	88		Interval Width	6	
8	5	91				
9	6	102		Upper Limit of Bin	IQ Score	Frequency
10	7	95		62	62 or smaller	0
11	8	120		68	63-68	8
12	9	97		74	69-74	20
13	10	129		80	74-80	35
14	11	95		86	81-86	53
15	12	103		92	87-92	75
16	13	117		98	93-98	92
17	14	66		104	99-104	90
18	15	133		110	105-110	73
19	16	124		116	111-116	66
20	17	108		122	117-122	40
21	18	127		128	123-128	35
22	19	92		134	129-134	7
23	20	94		140	135-140	6
24	21	78			141 or larger	0

shown in Figure 3.1a. It yields a result of 6, as shown in Figure 3.1b, which we will use for the interval width.

Step 3: Construct the frequency distribution with a frequency array function or a PivotTable. We show two methods in Excel to construct a frequency distribution. The first method, a frequency array function, facilitates a fundamental understanding of what a frequency distribution represents. The second method, a more widely used PivotTable, yields the same results but tends to move away from the fundamental mechanics of constructing a frequency distribution.

First, we construct a frequency distribution using the frequency array function. In Excel the term *array* refers to a range of cells. An array function is more complex than other functions that we demonstrate in this text. **Array functions** perform complex calculations based on information from a range of cells. In this case, the calculation will be the number of values that fall within an interval width. The complexity is that the interval widths are defined by Excel comparing values across cells rather than referring to just one cell.

An **array function** is an Excel function that performs complex calculations based on information from a range of cells.

We divide this into three stages: Stage 1: Find the upper limit of each interval. Stage 2: Create labels for each interval. Stage 3: Count the scores within the interval. The frequency array function in Excel first creates an interval, which it calls a **bin**, to catch all scores lower than a specific value. The next bin contains all scores that are larger than the previous bin up to a specified interval width. For clarity we will type some more precise labels for each bin of IQ Scores. We then use the array function called FREQUENCY to count the number of scores in each bin.

We start by typing into the following cells the labels to the right of the cell address, as shown in Figure 3.1:

D9: Upper Limit of Bin

E9: IQ Score

F9: Frequency

Stage 1: Find the upper limit of each bin. Let us start defining the upper limit of each bin. Because values in the first bin in Excel are smaller than a selected value, we will type 62 in D10. We can confirm that there are no values equal to or lower than 62 in our distribution by looking at cell E4, which shows a smallest value of 63, as shown in Figure 3.1b.

The sizes of subsequent bins are determined by the interval width that we calculated in cell E7. Excel counts values that are larger than those in the previous bin but equal to or smaller than those at the upper limit of the current bin. To get the upper limit of the next bin, we add 6 to the upper limit of the previous bin. (All the values in this data set are whole numbers; we do not need to be concerned about decimals. However, we could enter decimal values if we chose to do so.)

In cell D11, type =D10+E$7, which returns a value of 68, as shown in Figure 3.1. This is the first of our 13 bins (i.e., our intervals). Select cell D10 and fill or paste its contents through D23. Now we have the upper limits in 13 bins. The last bin's upper limit is equal to the largest value in the data set, an IQ score of 140. See column D in Figure 3.1a and 3.1b.

Stage 2. Create labels for each interval. For clarity, we recommend typing into cells E10 to E24 the exact range of IQ scores contained in each interval. These labels provide two advantages. First, they are a clear and explicit statement of the interval for the data grouped into that bin. Second, they facilitate graphing the frequency distribution. (This step, however, is not necessary for using the array function FREQUENCY.) Cell D10 specifies all values of 62 or smaller. Therefore, type "62 or smaller" into cell E10. Cell D11 specifies values up to 68 that were not included in the previous bin. Therefore, type "63–68" in cell E11. Continue this pattern down to cell E23, as shown in column E in Figure 3.1. The array function FREQUENCY will also count any values above the upper limit of the largest bin that we specify. Thus, one additional bin will be created beyond the upper limit we specify. Type into cell E24 "141 or Larger".

> **Appendix B**
>
> See **Appendix B6**, p. 306, for anchoring cell references.
>
> See **Appendix B4**, p. 304, for how to highlight cells and paste and fill cell contents.

Bin is a term in the Excel array function FREQUENCY that is equivalent to interval width.

Stage 3. Count the scores within the Interval. When we use the array function FREQUENCY, Excel will use the upper limit of each bin to count all values equal to or less than that number but greater than the upper limit of the adjacent smaller bin. The function will do this up to the upper limit specified and then create one more bin for any values above the upper limit of the largest bin.

In cell F10, type =FREQUENCY(B4:B603,D10:D23), as shown in Figure 3.1a. Cells B4 to B603 compose the data array, the first argument in the function. Cells D10 to D23 compose the bins array, the second argument in the function. Hit Enter for Excel to calculate the frequency of all scores of 62 and smaller. As expected, this returns a value of 0, as shown in Figure 3.1b. Now we must have this function populate cells F11 to F24. This cannot be done by pasting or filling down. Array functions are executed by pressing simultaneously the key combination of Control + Shift + Enter (Return). (Array functions are sometimes called CSE functions for that key combination.) There are three components to completing the array function:

1. Specify where we want to place the array function by highlighting F10 (this is where the frequency function was entered) to F24.

2. Press the Function 2 (Fn2) key. Depending on your keyboard, this may be a combination of two keys, Fn and F2. Excel will now highlight in two different colors your data array and bins array.

3. Press and hold the Control and Shift keys and hit Enter (Return).

Excel calculates the frequencies in each of the bins defined by the upper limits in cells D10 to D23. Additionally, it counts and displays in F24 any values larger than 140. This last frequency shown in cell F24 is also 0, as expected. See column F in Figure 3.1a and 3.1b.

Normal Distribution Created With a PivotTable

Now that we are more familiar with what a frequency distribution represents, we can create the same distribution using a PivotTable. To create a PivotTable, we need at least two columns of data. In this example, column A contains a unique number for each participant and column B contains IQ scores. To create the PivotTable, click anywhere in column A or B, then click the Insert tab, and click PivotTable.

Excel will select the labels we entered in row 3 and the 600 contiguous cells containing participant numbers and IQ scores. In the Create PivotTable dialog box that appears in Figure 3.2, the upper part displays the highlighted cell range, which you can change as needed. In the lower part, select "Existing worksheet," and then click in the cell you want to be the upper left of the PivotTable. For comparison, we can make this line up with the one we have already created with the frequency array function by selecting cell H10.

Click OK in the Create PivotTable dialog box to display the PivotTable Fields dialog box, as shown in Figure 3.3a. The labels "Child" and "IQ Score" in cells A3 and B3 indicate the sources of the fields used in the PivotTable. At the top of the

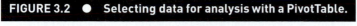

FIGURE 3.2 • Selecting data for analysis with a PivotTable.

Create PivotTable

Choose the data that you want to analyze.

◉ **Select a table or range**

    Table/Range: | IQ_Scores_Disrtibution!$A$3:$B$603 |

◯ **Use an external data source**

    | Choose Connection... | No data fields have been retrieved.

Choose where to place the PivotTable.

◯ New worksheet

◉ Existing worksheet

    Table/Range: | IQ_Scores_Disrtibution!$H$10 |

    | Cancel | | OK |

In Excel for Windows, the lower part of the dialog box is labeled "Location".

PivotTable Fields dialog box (top of Figure 3.3a), select the field Child to appear in Values (lower right of Figure 3.3a). This defaults to a sum. In the PivotTable (cell H10 at the moment), right click on Sum of Child, Figure 3.3b, select Value Field Settings, to bring up a new dialog box, PivotTable Field in Figure 3.3c. Select Count as in Figure 3.3c. The name of the field changes to "Count of Child". At the top of the PivotTable Fields dialog box again (Figure 3.3a), select the field IQ score to appear in Rows (lower left of Figure 3.3a). Starting in cell H11, the PivotTable reports each IQ score that occurs, from smallest to largest. It skips scores that do not occur. In column I appear the frequencies of each IQ score.

Because the default setting is to report frequencies for each score, we have more intervals than we need. We can group these data with the same interval widths as we did in the array function that appears to the left of the PivotTable we created. Right click on any interval (IQ score) in column H. Select Group and Outline (Mac only), as shown in Figure 3.4a. Then select Group. . . (Mac and Windows). The dialog box Group appears with the default low and high scores, 63 and 140, as the limits of the intervals in the first two boxes, as shown in Figure 3.4b. It now prepopulates the By box with 10, a suggested interval width. We will change that to 6, as shown in Figure 3.4b, to match our first frequency distribution. Although the PivotTable gives different labels for each interval, the frequency counts for the 13 intervals are the same as our first frequency distribution. Compare cells F11 to F23 in Figure 3.1b with cells I11 to I23 in Figure 3.5.

FIGURE 3.3 ● **Specifying how the PivotTable will summarize data. (a) Specify that rows will contain IQ scores and will summarize data on the column "Child." (b) Specifying that it will count the frequencies of the IQ Scores.**

(a)

(b)
(c)
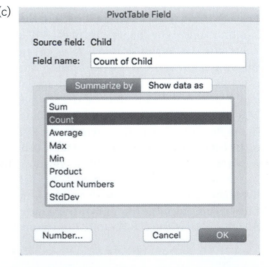

FIGURE 3.4 • Specifying how intervals of IQ scores will be calculated. (a) Menu options. (b) Dialog box for specifying parameters of intervals.

(a)
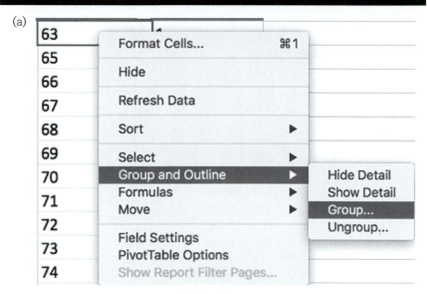

On a Windows system, select "Group . . ." from the menu.

(b)
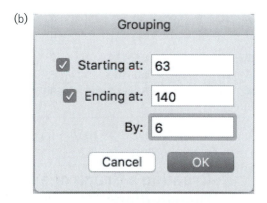

Excel gives the default labels in cells H10 and I10 Row Labels and Count of child, respectively. We can click in those cells and change the labels to IQ Score and to frequency, respectively (Figure 3.5). The final product is a frequency table that looks exactly like the one we created with the frequency array function. Compare IQ scores and frequency in columns E and F of Figure 3.1b to the IQ score and frequency in columns H and I in Figure 3.5.

FIGURE 3.5 ● Frequency distribution created as a PivotTable.

	A	B	H	I
1				
2		IQ		
3	Child	Score		
4	1	116		
5	2	89		
6	3	73		
7	4	88		
8	5	91		
9	6	102		
10	7	95	IQ score ▾	frequency
11	8	120	63-68	8
12	9	97	69-74	20
13	10	129	75-80	35
14	11	95	81-86	53
15	12	103	87-92	75
16	13	117	93-98	92
17	14	66	99-104	90
18	15	133	105-110	73
19	16	124	111-116	66
20	17	108	117-122	40
21	18	127	123-128	35
22	19	92	129-134	7
23	20	94	135-140	6
24	21	78	Grand Total	600

Appendix B

See **Appendix B7**, p. 307, for how to create and format a chart.

Creating a Graph of a Frequency Distribution

A final tool that adds meaning to a data set is a graph of the frequency distribution. We can do this in Excel by selecting the Insert tab. Highlight the 13 pairs of cells that contain the descriptions of the intervals and the frequency counts to their right. You can graph the frequency distribution created either with the frequency array or with the PivotTable. Your chart should look similar to the one in Figure 3.6.

FIGURE 3.6   ●   Graphs of frequency distribution data.

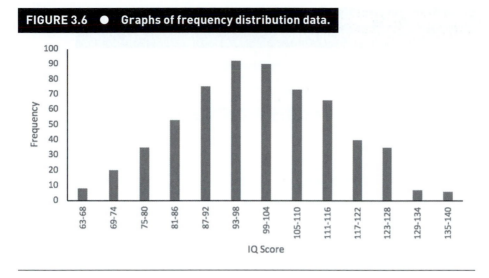

An informative chart has no unnecessary features and has appropriate labels. We model our charts after recommendations from the *Publication Manual of the American Psychological Association* (American Psychological Association, 2010).

Skewed Distribution Created With a PivotTable

We will create one more distribution with a different shape as compared to the one that we just created. This next distribution of household income is asymmetrical because of the extreme scores at the upper end of household income.

Download Household_Income_Distribution.xlsx from the student study site: http://study.sagepub.com/priviteraexcel1e. This workbook contains a single spreadsheet with participant identification numbers in column A and household income in column B.

Following the directions above for creating a PivotTable, create a PivotTable for the data from A3 to B1003. Select income $US for Rows and count of households for Values (Figure 3.7).

Recall that *you* decide the number of intervals and their width. If we stuck with the rule of thumb of no more than 20 intervals, each interval would be a little more than $30,000 in width. The trouble is that median household income in the United States of America in 2015 was below $60,000 (U.S. Census Bureau, 2016). We would lose resolution on the left side of the graph, with 50% of scores falling in the first two intervals. So we will create this distribution starting at $0 with interval widths of $11,000 (Figure 3.8). Although these parameters yield 53 intervals, they do preserve some resolution among the range of incomes in the lower half of the distribution (Figure 3.9). In this case, then, these parameters allow for a more representative or accurate depiction of the data.

FIGURE 3.7 ● Specifying how the PivotTable will summarize data of household income.

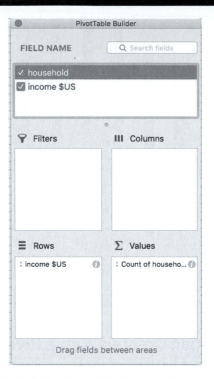

FIGURE 3.8 ● Specifying how intervals of household income will be calculated.

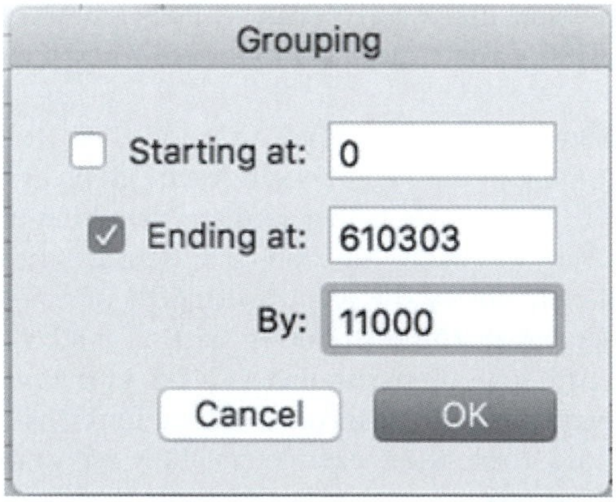

FIGURE 3.9 ● Frequency distribution of household income in the United States.

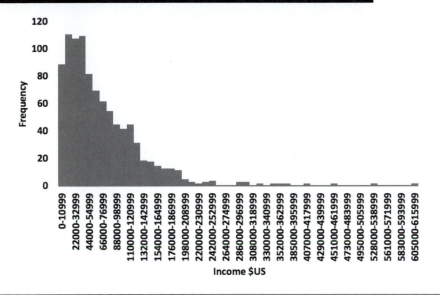

Probability

In your experiences with college, it is most certain that you have considered your *chances* along the way. Surely you were interested in your chances of being selected by a college, and considered your chances of graduating college, and even of obtaining a job after you graduate college. From college applications to job applications, you were and are interested in your chances or the *likelihood* that you will find success. In each example, you are applying probability to meaningfully navigate your path from college to employment and beyond.

You are applying probability any time you ask, "How likely is something to occur?" It is not uncommon at all for questions like this to be asked. For instance, probability is often used in sports (e.g., the likelihood that a team will win or lose a game), in the news (e.g., the likelihood that a crime will occur in a neighborhood), at an airport (e.g., the likelihood that a flight will be delayed), in a weather report (e.g., the chance of rain in the forecast), in an advertisement (e.g., over 97% of customers recommend a product) and even for emphasis in everyday conversation (e.g., you may exclaim, "I'm 99% confident!"). These examples highlight how common probabilities are in our everyday experiences.

Understanding the likelihood of the observations we make is fundamental to the application of statistics. Many or even most behaviors that we observe are normally distributed, where most people are behaving near the mean with few people at the extremes relative to all others in a given general population. It is therefore especially useful to understand probability as it relates to this type of distribution. Ultimately statistics provides a useful way to measure probability, which is instrumentally important to the decisions that researchers make. In this section, we will introduce many ways in which researchers use probability to understand the likelihood of the observations they make.

LEARNING
UNIT
4

Probability and the Normal Distribution

Excel Toolbox

Mathematical operators

- +
- /

Functions

- IF
- RANDBETWEEN
- COUNTIF
- AVERAGE
- STDEV.P
- SKEW
- KURT

Other tools

- freeze panes
- fill down or paste

(Continued)

(Continued)

- anchor cell references
- summarize with PivotTable
- format cells
- create chart
- format chart

Probability is used to describe the likelihood that an outcome will occur. A weather forecaster may tell you that there is a 30% chance of rain, the favored horse in the Kentucky Derby might have 2-to-1 odds of winning, or an all-star baseball player has a 3-in-10 chance of getting a hit. Probabilities are important in research as well. Researchers may report that the likelihood of detecting a disorder is 72%, that 1 in 4 women marry by their 20th birthday, or that about 24% of Americans age 25 or older have earned a bachelor's degree.

Probability can be used to predict any **random event**—any event in which the outcomes observed can vary. For example, if you flip a coin one time (the event), then it can land heads up or tails up (the outcomes). We can predict the likelihood of one outcome or the other, but the outcome itself can vary from one observation to the next. Probability is unnecessary in a **fixed event**—any event in which the outcome observed does not change. For example, what is the probability that a life (the event) will end (the outcome)? The event is fixed: All living things die eventually. Estimating the probability of this event is not valuable. Yet, suppose we ask what the probability is that a car accident (the event) will result in loss of life (the outcome)? Now the event is random: Not all car accidents result in death.

Calculating Probability

In this section, we demonstrate how probabilities are calculated. By definition, probability is the frequency of times an outcome occurs divided by the total number of possible outcomes.

To calculate probability, we need to know two things. First, we need to know the number of total possible outcomes. For example, if we flip a fair coin one time, then one of two total outcomes is possible: heads or tails. The total number of possible outcomes is called the **sample space**.

Second, we need to know how often an outcome of interest occurs. If we want to know how often heads occurs in one flip of a fair coin, we can count the number of times heads occurs in the total sample space. In this case, heads can occur one time per flip of a fair coin.

Probability (symbolized as *p*) is the frequency of times an outcome occurs divided by the total number of possible outcomes.

A **random event** is any event in which the outcomes observed can vary.

A **fixed event** is any event in which the outcome observed is always the same.

The **sample space**, also called the **outcome space**, is the total number of possible outcomes that can occur in a given random event.

For any given random event, the probability, p, of an outcome, x, is represented as $p(x)$. The frequency, f, of an outcome, x, is represented as $f(x)$. The formula for probability then is the frequency of times an outcome occurs, $f(x)$, divided by the sample space or the total number of possible outcomes:

$$p(x) = \frac{f(x)}{\text{sample space}}$$

To compute probability, we follow two steps: (1) find the sample space, and (2) find $f(x)$. We will use these steps to compute probability in two experiments.

Suppose we flip a fair coin one time and want to know what the probability is that we will flip heads. In Step 1, we find the sample space. The sample space for all possible outcomes is two: heads and tails:

Sample space: 2 (Heads, Tails).

In Step 2, we find $f(x)$. In this example, we want to know the probability of flipping heads. Hence, we want to know how often heads will be the outcome. When we count the number of times heads occurs in our sample space, we find that heads occurs one time. We can now state the probability of flipping heads (the outcome) with one flip of a fair coin (the event) as follows:

$$p(\text{flipping heads}) = \frac{1}{2}$$

Here are a few more examples to reinforce the concept of probability.

The sample space for a deck of cards is 52 once jokers are removed. We can calculate the probability of drawing a red card, or of drawing a heart, or of drawing a queen. Respectively, these probabilities are

p (red card) = 26/52 = ½

p (heart) = 13/52 = ¼

p (queen) = 4/52 = $\frac{1}{13}$

When you solve the probability formula, you can use two rules about probability to verify your answer:

1. **Probability varies between 0 and 1**. There are various ways to express a probability: It can be written as a fraction, decimal, percentage, or proportion. No matter how you express the probability, its value must vary between 0 and 1. The probability of flipping heads in our previous example was written as a fraction, but it would have been just as accurate if we wrote it as a decimal ($p = .50$), a percentage ($p = 50\%$), or a proportion ($p = 1{:}1$, where the proportion is stated as heads to tails). Similarly, the probability of selecting a heart in our second example was stated as a fraction, but it would have been just as accurate if we wrote it as a decimal ($p = .25$), a percentage ($p = 25\%$), or a

proportion (p = 1:4, where the proportion is stated as hearts to total cards). The closer to 1, the more probable an event is; the closer to 0, the less probable an event is.

2. **Probability can never be negative**. An event is either probable (its probability is greater than 0) or improbable (its probability is equal to 0).

Expected Value and the Binomial Distribution

We consider here a simple case of calculating the mean and standard deviation of a probability distribution with only two outcomes. The distribution of probabilities for each outcome of a random variable with two possible outcomes is called a **binomial probability distribution**. A binomial probability distribution can occur naturally—for example, the outcomes of flipping one fair coin are heads and tails. A binomial probability distribution can also occur by manipulation—for example, the level of self-esteem among children (self-esteem: low, high) or whether students graduate college (graduated: yes, no). We could define self-esteem and student graduation as having more than two outcomes, but we classified the measures such that only two outcomes were possible.

Appendix A

See **Appendix A6**, p. 287, for an explanation of expected value as a long-term mean for any number of outcomes.

Binomial probability distributions are common in behavioral research. In this section, we introduce how researchers compute the mean, variance, and standard deviation of random variables with only two possible outcomes.

The Mean of a Binomial Distribution

A **binomial probability distribution**, or **binomial distribution**, is the distribution of probabilities for each outcome of a bivariate random variable.

A **bivariate random variable** or **dichotomous variable** is any random variable with only two possible outcomes.

A random variable that has only two possible outcomes is called a **bivariate random variable** or **dichotomous variable**. When a random variable has only two possible outcomes, we can use a simple formula to estimate the expected value or expected outcome of the random variable. When there are only two outcomes for a random variable, x, we calculate the mean of the binomial probability distribution as

$$\mu = np.$$

The mean (μ) of a binomial distribution is the product of the number of times the bivariate random variable is observed (n) and the probability of the outcome of interest on an individual observation (p). For example, if we flip one fair coin 10 times (n = 10), then the expected value of flipping heads is as follows:

$$\mu = 10 \times .5 = 5 \text{ heads}$$

where p (heads) is .5 per flip. We expect to flip 5 heads in 10 flips of one fair coin.

The Variance and Standard Deviation of a Binomial Distribution

As with the mean, we can also simplify calculations of variance and standard deviation when there are only two outcomes of a random variable. The formula for the variance of a binomial probability distribution is

$$\sigma^2 = np(1-p)$$

or

$$\sigma^2 = npq$$

The formula for the standard deviation of a binomial probability distribution is the square root of the variance.

$$\sigma = \sqrt{\sigma^2} = \sqrt{np(1-p)}$$

or

$$\sigma = \sqrt{\sigma^2} = \sqrt{npq}$$

In each formula, n is the number of times the random variable is observed, p is the probability of the outcome of interest, and q is the probability of the complementary binomial outcome. Keep in mind that p and q are complementary outcomes, so $q = (1-p)$.

Each set of 10 flips of a fair coin will not always produce 5 outcomes with heads. We can estimate how far a set of 10 flips will deviate from the expected value of 5 heads. The estimated variance is as follows:

$$\sigma^2 = 10 \times .5 \times .5 = 2.5$$

The estimated standard deviation is the square root of the variance:

$$\sigma = \sqrt{\sigma^2} = \sqrt{2.5} = 1.58$$

Actual Values From an Unbiased "Coin"

We will now use Excel to demonstrate the values of a binomial distribution over many trials. This will lead us to a discussion of the distribution of these outcomes as an example of a normal distribution.

Open a blank Excel workbook and save it with the title Coin_Flips.xlsx. As shown in Figure 4.1, use the following cells in the first two rows to enter the labels listed to the right of the cell address:

A2: Trial

B1 (merged with C1 and centered): Frequency

B2: of H

C2: of T

E1 (merged with cells through N1 and centered): Coin Flip Number

E2 through N2: numbered 1 through 10

Appendix B

See **Appendix B2,** p. 301, for formatting cells.

See **Appendix B3,** p. 303, for freezing the display of some rows and columns.

We will simulate 20,000 trials of 10 flips of an unbiased "coin" in each trial. Column A contains the trial number from 1 to 20,000. Columns B and C contain the frequencies of obtaining either heads or tails, respectively. Columns E through N contain the outcomes of individual flips of the coin on each of the 10 flips composing a trial.

We start in cell A3 by typing the number 1 for the first trial, as shown in Figure 4.1a. Cell B3 will count the number of heads in trial one. In that cell type =COUNTIF(E3:N3,"H"), as shown in Figure 4.1a. This function counts the frequency of the letter H in the 10 cells from cell E3 to N3. Similarly, in cell C3 type =COUNTIF(E3:N3,"T"), as shown in Figure 4.1a, to count the frequency of the letter T in the same range of cells.

FIGURE 4.1 ● Creating 20,000 trials, each with 10 flips of "coin." (a) Functions to create and count the outcomes of flips of a "coin." Coin flips 3 through 10 in columns G through N are simulated the same way as 1 and 2 shown in columns E and F. (b) The outcome of the flips of a "coin."

For each of the 10 flips of a coin, we take advantage of the random number generator in Excel to simulate the flip of an unbiased coin, an event with two outcomes with equal probability. Using the RANDBETWEEN(x,y) function returns a random number within the range you specify between the parentheses. Using 1 to 2 as the range, we will assign the value H to 1 and the value T to 2. We embed the RANDBETWEEN function within another function that counts values we specify. In cell E3, type =IF(RANDBETWEEN(1,2)=1,"H","T"), as shown in Figure 4.1. The IF function requires a logical test, in this case in the first argument that the random number is 1. After that it requires instructions on what to do if the logical test is true in the second argument and if the logical test is false in the third argument. For our coin flip, a random number 1 returns a value of H for heads. Otherwise it returns the value of T for tails. (Note that we could have had it print the entire word but opted to have it print a single letter to save space.) Copy E3 and paste or fill through cell N3. Now we have 10 flips of an unbiased coin for the first trial.

Appendix B

See **Appendix B4,** p. 304, for highlighting, pasting, and filling.

From those 10 flips, the number of heads and the number of tails are displayed in cells B3 and C3, respectively. The result that you obtain may be different from the one in Figure 4.1, because your random numbers likely will be different from ours. Moreover, Excel will generate new random numbers each time the spreadsheet is changed. Thus, your numbers will keep changing through the exercise.

We now prepare row 4 for the second trial so that row 4 can be pasted or filled down for the remaining 19,998 trials. In cell A4, type =A3+1. This adds 1 to the previous trial number. Select cells B3 to N3 and paste or fill down to B4 to N4. Now every cell in row 4 contains a formula or function that can be pasted or filled to form the remaining 19,998 trials. Select cells A4 through N4. Paste or fill down through A20002 to N20002. A quick visual inspection of column B reveals many trials with 4, 5, or 6 heads and progressively fewer more extreme values of fewer than 4 or of more than 6.

We'll calculate descriptive statistics for the 20,000 trials, summarize them with a PivotTable as we did in Learning Unit 3 (pp. 36–40), and generate a frequency distribution chart.

As shown in Figure 4.2, type into cell P2 "*M* of Heads" and into P3 type "*SD* of Heads". Enter into cell Q2 =AVERAGE(B3:B20002) and into cell Q3 =STDEV.P (B3:B20002). Your values will likely differ slightly from the ones shown in Figure 4.2b. Theoretical values for the mean and standard deviation of a binomial distribution are 5.0 and 1.58, respectively, as calculated in the previous section "The Variance and Standard Deviation of a Binomial Distribution" on page 51. The actual values we just calculated should match or be very close to the theoretical values.

Select cells A2 to B20002. Select PivotTable from the ribbon of the Insert tab. Place "of H" in the Rows section of the dialog box (Figure 3.7). Select "Trial" and the number of each trial will be placed in the Values box. Click the "*i*" in the Values box to change the calculation from Sum to Count. Change the labels of the two columns of data in the PivotTable by clicking on and typing into them your desired label. The values displayed in the PivotTable are static. Although the result of H or T in each cell of the 20,000 replications will change, the PivotTable will remain the same

FIGURE 4.2 ● Summary of 20,000 trials of 10 flips of a coin. (a) Functions and formulas for calculating descriptive statistics. (b) Results of the calculation of functions and formulas.

(a)

	P	Q	R
1			
2	**M of Heads**	=AVERAGE(B3:B20002)	
3	**SD of Heads**	=STDEV.P(B3:B20002)	
4			
5	Number of Heads ▾	Frequency	**Rel Freq**
6	0	19	=Q6/Q$17
7	1	206	=Q7/Q$17
8	2	939	=Q8/Q$17
9	3	2360	=Q9/Q$17
10	4	4044	=Q10/Q$17
11	5	4851	=Q11/Q$17
12	6	4190	=Q12/Q$17
13	7	2324	=Q13/Q$17
14	8	859	=Q14/Q$17
15	9	184	=Q15/Q$17
16	10	24	=Q16/Q$17
17	**Grand Total**	**20000**	

(b)

	P	Q	R
1			
2	**M of Heads**	5.00	
3	**SD of Heads**	1.58	
4			
5	Number of Heads ▾	Frequency	**Rel Freq**
6	0	19	0.00095
7	1	206	0.01030
8	2	939	0.04695
9	3	2360	0.11800
10	4	4044	0.20220
11	5	4851	0.24255
12	6	4190	0.20950
13	7	2324	0.11620
14	8	859	0.04295
15	9	184	0.00920
16	10	24	0.00120
17	**Grand Total**	**20000**	

unless you choose to update the results. Updating the results can be done from the Data tab by clicking Refresh All or by right-clicking on the PivotTable and choosing Refresh Data.

Relative Frequency and Probability

When researchers summarize larger data sets (with thousands or even millions of counts), they often distribute the **relative frequency** of scores rather than counts. A relative frequency is a proportion from 0 to 1.0 that describes the portion of data in each interval. It is often easier to list the relative frequency of scores, because a list with very large frequencies in each interval can be more confusing to read. The calculation for a relative frequency is as follows:

$$\text{Relative Frequency} = \frac{\text{Observed Frequency}}{\text{Total Frequency Count}}$$

A **relative frequency** is a proportion from 0 to 1.0 that describes the portion of data in each interval.

Now we will calculate relative frequency for the outcomes of our trials of coin flips. In cell R5, type "Rel Freq" to keep track of what we calculate. In cell R6, type =Q6/Q$17, as shown in Figure 4.2a. This divides the observed frequency of 0 heads on 10 flips, 4, by the total frequency count or total number of trials, which is 20,000. Copy R6 and paste or fill through R16. This yields relative frequency for each possible outcome of the number of heads on 10 flips, from 0 heads to 10 heads, as shown in Figure 4.2b. The sum of relative frequencies across all intervals is 1.00, as the frequencies in Q6 through Q16 sum to 20,000: 20,000/20,000 = 1.00

The relative frequency formula looks strikingly similar to the calculation of a probability, which was first introduced above in the Calculating Probability section on page 48. Indeed, the relative frequency of an event is the probability of its occurrence. Both probability and relative frequency vary between 0 and 1 and can never be negative.

Normal Distribution

When researchers study behavior, they find that in many physical, behavioral, and social measurement studies, the data are normally distributed. Most measured values cluster around the center with very few values at the extremes. For example, most people express some level of aggression, a few are entirely passive, and a few express an abnormally high level of aggression. Most people have some moderate level of intelligence, a few score very low on intelligence, and a few score very high using the intelligence quotient (IQ) to measure intelligence.

Earlier in this learning unit we introduced probability of obtaining certain outcomes. We know that scores closer to the mean are more probable or likely than scores farther from the mean. Obtaining 4, 5, or 6 heads in 10 flips of a coin is more probable than is obtaining 0 or 10. Using probability in conjunction with standard deviation, we extend the concepts of probability to include situations in which we locate probabilities for scores in a **normal distribution**.

Characteristics of the Normal Distribution

In 1733, Abraham de Moivre introduced the normal distribution as a mathematical approximation to the binomial distribution, although de Moivre's 1733 work was not widely recognized until the accomplished statistician Karl Pearson rediscovered it in 1924. The shape of the curve in a normal distribution can drop suddenly at the tails, or the tails can be stretched out. Figure 4.3 shows three examples of normal distributions—notice in the figure that a normal distribution can vary in appearance. So, what makes a set of data normally distributed? In this section, we introduce eight characteristics that make a set of data normally distributed:

1. **The normal distribution is mathematically defined.** The shape of a normal distribution is specified by an equation relating each score (distributed along the x-axis) with each frequency (distributed along the y-axis):

$$Y = \left[\frac{1}{\sigma\sqrt{2\pi}} e^{-\frac{1}{2}\left[\frac{x-\mu}{\sigma}\right]^2} \right]$$

It is not necessary to memorize this formula. It is important to understand that rarely do behavioral data fall exactly within the limits of this formula. When we say that data are normally distributed, we mean that the data approximate a normal distribution. The normal distribution is so exact that it is simply impractical to think that behavior can fit exactly within the limits defined by this formula.

A **normal distribution** is a theoretical distribution with data that are symmetrically distributed around the mean, median, and mode; also called a **symmetrical, Gaussian,** or **bell-shaped distribution.**

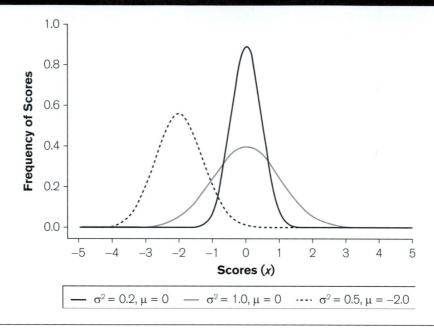

FIGURE 4.3 ● Three examples of a normal distribution with different means and standard deviations.

2. **The normal distribution is theoretical.** This characteristic follows from the first, in that it emphasizes that data can be normally distributed in theory—although rarely do we observe behaviors that are exactly normally distributed. Instead, behavioral data typically approximate a normal distribution. As you will see in this learning unit, we can still use the normal distribution to describe behavior so long as the behaviors being described are approximately normally distributed.

3. **The mean, the median, and the mode are all located at the 50th percentile.** In a normal distribution, the mean, the median, and the mode are the same value at the center of the distribution. Half the data (50%) in a normal distribution fall above the mean, the median, and the mode, and half the data (50%) fall below these measures.

4. **The normal distribution is symmetrical.** The normal distribution is symmetrical, in that the distribution of data above the mean is the same as the distribution of data below the mean. If you were to fold a normal curve in half, both sides of the curve would exactly overlap.

5. **The mean can equal any value.** The normal distribution can be defined by its mean and standard deviation. The mean of a normal distribution can equal any number from positive infinity (∞) to negative infinity ($-\infty$):

$$-\infty \leq M \leq +\infty.$$

6. **The standard deviation can equal any positive value.** The standard deviation (*SD*) is a measure of variability. Data can vary (*SD* > 0) or not vary (*SD* = 0). A negative standard deviation is meaningless. In the normal distribution, then, the standard deviation can be any positive value greater than 0.

7. **The total area under the curve of a normal distribution is equal to 1.0.** The area under the normal curve has the same characteristics as probability: Portions of it vary between 0 and 1 and can never be negative. In this way, the area under the normal curve can be used to determine the probabilities at different points along the distribution. In Characteristic 3, we stated that 50% of all data fall above and 50% fall below the mean. This is the same as saying that half (.50) of the area under the normal curve falls above and half of the area (.50) falls below the mean. The total area, then, is equal to 1.0. Figure 4.4 shows the proportions of area under the normal curve 3 *SD* above and below the mean.

8. **The tails of a normal distribution are asymptotic.** In a normal distribution, the tails are asymptotic, meaning that as you travel away from the mean the tails of the distribution are always approaching the *x*-axis but never touch it. Because the tails of the normal distribution go out to infinity, this characteristic allows for the possibility of outliers (or scores far from the mean) in a data set.

We now return to the spreadsheet that we created on simulated coin flips to draw a graph of the distribution and examine the proportions of trials within 1, 2, and 3 standard deviations of the mean.

Select the Insert tab. Highlight the 11 pairs of cells that contain the number of heads in 10 flips of a coin and the frequency counts to their right, cells P6 through Q16. In the toolbar of the Insert tab, select a column chart from Recommend Charts or hover over the upper left icon of a column chart. Clicking on Recommended Charts

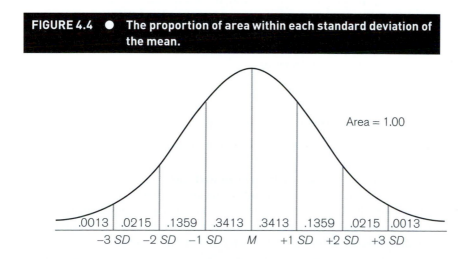

FIGURE 4.4 ● **The proportion of area within each standard deviation of the mean.**

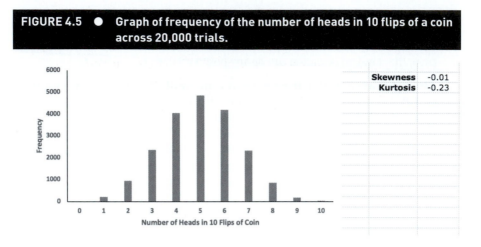

FIGURE 4.5 ● Graph of frequency of the number of heads in 10 flips of a coin across 20,000 trials.

Appendix B

See **Appendix B7**, p. 307, for how to insert and format a chart.

previews how selected data will appear in a graph. Select the one with columns. Reposition and resize the chart to your liking by clicking and dragging. Your chart should look similar to the one in Figure 4.5.

Figure 4.5 clearly approximates the normal distributions depicted in Figure 4.4. The mean, median, and mode are at the center (Characteristic 3). The distribution is symmetrical (Characteristic 4). Relatively few values are far from the mean, giving the tails the appearance of being asymptotic (Characteristic 8).

The Normal Distribution and Standard Deviation

The **empirical rule** states that for data that are normally distributed, at least 99.7% of data lie within three standard deviations of the mean, at least 95% of data lie within two standard deviations of the mean, and at least 68% of data lie within one standard deviation of the mean.

The standard deviation is an estimate for the average distance that scores deviate from the mean. When scores are concentrated near the mean, the standard deviation is small; when scores are scattered far from the mean, the standard deviation is larger. Yet, the standard deviation is more informative than this, particularly for data that are normally distributed. For normal distributions with any mean and any variance, we can make the following three statements:

1. At least 68% of all scores lie within one standard deviation of the mean.

2. At least 95% of all scores lie within two standard deviations of the mean.

3. At least 99.7% of all scores lie within three standard deviations of the mean.

These statements are often called the **empirical rule**. Empiricism is *to observe*. The name of this rule arises because many of the behaviors that researchers *observe* are approximately normally distributed. The empirical rule, then, is an approximation—the percentages are correct, give or take a few fractions of a standard deviation. Nevertheless, this rule is critical because of how specific it is for describing behavior.

We will continue to use our example of 20,000 coin flips as an example that approximates a normal distribution. For the 20,000 trials of 10 flips each, we will calculate the proportion that fall within one, two, and three standard deviations. The proportions below refer to the relative frequencies calculated in Figure 4.2.

We calculated the theoretical standard deviation to be 1.58 heads; the actual standard deviation in our approximation was 1.58 heads, as shown in Figure 4.2b. To approximate the proportion of trials within one standard deviation of the mean, the interval at the center, 5 heads, is divided in half for 0.5 heads. To that we add the whole interval on either side, 4 heads and 6 heads, and 0.08 heads from the next two intervals, 3 and 7 heads, yielding 1.58 heads on either side of the center of the distribution.

One standard deviation below the mean:

$$0.5 * 0.24255 + 1.0 * 0.20220 + 0.08 * 0.11800 = 0.33292$$

One standard deviation above the mean:

$$0.5 * 0.24255 + 1.0 * 0.20950 + 0.08 * 0.11620 = 0.34007$$

Yielding 0.67299, or 67.299% of all scores within one standard deviation of the mean. Table 4.1 presents calculation of proportions of scores within one, two, and three standard deviations of the mean.

Describing Departures From a Normal Distribution

We have emphasized that the data set used in the examples approximates a normal distribution. This raises the issue of how to describe distributions that depart from the characteristics of a normal distribution. Distributions can depart from normal because one of the two tails contains a greater number of extreme values or because both tails contain an unusually high or low number of extreme values.

Some data sets can have scores that are unusually high or low that skew (or distort) a data set. The distribution of such a set of scores is asymmetrical. A **skewed distribution** occurs whenever a data set includes a score or group of scores that fall substantially above (**positively skewed distribution**) or substantially below (**negatively skewed distribution**) most other scores in a distribution.

Some data sets can have few scores that are extreme (high and low) or can have many scores that are extreme (high and low). **Kurtosis** describes the frequency of extreme scores in the tails of a distribution. A **leptokurtic distribution** has very few extreme scores in both tails; the curve fitted to the data appears taller and thinner than a normal distribution. A **platykurtic distribution** has many extreme scores in both tails; the curve fitted to the data appears shorter and wider than a normal distribution.

We'll now illustrate how to obtain with Excel skewness and kurtosis indices of a distribution. The actual calculation of indices of skewness and kurtosis exceeds

A **skewed distribution** is a distribution of scores that includes scores that fall substantially above or below most other scores in a data set.

A **positively skewed distribution** is a distribution of scores that includes scores that are substantially larger (toward the right tail in a graph) than most other scores.

A **negatively skewed distribution** is a distribution of scores that includes scores that are substantially smaller (toward the left tail in a graph) than most other scores.

Kurtosis describes the frequency of scores that fall in the tails of a distribution; distributions with large kurtosis include data well beyond 3 SD in a normal distribution.

A **leptokurtic distribution** is a distribution that has very few extreme scores in both tails.

A **platykurtic distribution** is a distribution that has many extreme scores in both tails.

TABLE 4.1 ● Proportion of scores within (a) one, (b) two, and (c) three standard deviations of the mean. See page 59 for additional explanation of the approximation of the proportion of scores within one standard deviation of the mean.

(a)

# of Heads	Proportion of Trials	Multiplier	Proportion — One Standard Deviation — Below	Above	Total
0	0.00095				
1	0.01030				
2	0.04695				
3	0.11800	0.08	0.00944		
4	0.20220	1.00	0.20220		
5	0.24255	0.50	0.12128	0.12128	
6	0.20950	1.00		0.20950	
7	0.11620	0.08		0.00930	
8	0.04295				
9	0.00920				
10	0.00120				
			0.33292	0.34007	**0.67299**

(b)

# of Heads	Proportion of Trials	Multiplier	Proportion — Two Standard Deviations — Below	Above	Total
0	0.00095				
1	0.01030				
2	0.04695	0.66	0.03099		
3	0.11800	1.00	0.11800		
4	0.20220	1.00	0.20220		
5	0.24255	0.50	0.12128	0.12128	
6	0.20950	1.00		0.20950	
7	0.11620	1.00		0.11620	
8	0.04295	0.66		0.02835	
9	0.00920				
10	0.00120				
			0.47246	0.47532	**0.94778**

(c)

# of Heads	Proportion of Trials	Multiplier	Proportion		
			Three Standard deviations		
			Below	Above	Total
0	0.00095	0.24	0.00023		
1	0.01030	1.00	0.01030		
2	0.04695	1.00	0.04695		
3	0.11800	1.00	0.11800		
4	0.20220	1.00	0.20220		
5	0.24255	0.50	0.12128	0.12128	
6	0.20950	1.00		0.20950	
7	0.11620	1.00		0.11620	
8	0.04295	1.00		0.04295	
9	0.00920	1.00		0.00920	
10	0.00120	0.24		0.00029	
			0.49895	0.49941	**0.99837**

the scope of this introductory text. At this point in the learning unit, we aim only to make you aware of descriptors of skewness and kurtosis. We will use Excel to do this.

For these calculations, results close to zero indicate a greater resemblance to normal distribution. The greater the departure from zero in either the negative or positive direction, the greater the departure from resemblance to the normal distribution. For skewness, a negative skew index indicates more extreme values toward the left side of the distribution, and a positive skew index indicates more extreme values toward the right side of the distribution. For kurtosis, a negative kurtosis index indicates more extreme values in the tails, and a positive kurtosis index indicates fewer extreme values in the tails.

Return to the spreadsheet that you created with 20,000 trials of 10 flips of a coin. In cells V21 and V22, type, respectively, "Skewness" and "Kurtosis" to keep track of what we are calculating. In cell W21, type =SKEW.P(B3:B20002); in cell W22, type =KURT(B3:B20002). The values that you obtain should resemble the values close to zero that are shown to the right of the graph in Figure 4.5. For both skewness and kurtosis, values relatively close to zero indicate that the distribution does not deviate much from a normal distribution.

To put into perspective the skew and kurtosis indices for our approximation of a normal distribution with 20,000 trials of 10 flips of a coin, we will examine two other distributions that depart from normality. Download Age_At_Death_Probability_ Distribution.xlsx from the student study site: http://study.sagepub.com/priviteraexcel1e. This spreadsheet reconstructs the characteristics of the data set from a New York State Department of Health report on people who died in 2015 in the five counties that it designates as part of the New York City region. Column A contains a case number for each person. Column B contains the age at which that person died. Following the instructions earlier in this learning unit (p. 36), create a frequency distribution and a graph for these data. As shown in Figures 4.6 and 4.7, we grouped the data in intervals of 7 years. Looking just at the frequency distribution (Figure 4.6) alone, it is clear that the peak of scores is on the right, with a very small tail on the left.

The graph of the data illustrates the skewed distribution more clearly. Compared to the adjacent interval of 7–14 years, there are more than five times the number of deaths in the interval of 0–7 years. This is primarily due to high mortality rate in the first year of life.

We complete the discussion of departures from a normal distribution with one more example. The example simulates the results of 20,000 rolls of an unbiased

FIGURE 4.6 ● Frequency of deaths within each age group.

	D	E
2	**M of Age**	73.8
3	**SD of Age**	18.2
4		
5	Age at Death	Frequency
6	0-7	560
7	7-14	102
8	14-21	183
9	21-28	536
10	28-35	768
11	35-42	827
12	42-49	1705
13	49-56	3144
14	56-63	4517
15	63-70	6057
16	70-77	7631
17	77-84	8367
18	84-91	11316
19	91-98	6324
20	98-105	1236
21	**Grand Total**	**53273**

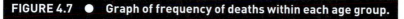

FIGURE 4.7 ● Graph of frequency of deaths within each age group.

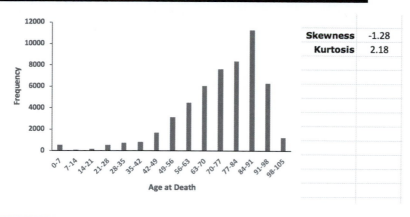

die (the singular of dice). The spreadsheet, Roll_Of_Die.xlsx, is available for download from the student study site: http://study.sagepub.com/priviteraexcel1e. We have already created the frequency distribution and the graph; they are shown in Figures 4.8a and 4.8b, respectively. The six possible results of the roll of an unbiased die have equal probabilities of occurrence, 0.167. Over the simulation of 20,000 rolls, we expect each value to occur about 3333 times. The distribution is symmetrical with a skew index of 0.01. The lack of a clear peak, because there are no extreme values in the tails, results in a kurtosis index of –1.27.

FIGURE 4.8 ● Summary of 20,000 rolls of a die. (a) Frequency of value on die. (b) Graph of frequency distribution.

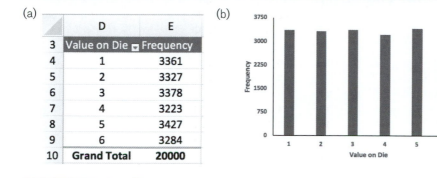

(a)

	D	E
3	Value on Die	Frequency
4	1	3361
5	2	3327
6	3	3378
7	4	3223
8	5	3427
9	6	3284
10	**Grand Total**	**20000**

LEARNING UNIT 5

The Standard Normal Distribution: *z* Scores

The Standard Normal Distribution

In a normal distribution, the mean can be any positive or negative number, and the standard deviation can be any positive number. For this reason, we could combine values of the mean and standard deviation to construct an infinite number of normal distributions. To find the probability of a score in each and every one of these normal curves would be quite overwhelming.

As an alternative, statisticians found the area under one normal curve, called the "standard," and stated a formula to convert all other normal distributions to this standard. The area under the normal curve is a probability at different points along the distribution. The "standard" curve is called the **standard normal distribution**, or **z distribution**, which has a mean of 0 and a standard deviation of 1. Scores on the x-axis in a standard normal distribution are called **z scores**.

Figure 5.1 shows the area, or probabilities, under the standard normal curve at each z score. The numerical value of a z score specifies the distance or standard deviation of a value from the mean. (Thus, $z = 1$ is one standard deviation above the mean, $z = -1$ is one standard deviation below the mean, and so on.) Notice that the probabilities given for the standard normal distribution are the same as those shown in Figure 5.2. The probabilities are the same because the proportion of area under the normal curve is the same at each standard deviation for all normal distributions.

Because we know the probabilities under a standard normal curve, we can convert all other normal distributions to this standard. By doing so, we can find the probabilities of scores in any normal distribution using probabilities listed for the standard normal distribution. To convert any normal distribution to a standard

The **standard normal distribution**, or **z distribution**, is a normal distribution with a mean equal to 0 and a standard deviation equal to 1. The standard normal distribution is distributed in z score units along the x-axis.

A **z score** is a value on the x-axis of a standard normal distribution. The numerical value of a z score specifies the distance or the number of standard deviations that a value is above or below the mean.

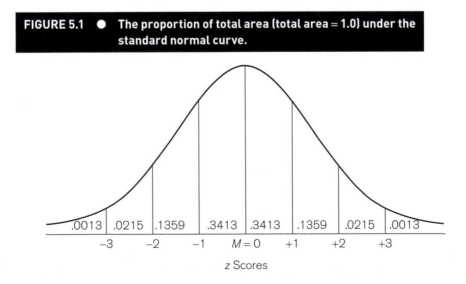

FIGURE 5.1 ● **The proportion of total area (total area = 1.0) under the standard normal curve.**

| .0013 | .0215 | .1359 | .3413 | .3413 | .1359 | .0215 | .0013 |

−3   −2   −1   M = 0   +1   +2   +3

z Scores

The standard normal distribution is one example of a normal distribution.

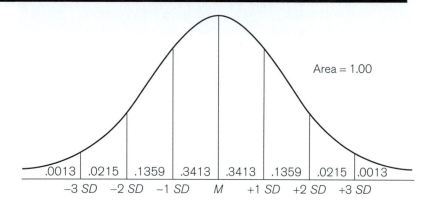

FIGURE 5.2 ● The proportion of area within each standard deviation of the mean.

Area = 1.00

.0013 | .0215 | .1359 | .3413 | .3413 | .1359 | .0215 | .0013

−3 *SD* −2 *SD* −1 *SD* *M* +1 *SD* +2 *SD* +3 *SD*

normal distribution, we compute the **standard normal transformation**, or **z transformation**. The formula for the *z* transformation is

$$z = \frac{x - \mu}{\sigma}$$

for a population of scores, or

$$z = \frac{x - M}{SD}$$

for a sample of scores.

We use the *z* transformation to locate where a score in any normal distribution would be in the standard normal distribution.

To illustrate, we will compute a *z* transformation. A researcher measures the farthest distance (in meters) that students moved from a podium during a class presentation. The data were normally distributed with *M* = 3 meters (approximately 12 feet) and *SD* = 0.5 meters (approximately 1.5 feet). What is the *z* score for *x* = 3.5 meters?

Because *M* = 3 and *SD* = 0.5, we can find the *z* score for *x* = 3.5 by substituting these values into the *z* transformation formula:

$$z = \frac{3.5 - 3}{0.5} = \frac{0.5}{0.5} = 1.0$$

Figure 5.3a shows the original normal distribution of scores (*x*) with *M* = 3 meters and *SD* = 0.5 meters. Notice that in Figure 5.3b, a score of *x* = 3.5 in the original distribution is exactly one *z* score, or one standard deviation, above the mean in a standard normal distribution.

The **standard normal transformation**, or ***z* transformation**, is a formula used to convert any normal distribution with any mean and any variance to a standard normal distribution with a mean equal to 0 and a standard deviation equal to 1.

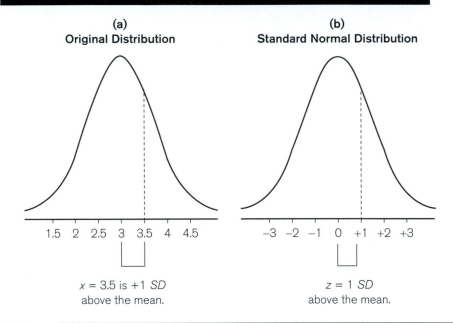

FIGURE 5.3 ● Computing a z transformation for a sample with M = 3 and SD = 0.5. A score of x = 3.5 in the original distribution is located at z = 1.0 in a standard normal distribution, or 1 SD above the mean.

(a)
Original Distribution

1.5 2 2.5 3 3.5 4 4.5

$x = 3.5$ is $+1$ SD
above the mean.

(b)
Standard Normal Distribution

−3 −2 −1 0 +1 +2 +3

$z = 1$ SD
above the mean.

Of course, z scores can be negative. Following the reasoning above, for a score of 2 meters from the podium, we can substitute into the z transformation formula as follows:

$$z = \frac{2-3}{0.5} = \frac{-1}{0.5} = -2.0.$$

Notice that in Figure 5.3b, a score of $x = 2$ in the original distribution is exactly two z scores, or two standard deviations, below the mean in a standard normal distribution.

We now do this in Excel with a simulation of SAT math scores from 454 seniors graduating from high school. Download SAT.xlsx from the student study site: http://study.sagepub.com/priviteraexcel1e. Column A contains an identification number for each student, and column B contains that student's math SAT score. For ease of reference in this exercise, calculate the mean and standard deviation in the upper left of this worksheet. As shown in Figure 5.4, type in cells A1 and A2, respectively, "M" and "SD" to keep track of calculations. As shown in Figure 5.4a, enter into cell B1 =AVERAGE(B5:B458), and in B2 =STDEV.S(B5:B458). Consistent with the construction of the SAT, the mean is approximately 500 and the standard deviation approximately 100.

We demonstrate two ways of calculating a *z* score. The first is with a formula that we build to help understand what a *z* score expresses; the second is with a function included in Excel. As shown in Figure 5.4, type into cell C3 "*z* Score Method" to keep track of calculations. Merge and center C3 and D3. We will use a formula in column C and the Excel function in column D. In cells C4 and D4, respectively, type "Formula" and "Function".

Following the formula described above, we calculate in column C the *z* score for each raw score. Enter into cell C5 =(B5-B$1)/B$2, as shown in Figure 5.4a. This formula subtracts the mean (cell B1) from the raw score (cell B5) and divides the difference by the standard deviation (cell B2) to obtain the *z* score. To get *z* scores for the remaining raw scores, select cell C5 and paste or fill down to cell C458.

> **Appendix B**
>
> See **Appendix B2,** p. 301, for merging cells, centering content, and changing cell borders.
>
> See **Appendix B3,** p. 303, for freezing panes.

> **Appendix B**
>
> See **Appendix B6,** p. 306, for anchoring cell references.

A quick examination of raw and *z* scores in Figure 5.4b confirms their correspondence to expectation. With a mean of approximately 500 and a standard deviation of approximately 100, we would expect a raw score of 500 to correspond to a *z* score of approximately 0. Cells B5 (raw score) and C5 and D5 (*z* score) confirm that expectation. A raw score of 600 (cell B6), approximately one standard deviation above the mean, yields a *z* score close to 1 (cell C6). A raw score of 400 (cell B8), approximately one standard deviation below the mean, yields a *z* score of approximately 1 standard deviation below the mean (cell C8). Raw scores of 300 and 700 yield *z* scores two standard deviations below and above the mean, respectively.

Now that we have further insight into what a *z* score expresses, we will work with the function that Excel provides to calculate a *z* score. The arguments required by the function are, of course, the same as those we used in the formula that we built: the raw score, the mean, and the standard deviation. As shown in Figure 5.4a, enter into cell D5 =STANDARDIZE(B5,AVERAGE(B$5:B$458),STDEV.S(B$5:B$458)). This function uses the same three pieces of information to perform the same calculation that we did in the formula. We could have also referred to cells B1 and B2 that we used in the formula that we built above. Embedding the AVERAGE and STDEV.S functions and anchoring the cell references allowed us to skip that step. Although the function does not seem to be more efficient to use as compared to the formula, the function does provide a means of checking the formula, if desired. You should find that your *z* scores in column C are the same as those in column D.

In the next section we will examine these data in relation to the unit normal table and graph the data to help visualize that relationship.

The Unit Normal Table: A Brief Introduction

The proportion of area under the standard normal distribution is given in the **unit normal table**, or **z table**, in Table C.1 in Appendix C. A portion of the table is shown in Table 5.1. The unit normal table has three columns: A, B, and C. This section will familiarize you with each column in the table.

The **unit normal table** or **z table** is a type of probability distribution table displaying a list of *z* scores and the corresponding probabilities (or proportions of area) associated with each *z* score listed.

**FIGURE 5.4 ●   Calculation of z scores. (a) Formulas and by functions.
(b) Results of the calculations of formulas and functions.**

(a)

	A	B	C	D
1	M	=AVERAGE(B5:B458)		
2	SD	=STDEV.S(B5:B458)		
3				z Score Method
4	Student	Math SAT	Formula	Function
5	1	500	=(B5-B$1)/B$2	=STANDARDIZE(B5,AVERAGE(B$5:B$458),STDEV.S(B$5:B$458))
6	2	600	=(B6-B$1)/B$2	=STANDARDIZE(B6,AVERAGE(B$5:B$458),STDEV.S(B$5:B$458))
7	3	620	=(B7-B$1)/B$2	=STANDARDIZE(B7,AVERAGE(B$5:B$458),STDEV.S(B$5:B$458))
8	4	400	=(B8-B$1)/B$2	=STANDARDIZE(B8,AVERAGE(B$5:B$458),STDEV.S(B$5:B$458))
9	5	310	=(B9-B$1)/B$2	=STANDARDIZE(B9,AVERAGE(B$5:B$458),STDEV.S(B$5:B$458))
10	6	490	=(B10-B$1)/B$2	=STANDARDIZE(B10,AVERAGE(B$5:B$458),STDEV.S(B$5:B$458))
11	7	300	=(B11-B$1)/B$2	=STANDARDIZE(B11,AVERAGE(B$5:B$458),STDEV.S(B$5:B$458))
12	8	470	=(B12-B$1)/B$2	=STANDARDIZE(B12,AVERAGE(B$5:B$458),STDEV.S(B$5:B$458))
13	9	700	=(B13-B$1)/B$2	=STANDARDIZE(B13,AVERAGE(B$5:B$458),STDEV.S(B$5:B$458))
14	10	480	=(B14-B$1)/B$2	=STANDARDIZE(B14,AVERAGE(B$5:B$458),STDEV.S(B$5:B$458))
15	11	450	=(B15-B$1)/B$2	=STANDARDIZE(B15,AVERAGE(B$5:B$458),STDEV.S(B$5:B$458))
16	12	550	=(B16-B$1)/B$2	=STANDARDIZE(B16,AVERAGE(B$5:B$458),STDEV.S(B$5:B$458))

(b)

	A	B	C	D
1		M 497.86		
2		SD 104.44		
3			z Score Method	
4	Student	Math SAT	Formula	Function
5	1	500	0.02	0.02
6	2	600	0.98	0.98
7	3	620	1.17	1.17
8	4	400	-0.94	-0.94
9	5	310	-1.80	-1.80
10	6	490	-0.08	-0.08
11	7	300	-1.89	-1.89
12	8	470	-0.27	-0.27
13	9	700	1.94	1.94
14	10	480	-0.17	-0.17
15	11	450	-0.46	-0.46
16	12	550	0.50	0.50

Column A lists the z scores. The table lists only positive z scores, meaning that only z scores at or above the mean are listed in the table. For negative z scores below the mean, you must know that the normal distribution is symmetrical. The areas listed in Columns B and C for each z score below the mean are the same as those for z scores listed above the mean in the unit normal table. In Column A, z scores are listed from $z = 0$ at the mean to $z = 4.00$ above the mean.

Column B lists the area between a z score and the mean. The first value for the area listed in Column B is .0000, which is the area between the mean ($z = 0$) and $z = 0$ (the mean). Notice that the area between the mean and a z score of 1.00 is .3413—the same value given in Figure 5.1. As a z score moves away from the mean, the proportion of area between that score and the mean increases closer to .5000, or the total area above the mean.

TABLE 5.1 ● A portion of the unit normal table in Appendix C1.

z	Area Between Mean and *z*	Area Beyond *z* in Tail
0.00	.0000	.5000
0.01	.0040	.4960
0.02	.0080	.4920
0.03	.0120	.4880
0.04	.0160	.4840
0.05	.0199	.4801
0.06	.0239	.4761
0.07	.0279	.4721
0.08	.0319	.4681
0.09	.0359	.4641
0.10	.0398	.4602
0.11	.0438	.4562
0.12	.0478	.4522
0.13	.0517	.4483
0.14	.0557	.4443

Source: Based on J. E. Freund (2004), *Modern elementary statistics* (11th ed.). Upper Saddle River, NJ: Pearson Prentice Hall.

Column C lists the area from a *z* score toward the tail. The first value for the area listed in Column C is .5000, which is the total area above the mean. As a *z* score increases and therefore moves closer to the tail, the area between that score and the tail decreases closer to .0000.

We can illustrate the correspondence between the unit normal table and the math SAT scores. Create a frequency distribution by highlighting cells A4 to B458 and selecting PivotTable from the Insert tab. Select Existing worksheet and cell F4 for the start of the PivotTable. Select Math SAT to appear in rows and Student in values. Click in the "*i*" icon in values, and select Count rather than Sum. The resulting PivotTable should look like columns F and G in Figure 5.5.

This frequency distribution has 29 intervals, 210 to 490, below the mean, and 29 intervals, 500 to 790, above the mean. As expected with a normal distribution,

FIGURE 5.5 ● For each math SAT score: frequency, relative proportion, proportion of scores at or below, proportion of scores above.

(a)

	F	G	H	I	J
3				Proportion	
4	Math SAT	Frequency	Relative	At or Below	Above
5	210	1	=G5/G$63	=H5	=1-I5
6	220	1	=G6/G$63	=I5+H6	=1-I6
7	230	1	=G7/G$63	=I6+H7	=1-I7
8	240	2	=G8/G$63	=I7+H8	=1-I8
9	250	1	=G9/G$63	=I8+H9	=1-I9
10	260	2	=G10/G$63	=I9+H10	=1-I10
11	270	2	=G11/G$63	=I10+H11	=1-I11
12	280	2	=G12/G$63	=I11+H12	=1-I12
13	290	3	=G13/G$63	=I12+H13	=1-I13
14	300	3	=G14/G$63	=I13+H14	=1-I14
15	310	4	=G15/G$63	=I14+H15	=1-I15
16	320	3	=G16/G$63	=I15+H16	=1-I16
17	330	4	=G17/G$63	=I16+H17	=1-I17
18	340	4	=G18/G$63	=I17+H18	=1-I18
19	350	5	=G19/G$63	=I18+H19	=1-I19
20	360	6	=G20/G$63	=I19+H20	=1-I20
21	370	6	=G21/G$63	=I20+H21	=1-I21
22	380	8	=G22/G$63	=I21+H22	=1-I22
23	390	9	=G23/G$63	=I22+H23	=1-I23
24	400	10	=G24/G$63	=I23+H24	=1-I24
25	410	10	=G25/G$63	=I24+H25	=1-I25
26	420	12	=G26/G$63	=I25+H26	=1-I26
27	430	14	=G27/G$63	=I26+H27	=1-I27
28	440	16	=G28/G$63	=I27+H28	=1-I28
29	450	18	=G29/G$63	=I28+H29	=1-I29
30	460	19	=G30/G$63	=I29+H30	=1-I30
31	470	18	=G31/G$63	=I30+H31	=1-I31
32	480	21	=G32/G$63	=I31+H32	=1-I32
33	490	22	=G33/G$63	=I32+H33	=1-I33
34	500	21	=G34/G$63	=I33+H34	=1-I34
35	510	19	=G35/G$63	=I34+H35	=1-I35
36	520	18	=G36/G$63	=I35+H36	=1-I36
37	530	17	=G37/G$63	=I36+H37	=1-I37
38	540	15	=G38/G$63	=I37+H38	=1-I38
39	550	15	=G39/G$63	=I38+H39	=1-I39
40	560	12	=G40/G$63	=I39+H40	=1-I40
41	570	14	=G41/G$63	=I40+H41	=1-I41
42	580	11	=G42/G$63	=I41+H42	=1-I42
43	590	12	=G43/G$63	=I42+H43	=1-I43
44	600	8	=G44/G$63	=I43+H44	=1-I44
45	610	7	=G45/G$63	=I44+H45	=1-I45
46	620	7	=G46/G$63	=I45+H46	=1-I46
47	630	5	=G47/G$63	=I46+H47	=1-I47
48	640	7	=G48/G$63	=I47+H48	=1-I48
49	650	5	=G49/G$63	=I48+H49	=1-I49
50	660	5	=G50/G$63	=I49+H50	=1-I50
51	670	5	=G51/G$63	=I50+H51	=1-I51
52	680	3	=G52/G$63	=I51+H52	=1-I52
53	690	3	=G53/G$63	=I52+H53	=1-I53
54	700	3	=G54/G$63	=I53+H54	=1-I54
55	710	2	=G55/G$63	=I54+H55	=1-I55
56	720	2	=G56/G$63	=I55+H56	=1-I56
57	730	3	=G57/G$63	=I56+H57	=1-I57
58	740	2	=G58/G$63	=I57+H58	=1-I58
59	750	2	=G59/G$63	=I58+H59	=1-I59
60	760	2	=G60/G$63	=I59+H60	=1-I60
61	770	1	=G61/G$63	=I60+H61	=1-I61
62	790	1	=G62/G$63	=I61+H62	=1-I62
63	Grand Total	454			

(b)

	F	G	H	I	J
3				Proportion	
4	Math SAT	Frequency	Relative	At or Below	Above
5	210	1	.0022	.0022	.9978
6	220	1	.0022	.0044	.9956
7	230	1	.0022	.0066	.9934
8	240	2	.0044	.0110	.9890
9	250	1	.0022	.0132	.9868
10	260	2	.0044	.0176	.9824
11	270	2	.0044	.0220	.9780
12	280	2	.0044	.0264	.9736
13	290	3	.0066	.0330	.9670
14	300	3	.0066	.0396	.9604
15	310	4	.0088	.0485	.9515
16	320	3	.0066	.0551	.9449
17	330	4	.0088	.0639	.9361
18	340	4	.0088	.0727	.9273
19	350	5	.0110	.0837	.9163
20	360	6	.0132	.0969	.9031
21	370	6	.0132	.1101	.8899
22	380	8	.0176	.1278	.8722
23	390	9	.0198	.1476	.8524
24	400	10	.0220	.1696	.8304
25	410	10	.0220	.1916	.8084
26	420	12	.0264	.2181	.7819
27	430	14	.0308	.2489	.7511
28	440	16	.0352	.2841	.7159
29	450	18	.0396	.3238	.6762
30	460	19	.0419	.3656	.6344
31	470	18	.0396	.4053	.5947
32	480	21	.0463	.4515	.5485
33	490	22	.0485	.5000	.5000
34	500	21	.0463	.5463	.4537
35	510	19	.0419	.5881	.4119
36	520	18	.0396	.6278	.3722
37	530	17	.0374	.6652	.3348
38	540	15	.0330	.6982	.3018
39	550	15	.0330	.7313	.2687
40	560	12	.0264	.7577	.2423
41	570	14	.0308	.7885	.2115
42	580	11	.0242	.8128	.1872
43	590	12	.0264	.8392	.1608
44	600	8	.0176	.8568	.1432
45	610	7	.0154	.8722	.1278
46	620	7	.0154	.8877	.1123
47	630	5	.0110	.8987	.1013
48	640	7	.0154	.9141	.0859
49	650	5	.0110	.9251	.0749
50	660	5	.0110	.9361	.0639
51	670	5	.0110	.9471	.0529
52	680	3	.0066	.9537	.0463
53	690	3	.0066	.9604	.0396
54	700	3	.0066	.9670	.0330
55	710	2	.0044	.9714	.0286
56	720	2	.0044	.9758	.0242
57	730	3	.0066	.9824	.0176
58	740	2	.0044	.9868	.0132
59	750	2	.0044	.9912	.0088
60	760	2	.0044	.9956	.0044
61	770	1	.0022	.9978	.0022
62	790	1	.0022	1.0000	.0000
63	Grand Total	454			

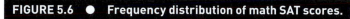

FIGURE 5.6 ● Frequency distribution of math SAT scores.

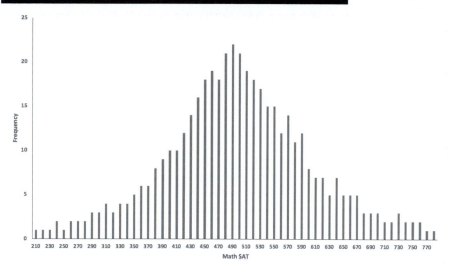

the scores are clustered near the center. Notice especially the large number of scores between 400 and 600. Notice also that there are relatively few scores below 400 and above 600. See Figures 5.5 and 5.6. Notice that Figure 5.6 looks nearly exactly like the theoretical normal distribution in Figure 5.1.

Next we take a step away from the raw scores to calculate proportions of scores at each value. As shown in Figure 5.5, to keep track of the proportions calculated, type "Proportion" in cell H3, merge with cells through J3, then center. We will calculate three types of proportions in three columns. Type into cells H4, I4, and J4, respectively, "Relative", "At or Below", and "Above". As shown in Figure 5.5a, enter into cell H5 =G5/G$63 to calculate the proportion of all 454 scores that had the value of 210. For the moment, copy H5 and paste it to H6. Enter into cell I5 =H5. In cell I6, type =I5+H6 to calculate the cumulative proportion of scores at or below the value of 220. In cell J5, type =1–I5 to reveal the proportion of scores above the value of 210. Copy J5 and paste to J6. Notice that as we move from scores of 210 to 220, the proportion of scores at or below the value for the given SAT score goes up, and the proportion of scores above the value goes down.

Appendix B

See **Appendix B7,** p. 307, for inserting and formatting a chart.

To complete the picture, highlight H6 through J6 and paste or fill down through H62 to J62. Your results should look like those in columns H, I, and J in Figure 5.5b. Notice again that with each increase in score, the proportion of scores at or below the value goes up and the proportion of scores above the value goes down.

Keep in mind that the normal distribution is used to determine the probability of a certain outcome in relation to all other outcomes. We can see how closely the math SAT data conform to a normal distribution. To describe data that are normally distributed, we ask questions, for example, about observing scores less than one standard deviation below the mean. The unit normal table tells us that a proportion of .1587 of scores fall below that value. The distribution of the math SAT data conforms to that with a proportion of .1696 (cell I24 in Figure 5.5b) falling at or below 400. The unit normal table also tells us that a proportion of .3413 of scores can be found within one standard deviation below the mean and .3413 above the mean. This yields .6826 (.3413 × 2) within one standard deviation above and below the mean. The distribution of math SAT data approximates the theoretical values with a proportion of (.5000 − .1476) = .3524 within a standard deviation below the mean and (.5000 − .1278) = .3722 within one standard deviation above the mean. This yields a proportion of .7246 within one standard deviation above and below the mean, slightly higher than the theoretical values. The unit normal table tells us that a proportion of .0228 of scores fall beyond two standard deviations above the mean. The distribution of the math SAT data conforms to that proportion with .0286 of scores falling two standard deviations above the mean.

Appendix A

See **Appendix A7,** p. 288, for the informativeness of the mean and standard deviation to find probabilities.

LEARNING UNIT 6

Sampling Distributions

(Continued)

- fill down or paste
- anchor cell reference
- summarize with PivotTable
- create chart
- format chart

In a broader context, it is important to be critical about the informativeness of samples for drawing conclusions about populations. How well do observations with samples truly generalize or inform us about a population? Can we trust the findings reported when samples of data are used? The most commonly reported and highly utilized statistic to describe behavior is the sample mean. At a fundamental level, it is practical to ask, "Is the sample mean unbiased?" In other words, on average, does it correctly estimate a population mean; and if it does not correctly estimate the population mean, then how far "off" is it, or how much of an "error" will we make?

When researchers measure sample statistics such as the mean and variance, they do so to estimate the value of the mean and variance in a population. But how well do sample statistics, such as the sample mean and sample variance, estimate the value of population parameters, such as the population mean and population variance? What is the probability that a sample statistic will be smaller than, larger than, or exactly equal to the value of a population parameter? These questions can be answered, in part, by applying our knowledge of normal distributions. In this learning unit, we explore the relationship between characteristics in a sample and characteristics of the population of interest, from which the sample was selected. Given that most research is conducted using samples in the behavioral sciences, it should not surprise you that samples are actually quite informative about the populations from which they are selected.

Selecting Samples From Populations

Inferential Statistics and Sampling Distributions

In inferential statistics, researchers select a sample or portion of data from a much larger population. The next step is to measure a sample statistic in the sample they selected, such as the mean or variance. The purpose of selecting the sample is to measure sample statistics such as the mean and variance, to estimate the value of the mean and variance in a population. To illustrate, Figure 6.1 gives an example of where you may ask a few students (the sample) how they scored on an exam to compare your score to theirs. You do this, though, to learn more about how you did compared to the

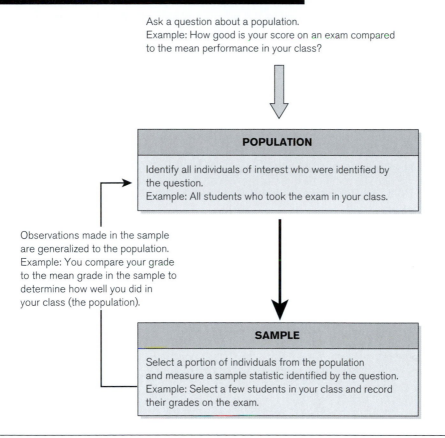

•FIGURE 6.1 ● Selecting samples from populations.

Ask a question about a population.
Example: How good is your score on an exam compared
to the mean performance in your class?

POPULATION

Identify all individuals of interest who were identified by
the question.
Example: All students who took the exam in your class.

Observations made in the sample
are generalized to the population.
Example: You compare your grade
to the mean grade in the sample to
determine how well you did in
your class (the population).

SAMPLE

Select a portion of individuals from the population
and measure a sample statistic identified by the question.
Example: Select a few students in your class and record
their grades on the exam.

In inferential statistics, researchers use the sample statistics they measure in a sample to make inferences
about the characteristics, or population parameters, in a population of interest.

entire class (the population), not just those few students. In a similar way, researchers
select samples to learn more about populations.

When researchers measure sample statistics such as the mean and variance, they
do so to estimate the value of the mean and variance in a population. But how well do
sample statistics, such as the sample mean and sample variance, estimate the value of
population parameters, such as the population mean and population variance? What
is the probability that a sample statistic will be smaller than, larger than, or exactly
equal to the value of a population parameter? These questions can be answered, in
part, by applying our knowledge of normal distributions.

In this learning unit, we compare the mean and variance in a sample to the mean
and variance in a population to show the relationship between samples and populations. We make this comparison by constructing a **sampling distribution**, which
is a distribution of the mean and variance for all possible samples of a given size from

A **sampling
distribution** is a
distribution of all
sample means or
sample variances
that could be
obtained in samples
of a given size
from the same
population.

a population. We can then compare the statistics we obtain in the samples to the value of the mean and variance in the hypothetical population. By doing so, we will answer the two questions asked in the previous paragraph. We will further use Excel to construct sampling distributions for large samples.

Selecting a Sample: Who's In and Who's Out?

Once we identify a population of interest, we need to determine a **sample design** for selecting samples from the population. A sample design is a plan for how individuals will be selected from a population of interest. There are many appropriate sample designs, and all of them address the following two questions:

1. Does the order of selecting participants matter?

2. Do we replace each selection before the next draw?

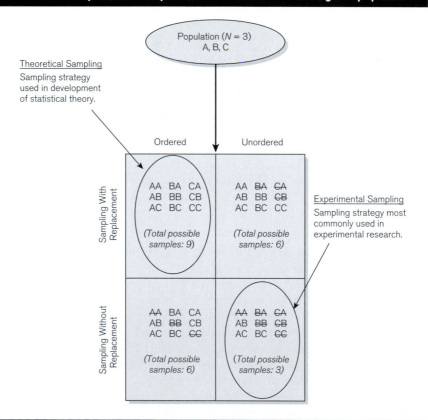

FIGURE 6.2 ● The effect of replacement and order changes on the many possible samples that can be drawn from a given population.

In this example, all possible samples of the size 2 ($n = 2$) are taken from this population of size 3 ($N = 3$). Notice that theoretical sampling allows for the most possible samples (9), whereas experimental sampling allows for the fewest possible samples (3).

A **sample design** is a specific plan or protocol for how individuals will be selected or sampled from a population of interest.

The first question determines how often people in a population can be selected. Both questions determine the number of samples of a given size that can be selected from a given population. Answering both questions leads to two strategies for sampling, which we describe in this section. One strategy, called theoretical sampling, is used in the development of statistical theory. The second strategy, called experimental sampling, is the most common strategy used in behavioral research. Figure 6.2 shows how we can apply each strategy.

Sampling Strategy: The Basis for Statistical Theory

Statistics is a branch of mathematics used to summarize, analyze, and interpret a group of numbers or observations. This branch of mathematics is based on theoretical proofs that show how statistical methods can be used to describe and interpret observations. Theoretical sampling, then, is used in the development of the theories that have led to statistics as a branch of mathematics.

To develop theories of sampling, statisticians answered yes to both questions stated above. To select samples from populations, the order of selecting people mattered, and each person selected was replaced before selecting again. To illustrate, suppose we select as many samples of two participants as possible from a population of three individuals (A, B, and C). In theoretical sampling,

1. Order matters. If two participants (A and B) are selected from a population, then selecting Participant A first, then B, differs from selecting Participant B first, then A. Each of these samples is regarded as a different possible sample that can be selected from this population.

2. We sample with replacement. This means that a sample of Participant A and then Participant A again is a possible sample, because we replaced Participant A before making the second selection.

The upper left portion of Figure 6.2 shows that we can select nine possible samples of size 2 from a population of three people using theoretical sampling. To determine the total number of samples of any size that can be selected from a population of any size using theoretical sampling, use the following computation:

$$\text{Total number of samples possible} = N^n$$

Let us verify the results shown in Figure 6.2, in which we had samples of two participants ($n = 2$) from a population of three people ($N = 3$). If we substitute these values into the computation, we obtain the following:

$$N^n = 3^2 = 9 \text{ samples}$$

Sampling Strategy: Most Used in Behavioral Research

In practice, however, we select diverse samples. For most studies in behavioral science, order does not matter, because we do not necessarily care about the order in which participants are selected. Also, we usually do not want to select the same person twice for the same study, so we sample without replacement. Experimental sampling, then, is the strategy used by experimenters who engage in behavioral research.

To illustrate the sampling strategy used in behavioral research, suppose we select as many samples of two participants as possible from a population of three people (A, B, and C). In experimental sampling:

1. Order does not matter. If two participants, A and B, are selected from a population, then selecting Participant A first, then B, is the same as selecting Participant B first, then A. These samples are counted as one sample and not as separate samples. In the example given in the lower right portion of Figure 6.2, this was one criterion by which samples were crossed out for experimental sampling.

2. We sample without replacement. This means that the same participant can never be sampled twice. So samples of AA, BB, and CC from the population in this example are not possible. In the example given in the lower right portion of Figure 6.2, this was the second criterion by which samples were crossed out for experimental sampling.

Thus, three samples of size 2 can be obtained from a population of size 3 using experimental sampling. To determine the total number of samples of any size that can be selected from a population of any size using experimental sampling, use the following computation:

$$\text{Total number of samples possible} = \frac{N!}{n!(N-n)!}$$

Let us use this computation to verify the results in Figure 6.2 in which we selected as many samples as possible of two individuals ($n = 2$) from a population of three individuals ($N = 3$):

$$\frac{N!}{n!(N-n)!} = \frac{3!}{2!(3-2)!} = \frac{3 \times 2 \times 1}{2 \times 1} = 3$$

Sampling Distributions: The Mean

In behavioral research, we often measure a sample mean to estimate the value of a population mean. To determine how well a sample mean estimates a population mean, we need to identify a population of interest and then determine the distribution of the sample means for all possible samples of a given size that can be selected from that population—thus, we need to construct a sampling distribution.

Statisticians used theoretical sampling to learn about the characteristics of the mean. Because experimental sampling yields the same results, we also will use experimental sampling strategy to select samples from a population. We can use the sampling distribution we construct in this section to see how well a sample mean estimates the value of a population mean.

To construct a sampling distribution, let us first look at a small hypothetical population of three people ($N = 3$) who took a psychological assessment. Person A scored an 8, Person B scored a 5, and Person C scored a 2 on this assessment. Because we know all three scores in this population, we can identify the mean in this population. (We can also identify the variance, which we will do in a later section.) Then we can construct a sampling distribution of the mean to determine how the sample means we could select from this population compare to the population mean we calculated.

First, let's see what we know about the population mean. The population mean for $N = 3$: The population mean (μ) is computed by summing all scores in the population, then dividing by the population size:

$$\mu = \frac{8 + 5 + 2}{3} = 5$$

Next we will select all samples of size 2 that can be drawn from this population. To find the sampling distribution for $n = 2$, we use the theoretical sampling technique from Figure 6.2, which lists the samples of size 2 that can be drawn from a population of three people using theoretical sampling. In all, there are nine possible samples we could have selected to estimate the population mean. These nine samples are given in Table 6.1 along with the scores and sample means we would have measured in those samples using the assessment scores we listed for each person.

In the third column in Table 6.1, ΣM is the sum of the sample means. The average sample mean (μ_M) is computed by dividing the sum of the sample means (ΣM) by the total number of samples summed (nine samples). Using the data in this table, we will find that the sample mean is related to the population mean in three ways. The sample mean

   (i) is an unbiased estimator,

  (ii) follows the central limit theorem, and

 (iii) has a minimum variance.

Let's look briefly at each of these relationships, and then use Excel to illustrate the characteristics of the sample mean using a larger sample size.

The Sample Mean Is an Unbiased Estimator (i)

A sample mean is an **unbiased estimator** when the sample mean we obtain in a randomly selected sample equals the value of the population mean on average. Note that the population mean is $\mu = 5$. If the sample mean is unbiased in its estimate of the population mean, then if we select a sample of a given size (in this case a sample size of 2) from that population, on average, the sample mean should equal the value of the true population mean. In other words, on average, the sample mean should be equal to 5 in our example. Notice in Table 6.1 that this is exactly what we find. The mean of

An **unbiased estimator** is any sample statistic, such as a sample variance when we divide SS by $n - 1$, obtained from a randomly selected sample that equals the value of its respective population parameter, such as a population variance, on average.

TABLE 6.1 ● The participants, individual scores, and sample means for each possible sample of size 2 from a population of size 3.		
Participants Sampled ($n = 2$)	**Scores for Each Participant**	**Sample Mean for Each Sample (M)**
A, A	8, 8	8.0
A, B	8, 5	6.5
A, C	8, 2	5.0
B, A	5, 8	6.5
B, B	5, 5	5.0
B, C	5, 2	3.5
C, A	2, 8	5.0
C, B	2, 5	3.5
C, C	2, 2	2.0
$N^n = 9$ samples		$\Sigma M = 45$
		$\mu_M = \dfrac{45}{9} = 5.0$

the sampling distribution of sample means is the sum of the sample means we could select (ΣM) divided by the total number of samples summed:

$$\mu_M = \frac{45}{9} = 5.0$$

On average, we can expect the sample mean from a randomly selected sample to be equal to the population mean. The sample mean, then, is an unbiased estimator of the value of the population mean. In statistical terms, $M = \mu$, on average. We can state this as a rule for the sample mean:

$$\text{When } M = \frac{\Sigma x}{n}, \text{ then } M = \mu \text{ on average}$$

The Sample Mean Follows the Central Limit Theorem (ii)

The **central limit theorem** explains that regardless of the distribution of scores in a population, the sampling distribution of sample means selected at random from that population will approach the shape of a normal distribution, as the number of samples in the sampling distribution increases. Thus, we should expect that a

The **central limit theorem** explains that regardless of the distribution of scores in a population, the sampling distribution of sample means selected at random from that population will approach the shape of a normal distribution, as the number of samples in the sampling distribution increases; note that as sample size increases, the number of samples in a sampling distribution also increases.

sampling distribution is always approximately normally distributed, even when the population distribution is not normal. This is exactly what we find to be true here, as illustrated in Figure 6.3. Although the population of scores is not normally

FIGURE 6.3 ● The central limit theorem.

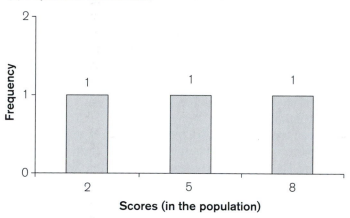

(a) Population Distribution

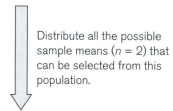

Distribute all the possible sample means ($n = 2$) that can be selected from this population.

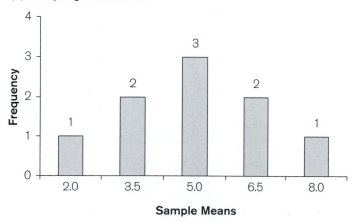

(b) Sampling Distribution

The hypothetical population has a nonmodal distribution (a), yet the possible sample means ($n = 2$) are approximately normally distributed (b).

distributed (the distribution is rectangular), the sample means selected from this population are normally distributed.

The central limit theorem has an important implication: It means that the probability distribution for obtaining a sample mean from a population is normal, and thus we can apply the empirical rule to find the probability of selecting a sample mean for a sample of a given size from a population of interest. From the empirical rule, for example, we know that at least 95% of all possible sample means we could select from a population are within two standard deviations (*SD*) of the true population mean—because we know the true population mean and the sample mean we can expect to select, on average, are the same (unbiased estimator).

The Sample Mean Has a Minimum Variance (iii)

What this characteristic emphasizes is that when we select a sample at random, not only will the sample mean be equal to the population mean on average (unbiased estimator), but when it does not equal the population mean, its variance––or how far "off" it is—will be minimal.

Critically, we can measure "error," or variability in how far "off" our estimates of the population mean can be, by taking the square root of the variance, which is the standard deviation. The standard deviation of a sampling distribution is called the **standard error of the mean** (*SEM* or σ_M), or simply the **standard error** (*SE*). The standard error tells us how far possible sample means deviate from the value of the population mean.

To compute the variance of the sampling distribution of sample means, divide the population variance (σ^2) by the sample size (*n*).

In our example, the population consisted of three people (A, B, C) with scores of 8, 5, and 2, respectively. The variance of 8, 5, and 2 is the population variance. The population variance is the sum of the squared deviation of scores from their mean (*SS*), divided by the population size (*N*):

$$\sigma^2 = \frac{(8-5)^2+(5-5)^2+(2-5)^2}{3} = 6.0$$

If we substitute the population variance (6) and sample size (2) from the original example into the formula, we find that the variance of the sampling distribution of sample means is equal to 3.0:

The **standard error of the mean**, or **standard error**, is the standard deviation of a sampling distribution of sample means. It is the standard error or distance that sample mean values deviate from the value of the population mean.

$$\sigma_M^2 = \frac{\sigma^2}{n} = \frac{6}{2} = 3.0$$

The standard error of the mean is the square root of the variance:

$$\sigma_M = \sqrt{\frac{\sigma^2}{n}} = \frac{\sigma}{\sqrt{n}}$$

$$\sigma_M = \sqrt{3.0} = 1.73$$

The value 1.73 is the smallest possible value we could obtain for the standard error. Researchers fully understand that when they select a sample, the mean they measure will not always be equal to the population mean. They understand that two random samples selected from the same population can produce different estimates of the same population mean, which is called **sampling error**. The standard error of the mean is a numeric measure of sampling error, with larger values indicating greater sampling error or greater differences that can exist from one sample to the next.

Minimizing Standard Error

The standard error can increase or decrease depending on the sample size and the value of the population standard deviation. In general, researchers are most interested in minimizing the "error" they can make, and thus have a desire to understand how to minimize standard error.

Two characteristics are useful for understanding how to minimize standard error. First, the smaller the population standard deviation (σ), the smaller the standard error. That is, the less scores in a population deviate from the population mean, the less possible it is that sample means will deviate from the population mean. Suppose, for example, that we select samples of size 2 ($n = 2$) from one of five populations having population standard deviations equal to $\sigma_1 = 4$, $\sigma_2 = 9$, $\sigma_3 = 16$, $\sigma_4 = 25$, and $\sigma_5 = 81$, respectively. Figure 6.4 shows that the standard error decreases as the population standard deviation decreases.

Second, the larger the sample size (n), the smaller the standard error. The larger the sample, the more data you collect, and the closer your estimate of the population mean will be. Suppose, for example, that we select samples of size 4 ($n = 4$), 9 ($n = 9$), 16 ($n = 16$), 25 ($n = 25$), and 81 ($n = 81$) from a single population with a standard deviation equal to 4. Figure 6.5 shows that the standard error decreases as the sample size increases. This result is called the **law of large numbers**.

Sampling error is the extent to which sample means selected from the same population differ from one another. This difference, which occurs by chance, is measured by the standard error of the mean.

The **law of large numbers** states that increasing the number of observations or samples in a study will decrease the standard error. Hence, larger samples are associated with closer estimates of the population mean on average.

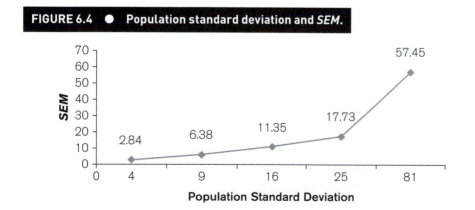

FIGURE 6.4 • Population standard deviation and *SEM*.

As the standard deviation in the population decreases, the standard error of the mean (*SEM*), or the distance that sample means deviate from the population mean, also decreases.

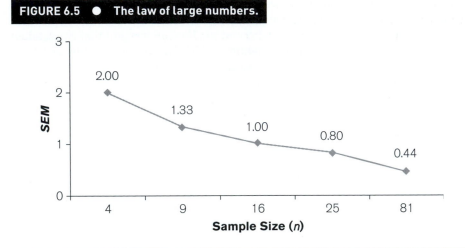

FIGURE 6.5 ● The law of large numbers.

As the sample size increases, the standard error of the mean (*SEM*) decreases, so sample means deviate closer to the population mean as sample size increases.

Overview of the Sample Mean

In all, three characteristics of the sample mean make it a good estimate of the value of the population mean:

1. The sample mean is an unbiased estimator. On average, the sample mean we obtain in a randomly selected sample will equal the value of the population mean.

2. A distribution of sample means follows the central limit theorem. That is, regardless of the shape of the distribution in a population, the distribution of sample means selected from the population will approach the shape of a normal distribution, as the number of samples in the sampling distribution increases.

3. A distribution of sample means has minimum variance. The sampling distribution of sample means will vary minimally from the value of the population mean.

Computing Characteristics of the Sample Mean Using Excel

With a larger data set in Excel, we can illustrate the characteristics of the sampling distribution for the sample mean. Download Age_At_Death_Sampling_Distribution.xlsx from the student study site: http://study.sagepub.com/priviteraexcel1e. Although these data are used in another learning unit, we have modified the data set in two ways. First we have again randomized the order of the numbers to be certain there is no systematic pattern as we go down the list of age at death. Second, we have limited the data set to the 53,000 cases. Let us consider this data set as the population of people who died in the New York City area in 2015.

With this larger data set, we will illustrate the characteristics of samples drawn from the population. Although we cannot reasonably perform theoretical or experimental sampling (both of which yield a number of samples that is several hundred digits in length), we can approximate diverse experimental sampling. To do this, we take 530 samples of 100 cases each without replacement.

We establish what can be known about this population. As shown in Figure 6.6a, type into cell D1 "Description of", and merge and center with E1. Type into cell D2 "Population", and merge and center with E2. List in column D from rows 3 to 8 some parameters of the population:

D3: *M*

D4: *SD*

D5: Skewness

D6: Kurtosis

D7: Minimum

D8: Maximum

We calculate these parameters in column E:

E3: =AVERAGE(B3:B53002)

E4: =STDEV.P(B3:B53002)

E5: =SKEW(B3:B53002)

E6: =KURT(B3:B53002)

E7: =MIN(B3:B53002)

E8: =MAX(B3:B53002).

Figure 6.6b shows the results of those calculations. The mean age at death is 73.81 years with an average deviation of 18.18 years. Age at death ranges from 0.1 years to 104.9 years. The skew index of –1.28 tells us that within that range of ages at death, there are a larger number of extreme scores to the left of the distribution than to the right. In practical terms, some people died very young. Most people lived for at least five or six decades, but not many lived beyond eight decades.

Appendix B

See **Appendix B2,** p. 301, for formatting cells.

See **Appendix B3**, p. 303, for freezing panes.

FIGURE 6.6 ● **Summarizing data about deaths in the New York City area in 2015. (a) Functions used to describe the population. (b) Results of the calculations of those functions.**

(a)

	A	B	C	D	E
1					Description of
2	Case #	Age at Death			Population
3	1	53.8		*M*	=AVERAGE(B3:B53002)
4	2	95.8		*SD*	=STDEV.P(B3:B53002)
5	3	91		Skewness	=SKEW(B3:B53002)
6	4	68.5		Kurtosis	=KURT(B3:B53002)
7	5	87.4		Minimum	=MIN(B3:B53002)
8	6	77.1		Maximum	=MAX(B3:B53002)
9	7	82.3			
10	8	92.4			
11	9	59			
12	10	74.1			

(b)

	A	B	C	D	E
1					Description of
2	Case #	Age at Death			Population
3	1	53.8		*M*	73.81
4	2	95.8		*SD*	18.18
5	3	91.0		Skewness	-1.28
6	4	68.5		Kurtosis	2.18
7	5	87.4		Minimum	0.1
8	6	77.1		Maximum	104.9
9	7	82.3			
10	8	92.4			
11	9	59.0			
12	10	74.1			

Because we randomized the order of the ages, we can treat each successive set of 100 cases in order as a random sample of the population of 53,000 cases. This yields 530 random samples for which we can calculate descriptions of the samples. As shown in Figure 6.7, type into cell H1 "Cases" and merge and center through cell K1. Next, we label the contents of each column:

H2: From

I2: To

J2: Mean

K2: Variance

Appendix B

See **Appendix B2,** p. 301, for formatting cells.

Beneath these labels, each row will identify which set of cases for mean and variance are calculated. Columns H and I will keep track of which set of 100 cases is represented. Columns J and K, respectively, report the mean and variance for that set of 100 cases. As shown in Figure 6.7a, enter into H3 and I3, respectively, the values 1 and 100. Into cell H4 enter =H3+100; into cell I4 enter =I3+100. This adds 100 to the value in the cell above and indicates that row 4 contains information on cases 101 to 200. Highlight H4 and I4 and paste or fill down through H532 and I532. This labels the range of cases contained in each of the 530 samples.

To calculate the means of samples, it will not be possible to use the simple =AVERAGE([cell range]) function to specify a cell range and then paste or fill this function into the cells below. That is because although the =AVERAGE([cell range]) function will adjust by one row number as we fill down or paste, the cases we want to include in the calculation are not one row apart. They are 100 rows apart. It's not necessary to type in all 530 individual cell ranges in column J. We can embed the

FIGURE 6.7 ● **Approximating experimental sampling with 530 samples, each of 100 scores. (a) Formulas and functions identifying samples and calculating means and variances. (b) Result of calculations of formulas and functions.**

(a)

	H	I	J	K
1			Cases	
2	From	To	Mean	Variance
3	1	100	=AVERAGE(OFFSET($B$3,(ROW()-ROW($J$3))*100,,100,))	=VAR.S(OFFSET($B$3,(ROW()-ROW($J$3))*100,,100,))
4	=H3+100	=I3+100	=AVERAGE(OFFSET($B$3,(ROW()-ROW($J$3))*100,,100,))	=VAR.S(OFFSET($B$3,(ROW()-ROW($J$3))*100,,100,))
5	=H4+100	=I4+100	=AVERAGE(OFFSET($B$3,(ROW()-ROW($J$3))*100,,100,))	=VAR.S(OFFSET($B$3,(ROW()-ROW($J$3))*100,,100,))
6	=H5+100	=I5+100	=AVERAGE(OFFSET($B$3,(ROW()-ROW($J$3))*100,,100,))	=VAR.S(OFFSET($B$3,(ROW()-ROW($J$3))*100,,100,))
7	=H6+100	=I6+100	=AVERAGE(OFFSET($B$3,(ROW()-ROW($J$3))*100,,100,))	=VAR.S(OFFSET($B$3,(ROW()-ROW($J$3))*100,,100,))
8	=H7+100	=I7+100	=AVERAGE(OFFSET($B$3,(ROW()-ROW($J$3))*100,,100,))	=VAR.S(OFFSET($B$3,(ROW()-ROW($J$3))*100,,100,))
9	=H8+100	=I8+100	=AVERAGE(OFFSET($B$3,(ROW()-ROW($J$3))*100,,100,))	=VAR.S(OFFSET($B$3,(ROW()-ROW($J$3))*100,,100,))
10	=H9+100	=I9+100	=AVERAGE(OFFSET($B$3,(ROW()-ROW($J$3))*100,,100,))	=VAR.S(OFFSET($B$3,(ROW()-ROW($J$3))*100,,100,))
11	=H10+100	=I10+100	=AVERAGE(OFFSET($B$3,(ROW()-ROW($J$3))*100,,100,))	=VAR.S(OFFSET($B$3,(ROW()-ROW($J$3))*100,,100,))
12	=H11+100	=I11+100	=AVERAGE(OFFSET($B$3,(ROW()-ROW($J$3))*100,,100,))	=VAR.S(OFFSET($B$3,(ROW()-ROW($J$3))*100,,100,))

(b)

	H	I	J	K
1			Cases	
2	From	To	Mean	Variance
3	1	100	71.88	429.97
4	101	200	77.32	276.55
5	201	300	76.70	274.16
6	301	400	75.30	207.86
7	401	500	71.40	308.40
8	501	600	74.22	275.33
9	601	700	73.22	349.03
10	701	800	71.44	458.60
11	801	900	75.68	297.00
12	901	1000	71.59	371.86

OFFSET and ROW functions within the AVERAGE function to move the calculation down to the next 100 scores in column B.

As shown in Figure 6.7a, enter into cell J3 =AVERAGE(OFFSET($B$3,(ROW()-ROW($J$3))*100,,100,)). This is a complicated function nested within the AVERAGE function. We will explain its components separately.

1. The first argument in the OFFSET function specifies $B$3 as a reference cell. The "$" anchors this cell reference when we paste or fill down to the cells below.

2. Next we need to know how far from the reference cell to start including numbers in the average. Our first average for cases 1 to 100 will actually begin on the same row as the reference cell, row 3. So (ROW()-ROW($J$3)) gives 0 offset. This argument uses the value of the current row, (ROW()), in which the mean is being calculated minus 3 (ROW($J$3)), the value of the row for the reference cell, B3, which equals 0. Zero times 100 equals 0, meaning we start zero rows down from B3, or exactly at B3 to calculate the first mean of cases 1 to 100.

3. The next argument, between two commas, is left blank; there is no column offset from B3, so we start in column B.

4. The next argument has the value 100 to include the 100 cells from the starting point down, B3 to B102. The last argument, after the last comma, is left blank; the calculation includes only one column, which is B. Because all of this is nested within the AVERAGE function, the value returned is the average of cells B3 to B102.

Appendix B

See **Appendix B4,** p. 304, for highlighting, pasting, and filling cells.

See **Appendix B6,** p. 306, for anchoring cell references.

Select cell J3 and paste or fill down to J532. When filling down or pasting to the cells below, references anchored by the "$" remain the same. One value that changes is the ROW() function that returns the value of the current row in which the mean is being calculated. So in row 4, (ROW()-ROW($J$3)) yields 4 (the value of the row in which the mean is being calculated) minus 3 (the value of row for the reference cell, B3), which equals 1. One times 100 equals 100, meaning we start down 100 cells after B3, at B103. Starting with B103, we include 100 cells, B103 to B202. Because this is nested with the AVERAGE function, it returns the average of cells B103 to B202. Following the same example, in row 5, 5 minus 3 equals 2, specifying we start down 200 cells after B3, at B203. This gives the average of the next 100 cases in B203 through B302. The pattern is the same all the way down to cell I532. The first 10 sample means are in J3 through J12 in Figure 6.7b.

In column K, we calculate the sample variance by following the same procedure that we used to calculate sample means. As shown in Figure 6.7b, enter into cell K3 =VAR.S(OFFSET($B$3,(ROW()-ROW($J$3))*100,,100,)). Select cell K3 and fill down to K532, or copy K3 and paste from K4 to K532. The first 10 sample variances are in K3 through K12 in Figure 6.7.

As shown in Figure 6.8, in columns M and N, we describe the sample means and sample variances just calculated in columns J and K. Type into cell M1 "Description of" and merge and center with N1. Type into cell M2 "530 Samples" and merge and center with N2. List in column M from rows 3 to 10 some parameters of the population:

M3: *M* of Samples

M4: *SE* (*SD* of Samples)

M5: Skewness

M6: Kurtosis

M7: Minimum Sample Mean

M8: Maximum Sample Mean

M9: Minimum Sample Variance

M10: Maximum Sample Variance

We calculate these parameters in column N:

N3: =AVERAGE(J3:J532)

N4: =STDEV.P(J3:J532)

N5: =SKEW(J3:J532)

N6: =KURT(J3:J532)

N7: =MIN(J3:J532)

N8: =MAX(J3:J532)

N9: =MIN(K3:K532)

N10: =MAX(K3:K532)

The mean of the sample means (μ_M), shown in cell N3 in Figure 6.8b, is 73.81. This represents 53,000 cases in 530 samples of 100 scores each. As expected, this is identical to the mean taken from all 53,000 cases, shown in cell E3 in Figure 6.6b. For the raw data, large indices of skewness in cell E5 and kurtosis in cell E6 reveal that many scores were to the extreme left in the distribution. In contrast, for the sampling distribution, small indices of skewness shown in cell N5 and kurtosis in N6 of Figure 6.8 indicated that the distribution of sample means is essentially normal. This is consistent with the central limit theorem, which states that the sampling distribution of the sample means will be normally distributed, even if the population of 53,000 scores was negatively skewed.

By creating a frequency distribution of the sample means and a column graph, we can see more easily that the shape of the distribution of sample means is approximately normally distributed. Select cells J2 to K532. Click the Insert tab, and then select PivotTable. Under Choose where to place the PivotTable, select Existing worksheet, and click on cell P2. Place "Mean" in the Rows section of the dialog box. Select "To" for placement in the Values box. Click "i" in the Values box to change the calculation from Sum to Count. Close the PivotTable builder. In cell P2 type "Sample

FIGURE 6.8 ● Summarizing the sampling distribution of people who died in the New York City area in 2015. (a) Functions used to describe the sampling distribution. (b) Results of the calculations of those functions.

(a)

	M	N
1	Description of	
2	530 Samples	
3	*M* of Samples	=AVERAGE(J3:J532)
4	*SE* (*SD* of Samples)	=STDEV.P(J3:J532)
5	Skewness	=SKEW(J3:J532)
6	Kurtosis	=KURT(J3:J532)
7	Minimum Sample Mean	=MIN(J3:J532)
8	Maximum Sample Mean	=MAX(J3:J532)
9	Minimum Sample Variance	=MIN(K3:K532)
10	Maximum Sample Variance	=MAX(K3:K532)

(b)

	M	N
1	Description of	
2	530 Samples	
3	*M* of Samples	73.81
4	*SE* (*SD* of Samples)	1.78
5	Skewness	-0.23
6	Kurtosis	0.23
7	Minimum Sample Mean	67.75
8	Maximum Sample Mean	79.17
9	Minimum Sample Variance	188.70
10	Maximum Sample Variance	579.71

Mean"; in cell Q2 type "Frequency". Right-click on the PivotTable to bring up a dialog box with Group and Outline. Select Group. . . to determine the bins for grouping scores. We know from cells N7 and N8 in Figure 6.8b that the range of sample means is from 67.75 to 79.17. For simplicity, we selected a starting score of 67 and an ending score of 80, increasing each bin by increments of 1. The frequency distribution should look like the one in Figure 6.9.

As expected from the skew and kurtosis indices of the 530 sample means, the distribution of sample means in Figure 6.9 has a large cluster of scores in the middle

FIGURE 6.9   ●   Frequency distribution of sample means of age at death tends toward a normal distribution despite the negatively skewed distribution in the population.

Sample Mean	Frequency
67-68	2
68-69	2
69-70	6
70-71	23
71-72	48
72-73	75
73-74	124
74-75	117
75-76	80
76-77	35
77-78	16
78-79	1
79-80	1
Grand Total	**530**

FIGURE 6.10   ●   Distribution of sample means of age at death tends toward a normal distribution despite the negatively skewed distribution of the raw data.

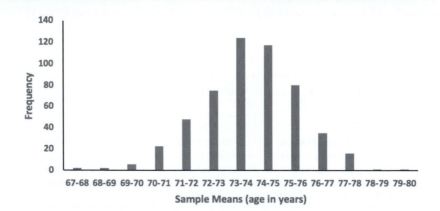

Sample Means (age in years)

with few scores in the extremes. Moreover, both left and right sides of the distribution appear approximately symmetrical.

We now create a graph of that distribution to compare it with the distribution generated with hypothetical data, Figure 6.3b. To create a column chart of the frequency distribution, select the Insert Tab and highlight cells P2 through Q15. In the toolbar of the Insert tab, select a column chart from Recommend Charts, or hover over the upper left icon of a column chart.

Appendix B

See **Appendix B7**, p. 307, for how to create and format a chart.

Clicking on Recommended Charts previews how selected data will appear in a graph. Select the one with columns. Reposition and resize the chart to your liking by clicking and dragging. Your chart should look like the one in Figure 6.10.

Sampling Distributions: The Variance

Not only are samples informative about the sample mean, but they are also informative about the sample variance. In this section, let us first begin with the same small hypothetical population of three people ($N = 3$) who took a psychological assessment. Person A scored an 8, Person B scored a 5 and Person C scored a 2 on this assessment. Because we know all three scores in this population, we can identify the variance in this population. (We computed the mean in the previous sections.) Then we can construct a sampling distribution of the variance to determine how the sample variances we could select from this population compare to the population variance we calculated.

First, let's see what we know about the population variance. The population variance (σ^2) is the sum of the squared deviation of scores from their mean (SS), divided by the population size (N):

$$\sigma^2 = \frac{(8-5)^2 + (5-5)^2 + (2-5)^2}{3} = 6$$

To calculate the sample variance, we can actually compute variance a little differently than we did for the population. To compute the sample variance, we compute the numerator the same way (SS), but in the denominator we divide by $n - 1$, also called *degrees of freedom (df) for variance*. Table 6.2 lists these nine samples, with the scores and sample variances that we would have measured in each of those samples.

Appendix A12

See **Appendix A12,** p. 298, for more on degrees of freedom for parametric tests.

Using the data in this table, when we divide SS by df, we find that the sample variance is related to the population variance in three ways. The sample variance

(i) is an unbiased estimator,

(ii) follows the skewed distribution rule, and

(iii) does not have minimum variance.

TABLE 6.2 ● The participants, individual scores, and sample variances for each possible sample of size 2 from a population of size 3.		
Participants Sampled ($n = 2$)	**Scores for Each Participant**	**Sample Variance for Each Sample ($SS/n-1$)**
A, A	8, 8	0
A, B	8, 5	4.50
A, C	8, 2	18.00
B, A	5, 8	4.50
B, B	5, 5	0
B, C	5, 2	4.50
C, A	2, 8	18.00
C, B	2, 5	4.50
C, C	2, 2	0
$N^n = 9$ samples		$\Sigma s^2 = 54$
		$\mu_{s^2} = \dfrac{54}{9} = 6.0$

Let's look briefly at each of these relationships, and then use Excel to illustrate the characteristics of the sample variance using a larger sample size.

The Sample Variance Is an Unbiased Estimator (i)

A sample variance is an *unbiased estimator* when the sample variance we obtain in a randomly selected sample equals the value of the population variance on average. We know that the population variance in the hypothetical example is equal to 6.0. The mean of the sampling distribution of sample variances (μ_{s_2}) is the sum of the sample variances we could select (Σs^2), divided by the total number of samples summed (N^n):

$$\mu_{s^2} = \frac{54}{9} = 6.0$$

On average, we can expect the sample variance from a randomly selected sample to equal the population variance when we divide SS by df. The sample variance, then, is an unbiased estimator of the value of the population variance. In statistical terms, $s^2 = \sigma^2$ on average. We can state this as a rule for the sample variance:

$$\text{When } s^2 = \frac{SS}{n-1} \text{ or } \frac{SS}{df}, \text{ then } s^2 = \sigma^2 \text{ on average}$$

If we divided *SS* by *n*, the result would be that we underestimate the population variance on average, which would make the sample variance a biased estimator of the population variance when we divide *SS* by *n*. Only when we divide *SS* by *df* will the sample variance be an unbiased estimator of the population variance. For this reason, we divide *SS* by *df* for sample variance to compute sample variance.

The Sample Variance Follows the Skewed Distribution Rule (ii)

We know that the sample variance is equal to the population variance, on average, when we divide *SS* by *df*. But what about all other possible outcomes we could obtain in the samples we select? We can distribute all other possible outcomes by listing the value of each possible sample variance on the *x*-axis of a graph and the number of times it occurs on the *y*-axis. Figure 6.11 shows that the sampling distribution of the sample variance selected from this population is approximately positively skewed. This result demonstrates the skewed distribution rule: Regardless of the distribution of scores in a population, the sampling distribution of sample variances selected at random from that population will approach the shape of a positively skewed distribution, as the number of samples in the sampling distribution increases.

The Sample Variance Does Not Have Minimum Variance (iii)

The variance of a skewed distribution can be any positive number. Defining the variance can give us an idea of how far the value of a sample variance can deviate from

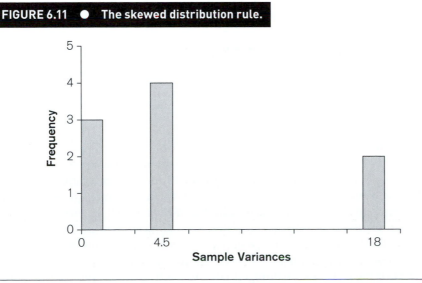

FIGURE 6.11 ● The skewed distribution rule.

The sampling distribution of sample variances tends toward a positively skewed distribution, regardless of the shape of the distribution in the population.

the population variance. When we divide *SS* by *df* to compute variance, however, we find that the sample variance does not vary minimally from the population variance. That is, when we select a sample variance that does not equal the population variance, its value can be quite far from the actual value of the population variance that we are trying to estimate, particularly for smaller sample sizes.

The distribution of sample variances is minimal only when we divide *SS* by *n*. Statisticians generally agree that it is better for the sample variance we measure to be unbiased (i.e., to be equal on average to the population variance) than for a distribution of sample variances to vary minimally from the population variance. For this reason, the sample variance is calculated by dividing *SS* by *df*.

Overview of the Sample Variance

In all, the sample variance is a good estimate of the value of the population variance because it is unbiased. The characteristics of the sample variance are as follows:

1. The sample variance is an unbiased estimator. On average, the sample variance we obtain in a randomly selected sample will equal the population variance when we divide *SS* by *df*, where $df = n - 1$.

2. A distribution of sample variances follows the skewed distribution rule. Regardless of the shape of the distribution in a population, the distribution of sample variances selected from the population will approach the shape of a positively skewed distribution, as the number of samples in the sampling distribution increases.

3. A distribution of sample variances has no minimum variance. The sampling distribution of sample variances will not vary minimally from the value of the population variance when we divide *SS* by *df*.

Computing Characteristics of the Sample Variance Using Excel

With a larger data set in Excel, we can illustrate the characteristics of the sampling distribution for the sample variance. Let us create a distribution of the variances that we calculated for each sample ($n = 100$) of the age-at-death data. In Figure 6.7, we calculated the variances for each of the samples; in Figure 6.12 the sample variances are distributed. We can see the positively skewed distribution of sample variances by creating a frequency distribution of the sample variances and a column graph. Select cells I2 to K532. Click the Insert tab, and then select PivotTable. Under Choose where to place the PivotTable, select Existing worksheet, and click on cell S2. Place "Variance" in the Rows section of the dialog box. Select "To" for placement in the Values box. Click "i" in the Values box to change the calculation from Sum to Count. Close the PivotTable builder. Type "Sample Variance" in cell S2 and "Frequency" in cell T2. Right-click on the PivotTable to bring up a dialog box with Group and Outline. Select Group. . . to determine the bins for grouping variances. We know from cells L9 and L10 that the sample variances range from 188.70 to 579.71. For simplicity, we selected

FIGURE 6.12 ● Frequency distribution of sample variances of age at death tends toward positively skewed despite the negatively skewed distribution of raw scores in the population.

Sample Variance	Frequency
188-212.5	15
212.5-237	19
237-261.5	43
261.5-286	67
286-310.5	74
310.5-335	67
335-359.5	81
359.5-384	57
384-408.5	39
408.5-433	27
433-457.5	17
457.5-482	14
482-506.5	5
506.5-531	3
531-555.5	1
555.5-580	1
Grand Total	**530**

a starting variance of 188 and an ending variance of 580, and created a bin width of 24.5. The frequency distribution should look like the one in Figure 6.11. The majority of sample variances fall just to the left of the center with more extreme sample variances on the right.

We now create a graph of that distribution of sample variances to compare it with the distribution generated with hypothetical data. To create a column chart of the frequency distribution, select the Insert tab, and highlight cells T2 through U18. In the toolbar of the Insert tab, select a column chart from Recommend Charts, or hover over the upper left icon of a column chart.

Appendix B

See **Appendix B7**, p. 307, for how to create and format a chart.

Clicking on Recommended Charts previews how selected data will appear in a graph. Select the one with columns. Reposition and resize the chart too your liking by clicking and dragging. Your chart should look like the one in Figure 6.13.

In this learning unit we evaluated the sample mean and the sample variance in terms of how informative these descriptive statistics are for parameters in the population (i.e., the population mean and the population variance). Our exploration in this learning unit revealed that both the sample mean and sample variance are quite informative.

While the sample mean, but not the sample variance, has minimum variance, both statistics are unbiased estimators of their respective parameters, meaning that for a

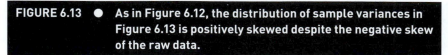

FIGURE 6.13 ● As in Figure 6.12, the distribution of sample variances in Figure 6.13 is positively skewed despite the negative skew of the raw data.

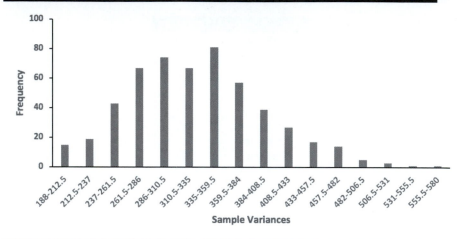

randomly selected sample, the sample mean will equal the population mean on average, and the sample variance will equal the population variance on average when we divide *SS* by *df*. The sampling distribution for both sample statistics also follows a consistent pattern, with the sampling distribution of the sample mean tending toward a normal distribution, and the sampling distribution of the sample variance tending toward a positive skewed distribution. Using Excel helps to illustrate the use of formulas and functions to quickly evaluate the characteristics of large samples, as we did in this learning unit.

Evaluating the Nature of Effects

The word *hypothesis* is loosely used in everyday language to describe an educated guess. We often informally state hypotheses about behaviors (e.g., who is the most outgoing among our friends) and events (e.g., which team will win the big game). Informally stating hypotheses in everyday language helps us describe or organize our understanding of the behaviors and events we experience from day to day.

In science, hypotheses are stated and tested more formally with the purpose of acquiring knowledge. The value of understanding the basic structure of the scientific process requires an understanding of how researchers test their hypotheses. Behavioral science is about understanding behaviors and events. You are in many ways a behavioral scientist in that you already hypothesize about many behaviors and events, albeit informally. Formally, hypothesis testing in science is similar to a board game, which has many rules to control, manage, and organize how you are allowed to move game pieces on a game board. Most board games, for example, have rules that tell you how many spaces you can move on the game board at most at a time, and what to do if you pick up a certain card or land on a certain spot on the game board. The rules, in essence, define the game. Each board game makes most sense if players follow the rules.

Likewise, in science, we ultimately want to gain an understanding of the behaviors and events we observe. The steps we follow in hypothesis testing allow us to gain this understanding and draw conclusions from our observations with certainty. In a board game, we follow rules to establish a winner; in hypothesis testing, we follow rules or steps to establish conclusions from the observations we make. In this learning unit, we explore the nature of hypothesis testing as it is used in science and the types of information it provides about the observations we make. This section provides information that is essential for understanding the context of and logic for hypothesis testing, which is applied in Sections IV and V.

LEARNING
UNIT
7

Hypothesis Testing: Significance, Effect Size, and Confidence Intervals

Making observations is something all of us are familiar with. We may observe friends "in love" or athletes "in the zone" or maybe you observe people "overreacting" to a situation. In each case, simply making the observation is not sufficient for science. From a scientific viewpoint, we must first structure our observations such that other people could observe the same things we did. In other words, how do you structure your observations to know what constitutes friends showing that they are "in love" or that an athlete is "in the zone" or that people are "overreacting" to a situation—in such a way that you could gain consensus from others using the same set of procedures to make those observations.

To address this question, we need to know what we expect to observe. In other words, we need to begin with hypotheses that help us to structure our observations. An equally critical step will be in how we test our hypotheses by analyzing the data we collect from our observations. By analyzing data, we can draw conclusions from the observations we make—we can understand the nature of the "effects" we observe. This learning unit provides an essential introduction to understanding the context of and logic for hypothesis testing, which is applied in Sections IV and V. Although we will not use Excel to introduce the nature of hypothesis testing in this learning unit, we will make extensive use of Excel in Sections IV and V, where we apply the general procedures described here for hypothesis testing.

Inferential Statistics and Hypothesis Testing

Inferential statistics allow us to observe samples to learn about behavior in populations that are often too large or inaccessible to observe. We use samples because we know how they are related to populations. For example, suppose the average score on a standardized exam in a given population is 150. The sample mean is an *unbiased estimator* of the population mean—if we select a random sample from a population, then on average the value of the sample mean will equal the value of the population mean. In our example, if we select a random sample from this population with a mean of 150, then, on average, the value of a sample mean will equal 150. On the basis of the *central limit theorem*, we know that the probability of selecting any other sample mean value from this population is normally distributed. This was one of the major themes in Learning Unit 6.

In behavioral research, we select samples to learn more about populations of interest to us. In terms of the mean, we measure a sample mean to learn more about the mean in a population. Therefore, we will use the sample mean to describe the population mean. We begin by stating a **hypothesis** about the value of a population mean, and then we select a sample and measure the mean in that sample. On average, the value of the sample mean will equal that of the population mean. The larger the difference or discrepancy between the sample mean and population mean, the less likely it will be that the value of the population mean we hypothesized is correct. This type of experimental situation, using the example of standardized exam scores, is illustrated in Figure 7.1. Although subsequent learning units will cover a variety of questions, research designs, and statistical tests, the underlying reasoning used here applies to research designs associated with various statistical tests.

The method of evaluating samples to learn more about characteristics in a given population is called **hypothesis testing**. Hypothesis testing is really a systematic way to test claims or ideas about a group or population. To illustrate, let us use a simple example concerning social media use. According to estimates reported by Mediakix (2016),

> A **hypothesis** is a statement about or proposed explanation for an observation, a phenomenon, or a scientific problem that can be tested using the research method. A hypothesis is often a statement about the value for a parameter in a population.
>
> **Hypothesis testing** or **significance testing** is a method for testing a claim or hypothesis about a parameter in a population, using data measured in a sample. In this method, we test a hypothesis by determining the likelihood that a sample statistic would be selected if the hypothesis regarding the population parameter were true.

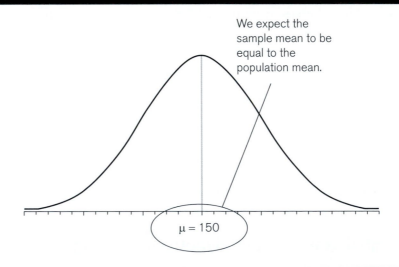

FIGURE 7.1 ● The sampling distribution for a population with a mean equal to 150.

We expect the sample mean to be equal to the population mean.

$\mu = 150$

If 150 is the correct population mean, then the sample mean will equal 150, on average, with outcomes farther from the population mean being less and less likely to occur.

the average consumer spends roughly 120 minutes (or 2 hours) a day on social media. Suppose we want to test how the social media use of premillennial consumers (i.e., those born before the millennial generation) compares to that of the average consumer. To make a test, we record the time (in minutes) that a sample of older consumers uses social media per day, and compare this to the average of 120 minutes per day that all consumers (the population) use social media. The mean we measure for these premillennial consumers is a sample mean. We can then compare the mean in our sample to the population mean for all consumers ($\mu = 120$ minutes).

The method of hypothesis testing can be summarized in four steps. We describe each of these four steps in greater detail in the next section. These four steps guide us through various statistical tests in Sections IV and V of this book, whether the statistical tests evaluate means or evaluate variance.

1. To begin, we identify a hypothesis or claim that we feel should be tested. For example, we decide to test whether the mean number of minutes per day that premillennial consumers spend on social media is 120 minutes per day (i.e., the average for all consumers).

2. We select a criterion upon which we decide whether the hypothesis being tested should be accepted or not. For example, the hypothesis is whether or not premillennial consumers spend 120 minutes using social media per day. If premillennial consumers' use of social media is similar to that of the average consumer, then we expect the sample mean will be about 120 minutes. If premillennial consumers spend more or less than 120 minutes using social media per day, then we expect the sample mean will be some value much lower or higher than 120 minutes. However, at what point do we decide that the discrepancy between the sample mean and 120 minutes (i.e., the population mean) is so big that we can reject the notion that premillennial consumers' use of social media is similar to that of the average consumer? In Step 2 of hypothesis testing, we answer this question.

3. Next, we select a sample from the population and measure the sample mean. For example, we can select a sample of 1,000 premillennial consumers and measure the mean time (in minutes) that they use social media per day.

4. Finally, we compare what we observe in the sample to what we expect to observe if the claim we are testing—that premillennial consumers spend 120 minutes using social media per day—is true. We expect the sample mean will be around 120 minutes. The smaller the discrepancy between the sample mean and population mean, the more likely we are to decide that premillennial consumers' use of social media is similar to that of the average consumer (i.e., about 120 minutes per day). The larger the discrepancy between the sample mean and population mean, the more likely we are to decide to reject that claim.

Four Steps to Hypothesis Testing

The goal of hypothesis testing is to determine the likelihood that a sample statistic would be selected if the hypothesis regarding a population parameter were true. In this section, we describe the four steps of hypothesis testing that were briefly introduced in the previous section:

Step 1: State the hypotheses.

Step 2: Set the criteria for a decision.

Step 3: Compute the test statistic.

Step 4: Make a decision.

Step 1: State the hypotheses. We begin by stating the value of a population mean in a **null hypothesis**, which we presume is true. For the example of social media use, we can state the null hypothesis (H_o) that premillennial consumers use an average of 120 minutes of social media per day: ($\mu = 120$ minutes).

This is a starting point so that we can decide whether or not the null hypothesis is likely to be true, similar to the presumption of innocence in a courtroom. When a defendant is on trial, the jury starts by assuming that the defendant is innocent. The basis of the decision is to determine whether this assumption is true. Likewise, in hypothesis testing, we start by assuming that the hypothesis or claim we are testing is true. This is stated in the null hypothesis. The basis of the decision is to determine whether this assumption is likely to be true.

The key reason we are testing the null hypothesis is because we think it is wrong. We state what we think is wrong about the null hypothesis in an **alternative hypothesis**. In a courtroom, the defendant is assumed to be innocent (this is the null hypothesis, so to speak), so the burden is on a prosecutor to conduct a trial to show evidence that the defendant is not innocent. In a similar way, we assume the null hypothesis is true, placing the burden on the researcher to conduct a study to show evidence that the null hypothesis is unlikely to be true. Regardless, we always make a decision about the null hypothesis (that it is likely or unlikely to be true). The alternative hypothesis is needed for Step 2.

The null and alternative hypotheses must encompass all possibilities for the population mean. For the example of social media use, we can state that the value in the null hypothesis is equal to 120 minutes. In this way, the null hypothesis value ($\mu = 120$ minutes) and the alternative hypothesis (H_1) value ($\mu \neq 120$ minutes) encompass all possible values for the population mean. If we believe that premillennial consumers use more than (>) or less than (<) 120 minutes of social media per day, then we can make a "greater than" or "less than" statement in the alternative hypothesis—this type of alternative is described in Step 2. Regardless of the decision alternative, the null and alternative hypotheses must encompass all possibilities for the value of the population mean.

Step 2: Set the criteria for a decision. To set the criteria for a decision, we state the **level of significance** for a hypothesis test. This is similar to the criterion that jurors use in a criminal trial. Jurors decide whether the evidence presented shows guilt *beyond a reasonable doubt* (this is the criterion). Likewise, in hypothesis testing, we collect data to test whether or not the null hypothesis is retained, based on the likelihood of selecting a sample mean from a population (the likelihood is the criterion). The likelihood or level of significance is typically set at 5% in behavioral research studies.

The **null hypothesis** (H_0), stated as the *null*, is a statement about a population parameter, such as the population mean, that is assumed to be true, and a hypothesis test is structured to decide whether or not to reject this assumption.

An **alternative hypothesis** (H_1) is a statement that directly contradicts a null hypothesis by stating that the actual value of a population parameter is less than, greater than, or not equal to the value stated in the null hypothesis.

Level of significance, or **significance level**, is a criterion of judgment upon which a decision is made regarding the value stated in a null hypothesis. The criterion is based on the probability of obtaining a statistic measured in a sample if the value stated in the null hypothesis were true.

When the probability of obtaining a sample mean would be less than 5% if the null hypothesis were true, then we conclude that the sample we selected is too unlikely, and thus we reject the null hypothesis.

The alternative hypothesis is identified so that the criterion can be specifically stated. Remember that the sample mean will equal the population mean on average if the null hypothesis is true. All other possible values of the sample mean are normally distributed (central limit theorem). The empirical rule tells us that at least 95% of all sample means fall within about 2 standard deviations (*SD*) of the population mean, meaning that there is less than a 5% probability of obtaining a sample mean that is beyond approximately 2 *SD* from the population mean. For the example of social media use, we can look for the probability of obtaining a sample mean beyond 2 *SD* in the upper tail (greater than 120), the lower tail (less than 120), or both tails (not equal to 120). Figure 7.2 shows the three decision alternatives for a hypothesis test; to conduct a hypothesis test, you choose only one alternative. How to choose an alternative is described in this learning unit. No matter what test you compute, the null and alternative hypotheses must encompass all possibilities for the population mean.

Step 3: Compute the test statistic. Suppose we observe the sample and record a sample mean equal to 100 minutes ($M = 100$) that premillennial consumers use social media per day. Of course, we did not observe everyone in the population, so to make a decision, we need to evaluate how likely this sample outcome is if the

FIGURE 7.2 ● The three decision alternatives for a hypothesis test.

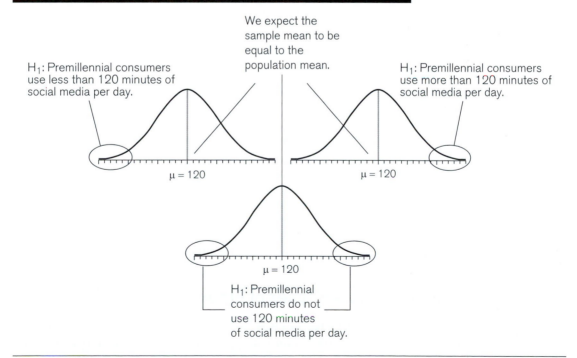

H_1: Premillennial consumers use less than 120 minutes of social media per day.

We expect the sample mean to be equal to the population mean.

H_1: Premillennial consumers use more than 120 minutes of social media per day.

$\mu = 120$

$\mu = 120$

$\mu = 120$

H_1: Premillennial consumers do not use 120 minutes of social media per day.

Although a decision alternative can be stated in only one tail, the null and alternative hypotheses should encompass all possibilities for the population mean.

population mean stated in the null hypothesis (120 minutes per day) is true. To determine this likelihood, we use a **test statistic**, which tells us how far, or how many standard deviations, a sample mean is from the population mean. The larger the value of the test statistic, the farther the distance, or number of standard deviations, a sample mean outcome is from the population mean stated in the null hypothesis. The value of the test statistic is used to make a decision in Step 4.

Step 4: Make a decision. We use the value of the test statistic to make a decision about the null hypothesis. The decision is based on the probability of obtaining a sample mean, given that the value stated in the null hypothesis is true. If the probability of obtaining a sample mean is less than or equal to 5% when the null hypothesis is true, then the decision is to reject the null hypothesis. If the probability of obtaining a sample mean is greater than 5% when the null hypothesis is true, then the decision is to retain the null hypothesis. In sum, there are two decisions a researcher can make:

> The **test statistic** is a mathematical formula that identifies how far or how many standard deviations a sample outcome is from the value stated in a null hypothesis. It allows researchers to determine the likelihood of obtaining sample outcomes if the null hypothesis were true. The value of the test statistic is used to make a decision regarding a null hypothesis.

1. Reject the null hypothesis. The sample mean is associated with a low probability of occurrence when the null hypothesis is true. For this decision, we conclude that the value stated in the null hypothesis is wrong; it is rejected.

2. Retain the null hypothesis. The sample mean is associated with a high probability of occurrence when the null hypothesis is true. For this decision, we conclude that there is insufficient evidence to reject the null hypothesis; this does not mean that the null hypothesis is correct. It is not possible to *prove* the null hypothesis.

> A *p* **value** is the probability of obtaining a sample outcome, given that the value stated in the null hypothesis is true. The *p* value for obtaining a sample outcome is compared to the level of significance or criterion for making a decision.

The probability of obtaining a sample mean, given that the value stated in the null hypothesis is true, is stated by the ***p* value**. The *p* value is a probability: It varies between 0 and 1 and can never be negative. In Step 2, we stated the criterion or probability of obtaining a sample mean at which we will decide to reject the value stated in the null hypothesis, which is typically set at 5% in behavioral research. To make a decision, we compare the *p* value to the criterion we set in Step 2.

When the *p* value is less than 5% ($p < .05$), we reject the null hypothesis, and when $p = .05$, the decision is also to reject the null hypothesis. When the *p* value is greater than 5% ($p > .05$), we retain the null hypothesis. The decision to reject or retain the null hypothesis is called **significance**. When the *p* value is less than or equal to .05, we *reach significance*; the decision is to reject the null hypothesis. When the *p* value is greater than .05, we *fail to reach significance*; the decision is to retain the null hypothesis. Figure 7.3 summarizes the four steps of hypothesis testing.

> **Significance**, or **statistical significance**, describes a decision made concerning a value stated in the null hypothesis. When the null hypothesis is rejected, we reach significance. When the null hypothesis is retained, we fail to reach significance.

Making a Decision: Types of Error

In Step 4, we decide whether to retain or reject the null hypothesis. Because we are observing a sample and not an entire population, it is possible that our decision about a null hypothesis is wrong. Table 7.1 shows that there are four decision alternatives regarding the truth and falsity of the decision we make about a null hypothesis:

FIGURE 7.3 ● A summary of the four steps of hypothesis testing.

STEP 1: State the hypotheses. A researcher states a null hypothesis about a value in the population (H_0) and an alternative hypothesis that contradicts the null hypothesis.

STEP 2: Set the criterion for a decision. A criterion is set upon which a researcher will decide whether to retain or reject the value stated in the null hypothesis.

A sample is selected from the population, and a sample mean is measured.

STEP 3: Compute the test statistic. This will produce a value that can be compared to the criterion that was set before the sample was selected.

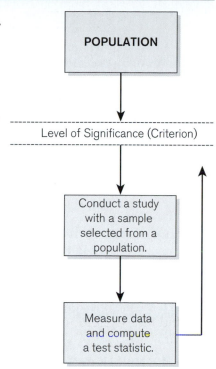

STEP 4: Make a decision. If the probability of obtaining a sample mean is less than or equal to 5% when the null is true, then reject the null hypothesis. If the probability of obtaining a sample mean is greater than 5% when the null is true, then retain the null hypothesis.

If 150 is the correct population mean, then the sample mean will equal 150, on average, with outcomes farther from the population mean being less and less likely to occur.

1. The decision to retain the null hypothesis is correct.
2. The decision to retain the null hypothesis is incorrect.
3. The decision to reject the null hypothesis is correct.
4. The decision to reject the null hypothesis is incorrect.

We investigate each decision alternative in this section. Because we will observe a sample, and not a population, it is impossible to know for sure the truth in the population. So for the sake of illustration, we will assume we know this. This assumption is labeled as Truth in the Population in Table 7.1. In this section, we introduce each decision alternative.

Decision: Retain the Null Hypothesis

When we decide to retain the null hypothesis, we can be correct or incorrect. The correct decision is to retain a true null hypothesis. This decision is called a null result or null finding. This is usually an uninteresting decision, because the decision is to retain what we already assumed. For this reason, a null result alone is rarely published in scientific journals for behavioral research.

TABLE 7.1 ● Four outcomes for making a decision.

		Decision	
		Retain the Null Hypothesis	**Reject the Null Hypothesis**
Truth in the Population	True	CORRECT $1 - \alpha$	TYPE I ERROR α
	False	TYPE II ERROR β	CORRECT $1 - \beta$ POWER

Type II error, or **beta (β) error**, is the probability of retaining a null hypothesis that is actually false.

Type I error is the probability of rejecting a null hypothesis that is actually true. Researchers directly control for the probability of committing this type of error by stating an alpha level.

An **alpha (α) level** is the level of significance or criterion for a hypothesis test. It is the largest probability of committing a Type I error that we will allow and still decide to reject the null hypothesis.

The **power** in hypothesis testing is the probability of rejecting a false null hypothesis. Specifically, it is the probability that a randomly selected sample will show that the null hypothesis is false when the null hypothesis is indeed false.

The incorrect decision is to retain a false null hypothesis: a "false negative" finding. This decision is an example of a **Type II error**, or **beta (β) error**. With each test we make, there is always some probability that the decision is a Type II error. In this decision, we decide not to reject previous notions of truth that are in fact false. While this type of error is often regarded as less problematic than a Type I error (defined in the next paragraph), it can be problematic in many fields, such as in medicine, where testing of treatments could mean life or death for patients.

Decision: Reject the Null Hypothesis

When we decide to reject the null hypothesis, we can be correct or incorrect. The incorrect decision is to reject a true null hypothesis: a "false positive" finding. This decision is an example of a **Type I error**. With each test we make, there is always some probability that our decision is a Type I error. A researcher who makes this error decides to reject previous notions of truth that are in fact true. Using the courtroom analogy, making this type of error is analogous to finding an innocent person guilty. To minimize this error, we therefore place the burden on the researcher to demonstrate evidence that the null hypothesis is indeed false.

Because we assume the null hypothesis is true, we control for Type I error by stating a level of significance. The level we set, called the **alpha level** (symbolized as α), is the largest probability of committing a Type I error that we will allow and still decide to reject the null hypothesis. This criterion is usually set at .05 ($\alpha = .05$) in behavioral research. To make a decision, we compare the alpha level (or criterion) to the p value (the actual likelihood of obtaining a sample mean, if the null were true). When the p value is less than the criterion of $\alpha = .05$, we decide to reject the null hypothesis; otherwise, we retain the null hypothesis.

The correct decision is to reject a false null hypothesis. In other words, we decide that the null hypothesis is false when it is indeed false. This decision is called the **power** of the decision-making process, because it is the decision we aim for. Remember that we are only testing the null hypothesis because we think it is wrong.

Deciding to reject a false null hypothesis, then, is the power, inasmuch as we learn the most about populations when we accurately reject false notions of truth about them. This decision is the most published result in behavioral research.

Nondirectional and Directional Alternatives to the Null Hypothesis

Recall that we can state one of three alternative hypotheses: A population mean is greater than (>), less than (<), or not equal to (≠) the value stated in a null hypothesis. The alternative hypothesis determines which tail of a sampling distribution to place the level of significance in, as illustrated in Figure 7.2.

For a **nondirectional**, or **two-tailed, test**, the alternative hypothesis is stated as *not equal to* (≠) the null hypothesis. For this test, we divide the level of significance, $p \leq .05$, into both tails of the sampling distribution. Now each tail has a rejection region of less than or equal to .025. We therefore stay neutral in terms of the alternative to the null hypothesis; we are interested in any alternative to the null hypothesis. This is the most common alternative hypothesis tested in behavioral science. In Figure 7.2, this test is illustrated in the bottom figure, where the rejection region is in both tails.

An alternative to the nondirectional test is a **directional**, or **one-tailed**, **test**, where the alternative hypothesis is stated as *greater than* (>) the null hypothesis or *less than* (<) the null hypothesis. For an upper-tail critical test, or a "greater than" statement, we place the level of significance, $p \leq .05$, in the upper tail of the sampling distribution. So we are interested in any alternative greater than the value stated in the null hypothesis. This test should only be used when it is impossible or highly unlikely that a sample mean will fall below the population mean stated in the null hypothesis. In Figure 7.2, this test is illustrated in the top right figure where the rejection region is in the upper tail only.

For a lower-tail critical test, or a "less than" statement, we place the level of significance or critical value in the lower tail of the sampling distribution. So we are interested in any alternative less than the value stated in the null hypothesis. This test should only be used when it is impossible or highly unlikely that a sample mean will fall above the population mean stated in the null hypothesis. In Figure 7.2, this test is illustrated in the top left figure where the rejection region is in the lower tail only.

For directional or one-tailed testing, it is important to consider that this testing creates the unique possibility of committing a **Type III error**. This type of error occurs when a decision would have been to reject the null hypothesis, but the researcher decides to retain the null hypothesis because the rejection region was located in the "wrong tail"—meaning that the effect or difference observed occurred in the opposite tail from where the rejection region was located. This type of error is not possible with a two-tailed test, because the rejection region is located in both tails for such tests. We take a closer look at one- versus two-tailed testing in the next section, where we further evaluate the strengths and limitations of such tests.

Nondirectional tests, or **two-tailed tests**, are hypothesis tests in which the alternative hypothesis is stated as *not equal to* (≠) a value stated in the null hypothesis. Hence, the researcher is interested in any alternative to the null hypothesis.

Directional tests, or **one-tailed tests**, are hypothesis tests in which the alternative hypothesis is stated as greater than (>) or less than (<) a value stated in the null hypothesis. Hence, the researcher is interested in a specific alternative to the null hypothesis.

A **Type III error** is a type of error possible with one-tailed tests in which a decision would have been to reject the null hypothesis, but the researcher decides to retain the null hypothesis because the rejection region was located in the wrong tail. The "wrong tail" refers to the opposite tail from where a difference was observed and would have otherwise been significant.

TAKING A CLOSER LOOK AT ONE-TAILED AND TWO-TAILED TESTING

Kruger and Savitsky (2006) conducted a study in which they performed two tests on the same data. They completed an upper-tail critical test at $\alpha = .05$ and a two-tailed test at $\alpha = .10$. As shown in Figure 7.8, these are similar tests, except in the upper-tail test, all the alpha level is placed in the upper tail, and in the two-tailed test, the alpha level is split so that .05 is placed in each tail. When the researchers showed these results to a group of participants, they found that participants were more persuaded by a significant result when it was described as a one-tailed test, $p < .05$, than when it was described as a two-tailed test, $p < .10$. This was interesting because the two results were identical—both tests were associated with the same critical value in the upper tail.

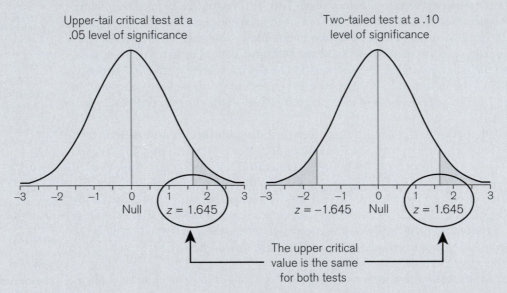

When $\alpha = .05$, all of that value is placed in the upper tail for an upper-tail critical test. The two-tailed equivalent would require a test with $\alpha = .10$, such that .05 is placed in each tail. Note that the normal distribution is symmetrical, so the cutoff in the lower tail is the same distance below the mean (–1.645; the upper tail is +1.645).

Most editors of peer-reviewed journals in behavioral research will not publish the results of a study where the level of significance is greater than .05. Although the two-tailed test, $p < .10$, was significant, it is unlikely that the results would be published in a peer-reviewed scientific journal. Reporting the same results as a one-tailed test, $p < .05$, makes it more likely that the data will be published.

The two-tailed test is more conservative; it makes it more difficult to reject the null hypothesis. It also eliminates the possibility of committing a Type III error. The one-tailed test, though, is associated with greater power. If the value stated in the null hypothesis is false, then a one-tailed test will make it easier to detect this (i.e., lead to a decision to reject the null hypothesis). Because the one-tailed test makes it easier to reject the null hypothesis, it is important that we justify that an outcome can occur in only one direction. Justifying that an outcome can occur in only one direction is difficult for much of the data that behavioral researchers measure. For this reason, most studies in behavioral research are two-tailed tests.

Effect Size

A decision to reject the null hypothesis means that an **effect** is significant. Hypothesis testing identifies whether or not an effect exists in a population. When a sample mean would be likely to occur if the null hypothesis were true ($p > .05$), we decide that an effect does not exist in a population; the effect is not significant. When a sample mean would be unlikely to occur if the null hypothesis were true (typically less than a 5% likelihood, $p < .05$), we decide that an effect does exist in a population; the effect is significant. Hypothesis testing does not, however, inform us of how big the effect is.

To determine the size of an effect, we compute **effect size**. There are two ways to calculate the size of an effect.

- *A change or shift in the population,* typically reported in standard deviation units (e.g., a seasonal promotion during an event increased the number of volunteers at the event 0.50 standard deviations above expected rates)

- *A proportion or percentage of variance accounted for,* typically reported as a proportion from 0 to 1.0 or as a percentage from 0% to 100% (e.g., 10% of the variance in academic achievement can be accounted for by the quality of instruction)

Effect size is most meaningfully reported with significant effects when the decision was to reject the null hypothesis. If an effect is not significant, as in instances when we retain the null hypothesis, then we are concluding that an effect does not exist in a population. It makes little practical sense to compute the size of an effect that we just concluded does not exist.

Estimation and Confidence Intervals

Beyond hypothesis testing, we can also learn more about the mean in a population using a different procedure without ever deciding to retain or reject a null hypothesis. An alternative approach requires only that we set limits for a population parameter within which it is likely to be contained. The goal of this alternative approach, called **estimation**, is the same as that in hypothesis testing—to learn more about the value of a mean in a population of interest.

There are two types of estimates: a point estimate and an interval estimate. When using one sample, a **point estimate** is the sample mean we measure. The advantage of using point estimation is that the *point estimate,* or sample mean, is an unbiased estimator—that is, the sample mean will equal the population mean on average. The disadvantage of using point estimation is that we have no way of knowing for sure whether a sample mean equals the population mean. One way to resolve this disadvantage is to identify a range of values (instead of giving just one value) within which we can be confident that any one of those values is equal to the population mean. The interval or range of possible values within which a population parameter is likely to be contained is called the **interval estimate**. Most often, the point estimate and interval estimate are given together. Thus, researchers report the sample mean (a point estimate) and give an interval within which a population mean is likely to be

---

An **effect** is a difference or disparity between what is thought to be true in a population and what is observed in a sample. In hypothesis testing, an effect is not significant when we retain the null hypothesis; an effect is significant when we reject the null hypothesis.

Effect size is a statistical measure of the size of an effect in a population, which allows researchers to describe how far scores shifted in the population, or the percentage of variance that can be explained by a given variable.

Estimation is a statistical procedure in which a sample statistic is used to estimate the value of an unknown population parameter. Two types of estimation are point estimation and interval estimation.

A **point estimate** is the use of a sample statistic (e.g., a sample mean) to estimate the value of a population parameter (e.g., a population mean).

An **interval estimate**, often reported as a **confidence interval**, is an interval or range of possible values within which a population parameter is likely to be contained.

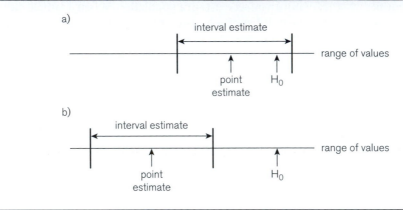

FIGURE 7.4 ● Point estimates and interval estimates on a range of values. (a) The interval estimate overlaps H_0. (b) The interval estimate does not overlap H_0.

contained (an *interval estimate*). The interval estimate, often reported as a **confidence interval**, is stated within a given **level of confidence**, which is the likelihood that an interval contains an unknown population mean.

Using estimation, we use the sample mean as a point estimate, and we use the variability as an estimate of the interval. Using the variability helps find a range of sample means within which the population mean is likely to be contained. While we do not "make a decision" per se using estimation, we can use the confidence limits to determine what the decision would have been using hypothesis testing. In terms of the decisions we make in hypothesis testing,

1. If the value stated by a null hypothesis is inside a confidence interval (Figure 7.4a), the decision is to retain the null hypothesis (not significant).

2. If the value stated by a null hypothesis is outside the confidence interval (Figure 7.4b), the decision is to reject the null hypothesis (significant).

Delineating Statistical Effects for Hypothesis Testing

A **level of confidence** is the probability or likelihood that an interval estimate will contain an unknown population parameter (e.g., a population mean).

At a macro level, hypothesis testing provides four core levels of information that can be used not only to make decisions about hypotheses, but also to help describe the nature of the effects being tested. Significance, effect size, and confidence intervals are three levels of information. Table 7.2 summarizes the information provided by each level, and adds a fourth level that is introduced in the next learning unit (Learning Unit 8).

- *Significance.* Is there an effect in the population?

- *Effect size.* What is the size of the effect in the population?

- *Confidence intervals.* Where is the effect likely to be in the population?

- *Power.* What is the likelihood of detecting the effect, if it exists?

When properly understood, addressing each of these levels of information—by answering each of the questions identified—can substantially bolster the comprehensiveness and informativeness of decisions made across hypothesis testing.

TABLE 7.2 ● Delineating significance, effect size, confidence intervals, and power.		
Type of Analysis	**Informativeness**	
Significance	Question Answered	Is there an effect in the population?
	Decision	Reject or retain the null hypothesis
Effect Size	Question Answered	What is the size of an effect in the population?
	Decision	Shift in the population (in standard deviations), or proportion of variance accounted for (as a proportion from 0 to 1.0)
Confidence Intervals	Question Answered	Where is the effect likely to be in the population?
	Decision	Interval or range of possible values within which the parameter we are estimating is likely to be contained
Power	Question Answered	What is the likelihood of detecting an effect, if it exists?
	Decision	Likelihood that an effect, if it exists, will lead to a "reject the null hypothesis" decision

LEARNING UNIT 8

Power

Detecting "Effects"

Suppose you know that more Americans use Instagram than Twitter—this is true according to a 2018 poll by the Pew Research Center showing that 35% of Americans say they use Instagram, compared to only 24% who say they use Twitter. Being a skeptic, you want to test this yourself. Suppose you take your own poll of 100 friends or 100 classmates selected at random. How likely are you to find similar results? Even if the results of your poll are similar to those of the Pew Research Center, is it necessarily true that you will always find the same results the Center finds?

Power, defined in Learning Unit 7 and again defined here, represents this likelihood. It is the likelihood of detecting an effect, if it exists. An *effect*, defined in Learning Unit 7 and again defined here, is a difference or disparity between what is thought to be true in a population and what is observed in a sample. In hypothesis testing, we conclude that an effect does not exist (i.e., it is not significant) when we retain the null hypothesis; we conclude that an effect does exist (i.e., it is significant) when we reject the null hypothesis.

In the example above, the social media *effect* being tested is the difference in users of Instagram and Twitter. But how much power do you have to detect the effect? In truth, it is not necessarily true that you will always detect the effect. The question is this: Assuming that the social media effect is true, what is the likelihood that you will detect the effect? The answer to this question is given by the power of your study. Power can range from 0% to 100%; the greater the power, the more likely it is that you will detect the effect.

As a general rule, in behavioral research, 80% power is regarded as the minimal standard. In other words, assuming there is an effect, researchers should ensure that at least 80% of the time they look for the effect, they will find it—again, assuming the effect actually exists. In this learning unit, we briefly evaluate two critical factors that tend to be given the greatest focus in terms of their impact on power: Effect size and sample size. *Effect size*, defined in Learning Unit 7 and again defined here, is a statistical measure of the size of an effect in a population, which allows researchers to describe how far scores shifted in the population, or the percentage of variance that can be explained by a given variable. Understanding the influence that effect size and sample size have on power can help illustrate what power is and why increasing power is optimal in science.

Effect Size, Power, and Sample Size

One advantage of knowing effect size, *d*, is that its value can be used to determine the power of detecting an effect in hypothesis testing. The likelihood of detecting an effect, called *power*, is critical in behavioral research, because it lets the researcher know the probability that a randomly selected sample will lead to a decision to reject the null hypothesis, if the null hypothesis is false. In this section, we describe how effect size and sample size are related to power.

The Relationship Between Effect Size and Power

As effect size increases, power increases. If we think of power as the ability to detect a signal, the stronger a signal relative to a distracting background, the more likely we are to detect that signal. As an example, consider the way to calculate effect size that we described in Learning Unit 7: measuring how far scores shifted in a population. Mathematically, we express effect size as the number of standard deviations an effect is shifted above or below the population mean stated by the null hypothesis:

$$\text{Effect Size: } d = \frac{\text{observed difference} - \text{null hypothesis}}{\text{population standard deviation}} = \frac{M - \mu}{\sigma}$$

It should be clear that effect size changes when either the numerator or the denominator changes. All other things being equal, effect size increases when

1. the distance between the observed difference and the hypothesized difference increases, or

2. the population standard deviation (or our estimate of the population standard deviation) decreases.

Simply stated, if we claim an effect exists, it would be nice to know the likelihood we will find it, if we are correct. In other words, it would be nice to know we can actually show that we are correct. Power will tell us this likelihood.

Here, we will illustrate how power and effect size are related using hypothetical statistics quiz scores for three classes of 30 randomly sampled students. Suppose we know, based on frequent testing, that the average score in the population on each quiz is 38 ($\mu = 38$). For Class 1 and Class 2, the population standard deviation is the same ($\sigma = 10$), but the effect size (*d*) differs based on differences in average performance (*M*) for each class:

$$\text{Class 1 Effect Size } (M = 40): d = \frac{M - \mu}{\sigma} = \frac{40 - 38}{10} = 0.20$$

$$\text{Class 2 Effect Size } (M = 48): d = \frac{M - \mu}{\sigma} = \frac{48 - 38}{10} = 1.00$$

For Class 3, introduced later, the effect will be the same as that of Class 1 ($M = 40$), but the standard deviation will be smaller ($\sigma = 2$):

$$\text{Class 3 Effect Size } (M = 40): d = \frac{M - \mu}{\sigma} = \frac{48 - 38}{2} = 1.00$$

For this example, think of the difference in performance as the strength of the signal. The louder the signal (i.e., the better the performance compared to μ) the easier it should be to detect the signal (i.e., the easier it should be to detect the differences). Let us look first at how this is true by comparing the power for Classes 1 and 2.

Class 1 and Class 2. In Class 1, students scored 40 points ($M = 40$)—2 points higher than the mean in the population, which was 38 points ($\mu = 38$). For this example, the population standard deviation is 10 points ($\sigma = 10$). This yields an effect size:

$$d = \frac{M - \mu}{\sigma} = \frac{48 - 38}{10} = 0.20$$

In Class 2, students scored 48 points ($M = 48$)—10 points higher than the mean in the population, which was 38 points ($\mu = 38$). For this example, the population standard deviation is again 10 points ($\sigma = 10$). This yields an effect size:

$$d = \frac{M - \mu}{\sigma} = \frac{48 - 38}{10} = 1.00$$

To determine power, we follow three steps:

1. Construct the sampling distribution for α (alpha), which is the type of error associated with assuming there is no effect, that is, assuming our decision for a hypothesis test is to retain the null hypothesis.

2. Construct the sampling distribution for β (beta), which is the type of error associated with assuming there is an effect as stated.

3. Compare the distributions to identify power.

Step 1: Construct the sampling distribution for α (alpha), which is the type of error associated with assuming there is no effect. For each class, we first construct the sampling distribution, assuming that $\mu = 38$ is indeed the correct average score, that is, assuming there is no effect. For Class 1, the mean of the sampling distribution, then, is equal to the population mean ($\mu = 38$).

The standard deviation of the sampling distribution, called the *standard error of the mean* (σ_M; see Learning Unit 6, p. 84), is equal to the population standard deviation divided by the square root of the sample size ($n = 30$ students):

$$\sigma_M = \frac{\sigma}{\sqrt{n}} = \frac{10}{\sqrt{30}} = 1.83$$

For simplicity, let us make a one-tailed test at a .05 level of significance. At .05, we can determine the cutoff for the rejection region—the region where we would decide to reject the null hypothesis that the population mean is 38. To do this, we compute a z transformation (see Learning Unit 5, p. 67) for a z score of 1.645—this is the cutoff on a z distribution for the top 5%; we want to determine what sample mean value is 1.645 standard deviations above 38 in a sampling distribution with a standard error of the mean of 1.83 for samples of size 30. The z transformation is

$$\frac{M - 38}{1.83} = 1.645$$

Solving for M,

$$M = 40.99$$

In the sampling distribution where we assume there is no effect, obtaining a sample mean equal to 40.99 or higher in Class 1 or in Class 2 will lead to a decision to reject the null hypothesis—which, if the null is actually true, would be an error, specifically, a *Type I error* (see Learning Unit 7, p. 109). To find power, we now need to move to Step 2.

Step 2: Construct the sampling distribution for β (beta), which is the type of error associated with assuming there is an effect as stated. The next step is then to actually assume the population mean ($\mu = 38$) is wrong; that the effect you observed is instead correct. For Class 1, this means that we will assume 40 is in fact the true population mean (a 2-point effect in the population). For Class 2, this means that we will assume 48 is in fact the true population mean (a 10-point effect in the population).

For Class 1 and Class 2, the standard deviation of the sampling distribution (called the standard error of the mean) for β—the type of error associated with false null hypotheses—does not change. What does change is the mean of the sampling distribution, which is always equal to the purported population mean. For Class 1 we state the mean of the sampling distribution as 40; for Class 2 we state the mean of the sampling distribution as 48.

Step 3: Compare the distributions to identify power. For Class 1 with a small effect size ($d = 0.20$), Figure 8.1 shows the sampling distribution for α (top figure) and the sampling distribution for β (the bottom figure—assuming there is a 2-point effect). Notice in the figure that the top and bottom figures overlap. In the bottom figure, which represents all the possible sample means we could select at random from this population, many of the sample means we could select do not fall in the rejection region. In other words, even if we are correct, and a 2-point effect does exist in the population, we would wrongly conclude to retain the null hypothesis; that is, we would fail to detect the effect. Power is represented as the percentage of sample mean outcomes that actually fall in the rejection region—in other words, the percentage of sample mean outcomes that would lead us to a decision that there is an effect (i.e., reject the null hypothesis). In this case, power is .2946 for Class 1: Even if we are correct, and there is a 2-point effect in this population, we will only detect this effect about 29% of the time we look for it.

For Class 2 with a large effect size ($d = 1.00$), Figure 8.2 shows the sampling distribution for α (top figure) and the sampling distribution for β (the bottom figure—assuming there is a 10-point effect). Notice in the figure that the top and bottom figures barely overlap. In the bottom figure, which represents all the possible sample means we could select at random from this population, nearly all of the sample means we could select fall in the rejection region. In other words, if we are correct, and a 10-point effect does exist in the population, nearly all of the sample means we could select at random would lead us to reject the null hypothesis decision; that is, we would detect the effect. Power—represented as the percentage of sample mean outcomes that actually fall in the rejection region—with a 10-point effect would lead us to a decision that there is an effect (i.e., reject the null hypothesis). In this case, power is .9999 for

FIGURE 8.1 ● Large standard deviation, small effect size, and low power for Class 1.

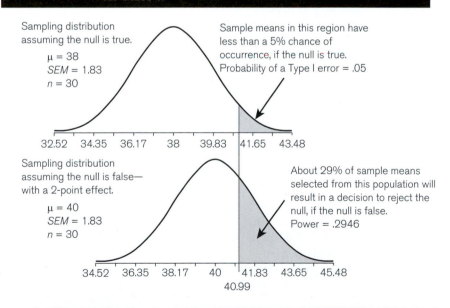

In this example, when alpha is .05, the critical value or cutoff for alpha is 38.61. When $\alpha = .05$, notice that practically any sample will detect this effect (the power). So if the researcher is correct, and the null is false (with a 2-point effect), nearly 100% of the samples he or she selects at random will result in a decision to reject the null hypothesis.

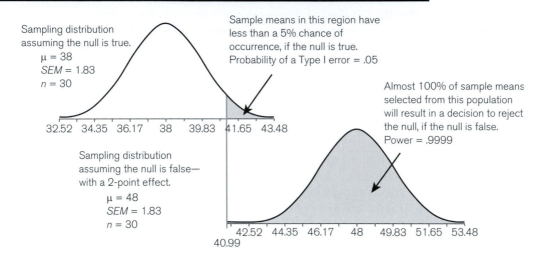

FIGURE 8.2 ● Large standard deviation, large effect size, and high power for Class 2.

Sampling distribution assuming the null is true.
$\mu = 38$
$SEM = 1.83$
$n = 30$

Sample means in this region have less than a 5% chance of occurrence, if the null is true. Probability of a Type I error = .05

Almost 100% of sample means selected from this population will result in a decision to reject the null, if the null is false. Power = .9999

32.52   34.35   36.17   38   39.83   41.65   43.48

Sampling distribution assuming the null is false— with a 2-point effect.
$\mu = 48$
$SEM = 1.83$
$n = 30$

40.99
42.52   44.35   46.17   48   49.83   51.65   53.48

In this example, when alpha is .05, the critical value or cutoff for alpha is 38.61. When $\alpha = .05$, notice that practically any sample will detect this effect (the power). So if the researcher is correct, and the null is false (with a 2-point effect), nearly 100% of the samples he or she selects at random will result in a decision to reject the null hypothesis.

Class 2: If we are correct, and there is a 10-point effect in this population, we detect this effect about 99% of the time we look for it.

Class 3. In the beginning of the section on effect size and power, we likened power to the ability to detect a signal. The stronger the signal relative to background noise, the more likely we are to detect the signal. The difference between Class 1 and Class 2 was the strength of the signal. The smaller 2-point difference (a weaker signal) in Class 1 would be harder to detect (power = .2946) as compared to the larger 10-point difference (a stronger signal) in Class 2 (power = .9999). A stronger signal translates to higher power.

Power can also vary with background noise. The background noise is represented by the population standard deviation. It is the variability in the population. Even with an effect being held constant, the more variability in the population, the greater the noise, and the more difficult it will be to detect an effect (i.e., the signal). To illustrate this, let us introduce Class 3, which has the same 2-point effect as Class 2, but with a smaller population standard deviation (i.e., less noise, which will make it easier to detect the signal; i.e., greater power).

For Class 1, power was .2946: If we are correct, and there is a 2-point effect in this population, we will only detect this effect about 29% of the time we look for it. Let us see how the power changes for the same 2-point effect, when the population standard deviation is smaller (i.e., when there is less noise).

Step 1: Construct the sampling distribution for α (alpha), which is the type of error associated with assuming there is no effect. We first construct the sampling distribution for Class 3, assuming that $\mu = 38$ is indeed the correct average score; that is, assuming there is no effect. For Class 3, the mean of the sampling distribution, then, is equal to the population mean ($\mu = 38$).

The standard deviation of the sampling distribution, called the *standard error of the mean* (σ_M; see Learning Unit 6, p. 84), is equal to the population standard deviation divided by the square root of the sample size ($n = 30$ students):

$$\sigma_M = \frac{\sigma}{\sqrt{n}} = \frac{2}{\sqrt{30}} = 0.37$$

For simplicity, let us again make a one-tailed test at a .05 level of significance. At .05, we can determine the cutoff for the rejection region—the region where we would decide to reject the null hypothesis that the population mean is 38. To do this, we compute a z transformation (see Learning Unit 5, p. 67) for a z score of 1.645—this is the cutoff on a z distribution for the top 5%; we want to determine what sample mean value is 1.645 standard deviations above 38 in a sampling distribution with a standard error of the mean of 0.37 for samples of size 30. The z transformation is

$$\frac{M - 38}{1.83} = 1.645$$

Solving for *M*,

$$M = 38.60$$

In the sampling distribution where we assume there is no effect, obtaining a sample mean equal to 38.60 or higher in Class 3 will lead to a decision to reject the null hypothesis—which, if the null is actually true, would be an error; specifically, a *Type I error* (see Learning Unit 7, p. 109). To find power, we now need to move to Step 2.

Step 2: Construct the sampling distribution for β (beta), which is the type of error associated with assuming there is an effect as stated. The next step is then to actually assume the population mean ($\mu = 38$) is wrong; that the effect you observed is instead correct. For Class 3, this means that we will assume 40 is in fact the true population mean (a 2-point effect in the population).

For Class 3, the standard deviation of the sampling distribution (called the standard error of the mean) for β—the type of error associated with false null hypotheses—does not change. What does change is the mean of the sampling distribution, which is always equal to the purported population mean. For Class 3 we state the mean of the sampling distribution as 40.

Step 3: Compare the distributions to identify power. For Class 3 with a large effect size ($d = 1.00$), Figure 8.3 shows the sampling distribution for α (top figure) and the sampling distribution for β (the bottom figure—assuming there is a 2-point effect). Notice in the figure that the top and bottom figures barely overlap. In the bottom figure, which represents all the possible sample means we could select at

FIGURE 8.3 ● Small standard deviation, large effect size, and high power for Class 3.

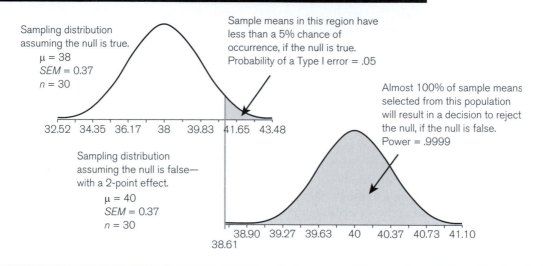

Sampling distribution assuming the null is true.
μ = 38
SEM = 0.37
n = 30

Sample means in this region have less than a 5% chance of occurrence, if the null is true.
Probability of a Type I error = .05

Almost 100% of sample means selected from this population will result in a decision to reject the null, if the null is false.
Power = .9999

32.52 34.35 36.17   38   39.83 41.65 43.48

Sampling distribution assuming the null is false— with a 2-point effect.
μ = 40
SEM = 0.37
n = 30

38.90 39.27 39.63   40   40.37 40.73 41.10
38.61

In this example, when alpha is .05, the critical value or cutoff for alpha is 38.61. When α = .05, notice that practically any sample will detect this effect (the power). So if the researcher is correct, and the null is false (with a 2-point effect), nearly 100% of the samples he or she selects at random will result in a decision to reject the null hypothesis.

random from this population, nearly all of the sample means we could select fall in the rejection region. In other words, if we are correct, and a 2-point effect does exist in the population, nearly all of the sample means we could select at random would lead to a rejection of the null hypothesis decision; that is, we would detect the effect. Power—represented as the percentage of sample mean outcomes that actually fall in the rejection region—with a 2-point effect would lead us to a decision that there is an effect (i.e., reject the null hypothesis). In this case, power is .9999 for Class 3: If we are correct, and there is a 2-point effect in this population, we detect this effect about 99% of the time we look for it.

Here, we can see that Class 3 (with a 2-point effect) has the same power as Class 2 (with a 10-point effect). For Class 2, the signal was louder (i.e., the mean difference was larger); for Class 3, the noise was lower (i.e., the population standard deviation was smaller). In each case, enhancing the signal and reducing the noise increased power.

The Relationship Between Sample Size and Power

Often, effects are small, and there is little we can do to change this. So how can we increase power, particularly in cases where the effect size itself is small? One common solution to overcoming low effect size is to increase the sample size. Increasing sample size decreases standard error (i.e., reduces the noise), thereby increasing power. To illustrate, let us return to Class 1 and compute a test statistic (computed as a z transformation; see Learning Unit 5, p. 67) using a one-tailed significance test.

With 30 students in Class 1 ($n = 30$), the class average was 40 ($M = 40$) and the standard error of the mean was 1.83 ($\sigma_M = 1.83$). For this class at $n = 30$, recall that the effect size was small ($d = 0.20$) and the power to detect effects was low (power = .2946).

For the upper tail, the critical value is still 1.645 for a test at a .05 level of significance. If the mean value of $M = 40$ falls 1.645 standard deviations or further from the population mean ($\mu = 38$), then we reject the null hypothesis (i.e., we detect an effect). We compute a z transformation to check this for $n = 30$:

$$z = \frac{M - \mu}{\frac{\sigma}{\sqrt{n}}} = \frac{40 - 38}{\frac{10}{\sqrt{30}}} = \frac{2}{1.83} = 1.10$$

When $n = 30$, we find that $M = 40$ is only 1.48 standard deviations from $\mu = 38$. In other words it is not different enough for us to reject the null hypothesis (i.e., it is not greater than the critical value of 1.645).

At $n = 30$, we failed to detect the effect. However, suppose we increase the sample size (i.e., by increasing the class size). Suppose we increase the sample size to $n = 100$ and again measure a sample mean of $M = 40$ with $\sigma = 10$. Effect size is still 0.20,

$$d = \frac{M - \mu}{\sigma} = \frac{40 - 38}{10} = 0.20$$

However, the standard error of the mean changes (it decreases from 1.83 to 1.00) because the sample size changed (it increased from 30 to 100),

$$\sigma_M = \frac{\sigma}{\sqrt{n}} = \frac{10}{\sqrt{100}} = 1.00$$

For the upper tail, the critical value is still 1.645 for a test at a .05 level of significance. If the mean value of $M = 40$ falls 1.645 standard deviations or further from the population mean ($\mu = 38$), then we reject the null hypothesis (i.e., we detect an effect). We compute a z transformation to check this for $n = 100$:

$$z = \frac{M - \mu}{\frac{\sigma}{\sqrt{n}}} = \frac{40 - 38}{\frac{10}{\sqrt{100}}} = \frac{2}{1.00} = 2.00$$

When $n = 100$, we find that $M = 40$ is 2.00 standard deviations from $\mu = 38$. In other words it is now greater than the critical value of 1.645, meaning that our decision would be to reject the null hypothesis (i.e., we detected the effect).

For this example, the actual power when $n = 100$ is .8594. This is much higher power than for the class with $n = 30$ (power = .2946). In this case, power is .8594 for Class 1 with $n = 100$: If we are correct, and there is a 2-point effect in this population, we detect this effect about 85% of the time we look for it. While Class 1 with $n = 30$ was well below the desired 80% minimal standard for power mentioned in the opening of this learning unit; by simply increasing the sample size to $n = 100$, we now exceed this minimum 80% standard.

Comparing Means: Significance Testing, Effect Size, and Confidence Intervals

A common way in which scientists test their hypotheses is to make comparisons between their observations and expected outcomes. At a most basic level, we can consider situations in which one group is compared to a criterion or standard. For example, we may want to compare student scores on a standardized assessment to the known national average score. For two groups, we may want to test whether students in an advanced class outperformed students in a basic class on a given assessment.

However, we would not be able to capture the full scope of a given behavior if our observations were limited to just one or two groups. Some variables naturally have more than two levels (seasons, months, or trimesters) or can be manipulated to have more than two levels (types of persuasion: ethos, pathos, logos, statistics, deliberation and refutation), and for some comparisons, a third or control group is needed (a "no treatment" group to compare to groups that receive two different treatments, A and B, for a mental health disorder).

In nature, rarely is one isolated factor causing changes in a dependent variable, and this is especially true in the behavioral sciences. It is reasonable to assume many causes impact our emotions, development, and performance at work, for example. Observing the combination of the levels of two factors can thus be advantageous. For example, we can observe how participant mood is influenced when observing foods that vary by their fat (low, high) and sugar (low, high) content. Here, we have two factors (fat, sugar), each with two levels (high, low). The combination of those levels creates the groups.

For the examples above, the class level, seasons, months, trimesters, types of persuasion, nutrient type, and nutrient level would be the independent variables or factors. The levels of each factor would be the groups, and we could observe different participants at each level or the same participants across all levels. To make our test, we test the null hypothesis that the group means (for the dependent variable) do not differ; the alternative hypothesis states that the group means do differ.

In the next three learning units, we will examine different statistical tests required by these variations in research designs.

LEARNING UNIT 9

t Tests: One-Sample, Two-Independent-Sample, and Related-Samples Designs

Excel Toolbox

Mathematical operators

- +
- –
- ( )
- *
- /
- ^2 [square]
- ^.5 [square root]

Functions

- AVERAGE
- COUNT
- STDEV.S
- SUM
- VAR.S
- T.TEST

(Continued)

(Continued)

Other tools

- format cells
- freeze panes
- fill down or paste
- inserting equations
- Analysis ToolPak

In this Learning Unit, we explore the nature of hypothesis testing when one group or two groups are observed; for two groups we explore situations in which the same or different participants are observed in each group. We further explore the informativeness of hypothesis testing for making decisions, and explore other ways of adding information about the nature of observed effects and how to appropriately interpret them. We do this with three different versions of a *t* test:

- one-sample *t* test,
- independent-sample *t* test, and
- related-samples *t* test.

Origins of the *t* Tests

An alternative to the *z* statistic was proposed by William Sealy Gosset (Student, 1908), a scientist working with the Guinness brewing company to improve brewing processes in the early 1900s. Because Guinness prohibited its employees from publishing "trade secrets," Gosset obtained approval to publish his work only under the condition that he used a pseudonym ("Student"). He proposed substituting the sample variance for the population variance in the formula for standard error. When this substitution is made, the formula for error is called the **estimated standard error (s_M)**:

$$\text{Estimated standard error: } s_M = \sqrt{\frac{s^2}{n}} = \frac{SD}{\sqrt{n}}$$

The substitution is possible because, as explained in learning units 2 and 7, the sample variance is an unbiased estimator of the population variance: On average, the sample variance equals the population variance. Using this substitution, an alternative test statistic can be introduced for one sample when the population variance is unknown. The formula, known as a ***t* statistic**, is as follows for one sample:

The **estimated standard error** is an estimate of the standard deviation of a sampling distribution of sample means selected from a population with an unknown variance. It is an estimate of the standard error, or standard distance that sample means can be expected to deviate from the value of the population mean stated in the null hypothesis.

The ***t* statistic**, known as ***t* observed** or ***t* obtained**, is an inferential statistic used to determine the number of standard deviations in a *t* distribution that a sample mean deviates from the mean value or mean difference stated in the null hypothesis.

$$t_{obt} = \frac{M - m}{s_M}, \text{where } s_M = \frac{SD}{\sqrt{n}}$$

Gosset showed that substituting the sample variance for the population variance led to a new sampling distribution known as the **t distribution,** which is also known as **Student's t,** referring to the pseudonym Gosset used when publishing his work. In Figure 9.1, you can see how similar the t distribution is to the normal distribution. The difference is that the t distribution has greater variability in the tails, because the sample variance is not always equal to the population variance. Sometimes the estimate for variance is too large; sometimes the estimate is too small. This leads to a larger probability of obtaining sample means farther from the population mean. Otherwise, the t distribution shares all the same characteristics of the normal distribution: It is symmetrical and asymptotic, and its mean, median, and mode are all located at the center of the distribution.

The Degrees of Freedom

The t distribution is associated with **degrees of freedom (df)**. In Learning Unit 2, we identified that the degrees of freedom for sample variance equal $n - 1$. Because the estimate of standard error for the t distribution is computed using the

---

FIGURE 9.1 ● A normal distribution and two *t* distributions.

The tails of a *t* distribution are thicker, which reflects the greater variability in values resulting from not knowing the population variance.

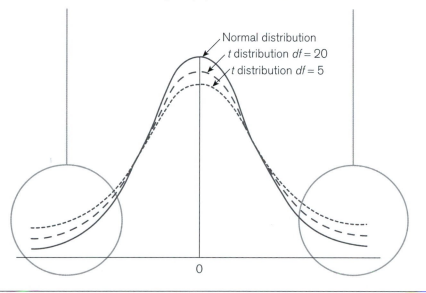

Normal distribution
t distribution *df* = 20
t distribution *df* = 5

0

Notice that the normal distribution has less variability in the tails; otherwise, these distributions share the same characteristics.

Source: www.unl.edu

The **t distribution,** or **Student's t,** is a normal-like distribution with greater variability in the tails than a normal distribution, because the sample variance is substituted for the population variance to estimate the standard error in this distribution.

The **degrees of freedom (df)** for a t distribution are equal to the degrees of freedom for sample variance for a given sample: $n - 1$. Each t distribution is associated with specified degrees of freedom; as sample size increases, the degrees of freedom also increase.

sample variance, the degrees of freedom for the t distribution are also $n - 1$. The t distribution is a sampling distribution in which the estimated standard error is computed using the sample variance in the formula. As sample size increases, the sample variance more closely approximates the population variance. The result is that there is less variability in the tails as sample size increases. So the shape of the t distribution changes (the tails approach the x-axis faster) as the sample size is increased. Each changing t distribution is thus associated with the same degrees of freedom as for sample variance: $df = n - 1$.

To locate probabilities and critical values in a t distribution, we use a t table, such as Table 9.1, which reproduces part of Table C.2 in Appendix C. In the t table, there are six columns of values listing alpha levels for one-tailed tests (top heading) and two-tailed tests (lower heading). The rows show the degrees of freedom (df) for a t distribution.

To use this table, you need to know the sample size (n), the alpha level (α), and the location of the rejection region (in one or both tails). For example, if we select a sample

Appendix A12

See **Appendix A12,** p. 298, for more on degrees of freedom for parametric tests.

TABLE 9.1 ● A portion of the t table adapted from Table C.2 in Appendix C.

	Proportion in One Tail					
	.25	.10	.05	.025	.01	.005
	Proportion in Two Tails Combined					
df	.50	.20	.10	.05	.02	.01
1	1.000	3.078	6.314	12.706	31.821	63.657
2	0.816	1.886	2.920	4.303	6.965	9.925
3	0.765	1.638	2.353	3.182	4.541	5.841
4	0.741	1.533	2.132	2.776	3.747	4.604
5	0.727	1.476	2.015	2.571	3.365	4.032
6	0.718	1.440	1.943	2.447	3.143	3.707
7	0.711	1.415	1.895	2.365	2.998	3.499
8	0.706	1.397	1.860	2.306	2.896	3.355
9	0.703	1.383	1.833	2.282	2.821	3.250
10	0.700	1.372	1.812	2.228	2.764	3.169

Source: Table III in Fisher, R. A., & Yates, F. (1974). *Statistical tables for biological, agricultural and medical research* (6th ed). London, England: Longman Group Ltd. (previously published by Oliver and Boyd Ltd., Edinburgh). Adapted and reprinted with permission of Addison Wesley Longman.

of 11 students, then $n = 11$, and $df = 10$ ($n - 1 = 10$). To find the *t* distribution with 10 degrees of freedom, we look for 10 listed in the rows. The critical values for this distribution at a .05 level of significance appear in the column with that probability listed: For a one-tailed test, the critical value is 1.812 for an upper-tail critical test and −1.812 for a lower-tail critical test. For a two-tailed test, the critical values are ±2.228. Each critical value identifies the cutoff for the rejection region, beyond which the decision will be to reject the null hypothesis for a hypothesis test.

Keep in mind that a *t* distribution is an estimate of a normal distribution. The larger the sample size, the more closely a *t* distribution estimates a normal distribution. When the sample size is so large that it equals the population size, we describe the sample size as infinite. In this case, the *t* distribution is a normal distribution. You can see this in the *t* table in Appendix C. The critical values at a .05 level of significance are ±1.96 for a two-tailed *t* test with infinite (∞) degrees of freedom and 1.645 (upper-tail critical) or −1.645 (lower-tail critical) for a one-tailed test. These are the same critical values listed in the unit normal table at a .05 level of significance. In terms of the null hypothesis, in a small sample, there is a greater probability of obtaining sample means that are farther from the value stated in the null hypothesis. As sample size increases, obtaining sample means that are farther from the value stated in the null hypothesis becomes less likely. The result is that critical values get smaller as sample size increases.

Computing the One-Sample *t* Test

In this section, we compute the **one-sample *t* test**, which is used to compare a mean value measured in a sample to a known value in the population. Specifically, this test is used to test hypotheses concerning a single group mean selected from a population with an unknown variance. To compute the one-sample *t* test, we make three assumptions:

1. *Normality.* We assume that data in the population being sampled are normally distributed. This assumption is particularly important for small samples. In larger samples ($n > 30$), the standard error is smaller, and this assumption becomes less critical as a result.

2. *Random sampling.* We assume that the data we measure were obtained from a sample that was selected using a random sampling procedure. It is considered inappropriate to conduct hypothesis tests with nonrandom samples.

3. *Independence.* We assume that each outcome or observation is independent, meaning that one outcome does not influence another. Specifically, outcomes are independent when the probability of one outcome has no effect on the probability of another outcome. Using random sampling usually satisfies this assumption.

Keep in mind that satisfying the assumptions for the *t* test is critically important. That said, for each example in this book, the data are intentionally constructed such that the assumptions for conducting the tests have been met. In Example 9.1 we

The **one-sample *t* test** is a statistical procedure used to compare a mean value measured in a sample to a known value in the population. It is specifically used to test hypotheses concerning the mean in a single population with an unknown variance.

follow the four steps to hypothesis testing introduced in Learning Unit 7 to compute a one-sample t test at a two-tailed .05 level of significance using an example adapted from published research.

Example 9.1. Learning is a common construct that behavioral sciences study. One common type of learning is the ability to recognize new objects, referred to as novelty recognition (Fisher-Thompson, 2017; Privitera, Mayeaux, Schey, & Lapp, 2013). An example with animals is the object recognition task. A mouse placed in an environment with two identical objects for five minutes is later returned to the same environment, but one of the objects has been replaced with a new or *novel* object. Because mice are naturally curious, we expect that the mouse will spend more time investigating the novel object, thus demonstrating object recognition. To operationalize, or make measurable, the percentage of time spent investigating the novel object relative to the familiar object, we make the following calculation:

$$\frac{\text{Time Spent Investigating Novel Object}}{\text{Time Spent Investigating Novel Object} + \text{Time Spent Investigating Familiar Object}} \times 100$$

Using this formula, if a mouse spends the same amount of time investigating each object (in other words, the mouse fails to show object recognition), then the result will be 50%. Thus, our standard we will compare against in the null hypothesis for this test will be 50%. A score below 50% indicates that subjects recognized the novel object but preferred the familiar object. Although unlikely, familiarity preference is a remote possibility.

Using a sample data set adapted from published research, we will use the four steps to hypothesis testing introduced in Learning Unit 7 to test whether the mean score in sample data significantly differs from the expected value of 50% at a .05 level of significance.

Step 1: State the hypotheses. The population mean is 50%, and we are testing whether or not the population mean differs from the sample mean:

$H_0 : \mu = 50\%$ For mice given the opportunity to investigate a novel and a familiar object, the mean percentage of time spent investigating the novel object is equal to 50%, as would be expected by chance.

$H_1 : \mu \neq 50\%$ For mice given the opportunity to investigate a novel and a familiar object, the mean percentage of time spent investigating the novel object is not equal to 50%.

Again, if a mouse spends the same amount of time investigating each object (in other words, the mouse fails to show object recognition), then the result will be 50%. Thus, our standard we will compare against in the null hypothesis for this test is 50%. The higher the percentage above 50%, the more time the mouse spent investigating the novel object, and thus the more likely we will be to reject the null hypothesis and conclude that object recognition occurred.

Step 2: Set the criteria for a decision. The level of significance for this test is .05. We are computing a two-tailed test with $n - 1$ degrees of freedom. We will use a data set with 15 scores, each from a different mouse, a sample size that is appropriate for this behavioral task in research with nonhumans. With $n = 15$, the degrees of freedom for this test are $15 - 1 = 14$. To locate the critical values, we find 14 listed in the rows of Table C.2 in Appendix C and go across to the column for a .05 proportion in two tails combined. The critical values are ±2.145.

We will compare the value of the test statistic with these critical values. If the value of the test statistic is beyond a critical value (either greater than 2.145 or less than 2.145), then there is less than a 5% chance we would obtain that outcome if the null hypothesis were correct, so we reject the null hypothesis; otherwise, we retain the null hypothesis.

> **Appendix A12**
>
> See **Appendix A12,** p. 298, for more on degrees of freedom for parametric tests.

Step 3: Compute the test statistic. Download Novel_Objects.xlsx from the student study site: http://study.sagepub.com/priviteraexcel1e. As shown in Figure 9.2, Column A contains an ID number for each animal; Column B contains the percentage of total investigation time each animal devoted to the novel object. Column C, which we save for use later, contains the expected percentage of time each animal would have devoted to the novel object if it did not show a preference for either the novel or the familiar object.

As shown in Figure 9.2, we insert in column D some labels to keep track of our calculations in column E for the one-sample *t* test:

D4: Mean (*M*)

D5: Sample size (*n*)

D6: Standard deviation (*SD*)

D7: Degrees of freedom (*df*)

D8: Critical value of *t* (t_{crit})

We covered mean in Learning Unit 1 and standard deviation in Learning Unit 2.

To the right of the cells mentioned above, we type these functions and formulas into column E:

E4: =AVERAGE(B4:B18)

E5: =COUNT(B4:B18)

E6: =STDEV.S(B4:B18)

E7: =E5–1

E8: 2.145

> **Appendix B**
>
> See **Appendix B2,** p. 301, for formatting cells.

At this point we have what we need to proceed with our calculation. From the values we have calculated already in rows 4 to 8, we prepare column D with three more labels:

D9: Estimated standard error (s_M)

D10: Obtained value of t (t_{obt})

D11: p value

On our way to finding the t statistic, we compute the estimated standard error. To compute the estimated standard error, we divide the sample standard deviation by the square root of the sample size:

$$s_M = \frac{SD}{\sqrt{n}}$$

In column E,

E9: =E6/E5^0.5

which yields

$$s_M = \frac{9.4}{\sqrt{15}} = 2.42$$

in cell E9 in Figure 9.2b.

We will compare the sample mean to the population mean stated in the null hypothesis: $\mu = 50$. The estimated sample standard deviation is the denominator of the t statistic.

$$t_{obt} = \frac{M - \mu}{s_M}$$

Find the t statistic by substituting the values for the sample mean, $M = 59.1$; the population mean stated in the null hypothesis, $\mu = 50$; and the estimated standard error we just calculated, $s_M = 2.42$. In column E,

E10: =(E4–50)/E9

which yields

$$t_{obt} = \frac{59.1 - 50}{2.42} = 3.74 \text{ in cell E10 in Figure 9.2b.}$$

Note that although there is no function in Excel to calculate a t value, there is a function to calculate the p value associated with a t test. To calculate an exact p value for a one-sample t test, we use a second column of expected values equal to 50% for each of the 15 mice, shown in column C in Figure 9.2. We use the T.TEST function built into Excel.

In column E,

E11: =T.TEST(B4:B18,C4:C18,2,1).

This function requires two cell ranges of data: B4:B18 contains the observed percentage of time spent investigating the novel object, and C4:C18 contains the expected percentage of time spent sniffing the novel object: 50% in each cell. After those two

FIGURE 9.2 ● One-sample *t* test. (a) Functions and formulas. (b) Resulting calculations from functions and formulas.

(a)

	A	B	C	D	E
1		Percentage of total			
2		time spent exploring	Expected		
3	Mouse #	novel object	percentage		
4	1	55	50	Mean (*M*)	=AVERAGE(B4:B18)
5	2	63	50	Sample size (*n*)	=COUNT(B4:B18)
6	3	56	50	Standard deviation (*SD*)	=STDEV.S(B4:B18)
7	4	73	50	Degrees of freedom (*df*)	=E5-1
8	5	54	50	Critical value of *t* (t_{crit})	2.145
9	6	74	50	Estimated standard error (s_M)	=E6/E5^0.5
10	7	57	50	Obtained value of *t* (t_{obt})	=(E4-50)/E9
11	8	53	50	*p* value	=T.TEST(B4:B18,C4:C18,2,1)
12	9	63	50		
13	10	76	50	Estimated Cohen's *d*	=(E4-50)/E6
14	11	45	50	Eta-squared (η^2)	=E10^2/(E10^2+E7)
15	12	46	50		
16	13	61	50	$t(s_M)$	=E8*E9
17	14	55	50	95% CI upper limit	=E4+E16
18	15	55	50	95% CI lower limit	=E4-E16

(b)

	A	B	C	D	E
1		Percentage of total			
2		time spent exploring	Expected		
3	Mouse #	novel object	percentage		
4	1	55	50	Mean (*M*)	59.1
5	2	63	50	Sample size (*n*)	15
6	3	56	50	Standard deviation (*SD*)	9.4
7	4	73	50	Degrees of freedom (*df*)	14
8	5	54	50	Critical value of *t* (t_{crit})	2.145
9	6	74	50	Estimated standard error (s_M)	2.42
10	7	57	50	Obtained value of *t* (t_{obt})	3.74
11	8	53	50	*p* value	.002
12	9	63	50		
13	10	76	50	Estimated Cohen's *d*	0.97
14	11	45	50	Eta-squared (η^2)	0.50
15	12	46	50		
16	13	61	50	$t(s_M)$	5.20
17	14	55	50	95% CI upper limit	64.3
18	15	55	50	95% CI lower limit	53.9

Appendix B

See **Appendix B2**, p. 301, on formatting cells to add superscripts.

ranges of data, the next argument required in the function is the number of tails, for which we specify 2. The final argument is the type of t test, which we specify as related-samples, which Excel terms "Paired," with a 1. As expected with such a large t_{obt}, the p value returned of .002 is small, shown in cell E11 in Figure 9.2b.

Step 4: Make a decision. To decide to reject or retain the null hypothesis, we compare the obtained value ($t_{obt} = 3.74$) to the critical values in the t table in Appendix C2. For $df = n - 1$, $15 - 1 = 14$, the critical value at $\alpha = .05$ is 2.145. Because t_{obt} of 3.74 exceeds the critical value, the decision is to reject the null hypothesis. This t_{obt} indicates that our observed value of 9.1 percentage points above the expected value of 50 percentage points is 3.74 times larger than the average deviation of 2.42 percentage points of a mean based on 15 samples. If this result were reported in a research journal, it would look something like this following APA format (APA, 2010):

> The percentage of time mice explored the novel object ($M = 59.1$, $SD = 9.4$) was significantly higher than the percentage expected by chance, $t(14) = 3.74$, $p = .002$. Thus, the results support the conclusion that the mice demonstrated object recognition.

Effect Size for the One-Sample t Test

As described in Learning Unit 7, hypothesis testing identifies whether an effect exists in a population. When we decide to retain the null hypothesis, we conclude that an effect does not exist in the population. When we decide to reject the null hypothesis, we conclude that an effect does exist in the population. However, hypothesis testing does not tell us how large the effect is.

In Example 9.1, we concluded that mice investigated a novel object more than they investigated a familiar object. To determine the size of an effect, we compute effect size, which gives an estimate of the size of an effect in the population. Two measures of effect size for the one-sample t test are described in this section: estimated Cohen's d and proportion of variance (eta squared).

To label these calculations, in column D we enter

D13: Estimated Cohen's d

D14: Eta squared (η^2)

Estimated Cohen's d. The estimate of effect size that is most often used with a t test is the **estimated Cohen's d**. As described at the beginning of this learning unit on the t test, when the population standard deviation is unknown, we use the sample standard deviation, because it gives an unbiased estimate of the population standard deviation. Similarly, with the estimated Cohen's d formula, we use the sample standard deviation as follows:

$$d = \frac{M - \mu}{SD}$$

Estimated Cohen's d is a measure of effect size in terms of the number of standard deviations that mean scores shifted above or below the population mean stated by the null hypothesis. The larger the value of d, the larger the effect in the population.

In column E,

E13: =(E4–50)/E6

which yields

$$d = \frac{59.1 - 50.0}{9.4} = \frac{9.1}{9.4} = 0.97$$

in cell E13 in Figure 9.2b.

We conclude that novelty of an object will increase investigation by mice of that object by 0.97 standard deviations above the expectation of equal investigation of familiar and novel objects. The effect size conventions (Cohen, 1988) given in the middle column of Table 9.2 show that this is a large effect size. We could report this measure with the significant *t* test in Example 9.1 by stating,

> The percentage of time mice explored the novel object (*M* = 59.1, *SD* = 9.4) was significantly higher than the percentage expected by chance, *t*(14) = 3.74, *p* < .01, *d* = 0.97. Thus, the results support the conclusion that the mice demonstrated object recognition.

Proportion of Variance: Eta squared (η^2). Another measure of effect size is to estimate the **proportion of variance** that can be accounted for by some **treatment**. A treatment, which is any unique characteristic of a sample or any unique way that a researcher treats a sample, can change the value of a dependent variable. A treatment is associated with variability in a study. Proportion of variance estimates how much of the variability in a dependent variable can be accounted for by the treatment. In the proportion of variance formula, the variability explained by a treatment is divided by the total variability observed:

$$\text{Proportion of variance} = \frac{\text{variance explained}}{\text{total variance}}$$

In Example 9.1, we found that mice investigated a novel object more than they investigated a familiar object. The unique characteristic of the sample in this study was that the mice encountered a novel object that attracted their attention, not just two familiar objects. The variable we measured (i.e., the dependent variable) was percentage of total time investigating that was devoted to the novel object. Measuring proportion of variance determines how much of the variability in the dependent variable (percentage of investigation time) can be explained by the treatment (the fact that one of the objects was novel). Here, we describe a measure of proportion of variance, eta squared (η^2).

Eta squared is a measure of proportion of variance that can be expressed in a single formula based on the result of a *t* test:

$$\eta^2 = \frac{t^2}{t^2 + df}$$

Proportion of variance is a measure of effect size in terms of the proportion or percentage of variability in a dependent variable that can be explained or accounted for by a treatment.

In hypothesis testing, a **treatment** is any unique characteristic of a sample or any unique way that a researcher treats a sample.

In this formula, t is the value of the t statistic, and df is the degrees of freedom. In this example, $t = 3.74$, and $df = 14$. To find variance, we square the standard deviation. Thus, in the eta squared formula, we square the value of t to find the proportion of variance. In column E,

    E14: =E10^2/(E10^2+E7)

which yields

$$\eta^2 = \frac{3.74^2}{3.74^2 + 14} = \frac{13.9876}{13.9876 + 14} = 0.50$$

in cell E14 in Figure 9.2b.

We conclude that 50% of the variability in the percentage of time spent investigating objects (the dependent variable) can be explained by the fact that one of the objects was novel (the treatment). We could report this measure with the significant t test in Example 9.1 by stating,

The percentage of time mice explored the novel object ($M = 59.1$, $SD = 9.4$) was significantly higher than the percentage expected by chance, $t(14) = 3.74$, $p < .01$ ($\eta^2 = .50$). Thus, the results support the conclusion that the mice demonstrated object recognition.

The third column in Table 9.2 displays guidelines for interpreting a trivial, small, medium, and large effect for a variety of measures for effect size, including η^2. Using this table, we find that $\eta^2 = .4998$ is a large effect. Although eta squared is a popular measure of proportion of variance, it tends to overestimate the proportion of variance explained by a treatment. To correct for this bias, many researchers use a modified eta squared formula, called omega-squared. Coverage of omega-squared is beyond the scope of this book.

TABLE 9.2 ● The size of an effect using estimated Cohen's d and proportion of variance (eta squared).

Description of Effect	d	η^2	ω^2
Trivial	—	$\eta^2 < .01$	$\omega^2 < .01$
Small	$d < 0.2$	$.01 < \eta^2 < .09$	$.01 < \omega^2 < .09$
Medium	$0.2 < d < 0.8$	$.10 < \eta^2 < .25$	$.10 < \omega^2 < .25$
Large	$d > 0.8$	$\eta^2 > .25$	$\omega^2 > .25$

Note that Cohen's d is interpreted the same with negative values. The sign (+, -) simply indicates the direction of the effect.

Confidence Intervals for the One-Sample *t* Test

In Example 9.1, we stated a null hypothesis regarding the value of the mean in a population. We can further describe the nature of the effect by determining where the effect is likely to be in the population by computing the confidence intervals.

As introduced in Learning Unit 7, there are two types of estimates: a point estimate and an interval estimate. When using one sample, a *point estimate* is the sample mean we measure. The interval estimate, reported as a *confidence interval*, is stated within a given *level of confidence*, which is the likelihood that an interval contains an unknown population mean.

To illustrate confidence intervals for the one-sample *t* test, we will revisit Example 9.1 to compute the confidence intervals at a 95% level of confidence for the data analyzed using the one-sample *t* test. To find the confidence intervals, we need to evaluate an estimation formula. We will use the estimation formula to identify the upper and lower confidence limits within which the unknown population mean is likely to be contained. The estimation formula for the one-sample *t* test is as follows:

$$M \pm t(s_M)$$

In all, we follow three steps to estimate the value of a population mean using a point estimate and an interval estimate:

Step 1: Compute the sample mean and standard error.

Step 2: Choose the level of confidence and find the critical values at that level of confidence.

Step 3: Compute the estimation formula to find the confidence limits.

Step 1: Compute the sample mean and standard error. We have already computed the sample mean, which is the point estimate of the population mean, $M = 59.1$ in cell E4 of Figure 9.2b. We have also already computed the standard error of the mean, which is the sample standard deviation divided by the square root of the sample size, $s_M = 2.42$ in cell E9 of Figure 9.2b.

Step 2: Choose the level of confidence and find the critical values at that level of confidence. In this example, we chose the 95% confidence interval (CI). The critical value at this level of confidence will be the same as we found in Step 2 for Example 9.1 using hypothesis testing. As shown in Table 9.3, the 95% level of confidence corresponds to a two-tailed test at a .05 level of significance using hypothesis testing. Thus, the critical value for the interval estimate is 2.145, as shown in cell E8 of Figure 9.2b.

To explain further how this critical value was determined, remember that in a sampling distribution, 50% of sample means fall above the sample mean we selected, and 50% fall below it. We are looking for the 95% of sample means that surround the sample mean we selected, meaning the 47.5% of sample means above and the 47.5% of sample means below the sample mean we selected. This leaves only 2.5% of sample means remaining in the upper tail and 2.5% in the lower tail. Table 9.3 shows how

TABLE 9.3 ● Levels of significance using hypothesis testing and the corresponding levels of confidence using estimation.	
Level of Confidence	**Level of Significance (α level, two-tailed)**
99%	.01
95%	.05
90%	.10
80%	.20

different levels of confidence using estimation correspond to different two-tailed levels of significance (α) using hypothesis testing. Referring to Table 9.3, we find that a 95% CI corresponds to a two-tailed test at a .05 level of significance. To find the critical value at this level of confidence, we look in the t table in Table C.2 in Appendix C. The degrees of freedom are 14 ($df = n - 1$ for a one-sample t test). The critical value for the interval estimate is 2.145. Multiplying the observed standard error of the mean by the critical value of t tells us how far above the sample mean 47.5% of all sample means would fall and how far below the mean another 47.5% of all sample means would fall. This range above and below the sample mean encompasses 95% of sample means.

Step 3: Compute the estimation formula to find the confidence limits for a 95% confidence interval. In column D,

D16: $t(s_M)$

D17: 95% CI upper limit

D18: 95% CI lower limit

To compute the formula, multiply t by the estimated standard error. In column E,

E16: =E8*E9

which yields

$$t(s_M) = 2.145(2.42) = 5.20$$

in cell E16 in Figure 9.2b.

Add 5.20 to the sample mean to find the upper confidence limit, and subtract 5.20 from the sample mean to find the lower confidence limit. In column E,

E17: =E4+E16

E18: =E4–E16

which yields

$$M + t(s_M) = 59.1 + 5.20 = 64.3$$

in cell E17 in Figure 9.2b, and

$$M - t(s_M) = 59.1 - 5.20 = 53.9$$

in cell E18 in Figure 9.2b.

As shown in Figure 9.3, the 95% confidence interval in this population is between a percentage of 53.9% and 64.3% of investigation time directed toward a novel object. We can estimate within a 95% level of confidence that the mean percentage of time investigating a novel object is between 53.9% and 64.3% in the population. We are 95% confident that the population mean falls within this range, because 95% of all sample means we could have selected from this population fall within the range of sample means we specified.

Computing the One-Sample
t Test Using the Analysis Toolpak

We can also calculate this *t* test using the Analysis ToolPak available in Excel for easy and accurate calculation. We'll guide you through the steps to do the analysis we did for the one-sample *t* test.

Return to the workbook Novel_Objects.xlsx. Click on the Data tab, and then on the Data Analysis icon all the way to the right. Select "t-Test: Paired Two Sample for Means," as shown in Figure 9.4a. As we mentioned above, we can get the same result from a one-sample *t* test as we can from a related-samples *t* test (which is called a Paired t-Test in Excel) when we pair the value predicted by the null hypothesis, column C in Figure 9.2, with each score that was measured, column B in Figure 9.2.

Selecting "t-Test: Paired Two Sample for Means" yields the dialog box in Figure 9.4b. For Variable 1, we select the observed values of the percentage of time spent exploring the novel object in cells B3 through B18, which includes in B3 a label for the data.

FIGURE 9.3 ● At a 95% CI, the trust population mean score falls between 53.9 and 64.3 in this population of curious mice.

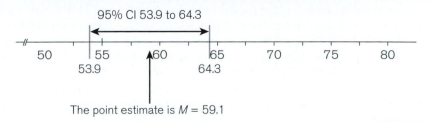

FIGURE 9.4 • Performing a one-sample *t* test with the Analysis ToolPak in Excel. (a) Selecting "t-Test: Paired Two Sample for Means" to perform a one-sample *t* test. (b) Specifying the location of the data and parameters for the *t* test.

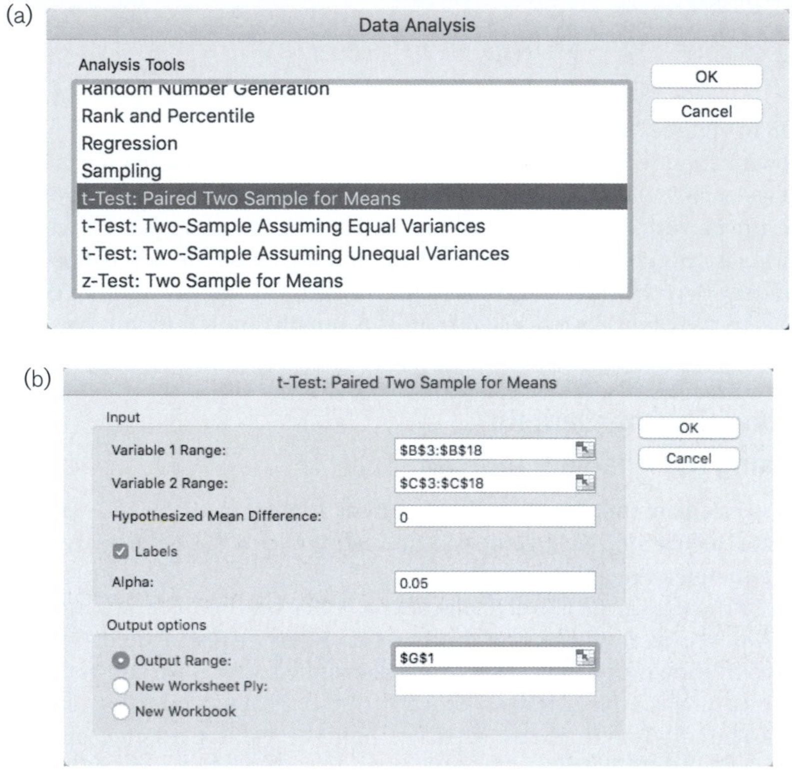

For Variable 2, we select the expected percentages in C3 through C18, all of which are 50, and include in C3 a label for the data. The Hypothesized Mean Difference we expect to be 0. (Zero is the default if this box remains blank.) Check the Labels box so that the output contains the labels from B3 and C3. We keep our output on the same page by selecting Output Range and clicking in cell G1.

Clicking OK on the dialog box returns the output table in Figure 9.5. The labels that we included in the cell range for the analysis are in H3 and I3. We can change these labels as we desire. Notice that in Figure 9.5, we get the same mean of 59.1% in cell H4, same t_{obt} of 3.74 in cell H10, and same two-tailed *p* value of .002 in cell H13 as we did in Figure 9.2b. Although neither an estimate of effect size nor confidence intervals are generated automatically, the output table gives the mean from which we would subtract the expected value of 50%, the variance, and the degrees of freedom. With this information we can calculate effect size and confidence intervals as we did above.

FIGURE 9.5 ● Results of one-sample *t* test using the Analysis ToolPak.

	G	H	I
1	t-Test: Paired Two Sample for Means		
2			
3		novel object	percentage
4	Mean	59.1	50.0
5	Variance	88.1	0
6	Observations	15	15
7	Pearson Correlation	#DIV/0!	
8	Hypothesized Mean Difference	0	
9	df	14	
10	t Stat	3.74	
11	P(T<=t) one-tail	.001	
12	t Critical one-tail	1.76	
13	P(T<=t) two-tail	.002	
14	t Critical two-tail	2.14	

Computing the Two-Independent-Sample *t* Test

In this section, we compute the **two-independent-sample *t* test**, which is used to compare the mean difference between two groups; specifically, to test hypotheses regarding the difference between two population means. In terms of the null hypothesis, we state the mean difference that we expect in the population and compare it to the difference we observe between the two sample means in our sample. Often, a visual inspection of data from two groups can be quite insightful in terms of determining whether groups differ. Appendix A8 provides an illustration for how to inspect grouped data visually. For a two-independent-sample *t* test concerning two population means, we make four assumptions:

1. *Normality.* We assume that data in each population being sampled are normally distributed. This assumption is particularly important for small samples, because the standard error is typically much larger. In larger sample sizes ($n > 30$), the standard error is smaller, and this assumption becomes less critical as a result.

2. *Random sampling.* We assume that the data we measure were obtained from samples that were selected using a random sampling procedure.

3. *Independence.* We assume that each measured outcome or observation is independent, meaning that one outcome does not influence another. Specifically, outcomes are independent when the probability of one outcome has no effect on the probability of another outcome. Using random sampling usually satisfies this assumption.

The **two-independent-sample *t* test** is a statistical procedure used to compare the mean difference between two independent groups. This test is specifically used to test hypotheses concerning the difference between two population means, where the variance in one or both populations is unknown.

4. *Equal variances.* We assume that the variances in each population are equal to each other. This assumption is usually satisfied when the larger sample variance is not greater than two times the smaller:

$$\frac{larger\ s^2}{smaller\ s^2} < 2$$

Appendix A8

See **Appendix A8,** p. 290, for how to visually inspect data to compare differences between two groups.

Keep in mind that satisfying the assumptions for the *t* test is critically important. That said, for each example in this book, the data are intentionally constructed such that the assumptions for conducting the tests have been met. In Example 9.2 we follow the four steps to hypothesis testing introduced in Learning Unit 7 to compute a two-independent-sample *t* test using an example adapted from published research.

Example 9.2. For an example, let us consider the impact of safety training in the workplace. Nonfatal workplace injuries can be expressed as a rate: the number of injuries per 200,000 hours worked by all employees. A nonfatal incidence rate of 5 means that 5 nonfatal injuries in 200,000 hours of work were accumulated by all employees at a company. Thus, the incident rate that we analyze has been adjusted for size of company.

Using a sample data set adapted from published research, we will use the four steps to hypothesis testing introduced in Learning Unit 7. We examine at a .05 level of significance whether safety training for 40 companies produces a difference in incidence rate as compared to 40 other companies without safety training.

Step 1: State the hypotheses. The null hypothesis states that there is no difference between the two groups, and we are testing whether or not there is a difference:

$H_0 : \mu_1 - \mu_2 = 0$ There is no difference; safety training has no effect on the incidence rate of nonfatal injuries.

$H_0 : \mu_1 - \mu_2 \neq 0$ Safety training does have an effect on the incidence rate of nonfatal injuries.

Step 2: Set the criteria for a decision. The level of significance for this test is .05. We are computing a two-tailed test, so we place the rejection region in both tails. For the *t* test, the degrees of freedom for each group or sample are *n* – 1. Table 9.4 compares degrees of freedom for one-sample and for two-independent-sample *t* tests. To find the degrees of freedom for two samples, then, we add the degrees of freedom in each sample. This can be found using one of three methods:

Method 1: *df* for two-independent-sample *t* test = $df_1 + df_2$

Method 2: *df* for two-independent-sample *t* test = $(n_1 - 1) + (n_2 - 1)$

Method 3: *df* for two-independent-sample *t* test = $N - 2$

As summarized in Table 9.4, we can add the degrees of freedom for each sample using the first two methods. In the third method, *N* is the total sample size for both groups combined, and we subtract 2 from this value. All three methods will produce the same result for degrees of freedom. The degrees of freedom for each sample here are 40 – 1 = 39. Thus, the degrees of freedom for the two-independent-sample *t* test are the sum of these degrees of freedom:

Appendix A12

See **Appendix A12,** p. 298, for more on degrees of freedom for parametric tests.

$$df = 39 + 39 = 78$$

In Table C.2 in Appendix C, p. 318, the degrees of freedom in the leftmost column increase by 1 up to $df = 30$. After 30, they increase by 10. Because there is no entry for $df = 78$, we use the next smallest value, which is $df = 60$. Move across the columns to find the critical value for a .05 proportion in two tails combined. The critical values for this test are ±2.000.

We will compare the value of the test statistic with these critical values. If the value of the test statistic is beyond a critical value (either greater than +2.000 or less than -2.000), then there is less than a 5% chance we would obtain that outcome if the null hypothesis were correct, so we reject the null hypothesis; otherwise, we retain the null hypothesis.

Step 3: Compute the test statistic. Download Employee_Safety_Training.xlsx from the student study site: http://study.sagepub.com/priviteraexcel1e. Column A contains the rate of nonfatal injuries per 200,000 hours that employees worked at companies

TABLE 9.4 ● Computing the degrees of freedom for a *t* test.

Participants	Teacher		Difference Scores
	Present	**Absent**	
1	220	210	(220 – 210) = 10
2	245	220	(245 – 220) = 25
3	215	195	(215 – 195) = 20
4	260	265	(260 – 265) = –5
5	300	275	(300 – 275) = 25
6	280	290	(280 – 290) = –10
7	250	220	(250 – 220) = 30
8	310	285	(310 – 285) = 25

with safety training; column B contains that same measure at companies without safety training. We can copy A2 to B3 and paste them to D2 to E3 as shown in Figure 9.6. These column headers label the two treatments of the independent variable.

Also as shown in Figure 9.6, we insert in column C labels to keep track of our calculations in columns D and E for the two-independent-sample t test:

C4: Mean (M)

C5: Sample size (n)

C6: Variance (s^2)

C7: Degrees of freedom (df)

To the right of the cells mentioned above, we type these functions and formulas into column D and E:

D4: =AVERAGE(A4:A43)   E4: =AVERAGE(B4:B43)

D5: =COUNT(A4:A43)   E5: =COUNT(B4:B43)

D6: =VAR.S(A4:A43)   E6: =VAR.S(B4:B43)

D7: =D5-1   E7: =E5-1

As mentioned above, the critical value of t taken from Table C.2 in Appendix C is 2.000.

C8: Critical value of t, $df = 60$ in Table C.2 (t_{crit})

 D8: 2.000

These values in D4 through E7 allow us to proceed with the calculation of the two-independent-sample t test and compare that result with the t_{crit} of 2.000. We prepare column C with six more labels:

C9: Sample mean difference ($M_1 - M_2$)

C10: Hypothesized mean difference ($\mu_1 - \mu_2$)

C11: Pooled sample variance (s_p^2)

C12: Standard error for difference ($s_{M_1 - M_2}$)

C13: Obtained value of t (t_{obt})

C14: p value

In the formula for a two-independent-sample t test, we subtract the mean difference between the sample means, cell D9, from the mean difference stated in the null, cell D10. To column D we add:

D9: =D4-E4

D10: 0

We divide this difference by the combined standard error in both samples, called the **estimated standard error for the difference**, which is computed as

$$s_{M_1-M_2} = \sqrt{\frac{s_p^2}{n_1} + \frac{s_p^2}{n_2}}$$

Notice that the numerator in the estimated standard error for the difference formula is s_p^2, which is called the **pooled sample variance.** The first step, then, to compute the estimated standard error for the difference is to compute the pooled sample variance. Because we have equal sample sizes in the two groups, we can average the two sample variances using the following formula:

$$s_p^2 = \frac{s_1^2 + s_2^2}{2}$$

Appendix A9 provides more detail regarding the calculation and interpretation of the pooled sample variance.

In column D11, we calculate pooled sample variance:

D11: =(D6+E6)/2

which yields

$$s_p^2 = \frac{3.61 + 4.92}{2} = 4.27$$

in cell D11 in Figure 9.6b.

Having the pooled sample variance allows us to then calculate the estimated standard error for the difference in column D (notice that 4.27 is now the numerator in the estimated standard error for the difference formula):

D12: =((D11/D5)+(D11/E5))^0.5

which yields

$$s_{M_1-M_2} = \sqrt{\frac{4.27}{39} + \frac{4.27}{39}} = 0.46$$

in cell D12 in Figure 9.6b.

Appendix B

See **Appendix B2**, p. 301, on formatting cells to add superscripts or subscripts.

See **Appendix B8**, p. 312, on inserting equations, especially to use both a superscript and subscript or add multiple subscripts.

Appendix A9

See **Appendix A9,** p. 292, for more detail regarding the calculation and interpretation of the pooled sample variance.

The **estimated standard error for the difference** is an estimate of the standard deviation of a sampling distribution of mean differences between two sample means. It is an estimate of the standard error or standard distance that mean differences can be expected to deviate from the mean difference stated in the null hypothesis.

The **pooled sample variance** is the mean sample variance of two samples. When the sample size is unequal, the variance in each group or sample is weighted by its respective degrees of freedom.

Now we have the three components needed to calculate the two-independent-sample t test:

$$t_{obt} = \frac{(M_1 - M_2) - (\mu_1 - \mu_2)}{s_{M_1 - M_2}}$$

In column D we insert

D13: =(D9-D10)/D12

which yields

$$t_{obt} = \frac{-1.95 - 0}{0.46} = -4.222$$

in cell D13 in Figure 9.6b.

Finally, in column D we calculate a p value:

D14: =T.TEST(A4:A43,B4:B43,2,2)

which yields a p value of .000065 in cell D14 in Figure 9.6b.

Step 4: Make a decision. The t_{obt} value in cell D13 is -4.222. This value far exceeds our two-tailed critical value at $\alpha = .05$ of 2.000 for $df = 60$ from Table C2 in Appendix C. In fact, the exact p value that we can calculate with Excel indicates that the probability of such an outcome occurring, if the null hypothesis were true, is very unlikely: $p = .000065$ in cell D14 in Figure 9.5b. If this result were reported in a research journal, it would look something like this following APA format (American Psychological Association, 2010):

The mean nonfatal incidence rate at companies with employee safety training ($M = 8.23$, $SD = 1.90$) was significantly lower than was the rate at companies without employee safety training ($M = 10.18$, $SD = 2.22$), $t(78) = -4.222$, $p < .001$.

Effect Size for the Two-Independent-Sample t Test

Hypothesis testing is used to identify whether an effect exists in one or more populations of interest. When we reject the null hypothesis, we conclude that an effect does exist in the population. When we retain the null hypothesis, we conclude that an effect does not exist in the population. In Example 9.2, we concluded that an effect does exist. We will compute effect size for the test in Example 9.2 to determine the effect size of this result or mean difference. We can identify two measures of effect

FIGURE 9.6 ● Two-independent-sample *t* test. (a) Functions and formulas. (b) Results of the calculations.

(a)

	A	B	C	D	E
1					
2	Training			Training	
3	With	Without		With	Without
4	8	13	Mean (*M*) =AVERAGE(A4:A43)		=AVERAGE(B4:B43)
5	4	6	Sample size (*n*) =COUNT(A4:A43)		=COUNT(B4:B43)
6	11	9	Variance (*s*²) =VAR.S(A4:A43)		=VAR.S(B4:B43)
7	6	9	Degrees of freedom (*df*) =D5-1		=E5-1
8	4	11	Critical value of *t*, *df*=60 in Table C.2 (*t*ᵣᵢₜ) 2		
9	8	12	Sample mean difference (M₁-M₂) =D4-E4		
10	10	14	Hypothesized mean difference (μ₁-μ₂) 0		
11	10	5	Pooled sample variance (*s*ₚ²) =(D6+E6)/2		
12	8	13	Standard error for difference (*s*ₘ₁₋ₘ₂) =((D11/D5)+(D11/E5))^0.5		
13	5	9	Obtained value of *t* (*t*ₒᵦₜ) =(D9-D10)/D12		
14	11	10	*p* value =T.TEST(A4:A43,B4:B43,2,2)		
15	7	11			
16	6	10	Estimated Cohen's *d* =(D4-E4)/D11		
17	10	13	Eta-squared (η²) =D13^2/(D13^2+78)		
18	11	11			
19	7	9	*t*(*s*ₘ₁₋ₘ₂) =D8*D12		
20	9	9	95% CI upper limit =D9+D19		
21	8	10	95% CI lower limit =D9-D19		

(b)

	A	B	C	D	E
1					
2	Training			Training	
3	With	Without		With	Without
4	8	13	Mean (*M*)	8.23	10.18
5	4	6	Sample size (*n*)	40	40
6	11	9	Variance (*s*²)	3.61	4.92
7	6	9	Degrees of freedom (*df*)	39	39
8	4	11	Critical value of *t*, *df*=60 in Table C.2 (*t*ᵣᵢₜ)	2.000	
9	8	12	Sample mean difference (M₁-M₂)	-1.95	
10	10	14	Hypothesized mean difference (μ₁-μ₂)	0	
11	10	5	Pooled sample variance (*s*ₚ²)	4.27	
12	8	13	Standard error for difference (*s*ₘ₁₋ₘ₂)	0.46	
13	5	9	Obtained value of *t* (*t*ₒᵦₜ)	-4.222	
14	11	10	*p* value	.000065	
15	7	11			
16	6	10	Estimated Cohen's *d*	-0.46	
17	10	13	Eta-squared (η²)	.19	
18	11	11			
19	7	9	*t*(*s*ₘ₁₋ₘ₂)	0.92	
20	9	9	95% CI upper limit	-1.03	
21	8	10	95% CI lower limit	-2.87	

size for the two-independent-sample t test: estimated Cohen's d and proportion of variance with eta squared.

To label these calculations, in column C we enter

C16: Estimated Cohen's d

C17: Eta squared (η^2)

Estimated Cohen's d. As stated in Example 9.1 above, estimated Cohen's d is most often used with the t test. When the estimated Cohen's d is used with the two-independent-sample t test, we place the difference between two sample means in the numerator and the **pooled sample standard deviation** (or square root of the pooled sample variance) in the denominator. The pooled sample standard deviation is an estimate for the pooled or mean standard deviation for the difference between two population means. The formula for an estimated Cohen's d for the two-independent-sample t test is

$$\frac{M_1 - M_2}{\sqrt{s_p^2}}$$

In column D, enter

D16: =(D4-E4)/D11

which yields

$$d = \frac{8.23 - 10.18}{4.27} = -0.46$$

in cell D 16 in Figure 9.6b.

We conclude safety training decreases nonfatal incident rate by 0.46 standard deviations below the mean as compared to no safety training. The effect size conventions given in the middle column of Table 9.2 show that this is a medium effect size. We could report this measure with the significant t test in Example 9.2 by stating,

Pooled sample standard deviation is the combined sample standard deviation of two samples. It is computed by taking the square root of the pooled sample variance. This measure estimates the standard deviation for the difference between two population means.

The mean nonfatal incidence rate at companies with employee safety training ($M = 8.23$, $SD = 1.90$) was significantly lower than was the rate at companies without employee safety training ($M = 10.18$, $SD = 2.22$), $t(78) = -4.222$, $p < .01$, $d = -0.46$.

Proportion of Variance: Eta squared (η^2). Another measure of effect size is proportion of variance, which estimates the proportion of variance in a dependent variable that can be explained by some treatment. In Example 9.2, this measure can describe the proportion of variance in the nonfatal incident rate (the dependent variable) that can be explained by whether companies did or did not have safety training (the treatment). One measure of proportion of variance for the two-independent-sample t test is eta squared, η^2 .

Eta squared can be expressed in a single formula based on the result of a *t* test:

$$\eta^2 = \frac{t^2}{t^2 + df}$$

In Example 9.2, $t = -4.22$, and $df = 78$. To find proportion of variance using the eta squared formula, we then square the value of *t* in the numerator and the denominator. In column D, insert:

D17: =D13^2/(D13^2+78)

which yields

$$\eta^2 = \frac{-4.222^2}{-4.222^2 + 78} = \frac{17.83}{17.83 + 78} = .19$$

in cell D17 in Figure 9.6b.

We conclude that only 19% of the variability in nonfatal incident rates can be explained by whether companies did or did not provide safety training. Based on the effect size conventions in Table 9.2, this result indicates a medium effect size. We can report this estimate with the significant *t* test in Example 9.2 by stating,

> The mean nonfatal incidence rate at companies with employee safety training ($M = 8.23$, $SD = 1.90$) was significantly lower than was the rate at companies without employee safety training ($M = 10.18$, $SD = 2.22$), $t(78) = -4.222$, $p < .01$, $\eta^2 = .19$.

Confidence Intervals for the Two-Independent-Sample *t* Test

In Example 9.2, we stated a null hypothesis regarding the mean difference in a population. We can further describe the nature of the effect by determining where the effect is likely to be in the population by computing the confidence intervals.

As introduced in Learning Unit 7, there are two types of estimates: a point estimate and an interval estimate. When comparing two samples, a *point estimate* is the sample mean difference we measure. The interval estimate, often reported as a *confidence interval*, is stated within a given *level of confidence*, which is the likelihood that an interval contains an unknown population mean difference.

To illustrate confidence intervals for the two-independent-sample *t* test, we will revisit Example 9.2, and using the same data, we will compute the confidence intervals at a 95% level of confidence using the three steps to estimation first introduced in Example 9.1. For a two-independent-sample *t* test, the estimation formula is

$$M_1 - M_2 \pm t\left(s_{M_1 - M_2}\right)$$

Step 1: Compute the sample mean and standard error. The difference between the two sample means is $M_1 - M_2 = -1.95$ nonfatal injuries per 200,000 hours that employees worked. Therefore, the mean difference or point estimate of the population mean difference is –1.95. (We already computed this value for Example 9.2 in Step 3 of hypothesis testing.)

The estimated standard error for the difference, $s_{M_1 - M_2}$, is equal to 0.46. (We already computed this value as well for Example 9.2 in Step 3 of hypothesis testing.)

Step 2: Choose the level of confidence and find the critical values at that level of confidence. In this example, we want to find the 95% confidence interval (CI), so we choose a 95% level of confidence. Remember, in a sampling distribution, 50% of the differences between two sample means fall above the mean difference we selected in our sample, and 50% fall below it. We are looking for the 95% of differences between two sample means that surround the mean difference we measured in our sample. A 95% CI corresponds to a two-tailed test at a .05 level of significance. To find the critical value at this level of confidence, we look in the t table in Table C.2 in Appendix C. As explained in Step 2 in Example 9.2, we use $df = 60$. The critical value for the interval estimate is $t = 2.000$.

Step 3: Compute the estimation formula to find the confidence limits for a 95% confidence interval. Refer again to Figure 9.6. In column C, insert

C19: $t(s_{M_1 - M_2})$

C20: 95% CI upper limit

C21: 95% CI lower limit

Because we are estimating the difference between two sample means in the population with an unknown variance, we use the $M_1 - M_2 \pm t(s_{M_1 - M_2})$ estimation formula. To compute the formula, multiply t by the estimated standard error for the difference:

$$t(s_{M_1 - M_2})$$

In column D,

D19: =D8*D12

which yields

$$t(s_{M_1 - M_2}) = 2.000(0.46) = 0.92$$

in cell D19 in Figure 9.6b.

Add 0.92 to the sample mean difference to find the upper confidence limit, and subtract 0.92 from the sample mean difference to find the lower confidence limit. In column D,

D20: =D9+D19

D21: =D9-D19

which yields

$$M_1 - M_2 + t\left(s_{M_1 - M_2}\right) = -1.95 + 0.92 = -1.03$$

in cell D20 in Figure 9.6b, and

$$M_1 - M_2 - t\left(s_{M_1 - M_2}\right) = -1.95 - 0.92 = -2.87$$

in cell D21 in Figure 9.6b.

As shown in Figure 9.7, the 95% confidence interval in this population is between a mean difference in nonfatal injury incidence rate of –2.87 and –1.03 per 200,000 hours worked. We can estimate within a 95% level of confidence that the difference between groups in nonfatal injury incidence rate is between –2.87 and –1.03 per 200,000 hours worked. We are 95% confident that the mean difference in the population falls within this range, because 95% of all sample mean differences we could have selected from this population fall within the range of sample mean differences we specified.

Computing the Two-Independent-Sample *t* Test Using the Analysis Toolpak

We can also use the Analysis ToolPak available in Excel for easy and accurate calculation. We'll guide you through the steps to do the analysis for the two-independent-sample *t* test.

Click on the Data tab, and then on the Data Analysis icon all the way to the right. Select "t-Test: Two-Sample Assuming Equal Variances" (Figure 9.8a). According to the fourth assumption of the two-independent-sample *t* test described above, variances in the two samples must be equal. The rule of thumb we use is that the larger variance is no more than twice the smaller variance. That is the case with these data, as is shown in Figure 9.6b, cells D6 and E6. The variances for the two groups are 3.61 and 4.92.

FIGURE 9.7 ● At a 95% CI, the mean difference nonfatal injury incidents falls between –2.87 and –1.03.

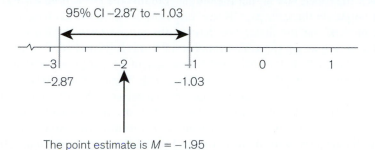

95% CI –2.87 to –1.03

–2.87

–1.03

The point estimate is *M* = –1.95

FIGURE 9.8 ● **Performing a two-independent-sample *t* test with the Analysis ToolPak in Excel. (a) Selecting "t-Test: Two-Sample Assuming Equal Variance" to perform a one-sample *t* test. (b) Specifying the location of the data and parameters for the *t* test.**

(a)

(b)

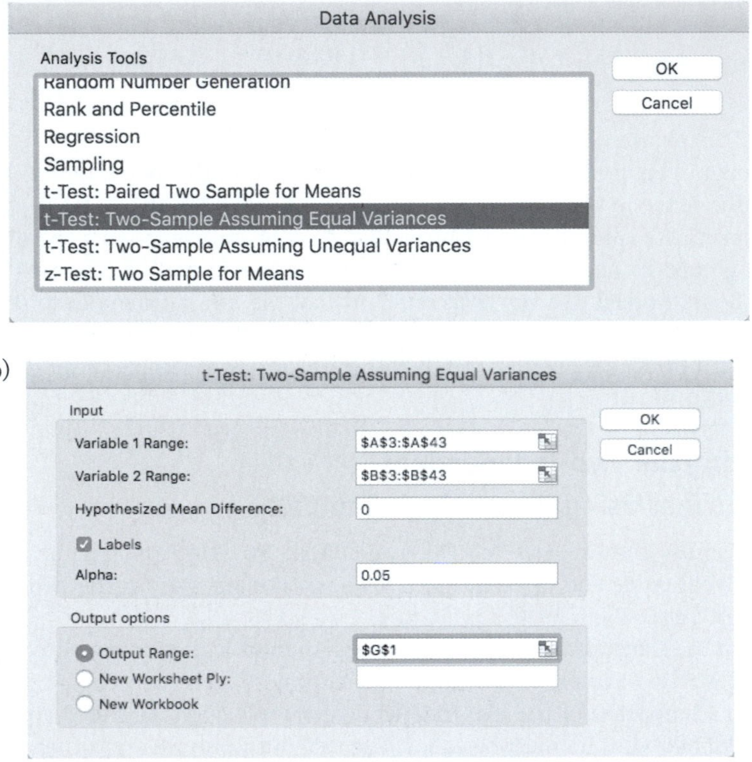

Selecting "t-Test: Two-Sample Assuming Equal Variance" yields the dialog box in Figure 9.8b. For Variable 1, we select the nonfatal injury incident rate for companies with safety training in cells A3 through A43, which includes in A3 a label for the data. For Variable 2, we select the data for companies without safety training in cells B3 through B43, and include in B3 a label for the data. The Hypothesized Mean Difference is 0. Check the Labels box so that the output contains the labels from A3 and B3. We keep our output on the same page by selecting Output Range and clicking in cell F3.

Clicking "OK" on the dialog box returns the output table in Figure 9.9. Notice that in Figure 9.9, we get the same means of 8.23 in cell H4 and 10.18 in cell I4 as we obtained in Figure 9.6b. We also get the same t_{obt} of −4.222 in cell H10 and same p value of .000065 in cell H13 as we did in Figure 9.7b. The t_{crit} in cell H14 in Figure 9.9 is for $df = 78$ and is thus more precise than the one stated in Step 2 above and shown in Figure 9.6. Although neither an estimate of effect size nor confidence intervals are generated automatically, the output table gives the means of the two groups, the variance, and the degrees of freedom. With this information we can calculate effect size and confidence intervals as we did above.

FIGURE 9.9 ● Results of two-independent-sample *t* test using the Analysis ToolPak.

	G	H	I
1	t-Test: Two-Sample Assuming Equal Variances		
2			
3		*With*	*Without*
4	Mean	8.23	10.18
5	Variance	3.61	4.92
6	Observations	40	40
7	Pooled Variance	4.27	
8	Hypothesized Mean Difference	0	
9	df	78	
10	t Stat	-4.222	
11	P(T<=t) one-tail	.000032	
12	t Critical one-tail	1.665	
13	P(T<=t) two-tail	.000065	
14	t Critical two-tail	1.991	

Computing the Related-Samples *t* Test

In this section, we compute the **related-samples *t* test**, which is used to compare the mean difference between pairs of scores. In terms of the null hypothesis, we start by stating the null hypothesis for the mean difference between pairs of scores in a population, and we then compare this to the difference we observe between paired scores in a sample. The related-samples *t* test is different from the two-independent-sample *t* test in that first we subtract one score in each pair from the other to obtain the **difference score** for each participant; then we compute the test statistic. Appendix A10 provides an overview for the reason we compute difference scores. For a related-samples *t* test, we make two assumptions:

1. *Normality.* We assume that data in the population of difference scores are normally distributed. Again, this assumption is most important for small sample sizes. With larger samples ($n > 30$), the standard error is smaller, and this assumption becomes less critical as a result.

2. *Independence within groups.* The samples are related or matched between groups. However, we must assume that difference scores were obtained from different individuals within each group or treatment.

Again, keep in mind that satisfying the assumptions for the *t* test is critically important. That said, for each example in this book, the data are intentionally constructed such that the assumptions for conducting the tests have been met. In Example 9.3, we follow the four steps to hypothesis testing introduced in Learning Unit 7 to compute a related-samples *t* test using an example adapted from published

The **related-samples *t* test** is a statistical procedure used to test hypotheses concerning two related samples selected from populations in which the variance in one or both populations is unknown.

A **difference score** is a score or value obtained by subtracting one score from another. In a related-samples *t* test, difference scores are obtained prior to computing the test statistic.

Appendix A10

See **Appendix A10,** p. 293, for more detail regarding why difference scores are calculated for a related-samples *t* test.

Appendix A11

See **Appendix A11,** p. 295, for more detail regarding the types of designs that are considered related-samples designs.

research. Note that there are many types of designs that fit into the category of *related-samples*. An overview of the types of designs that fit into this category is provided in Appendix A11.

Example 9.3. One area of focus in cognitive psychology is attention. Psychologists have examined what kinds of visual stimuli capture our attention most quickly. The course of human evolution may have predisposed us to notice animals more readily than we notice inanimate objects (Hagen & Laeng, 2016; New, Cosmides, & Tooby, 2007). In our evolutionary past, animals could have been predators that would harm us or food that would nourish us. Thus animal objects in the environment may have held more meaning than nonanimal objects such as plants or rocks. Changes to animate stimuli may capture our attention more quickly than changes in other stimuli. Suppose we conduct a study of whether people are faster to detect change in animate targets (e.g., people or animals) than in inanimate targets (e.g., plants, cars). We show participants several pairs of scenes that are virtually identical except for one change. That change could be to an animate object or to an inanimate object. For 35 participants, we record to the nearest 0.01 second the time taken for correct identification of a change. Using a sample data set adapted from published research, we will use the four steps to hypothesis testing introduced in Learning Unit 7 to test for a difference in their responses to each kind of change, animate versus inanimate, at a .05 level of significance.

Step 1: State the hypotheses. Because we are testing whether or not a difference exists, the null hypothesis states that there is no mean difference, and the alternative hypothesis states that there is a mean difference:

$H_0 : \mu_1 - \mu_2 = 0$ No difference; changes in animate as compared to inanimate objects do not differ in time to detection.

$H_0 : \mu_1 - \mu_2 \neq 0$ Changes in animate as compared to inanimate objects differ in time to detection.

Step 2: Set the criteria for a decision. The level of significance for this test is .05. This is a two-tailed test for the mean difference between two related samples. The degrees of freedom for this test are $df = 35 - 1 = 34$.

Because $df = 34$ is not available in Table C.2 in Appendix C, we take the closest smaller value, which is $df = 30$. Move across the columns to find the critical value for a .05 proportion in two tails combined. The critical values for this test are ±2.042.

Appendix A12

See **Appendix A12,** p. 298, for more on degrees of freedom for parametric tests.

We will compare the value of the test statistic with these critical values. If the value of the test statistic is beyond a critical value (either greater than +2.042 or less than −2.042), then there is less than a 5% chance we would obtain that outcome if the null hypothesis were correct, so we reject the null hypothesis; otherwise, we retain the null hypothesis.

Step 3: Compute the test statistic. Download Visual_Change.xlsx from the student study site: http://study.sagepub.com/priviteraexcel1e. As shown in Figure 9.10, participants are identified in column A, and their times to detect visual change in animate and inanimate objects are listed in the same row. Note that, in this spreadsheet, the information for a participant is all on one row, and that one row contains information from only a single participant.

To compute the test statistic, we (1) compute a difference score by subtracting for each participant one measure from the other measure; (2) compute the mean, variance, and standard deviation of difference scores; (3) compute the estimated standard error for difference scores; and then (4) compute the test statistic.

(1) Compute the difference scores. In cell D3, type "*D*" to signify that the column will contain difference scores, as in Figure 9.10. To calculate a difference score for the first participant, enter into cell D4 =B4-C4. Select cell D4. Fill down to cell D38, or copy D4 and paste from D5 to D38. Keep in mind that the sign (negative or positive) of difference scores matters when we compute the mean and standard deviation.

(2) Compute the mean, variance, and standard deviation of difference scores, and the **estimated standard error for the difference scores (s_{MD})**. We'll reserve column E for calculating D^2, which we need on our way to calculating the variance and standard deviation of the difference scores. Use column F, as in Figure 9.10, for labels to keep track of what we calculate:

F4: Mean difference score (M_D)

F5: Sample size (*n*)

F6: Variance of the difference scores (s_D^2)

F7: Standard deviation of difference scores (s_D)

F8: Standard error for difference scores (s_{MD})

To the right of the cells in column F mentioned above, type into Column G functions and formulas to calculate the values, as shown in Figure 9.10:

G4: =AVERAGE(D4:D38)

G5: =COUNT(D4:D38)

G6: =VAR.S(D4:D38)

> **Appendix B**
>
> See **Appendix B2**, p. 301, on formatting cells to add superscripts or subscripts.
>
> See **Appendix B8**, p. 312, on inserting equations, especially to use both a superscript and subscript or add multiple subscripts.

The **estimated standard error for difference scores (s_{MD})** is an estimate of the standard deviation of a sampling distribution of mean difference scores. It is an estimate of the standard error or standard distance that the mean difference scores deviate from the mean difference score stated in the null hypothesis.

FIGURE 9.10 ● Related-samples *t* test. (a) Functions and formulas. (b) Results of calculations.

(a)

	A	B	C	D	E	F	G
1							
2		Object Changed					
3	Participant	Animate	Inanimate	D			
4	1	1.82	2.54	=B4-C4		Mean difference score (M_D)	=AVERAGE(D4:D38)
5	2	0.64	0.27	=B5-C5		Sample size (n)	=COUNT(D4:D38)
6	3	2.89	4.98	=B6-C6		Variance of the difference scores (s_D^2)	=VAR.S(D4:D38)
7	4	1.06	2.23	=B7-C7		Standard deviation of difference scores (s_D)	=G6^0.5
8	5	2.38	5.96	=B8-C8		Standard error for difference scores (s_MD)	=G7/G5^0.5
9	6	0.75	2.29	=B9-C9		Degrees of freedom (df)	=G5-1
10	7	3.74	3.38	=B10-C10		Critical value of t (t_crit)	2.042
11	8	3.49	4.05	=B11-C11		Obtained value of t (t_obt)	=(G4-0)/G8
12	9	4.31	4.72	=B12-C12		p value	=T.TEST(B4:B38,C4:C38,2,1)
13	10	2.68	4.94	=B13-C13			
14	11	1.08	3.48	=B14-C14		Estimated Cohen's d	=G4/G7
15	12	0.85	4.16	=B15-C15		Eta-squared (η^2)	=G11^2/(G11^2+G9)
16	13	4.51	3.28	=B16-C16			
17	14	2.86	5.75	=B17-C17		t(s_MD)	=G10*G8
18	15	5.46	8.24	=B18-C18		95% CI upper limit	=G4+G17
19	16	2.46	0.66	=B19-C19		95% CI lower limit	=G4-G17

(b)

	A	B	C	D	E	F	G
1							
2		Object Changed					
3	Participant	Animate	Inanimate	D			
4	1	1.82	2.54	-0.72		Mean difference score (M_D)	-0.674
5	2	0.64	0.27	0.37		Sample size (n)	35
6	3	2.89	4.98	-2.09		Variance of the difference scores (s_D^2)	2.434
7	4	1.06	2.23	-1.17		Standard deviation of difference scores (s_D)	1.560
8	5	2.38	5.96	-3.58		Standard error for difference scores (s_MD)	0.264
9	6	0.75	2.29	-1.54		Degrees of freedom (df)	34
10	7	3.74	3.38	0.36		Critical value of t (t_crit)	2.042
11	8	3.49	4.05	-0.56		Obtained value of t (t_obt)	-2.555
12	9	4.31	4.72	-0.41		p value	.015
13	10	2.68	4.94	-2.26			
14	11	1.08	3.48	-2.40		Estimated Cohen's d	-0.432
15	12	0.85	4.16	-3.31		Eta-squared (η^2)	.161
16	13	4.51	3.28	1.23			
17	14	2.86	5.75	-2.89		t(s_MD)	0.539
18	15	5.46	8.24	-2.78		95% CI upper limit	-0.135
19	16	2.46	0.66	1.80		95% CI lower limit	-1.212

G7: =G6^0.5

G8: =G7/G5^.5

(3) Compute the test statistic. At this point we are ready to proceed with the calculation and evaluation of the related-samples *t* test. Use column F, as in Figure 9.10, for labels to keep track of what we calculate:

F9: Degrees of freedom (*df*)

F10: Critical value of *t* (t_{crit})

F11: Obtained value of *t* (t_{obt})

F12: *p* value

To the right of the cells in column F mentioned above, type into Column G functions and formulas to calculate the values, as shown in Figure 9.10:

G9: =G5-1

G10: 2.042

The test statistic for a related-samples *t* test estimates the number of standard deviations in a *t* distribution that a sample mean difference falls from the population mean difference stated in the null hypothesis. Similar to the other *t* tests, the mean difference is placed in the numerator, and the estimate of the standard error is placed in the denominator. By placing the mean differences in the numerator and the estimated standard error for difference scores in the denominator, we obtain the formula for the test statistic for a related-samples *t* test:

$$t_{obt} = \frac{M_D - \mu_D}{s_{MD}}$$

In column G,

G11: =(G4-0)/G8

which yields

$$t_{obt} = \frac{-0.674 - 0}{.264} = -2.555$$

in cell G11 in Figure 9.10b.

Excel allows us to calculate an exact *p* value, as shown in cell G12 in Figure 9.10a:

G12: =T.TEST(B4:B38,C4:C38,2,1)

This function requires two cell ranges of data: B4:B38 contains the times to identify change in the animate object, C4:C38 contains the times to identify change in the inanimate object. After those two ranges of data, the next argument required in the function is the number of tails, for which we specify 2. The final argument is the type of *t* test, which we specify as "paired" 1. "Paired" is the term used in Excel to calculate a related-samples *t* test. As expected with the t_{obt}, the *p* value is .015, as shown in cell G12 of Figure 9.10b.

Step 4: Make a decision. To make a decision, we compare the obtained value to the critical value. We reject the null hypothesis if the obtained value exceeds the critical value. Figure 9.10 reveals that the obtained value ($t_{obt} = -2.555$) exceeds the lower critical value; it falls in the rejection region. The decision is to reject the null hypothesis. If we were to report this result in a research journal, it would look something like this:

> Changes to animate objects were identified significantly more quickly than were changes to inanimate objects, $t(34) = -2.555$, $p = .015$.

Effect Size for the Related-Samples *t* Test

Hypothesis testing identifies whether or not an effect exists. In Example 9.3, we concluded that an effect does exist—people noticed changes to animate objects more quickly than they noticed changes to inanimate objects; we rejected the null hypothesis. The size of this effect is determined by measures of effect size. We will compute effect size for Example 9.3, because the decision was to reject the null hypothesis for that hypothesis test. There are two measures of effect size for the related-samples *t* test: estimated Cohen's *d* and proportion of variance with eta squared.

To label these calculations, in column C we enter

F14: Estimated Cohen's *d*

F15: Eta-squared (η^2)

Estimated Cohen's *d*. As stated in Example 9.1 above, estimated Cohen's *d* is most often used with the *t* test. When the estimated Cohen's *d* is used with the related-samples *t* test, it measures the number of standard deviations that mean difference scores shifted above or below the population mean difference stated in the null hypothesis. The larger the value of *d*, the larger the effect in the population. To compute estimated Cohen's *d* with two related samples, we place the mean difference between two samples in the numerator and the standard deviation of the difference scores to estimate the population standard deviation in the denominator:

$$d = \frac{M_D}{s_D}$$

In column G,

G14: =G4/G7

which yields

$$d = \frac{-0.674}{1.560} = -0.432$$

in cell G14 of Figure 9.10b.

We conclude that time to recognize a change in animate objects is 0.432 standard deviations shorter than time to recognize changes in inanimate objects. The effect size conventions listed in Table 9.2 show that this is a medium effect size ($-0.8 < d < -0.2$). We could report this measure with the significant *t* test in Example 9.3 by stating,

> Changes to animate objects were identified significantly more quickly than were changes to inanimate objects, $t(34) = -2.555$, $p < .05$ ($d = -0.432$).

Proportion of Variance: Eta squared (η^2). Another measure of effect size is proportion of variance, which estimates the proportion of variance in a dependent variable that can be explained by some treatment. In Example 9.3, this measure can describe the proportion of variance in the difference in recognition time (the dependent variable) that can be explained by whether the changed object was animate or inanimate (the treatment). One measure of proportion of variance for the two-independent-sample *t* test is eta squared, η^2.

Eta squared can be expressed in a single formula based on the result of a *t* test:

$$\eta^2 = \frac{t^2}{t^2 + df}$$

In column G,

G15: =G11^2/(G11^2+G9)

which yields

$$\eta^2 = \frac{-2.555^2}{-2.555^2 + 34} = \frac{6.528}{6.528 + 34} = .161$$

in cell G15 in Figure 9.10b.

Typically, we report proportions to the hundredths place. So with rounding, we conclude that 16% of the variability in reaction time can be explained by whether the object that changed was animate or inanimate. Based on the effect size conventions in Table 9.2, this result indicates a medium effect size. We can report this estimate with the significant *t* test in Example 9.3 by stating,

> Changes to animate objects were identified significantly more quickly than were changes to inanimate objects, $t(34) = -2.555$, $p < .05$ ($\eta^2 = .16$).

Confidence Intervals for the Related-Samples *t* Test

In Example 9.3, we stated a null hypothesis regarding the mean difference in a population. We can further describe the nature of the effect by determining where the effect is likely to be in the population by computing the confidence intervals.

As introduced in Learning Unit 7, there are two types of estimates: a point estimate and an interval estimate. When using two related samples, a *point estimate* is the sample mean difference score we measure. The interval estimate, often reported as a *confidence interval*, is stated within a given *level of confidence*, which is the likelihood that an interval contains an unknown population mean.

To illustrate confidence intervals for the related-samples *t* test, we will revisit Example 9.3, and using the same data, we will compute the confidence intervals at a 95% level of confidence using the three steps to estimation first introduced in Example 9.1. For a related-samples *t* test, the estimation formula is

$$M_D \pm t(s_{MD})$$

Step 1: Compute the sample mean and standard error. The mean difference, which is the point estimate of the population mean difference, is equal to $M_D = -0.674$. The estimated standard error for difference scores $s_{MD} = 0.264$.

Step 2: Choose the level of confidence and find the critical values at that level of confidence. In this example, we want to find the 95% confidence interval, so we choose a 95% level of confidence. Remember, in a sampling distribution, 50% of the mean differences fall above the mean difference we selected in our sample, and 50% fall below it. We are looking for the 95% of mean differences that surround the mean difference we selected in our sample. A 95% CI corresponds to a two-tailed test at a .05 level of significance. To find the critical value at this level of confidence, we look in the *t* table in Table C.2 in Appendix C. The degrees of freedom are 34 ($df = n_D - 1$) for two related samples. The critical value for the interval estimate is $t = 2.042$.

Step 3: Compute the estimation formula to find the confidence limits for a 95% confidence interval. In column G,

F17: $t(s_{MD})$

F18: 95% CI upper limit

F19: 95% CI lower limit

Because we are estimating the mean difference between two related samples from a population with an unknown variance, we use the $M_D \pm t(s_{MD})$ estimation formula.

To compute the formula, multiply *t* by the estimated standard error for difference scores. In column G,

G17: =G10*G8

which yields

$$t(s_{MD}) = 2.042(0.264) = 0.539$$

in cell G17 of Figure 9.10b.

Add 0.539 to the sample mean difference to find the upper confidence limit, and subtract 0.539 from the sample mean to find the lower confidence limit. In column G,

G18: =G4+G17

G19: =G4-G17

which yields

$$M_D + t(s_{MD}) = -0.674 + 0.539 = -0.135$$

in cell G18 of Figure 9.10b, and

$$M_D - t(s_{MD}) = -0.674 - 0.539 = -1.212$$

in cell G19 of Figure 9.10b.

As shown in Figure 9.11, the 95% confidence interval in this population is between −1.212 seconds and −0.135 seconds. We can estimate within a 95% level of confidence that people take more time to notice a change in an inanimate object than they take to notice a change in an animate object.

Computing the Related-Samples
t Test Using the Analysis Toolpak

We can also use the Analysis ToolPak available in Excel for easy and accurate calculation. We will guide you through the steps to do the analysis for the related-samples *t* test.

Click on the Data tab, and then on the Data Analysis icon all the way to the right. Select "t-Test: Paired Two Sample for Means," as shown in Figure 9.12a, which yields the dialog box in Figure 9.12b. For Variable 1, we select reaction times when the animate object changed, cells B3 through B38, which includes in B3 a label for the data. For Variable 2, we select reaction times when the inanimate object changed, cells C3 to C38, and include in C3 a label for the data. The Hypothesized Mean Difference is 0. Check the Labels box so that the output contains the labels from B3 and C3. We keep our output on the same page by selecting Output Range and clicking in cell I1.

Clicking "OK" on the dialog box returns the output table in Figure 9.13. Notice that we get the same t_{obt} of −2.555 as in cell G11 of Figure 9.10b, and the same *p* value of .015 as in cell G12 of Figure 9.10b. The t_{crit} for *df* = 34 in Figure 9.13 cell J14 is 2.032 .

FIGURE 9.11 ● At a 95% CI, the mean difference in response time falls between −1.212 and −0.135.

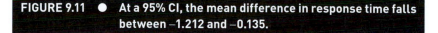

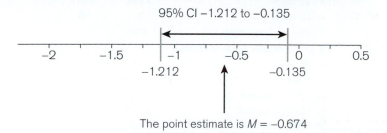

95% CI −1.212 to −0.135

−1.212

−0.135

The point estimate is *M* = −0.674

FIGURE 9.12 ● **Performing a one-sample *t* test with the Analysis ToolPak in Excel. (a) Selecting "t-Test: Paired Two Sample for Means" to perform a one-sample *t* test. (b) Specifying the location of the data and parameters for the *t* test.**

(a)

(b)

FIGURE 9.13 ● **Results of related-samples *t* test using the Analysis ToolPak.**

	I	J	K
1	t-Test: Paired Two Sample for Means		
2			
3		*Animate*	*Inanimate*
4	Mean	2.987	3.661
5	Variance	2.291	3.761
6	Observations	35	35
7	Pearson Correlation	.616	
8	Hypothesized Mean Difference	0	
9	df	34	
10	t Stat	-2.555	
11	P(T<=t) one-tail	.008	
12	t Critical one-tail	1.691	
13	P(T<=t) two-tail	.015	
14	t Critical two-tail	2.032	

One-Way Analysis of Variance: Between-Subjects and Repeated-Measures Designs

---

Excel Toolbox

Mathematical operators

- –
- ( )
- *
- /
- ^2 [square]
- ^.5 [square root]

Functions

- AVERAGE
- COUNT
- SUM

(Continued)

(Continued)

Other tools

- format cells
- freeze panes
- anchor cell reference
- fill down or paste
- Analysis ToolPak

In this learning unit, we explore the nature of hypothesis testing when observations are made across more than two levels of a factor, how to compute and interpret observed effects, and the informativeness of hypothesis testing for making such comparisons. We further explore other ways of adding information about the nature of observed effects and how to appropriately interpret them.

An Introduction to Analysis of Variance (ANOVA)

The **levels of the factor**, symbolized as k, are the number of groups or different ways in which an independent or quasi-independent variable is observed.

An **analysis of variance (ANOVA)** is a statistical procedure used to test hypotheses for one or more factors concerning the variance among two or more group means ($k \geq 2$) where the variance in one or more populations is unknown.

An **F distribution** is a positively skewed distribution derived from a sampling distribution of F ratios.

In hypothesis testing, the t tests are limited in that they can only be used to test for differences in one group or between two groups. However, researchers often ask questions that require the observation of more than two groups. In such research situations, we need a new test statistic, because as the number of groups increases, so does the number of comparisons that need to be made between groups.

To illustrate the need for a new test statistic, consider a research situation in which participants are given negative or positive feedback regarding an exam to see how that subsequently influences their self-esteem. In this example, there are only two groups; however, in a typical behavioral research study, it is essential to also include a control group in which feedback is not given—thus, a group in which the manipulation (type of feedback) is omitted. Now we have three groups, or three levels of the factor (feedback: positive, negative, and none), and, as illustrated in Figure 10.1, we also have three ways in which we can compare differences between these groups. The number of groups or **levels of the factor** are symbolized as k. When many pairs of group means can differ, we analyze the variance of group means using a new hypothesis test called an **analysis of variance (ANOVA)**. This parametric test, which is introduced in this learning unit, is one of the most popular hypothesis tests used in the behavioral sciences.

The distribution of possible outcomes for the test statistic of an ANOVA is positively skewed. The distribution, called the **F distribution**, is the distribution upon which we will decide to retain or reject the null hypothesis, and is derived from a sampling distribution of F ratios. The F distribution is illustrated in Figure 10.2. When group means at each level of a factor are exactly the same, the F ratio is equal to 0. The larger the differences are between group means, the larger the F ratio becomes.

FIGURE 10.1 ● Differences among groups when $k = 3$.

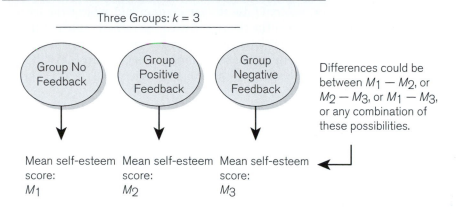

Three Groups: $k = 3$

Group No Feedback

Group Positive Feedback

Group Negative Feedback

Differences could be between $M_1 - M_2$, or $M_2 - M_3$, or $M_1 - M_3$, or any combination of these possibilities.

Mean self-esteem score: M_1

Mean self-esteem score: M_2

Mean self-esteem score: M_3

Note that as the number of groups increases, so does the number of pairs of group means that can differ.

FIGURE 10.2 ● The F distribution.

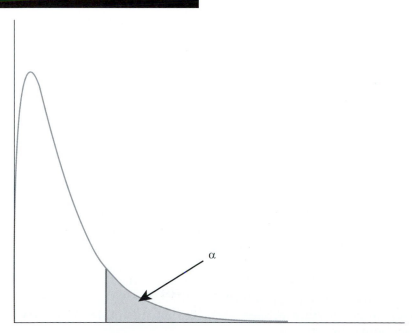

α

The rejection region or alpha level (α) is placed in the upper tail of an F distribution because values farther from 0 indicate outcomes that are less likely to occur if the null hypothesis is true.

In this learning unit, we introduce the ANOVA for one factor in which the same (*within-subjects*) or different (*between-subjects*) participants are observed at each level of the factor, or in each group. The word *subjects* refers to the design that describes how participants are observed—whether the same or different participants are observed.

When the same participants are observed across the levels of a factor, we use the within-subjects design. For example, to see whether students preferred celery or carrots as a healthy snack, we could use the same group and subject the participants to two treatments (e.g., first the celery and then the carrots). When different participants are observed at each level of a factor, we use the between-subjects design. For example, to see whether students preferred celery or carrots as a healthy snack, we could use two groups and give one group the celery and the other group the carrots.

In behavioral research, we select samples to learn more about populations of interest to us. In this learning unit, we explain and compute the two types of ANOVAs when comparing group means across the levels of a single factor: The one-way between-subjects ANOVA and the one-way within-subjects ANOVA.

One-Way Between-Subjects ANOVA

When data are measured on an interval or ratio scale and different participants are observed in each group or at each level of one factor with two or more levels, we compute the **one-way between-subjects ANOVA**. The *one-way* in the name of this hypothesis test indicates the number of factors being tested in the study. For a one-way test, then, we are testing across the levels of one factor. The between-subjects refers to the *between-subjects design*, which is the design used when different participants are observed in each group or at each level of a factor.

For a one-way between-subjects ANOVA, means can vary either between groups or within groups—each is called a **source of variation**: between groups and within groups.

The variance between the group means is called **between-groups variation**. This source of variation is the "effect" we are testing and is placed in the numerator of the test statistic. The variance attributed to error or chance is called **within-groups variation** or **error variation**. This source of variation is random variation that occurs within the groups and is placed in the denominator of the test statistic. Each source of variation is illustrated in Table 10.1 using an example in which we observe students in one of three classes.

The variances measured in an ANOVA are computed as mean squares. A mean square is a variance. The two terms, *variance* and *mean square*, are synonyms—they mean the same thing. The formula for the test statistic is the variance between groups, or **mean square between groups (MS_{BG})**, divided by the variance within groups, or **mean square within groups** (also called **mean square error**: MS_E). The formula for the test statistic is

$$F_{obt} = \frac{MS_{BG}}{MS_E} = \frac{\text{variance between groups}}{\text{variance within groups}}$$

The test statistic is used to determine how large or disproportionate the differences are between group means compared to the variance expected to occur by chance.

One-way between-subjects ANOVA is a statistical procedure used to test hypotheses for one factor with two or more levels concerning the variance among the group means. This test is used when different participants are observed at each level of a factor and the variance in any one population is unknown (10).

A **source of variation** is any variation that can be measured in a study. In the one-way between-subjects ANOVA, there are two sources of variation: variation attributed to differences between group means and variation attributed to error.

Between-groups variation is the variation attributed to mean differences between groups.

Within-groups variation or **error variation** is the variation attributed to mean differences within each group. This source of variation cannot be attributed to or caused by having different groups and is therefore called error variation.

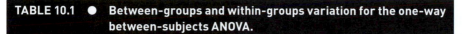

TABLE 10.1 ● Between-groups and within-groups variation for the one-way between-subjects ANOVA.

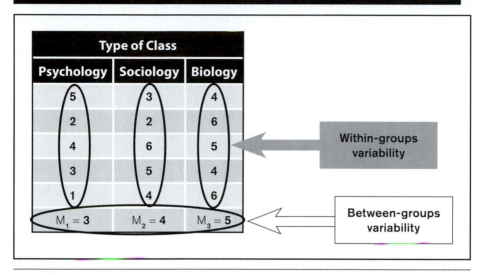

Between-groups variation is attributed to differences between group means. Within-groups variation is attributed to variation that has nothing to do with having different groups.

To understand the relationship between the test statistic, called the *F statistic*, and the null hypothesis, keep in mind that the *F* statistic evaluates how much variance is due to the groups (placed in the numerator) and how much variance is due to error (placed in the denominator). When the variance attributed to the groups is equal to the variance attributed to error, then $F = 1.0$. (The numerator and denominator are the same value; anything divided by itself is equal to 1.0.) Thus, the traditional expectation is that *F* will equal 1.0 when the null hypothesis is true that the group means do not differ. However, this assumes that the group means vary in some way (i.e., that the group means are not all exactly equal—so that a variance larger than 0 is computed in the numerator). When the group means are exactly the same value, however, $F = 0$ (because the variance of the group means is 0); this is also an expectation when the null hypothesis is true.

The notation used to identify the sample size for the ANOVA is different from that used with the *t* test. For the ANOVA, *n* represents the number of participants per group (not sample size), and *N* represents the number of total participants in a study (not population size).

$$n = \text{number of participants per group}$$

$$N = \text{total number of participants in a study}$$

The degrees of freedom for a one-way between-subjects ANOVA are equal to those for sample variance: $N - 1$. However, there are two sources of variation for the one-way between-subjects ANOVA. For this reason, we must split the total degrees of freedom $(N - 1)$ into two parts: one for each source of variation.

Mean square between groups (MS_{BG}) is the variance attributed to differences between group means. It is the numerator of the test statistic.

Mean square within groups or **mean square error** (MS_E) is the variance attributed to differences within each group. It is the denominator of the test statistic.

The variance in the numerator is attributed to differences between group means. The degrees of freedom for this variance are called the **degrees of freedom numerator** or **degrees of freedom between groups (df_{BG})**. The degrees of freedom for this variance are the number of groups (k) minus 1:

$$df_{BG} = k - 1$$

Appendix A12

See **Appendix A12,** p. 298, for more on degrees of freedom for parametric tests.

The variance in the denominator is attributed to error. The degrees of freedom for this variance are called the **degrees of freedom error (df_E)**, **degrees of freedom within groups**, or **degrees of freedom denominator**. The degrees of freedom for this variance are the total sample size (N) minus the number of groups (k):

$$df_E = N - k$$

The reason for the reference to numerator and denominator for degrees of freedom is that there are two sets of degrees of freedom: one for the variance placed in the numerator of the test statistic (between groups) and one for the variance placed in the denominator of the test statistic (error variance). This is shown here:

The **degrees of freedom between groups (df_{BG})** or **degrees of freedom numerator** are the degrees of freedom associated with the variance of the group means in the numerator of the test statistic. They are equal to the number of groups (k) minus 1.

$$F_{obt} = \frac{\text{variance between groups}}{\text{variance within groups}} \text{ Degrees of freedom for each variance are} \rightarrow \frac{k-1}{N-K}$$

Note that changing any one of the degrees of freedom will change the shape of the F distribution. As the value for k, N, or n increases, so too will the total degrees of freedom. As the total degrees of freedom increase, the F distribution becomes less skewed, meaning that the tails of the F distribution pull closer to the y-axis. In terms of the critical values for an ANOVA, as degrees of freedom increase, the critical values get smaller. Smaller critical values are associated with greater power. Hence, as the degrees of freedom increase, the power to detect an effect also increases.

The **degrees of freedom error (df_E)**, **degrees of freedom within groups**, or **degrees of freedom denominator** are the degrees of freedom associated with the error variance in the denominator. They are equal to the total sample size (N) minus the number of groups (k).

To locate the critical values for an ANOVA, we use an F table, which is given in Table C.3 in Appendix C. The F table in Appendix C lists the critical values at a .05 and .01 level of significance; the values in boldface are for a .01 level of significance. Table 10.2 shows a portion of the F table. To use the table, locate the degrees of freedom numerator listed in the columns and then the degrees of freedom denominator listed across the rows. The critical value is the entry found at the intersection of the two degrees of freedom. As an example, for a one-way ANOVA with 2 and 12 degrees of freedom at a .05 level of significance, the critical value is 3.89.

Keep in mind that the F distribution is positively skewed. It begins at 0 and is skewed toward positive values. So the critical value for all tests is placed in the upper tail. Negative outcomes are not possible in an F distribution.

TABLE 10.2 ● A portion of the *F* table.

		Degrees of Freedom Numerator			
		1	**2**	**3**	**4**
Degrees of Freedom Denominator	1	161 **4052**	200 **5000**	216 **5403**	225 **5625**
	2	18.51 **98.49**	19.00 **99.00**	19.16 **99.17**	19.25 **99.25**
	3	10.13 **34.12**	9.55 **30.92**	9.28 **29.46**	9.12 **28.71**
	4	7.71 **21.20**	6.94 **18.00**	6.59 **16.69**	6.39 **15.98**
	5	6.61 **16.26**	5.79 **13.27**	5.41 **12.06**	5.19 **11.39**
	6	5.99 **13.74**	5.14 **10.92**	4.76 **9.78**	4.53 **9.15**
	7	5.59 **13.74**	4.74 **9.55**	4.35 **8.45**	4.12 **7.85**
	8	5.32 **11.26**	4.46 **8.65**	4.07 **7.59**	3.84 **7.01**
	9	5.12 **10.56**	4.26 **8.02**	3.86 **6.99**	3.63 **6.42**
	10	4.96 **10.04**	4.10 **7.56**	3.71 **6.55**	3.48 **5.99**
	11	4.84 **9.65**	3.98 **7.20**	3.59 **6.22**	3.36 **5.67**
	12	4.75 **9.33**	3.89 **6.93**	3.49 **5.95**	3.26 **5.41**

The degrees of freedom numerator is listed in the columns; the degrees of freedom denominator is listed in the rows.

Computing the One-Way Between-Subjects ANOVA

In this section, we compute the one-way between-subjects ANOVA. There are four assumptions associated with the one-way between-subjects ANOVA:

1. *Normality.* We assume that data in the population or populations being sampled from are normally distributed. This assumption is particularly important for small sample sizes. In larger samples, the overall variance is reduced, and this assumption becomes less critical as a result.

2. *Random sampling.* We assume that the data we measure were obtained from a sample that was selected using a random sampling procedure. It is generally considered inappropriate to conduct hypothesis tests with nonrandom samples.

3. *Independence.* We assume that the probabilities of each measured outcome in a study are independent or equal. Using random sampling usually satisfies this assumption.

4. *Homogeneity of variance.* We assume that the variance in each population is equal to that of the others. Violating this assumption can inflate the value of the variance in the numerator of the test statistic, thereby increasing the likelihood of committing a Type I error.

Keep in mind that satisfying the assumptions for the ANOVA is critically important. That said, for each example in this book, the data are intentionally constructed such that the assumptions for conducting the tests have been met. In Example 10.1 we follow the four steps to hypothesis testing introduced in Learning Unit 7 to compute a one-way between-subjects ANOVA at a two-tailed .05 level of significance using an example adapted from published research.

The one-way between-subjects ANOVA is used to compare two or more group means, in which different participants are observed in each group. In terms of differences, the null hypothesis states that each mean is the same or equal: $H_0: \mu_1 = \mu_2 = \mu_k$, where k is the number of groups. However, we compute and compare variances in an ANOVA: the variance attributed to the groups and the variance attributed to error/chance. It is therefore most appropriate to state the null hypothesis and the alternative hypothesis in a way that mathematically matches the test we will compute, just as we did for the t tests when we compared mean differences. Strictly speaking, we compute variances, not differences, in an ANOVA. In terms of variance, which is directly measured to conduct this test, the null hypothesis states that group means (μ) do not vary (σ^2) in the population:

$$H_0 : \sigma_\mu^2 = 0$$

The alternative hypothesis states that group means (μ) in the population do vary (σ^2):

$$H_1 : \sigma_\mu^2 > 0$$

In terms of variance, group means either vary ($\sigma_\mu^2 > 0$) or do not vary ($\sigma_\mu^2 = 0$). A negative variance is meaningless. For this reason, the alternative hypothesis is always a "greater than" statement. Also, note that variance corresponds to differences. When group means vary, they also differ; when group means do not vary, they also do not differ.

Because we compute variance across groups, the sample size (n) must be equal in each group—it is necessary that the same number of scores is averaged in each group. Most researchers plan for equal samples by making sure that the same number of participants is observed in each group. Sometimes this is too difficult or impractical to accomplish. In these circumstances, the best alternative is to increase the sample size to minimize problems associated with averaging a different number of scores in each group.

We now follow the four steps in hypothesis testing to compute a one-way between-subjects ANOVA.

Example 10.1. Employee turnover is a common concern among businesses and organizational psychologists. Stress levels at a workplace are often cited as a key reason for increased employee turnover, which is the rate at which employees leave a company, thereby impacting costs needed to hire new employees (DeTienne, Agle, Phillips, & Ingerson, 2012; Morrell, 2016; Saridakis & Cooper, 2016). As an example of one such study in this area of research, suppose we ask new employees at a company how long they feel they will remain with the company. Employees are assigned to groups based on how stressful they rated the workplace: 30 employees rated the company as a high-stress workplace, 30 as moderately stressful, and 30 as low stress. The times in years that employees said they would stay with the company is the dependent variable. We will conduct an ANOVA to analyze the significance of these data at a .05 level of significance.

Step 1. State the hypotheses. In terms of differences, the null hypothesis states that each mean is the same as or equal to the others: $H_0 : \mu_1 = \mu_2 = \mu_k$, where k is the number of groups. In terms of variance, which is directly measured to conduct this test, the null hypothesis states that group means (μ) do not vary (σ^2) in the population. Thus, the null hypothesis states that group means in the population do not vary (variance = 0); the alternative hypothesis states that group means in the population do vary (variance > 0):

$H_0 : \sigma_\mu^2 = 0$. Group means do not vary between groups in the population of employees.

$H_1 : \sigma_\mu^2 > 0$. Group means do vary between groups in the population of employees.

Step 2: Set the criteria for a decision. The level of significance for this test is .05. The degrees of freedom for a one-way between-subjects ANOVA are equal to those for sample variance: $N - 1$. However, recall that there are two sources of variation for the one-way between-subjects ANOVA: one for each source of variation.

The variance in the numerator is attributed to differences between group means: the degrees of freedom between groups (df_{BG}). The degrees of freedom for this variance are the number of groups (k) minus 1: $k - 1$.

$$df_{BG} = 3 - 1 = 2$$

The variance in the denominator is attributed to error: the degrees of freedom error (df_E). The degrees of freedom for this variance are the total sample size (N) minus the number of groups (k): $N - k$.

$$df_E = 90 - 3 = 87$$

To locate the critical values, we find 2 in the columns, and 87 in the rows in Table C.3 in Appendix C. However, for the table in the back of the book, 87 is not listed. Note that as degrees of freedom increases, the critical values decrease. For this reason, and to be conservative, we read the row with the next smallest degrees of freedom: 60. In Table C.3, the critical value located where 2 and 60 intersect in Table C.3 is 3.15.

We will compare the value of the test statistic with this critical value. If the value of the test statistic falls beyond the critical value (at or greater than 3.15), then there is less than a 5% chance we would obtain that outcome if the null hypothesis were correct, so we reject the null hypothesis; otherwise, we retain the null hypothesis.

Step 3: Compute the test statistic. To compute the test statistic, we follow five stages:

- calculate n, N, group means, and grand mean;

- calculate between-group variance and sum of squares;

- calculate within-groups (error) variance and sum of squares;

- calculate the total variance and sum of squares; and

- complete the F table.

Because the total sum of squares equals the sum of squares between groups plus the sum of squares within groups ($SS_T = SS_{BG} + SS_E$), it is not strictly necessary to calculate all three terms separately. After calculating any two terms, the third can always be derived. Given the ease of calculation with Excel, we show the calculation of all three terms because it is a good way to check for mistakes.

Download Employee_Turnover.xlsx from the student study site: http://study.sagepub.com/priviteraexcel1e. Columns B, C, and D contain the time in years that employees said they would stay with the company among employees who rated the workplace as being low stress (column B), moderate stress (column C), or high stress (column D).

Stage 1. Calculating n, N, group means, and grand mean. Start by labeling cells A36 and A37, respectively, "*n*" and "Group Mean". Calculate *n* with the COUNT function, and calculate each group mean with the AVERAGE function, as in Figure 10.3a.

B36: =COUNT(B5:B34)

C36: =COUNT(C5:C34)

D36: =COUNT(D5:D34)

B37: =AVERAGE(B5:B34)

C37: =AVERAGE(C5:C34)

D37: =AVERAGE(D5:D34)

These yield *n* for each group in B36 through D36 and the group means in B37 through D37, as shown in Figure 10.3b.

Next, into the cells listed below, type the labels below, as shown in Figure 10.3:

C39-D39: All Groups

C40: *k*

C41: *N*

C42: Grand Mean

Then enter the functions into the cells listed below, as shown in Figure 10.3a, which yield the result shown in Figure 10.3b.

D40: =COUNT(B36:D36), yielding 3

D41: =SUM(B36:D36), yielding 90

D42: =AVERAGE(B5:D34), yielding 3.28

These calculations provide the numbers for the next three stages: calculating sums of squares and degrees of freedom.

> **Appendix B**
>
> See **Appendix B2,** p. 301, for formatting cells.
>
> See **Appendix B3,** p. 303, for freezing panes.

Stage 2. Calculating between-groups variance and SS_{BG}. To determine how much the groups differ from each other, we

- subtract the grand mean from each group mean,

- square each difference,

FIGURE 10.3 ● Raw data with *n* and mean for each group, *k*, *N*, and grand mean. (a) Formulas and functions. (b) Results of calculations.

(a)

	A	B	C	D
1		Years expected to remain at company		
2				
3		Perceived Stress Level of Workplace		
4		Low	Moderate	High
31		3.7	3.4	3.4
32		3.2	3.4	2.9
33		3.7	2.9	2.7
34		2.6	3.3	3.4
35				
36	*n*	=COUNT(B5:B34)	=COUNT(C5:C34)	=COUNT(D5:D34)
37	Group Mean	=AVERAGE(B5:B34)	=AVERAGE(C5:C34)	=AVERAGE(D5:D34)
38				
39			All Groups	
40			*k*	=COUNT(B36:D36)
41			*N*	=SUM(B36:D36)
42			Grand Mean	=AVERAGE(B5:D34)

(b)

	A	B	C	D
1		Years expected to remain at company		
2				
3		Perceived Stress Level of Workplace		
4		Low	Moderate	High
31		3.7	3.4	3.4
32		3.2	3.4	2.9
33		3.7	2.9	2.7
34		2.6	3.3	3.4
35				
36	*n*	30	30	30
37	Group Mean	3.42	3.36	3.05
38				
39			All Groups	
40			*k*	3
41			*N*	90
42			Grand Mean	3.28

- sum the squared differences, and

- multiply by n to yield the SS_{BG}.

To keep track of calculations, copy the Low, Moderate, and High labels from B4 through D4 and paste them in F4 through H4. In F3, label this section "Between-group variance: SS_{BG}". (Figure 10.4 includes in rows 1 and 2 a reminder of the calculation.) Subtract the grand mean from each of the group means; then square each of the differences, as in Figure 10.4. Anchoring the cell address of the grand mean, D42, as \$D\$42 allows you to type the formula into F5 and either fill or copy and paste to the other two cells, as shown in Figure 10.4a, yielding the results show in Figure 10.4b.

F5: =(B37-\$D\$42)^2*B36, yielding 0.616

G5: =(C37-\$D\$42)^2*C36, yielding 0.208

H5: =(D37-\$D\$42)^2*D36, yielding 1.541

To keep track of the next calculations, label cells G7 and H7, respectively, "SS_{BG}" and "df_{BG}". Then calculate those values, as shown in Figure 10.4a, yielding the results shown in Figure 10.4b.

G8: =SUM(F5:H5), yielding 2.366

H8: = D40-1, yielding 2

We enclosed G7 through H8 in a box to highlight these as the first portion of the F table for Stage 5.

Stage 3. Calculating within-groups variance, SS_E. As with variance in Learning Unit 2, in Step 3, to calculate the total variance within groups,

- subtract the group mean from each score in the group,

- square the difference, and

- sum the squared differences to yield SS_E.

FIGURE 10.4 ● Calculating sum of squares and degrees of freedom between groups. (a) Formulas and functions. (b) Results of calculations.

(a)

	F	G	H
1	Subtract grand mean from group mean,		
2	square the difference, multiply by n.		
3	Between-group variance: SS_{BG}		
4	Low	Moderate	High
5	=(B37-\$D\$42)^2*B36	=(C37-\$D\$42)^2*C36	=(D37-\$D\$42)^2*D36
6			
7		SS_{BG}	df_{BG}
8		=SUM(F5:H5)	=D40-1

(b)

	F	G	H
1	Subtract grand mean from group mean,		
2	square the difference, multiply by n.		
3	Between-group variance: SS_{BG}		
4	Low	Moderate	High
5	0.616	0.208	1.541
6			
7		SS_{BG}	df_{BG}
8		2.366	2

To keep track of calculations, copy the Low, Moderate, and High labels from B4 through D4 and paste them in J4 through L4. In J3, label this section "Within-group (error) variance: SS_E". (Figure 10.5 includes in rows 1 and 2 a reminder of the calculation.) Subtract the Low group's mean from the first score in that group, and square the difference by typing into cell J5: =(B5-B$37)^2. Anchoring the cell address of the group mean, B36, as B$36 allows the formula in J5 to be filled down through J34 or copied and pasted to J6 through J34. Selecting J5 to J34 allows filling right to K5 through L34 or copying and pasting from K5 through L34, the bottom four rows of which are shown in Figure 10.5a. This yields for the 30 scores in each group the squared deviations from their group mean, the bottom four rows of which are shown in Figure 10.5b.

To keep track of the next calculations, label cells K36 and L36, respectively, SS_E and df_E. Then we calculate those values, as shown in Figure 10.5a, yielding the results shown in Figure 10.5b.

K37: =SUM(J5:L34), yielding 13.875

L37: =D41-D40, yielding 87

We enclosed K36 through L37 in a box to highlight these as the second portion of the *F* table for Stage 5.

Stage 4. Calculating total variance: SS_T. To determine the total variance among all scores in the entire study, we

- subtract the grand mean from each of the scores,

- square each difference, and

- sum the squared differences to yield the SS_T.

FIGURE 10.5 ● Calculating sum of squares and degrees of freedom within groups (error). (a) Formulas and functions. (b) Results of calculations.

(a)

	J	K	L
1	Subtract group mean from each score		
2	in the group, square the difference.		
3	Within-group (error) variance: SS_E		
4	Low	Moderate	High
31	=(B31-B$37)^2	=(C31-C$37)^2	=(D31-D$37)^2
32	=(B32-B$37)^2	=(C32-C$37)^2	=(D32-D$37)^2
33	=(B33-B$37)^2	=(C33-C$37)^2	=(D33-D$37)^2
34	=(B34-B$37)^2	=(C34-C$37)^2	=(D34-D$37)^2
35			
36		SS_E	df_E
37		=SUM(J5:L34)	=D41-D40

(b)

	J	K	L
1	Subtract group mean from each score		
2	in the group, square the difference.		
3	Within-group (error) variance: SS_E		
4	Low	Moderate	High
31	0.078	0.002	0.122
32	0.048	0.002	0.023
33	0.078	0.212	0.123
34	0.672	0.004	0.122
35			
36		SS_E	df_E
37		13.875	87

To keep track of calculations, copy the Low, Moderate, and High labels from B4 through D4 and paste them in N4 through P4. In N3, label this section "Total variance: SS_T". (In Figure 10.6, rows 1 and 2 include a reminder of the calculation.) Subtract the grand mean from the first score in the Low group, and square the difference by typing into cell N5 =(B5-$D$42)^2. Anchoring the cell address of the group mean, D41, as $D$41 allows the formula in N5 to be filled down through N34 or copied and pasted to N6 through N34, the bottom four rows of which are shown in Figure 10.6a. Selecting N5 to N34 allows filling right to P5 through P34 or copying and pasting from O5 through P34. This yields for the 90 scores the squared deviations from their grand mean, as shown in Figure 10.6b.

> **Appendix B**
>
> See **Appendix B4**, p. 304, on highlighting, pasting, and filling.

To keep track of the next calculations, label cells O36 and P36, respectively, "SS_T" and "df_T". Then we calculate those values, as shown in Figure 10.6a, yielding the results shown in Figure 10.6b.

O37: =SUM(N5:P34), yielding 16.241

P37: =D41-1, yielding 89

We enclosed O36 through P37 in a box to highlight these as the third portion of the *F* table for Stage 5.

As mentioned at the beginning of Step 3, $SS_T = SS_{BG} + SS_E$. We can now confirm that $16.241 = 2.366 + 13.875$.

Stage 5. Completing the F table. The *F* table lists the sum of squares (*SS*), degrees of freedom (*df*), mean squares (*MS*), and value of the test statistic (*F*).

In cells R4 through V4, type the following headings: "Source of Variation", "SS", "df", "MS", and "F", as in Figure 10.7. In cells R5 through R7, below "Source of Variation",

---

FIGURE 10.6 ● Calculating total sum of squares and degrees of freedom. (a) Formulas and functions. (b) Results of calculations.

(a)

	N	O	P
1	Subtract grand mean from		
2	each score, square the difference.		
3		Total variance: SS_T	
4	Low	Moderate	High
31	=(B31-$D$42)^2	=(C31-$D$42)^2	=(D31-$D$42)^2
32	=(B32-$D$42)^2	=(C32-$D$42)^2	=(D32-$D$42)^2
33	=(B33-$D$42)^2	=(C33-$D$42)^2	=(D33-$D$42)^2
34	=(B34-$D$42)^2	=(C34-$D$42)^2	=(D34-$D$42)^2
35			
36		SS_T	df_T
37		=SUM(N5:P34)	=D41-1

(b)

	N	O	P
1	Subtract grand mean from		
2	each score, square the difference.		
3	Total variance: SS_T		
4	Low	Moderate	High
31	0.179	0.015	0.015
32	0.006	0.015	0.142
33	0.179	0.142	0.333
34	0.458	0.001	0.015
35			
36		SS_T	df_T
37		16.241	89

we list the sources that we have just calculated: "Between groups", "Within groups (error)", and "Total", as shown in Figure 10.7.

For the three values of *SS* and three values of *df*, we refer to the cells in which we have calculated these values in Stages 2, 3, and 4, as shown in Figure 10.7a.

Three values of *SS*:

S5: =G8 to display SS_{BG}

S6: =K37 to display SS_{E}

S7: =O37 to display SS_{T}

Selecting S5 through S7 and filling right to T5 through T7 or copying and pasting to T5 through T7 yields the cells containing the values for *df*, as shown in Figure 10.7a.

Three values of *df*:

T5: =H8 to display df_{BG}

T6: =L37 to display df_{E}

T7: =P37 to display df_{T}

Appendix B

See **Appendix B2**, p. 301, on formatting cells to add subscripts.

We use the values for *SS* and for *df* to calculate MS_{BG} and MS_{E}. The formula for variance is *SS* divided by *df*, so we divide across the row to compute each mean square.

To compute the variance or mean square between groups, we divide SS_{BG} by df_{BG}:

$$MS_{BG} = \frac{SS_{BG}}{df_{BG}}$$

In cell U5, enter =S5/T5. As shown in Figure 10.7b, this yields

$$MS_{BG} = \frac{2.366}{2} = 1.183$$

Likewise, to compute the variance or mean square within groups (error), we divide SS_{E} by df_{E}:

$$MS_{E} = \frac{SS_{E}}{df_{E}}$$

Select U5 and fill down to U6, or copy U5 and paste to U6 to get =S6/T6, as shown in Figure 10.7a, which yields

$$MS_{E} = \frac{13.875}{87} = 0.159$$

as shown in Figure 10.7b.

The formula for the F statistic is the mean square between groups divided by the mean square error:

$$F_{\text{obt}} = \frac{MS_{\text{BG}}}{MS_{\text{E}}}$$

In cell V5, enter =U5/U6 , as shown in Figure 10.7a, which yields

FIGURE 10.7 ● Summary table for one-way between-subjects ANOVA, calculating effect size and post hoc comparisons. (a) Formulas and functions. (b) Results of calculations.

(a)

	R	S	T	U	V
4	**Source of Variation**	**SS**	**df**	**MS**	**F**
5	**Between groups**	=G8	=H8	=S5/T5	=U5/U6
6	**Within groups (error)**	=K37	=L37	=S6/T6	
7	**Total**	=O37	=P37		
8					
9	**Effect size**				
10	η^2 =S5/S7				
11					
12	**Post hoc comparison difference**				
13	**Low Stress and High Stress** =B37-D37				
14	**Moderate Stress and High Stress** =C37-D37				
15	**Low Stress and Moderate Stress** =B37-C37				
16	q_α 3.41				
17	**critical value** =S16*(U6/B36)^0.5				

(b)

	R	S	T	U	V
4	**Source of Variation**	**SS**	**df**	**MS**	**F**
5	**Between groups**	2.366	2	1.183	7.418
6	**Within groups (error)**	13.875	87	0.159	
7	**Total**	16.241	89		
8					
9	**Effect size**				
10	η^2	.15			
11					
12	**Post hoc comparison difference**				
13	**Low Stress and High Stress**	0.37			
14	**Moderate Stress and High Stress**	0.31			
15	**Low Stress and Moderate Stress**	0.06			
16	q_α	3.41			
17	**critical value**	0.25			

$$F = \frac{1.183}{0.159} = 7.418$$

as shown in Figure 10.7b.

Step 4: Make a decision. To make a decision, we compare the obtained value to the critical value. As shown in cell V5 of Figure 10.7, the obtained value (7.418) is greater than the critical value (3.15); it falls in the rejection region. The decision is to reject the null hypothesis.

Measuring Effect Size With Eta Squared

In Example 10.1, we concluded that the group means significantly varied by group. We can also determine the size of this effect using the proportion of variance estimated with eta squared. A proportion of variance is used to measure how much variability in the dependent variable (time in years) can be accounted for by the levels of the factor (the perceived stress of the workplace).

Using eta squared, the symbol R^2 may be used instead of η^2. Eta squared is computed as the sum of squares between groups divided by the sum of squares total:

$$R^2 = \eta^2 = \frac{SS_{BG}}{SS_T}$$

For Example 10.1, into cell R10 type η^2, as shown in Figure 10.7a. Into cell S10 enter =S5/S7, which yields

$\eta^2 = \frac{2.366}{16.241} = .146$, as shown rounded to the hundredths place in Figure 10.7b in cell S10.

We conclude that 14.6% of the variability in how long employees said they would stay with their company can be accounted for by the perceived stress of the workplace. Based on the effect size conventions listed in the second column of Table 9.2 in Learning Unit 9 (p. 138), this is a medium effect size. Here is how we might report eta squared with the significant result:

> The one-way analysis of variance showed that how long employees stated that they would stay with the company depended on the stress level they perceived in the workplace, $F(2, 87) = 7.418$, $p < .05$ ($\eta^2 = .146$).

Post Hoc Test Using Tukey's HSD

When the decision is to retain the null hypothesis for an ANOVA, we stop the analysis. No pairs of group means are significantly different. As shown in Figure 10.8, following a decision to retain the null hypothesis, we stop, start over, consider an alternative study, and begin again.

The decision in Example 10.1, however, was to reject the null hypothesis: The test was significant. A significant ANOVA indicates that at least one pair of group means significantly differs. However, this test does not tell us which pairs of means differ. To determine which pairs differ, we compute **post hoc tests** or "after-the-fact" tests.

A **post hoc test** is a statistical procedure computed following a significant ANOVA to determine which pair or pairs of group means significantly differ. These tests are necessary when $k > 2$, because multiple comparisons are needed. When $k = 2$, only one comparison is made, because only one pair of group means can be compared.

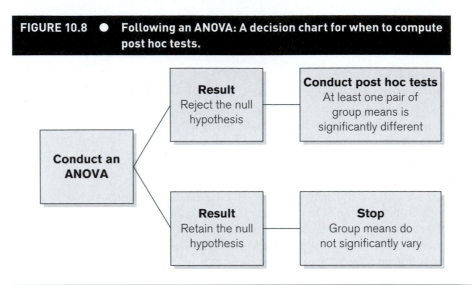

FIGURE 10.8 ● Following an ANOVA: A decision chart for when to compute post hoc tests.

These tests evaluate the difference for all possible pairs of group means, called **pairwise comparisons.** With only two groups ($k = 2$), post hoc tests are not needed because only one pair of group means can be compared. With more than two groups ($k > 2$), multiple comparisons must be made, so post hoc tests are necessary.

All post hoc tests are aimed at making sure that no matter how many tests we compute, the overall likelihood of committing a Type I error is .05. In other words, all post hoc tests control for **experimentwise alpha**, which is the overall alpha level for multiple tests conducted on the same data. The alpha level for each test is called **testwise alpha**.

In Example 10.1, we stated an experimentwise alpha equal to .05 for all tests. Post hoc tests are used to control for experimentwise alpha, thereby making the overall alpha or probability of a Type I error for all pairwise comparisons combined equal to .05. Figure 10.9 lists five tests commonly used to control for experimentwise alpha.

A **pairwise comparison** is a statistical comparison for the difference between two group means. A post hoc test evaluates all possible pairwise comparisons for an ANOVA with any number of groups.

Experimentwise alpha is the aggregated alpha level, or probability of committing a Type I error for all tests, when multiple tests are conducted on the same data.

Testwise alpha is the alpha level, or probability of committing a Type I error, for each test or pairwise comparison made on the same data.

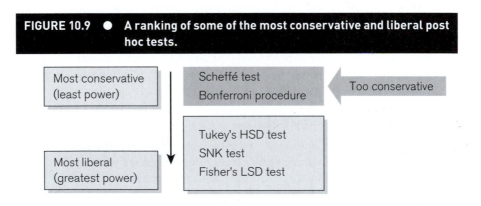

FIGURE 10.9 ● A ranking of some of the most conservative and liberal post hoc tests.

While the Scheffé test and Bonferroni procedure are good post hoc tests, they are generally considered too conservative for a between-subjects ANOVA design. HSD = honestly significant difference; LSD = least significant difference; SNK = Student-Newman-Keuls.

The tests in the figure are listed from most conservative (associated with the least power) to most liberal (associated with the greatest power).

For a between-subjects test, the two most conservative tests are the Scheffé test and the Bonferroni procedure. For a between-subjects design, that is, when different participants are observed in each group, both post hoc tests tend to be too conservative—in a way, these post hoc tests do too good of a job of controlling for experimentwise alpha. However, the Bonferroni procedure is only too conservative when the number of pairwise comparisons is greater than three. Because we made three pairwise comparisons in Example 10.1, this procedure would not have been too conservative in that case.

The remaining three post hoc tests are Fisher's least significant difference (LSD) test, the Student-Newman-Keuls (SNK) test, and Tukey's honestly significant difference (HSD) test. Each test has drawbacks as well, although all tend to have a better balance between making it too easy (too liberal) and making it too difficult (too conservative) to reject the null hypothesis. In this section, we describe the most conservative (Tukey's HSD) of these post hoc tests, which is also a commonly reported post hoc test.

The three steps to compute Tukey's HSD are as follows:

Step 1: Compute the test statistic for each pairwise comparison.

Step 2: Compute the critical value for each pairwise comparison.

Step 3: Make a decision to retain or reject the null hypothesis for each pairwise comparison.

Step 1: Compute the test statistic for each pairwise comparison. As shown in Figure 10.7, cells R12 through R17 label the components of the post hoc comparisons:

R12: Post hoc comparison

R13: Low Stress and High Stress

R14: Moderate Stress and High Stress

R15: Low Stress and Moderate Stress

R16: q_α

R17: critical value

Cell S12 designates the location for calculation of "difference". The test statistic for each pairwise comparison is the difference between the largest and the smallest group mean. We compute the test statistic in the same way for both post hoc tests. The test statistic for each comparison, as shown in cells S13 through S15 in Figure 10.7, is as follows:

S13: =B37-D37, which yields a difference of 0.37 years for Comparison 1;

S14: =C37-D37, which yields a difference of 0.31 years for Comparison 2; and

S15: =B37-C37, which yields a difference of 0.06 years for Comparison 3.

Here, we will compute the critical value (Step 2) and make a decision (Step 3) for Tukey's HSD.

Step 2: Compute the critical value for each pairwise comparison. The critical value is computed using the following statistic:

$$\text{Tukey's HSD: } q_\alpha \sqrt{\frac{MS_E}{n}}$$

In this formula, **q** is the **studentized range statistic**. We must find this value in the studentized range statistic table in Table C.4 in Appendix C, p. 323. To locate values for q in Table C.4, we need to know df_E and the real range (r). For Tukey's HSD test, the real range, r, is equal to the number of groups, k, in a study. In Example 10.1, we observed three groups; therefore, $r = 3$.

In Table C.4, we move across to 3 in the columns and down to 87 (the value for df_E) in the rows. Because 87 is not in the table, the most conservative rule is to use the next smallest value, which is 60 in the table. We use the q value at 3 and 60: $q = 3.41$, and enter that value in cell S16. For this test, $MS_E = 0.159$, shown in cell U6, and $n = 30$, shown in cell B36. To calculate the critical value in cell S17, enter =S16*(U6/B36)^.5, as shown in Figure 10.7a, which yields the critical value for Tukey's HSD:

$$3.41\sqrt{\frac{0.159}{30}} = 0.25$$

as shown in Figure 10.7b in cell S17.

Step 3: Make a decision to retain or reject the null hypothesis for each pairwise comparison. The value 0.25 is the critical value for each pairwise comparison. For each comparison, we decide that the two groups are significantly different if the test statistic is larger than the critical value we computed. The decision for each comparison is given below (an asterisk is included to indicate significance where applicable):

Comparison 1: Low Stress and High Stress: $3.42 - 3.05 = 0.37$ * (reject the null hypothesis; the test statistic value, 0.37, is larger than 0.25).

Comparison 2: Moderate Stress and High Stress: $3.36 - 3.05 = 0.31$ * (reject the null hypothesis; the test statistic value, 0.31, is larger than 0.25).

Comparison 3: Low Stress and Moderate Stress: $3.42 - 3.36 = 0.06$ (retain the null hypothesis; the test statistic value, 0.06, is less than 0.25).

Only Comparisons 1 and 2 are significant. Thus, we conclude that employees are willing to stay longer with a company if they perceive the workplace as a low- or moderate-stress environment compared to employees who perceive the same workplace as a high-stress environment. If we were to report this result in a research journal, it would look something like this:

The **studentized range statistic** **(q)** is a statistic used to determine critical values for comparing pairs of means at a given range. This statistic is used in the formula to find the critical value for Tukey's HSD post hoc test.

The one-way analysis of variance reached significance, $F(2, 87) = 7.418$, $p < .05$, with the time employees said they would stay with the company being significantly greater among employees who perceived the workplace environment as low or moderate stress compared to those who perceived the same workplace as a high-stress environment (Tukey's HSD, $p < .05$).

Computing the One-Way Between-Subjects ANOVA Using the Analysis Toolpak

We can also calculate this ANOVA using the Analysis ToolPak available in Excel for easy and accurate calculation. Return to the workbook Employee_Turnover.xlsx. Click on the Data tab, and then on the Data Analysis icon all the way to the right. Select "Anova: Single Factor," shown in Figure 10.10a, which yields the dialog box shown in Figure 10.10b. Our data are grouped so that each test condition in contained within a column. Enter $B$4:$D$34 for Input Range. Select the button next to Columns for the specification of Grouped By. Check the box to the left of Labels in first row so that the output will contain the names of the groups that we used. The value for alpha we

FIGURE 10.10 ● Performing a one-way between-subjects ANOVA with Analysis ToolPak in Excel. (a) Selecting "Anova: Single factor" to perform a one-way between-subjects ANOVA. (b) Specifying the location of the data and parameters for the ANOVA.

(a)
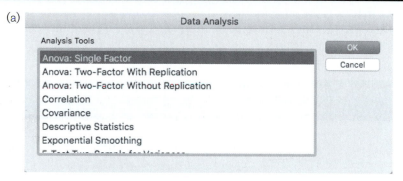

(b)
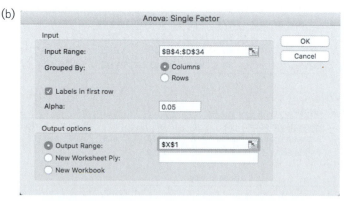

specify as .05. Select Output Range for the result to be displayed in the worksheet and click in the box to the right. Then click in cell X1 of the spreadsheet.

Clicking "OK" on the dialog box returns the output table in Figure 10.11. Notice that the values in the table for SS, df, MS, and F are the same as the ones we calculated. Because the F Table in Appendix C3 did not have a critical value for df 2 and 87, we used the more conservative critical value for 2 and 60. The output table generated by the Analysis ToolPak gives an exact critical value for df 2 and 87, which is 3.101 in cell AD12. Although the output table gives neither an estimate of effect size such as eta squared nor post hoc comparisons, it does provide the means for each group and all the components of the ANOVA summary table needed. Only the studentized range statistic, q, would need to be found in Appendix C4.

One-Way Within-Subjects ANOVA

When data are measured on an interval or ratio scale and the same participants are observed in each group or at each level of one factor with two or more levels, we compute the **one-way within-subjects ANOVA**. The *one-way* in the name of this hypothesis test indicates the number of factors being tested in the study. For a one-way test, then, we are testing across the levels of one factor. The within-subjects refers to the *within-subjects design*, also called the *repeated-measures design*, which is the design used when the same participants are observed in each group or at each level of a factor.

The test statistic is the same for the within-subjects and between-subjects designs using an ANOVA. It is the variance or mean square between groups divided by the variance or mean square error:

A **one-way within-subjects ANOVA**, also called a **one-way repeated-measures ANOVA**, is a statistical procedure used to test hypotheses for one factor with two or more levels concerning the variance among group means. This test is used when the same participants are observed at each level of a factor and the variance in any one population is unknown.

FIGURE 10.11 ● Results of the one-way between-subjects ANOVA using the Analysis ToolPak.

	X	Y	Z	AA	AB	AC	AD
1	Anova: Single Factor						
2							
3	SUMMARY						
4	Groups	Count	Sum	Average	Variance		
5	Low	30	102.6	3.42	0.2113		
6	Moderate	30	100.8	3.36	0.1335		
7	High	30	91.5	3.05	0.1336		
8							
9							
10	ANOVA						
11	Source of Variation	SS	df	MS	F	P-value	F crit
12	Between Groups	2.366	2	1.183	7.418	.001	3.101
13	Within Groups	13.875	87	0.159			
14							
15	Total	16.241	89				

$$F_{\text{obt}} = \frac{MS_{\text{BG}}}{MS_{\text{E}}} = \frac{\text{variance between groups}}{\text{variance within groups}}$$

There are three sources of variation in the one-way within-subjects ANOVA: between-groups, within-groups, and between-persons variation. The *between-groups variation* and *within-groups variation* are the same as that for the between-subjects design.

The within-groups and between-persons sources of variation are regarded as "error," or variation that cannot be explained by having different groups. The **between-persons variation**, which is a new source of variation, is calculated and removed from the denominator of the test statistic. It is a source of variation associated with the differences between person means averaged across groups. In a within-subjects design, we can assume that any differences in the characteristics of participants across groups are the same, because the same people are observed in each group. For this reason, between-persons variation can be measured and then removed from the error term in the denominator of the test statistic.

Although there are two sources of error in a within-subjects design, this does not mean that we have more error variation in this design compared to the between-subjects design. Think of error variation as a pie with two slices. In the between-subjects design, we measure the whole pie and place it all in the denominator of the test statistic. In the within-subjects design, we cut this same pie into two slices and then remove the between-persons slice. The remaining portion of pie is placed in the denominator of the test statistic.

Likewise, while the formula to compute degrees of freedom will be slightly different, we will still compute the same sets of degrees of freedom and look up critical values in the *F* table, the same as we did for the one-way between-subjects ANOVA. Again, the *F* distribution is positively skewed. It begins at 0 and is skewed toward positive values. So the critical value for all tests is placed in the upper tail. Negative outcomes are not possible in an *F* distribution.

Computing the One-Way Within-Subjects ANOVA

In this section, we compute the one-way within-subjects ANOVA. We make four assumptions to compute the one-way within-subjects ANOVA:

1. *Normality.* We assume that data in the population or populations being sampled from are normally distributed. This assumption is particularly important for small sample sizes. In larger samples, the overall variance of sample outcomes is reduced, and this assumption becomes less critical as a result.

2. *Independence within groups.* The same participants are observed between groups. Within each group, different participants are observed. For this reason, we make the assumption that participants are independently observed within groups but not between groups.

3. *Homogeneity of variance.* We assume that the variance in each population is equal to that in the others.

The **between-persons variation** is the variance attributed to differences between person means averaged across groups. Because the same participants are observed across groups using a within-subjects design, this source of variation is removed or omitted from the error term in the denominator of the test statistic for within-subjects designs.

4. *Homogeneity of covariance.* We assume that participant scores in each group are related, because the same participants are observed across or between groups. The reasons for this assumption are rather complex and beyond the scope of this book.

Together, the assumptions of homogeneity of variance and homogeneity of covariance are called *sphericity*. Note that if we violate the assumption of sphericity, then the value of the variance in the numerator of the test statistic can be inflated, which can increase the likelihood of committing a Type I error (or incorrectly rejecting the null hypothesis, defined in Learning Unit 7, p. 108).

Example 10.2. An important area of research targets efforts to reduce drug use to include the use of antismoking advertisement campaigns that facilitate the cessation and prevention of smoking among teens and adults (Farrelly et al., 2012; Institute of Medicine, 2015; Lee, Cappella, Lerman, & Strasser, 2013). As an example of a research study in this area, suppose a researcher wants to determine which of three advertisements is most likely to encourage teens not to smoke. To assess the impact of each advertisement, she asks a sample of 15 teenagers to view each ad and to rate the ad's effectiveness on a scale from 1 (*not at all effective*) to 7 (*very effective*). One ad uses words only (no-cues condition). A second ad uses a generic abstract picture (generic-cues condition). A third ad shows a picture of a teenager smoking and coughing (smoking-related-cues condition). We will conduct the one-way within-subjects ANOVA to analyze the significance of these data at a .05 level of significance.

Step 1: State the hypotheses. The null hypothesis states that group means in the population do not vary (variance = 0); the alternative hypothesis states that group means in the population do vary (variance = 0):

$H_0 : \sigma_\mu^2 = 0$. Group means do not vary among groups in the population of teenagers.

$H_1 : \sigma_\mu^2 > 0$. Group means do vary among groups in the population of teenagers.

Step 2: Set the criteria for a decision. The level of significance for this test is .05. The total degrees of freedom are $(kn) - 1$, which is $(3 \times 15) - 1 = 44$. We will split these total degrees of freedom into three parts for each source of variation.

The degrees of freedom between groups are $k - 1$: $df_{BG} = 3 - 1 = 2$.

The **degrees of freedom between persons** are $n - 1$: $df_{BP} = 15 - 1 = 14$.

The degrees of freedom error are $(k - 1)(n - 1)$: $df_E = (3 - 1) \times (15 - 1) = 28$.

The **degrees of freedom between persons** (df_{BP}) are the degrees of freedom associated with the variance of person means averaged across groups. They are equal to the number of participants (n) minus 1.

The corresponding degrees of freedom for the test statistic are the degrees of freedom numerator or between groups ($df_{BG} = 2$) and the degrees of freedom denominator or error ($df_E = 28$). Thus, we test only for between-groups variation (not between persons).

To locate the critical value with 2 and 28 degrees of freedom, find where these degrees of freedom intersect in Table C.3 in Appendix C. The critical value for this test is 3.34 at $\alpha = .05$.

We will compare the test statistic with this critical value. If the value of the test statistic falls beyond the critical value (at or greater than 3.34), then there is less than a 5% chance we would obtain that outcome if the null hypothesis were correct, so we reject the null hypothesis; otherwise, we retain the null hypothesis.

Step 3: Compute the test statistic. We compute the F statistic to determine the total variance attributed to differences between group means relative to the variance attributed to error. We will describe this analysis in six stages:

- calculate n, N, group means, participant (person) means, and grand mean

- calculate between-group variance and sum of squares

- calculate between-person variance and sum of squares

- calculate within-group (error) variance and sum of squares

- calculate the total variance and sum of squares

- complete the F table

Because the total sum of squares equals the total sum of squares from the other terms, it is not strictly necessary to calculate all the terms separately. Given the ease of calculation with Excel, we show the calculation of all the terms, because it is a good way to check for mistakes.

Download Antismoking_Advertisement.xlsx from the student study site: http://study.sagepub.com/priviteraexcel1e. Column A contains a single letter for identification of different participants. Columns B, C, and D contain ratings of the effectiveness of advertisements with no cues (column B), generic cues (column C), and smoking-related cues (column D).

Stage 1. Calculating n, N, group means, participant (person) means, and grand mean. Start by calculating a mean across the three test conditions for each person. As shown in Figure 10.12a, label E4 "Person Mean", and enter =AVERAGE(B5:D5) in cell E5. Select E5 and paste or fill down through E19.

Label cells A21 and A22, respectively, "n" and "Group means". Calculate n with the COUNT function, and calculate each group mean with the AVERAGE function, as in Figure 10.12a.

B21: =COUNT(B5:B19)

C21: =COUNT(C5:C19)

D21: =COUNT(D5:D19)

E21: =COUNT(E5:E19)

B22: =AVERAGE(B5:B19)

C22: =AVERAGE(C5:C19)

D22: =AVERAGE(D5:D19)

These yield n in each test condition in B21 through D21, the total number of participants in E21, and the group means in B22 through D22, as shown in Figure 10.12b.

Next label cells D24 through D26, respectively, *"k"*, *"k*n"*, and "Grand mean". Then calculate these values in column E, as in Figure 10.12a.

E24: =COUNT(B21:D21)

E25: =E24*E21

E26: =AVERAGE(E5:E19).

Appendix B

See **Appendix B2,** p. 301, for formatting cells.

See **Appendix B3,** p. 303, for freezing panes.

These calculations provide numbers for the next four stages: calculating sums of squares and degrees of freedom.

Stage 2. Calculating between-groups variance and SS_{BG}. To determine how much the scores in the three test conditions differ from each other, we

- subtract the grand mean from each of the test condition means,
- square each difference,
- sum the squared differences, and
- multiply by *n* to yield the SS_{BG}.

Appendix B

See **Appendix B2**, p. 301, on formatting cells to add subscripts.

See **Appendix B4**, p. 304, on highlighting, pasting, and filling.

To keep track of calculations, copy the No Cues, Generic Cues, and Smoking-Related Cues labels from B4 through D4 and paste them in G4 through I4. In G3 through I3, label this section "Between-group variance: SS_{BG}". (Figure 10.13 includes in rows 1 and 2 a reminder of the calculation.) Subtract the grand mean from each of the group means, square each of the differences, and multiply each difference by *n*, as in Figure 10.13a. Anchoring the cell address of the grand mean, E26, as $E$26 allows you to type the formula into G5 and either fill or copy and paste to the other two cells, as shown in Figure 10.13a, yielding the results shown in Figure 10.13b.

G5: =B22-$E$26^2*B21, yielding 10.696

H5: =C22-$E$26^2*C21, yielding 7.585

I5: =D22-$E$26^2*D21, yielding 36.296

To keep track of the next calculations, label cells H7 and I7, respectively, SS_{BG} and df_{BG}. Then we calculate those values, as shown in Figure 10.13a, yielding the results shown in Figure 10.13b

H8: =SUM(G5:I5) yielding 54.578

I8: =E24-1, yielding 2

FIGURE 10.12 ● Raw data with *n* and mean for each group, *k*, and grand mean. (a) Formulas and functions. (b) Results of calculations.

(a)

	A	B	C	D	E
1		Rating of advertisements			
2					
3			Cues		
4	Person	No Cues	Generic Cues	Smoking-Related Cues	Person mean
5	A	2	4	7	=AVERAGE(B5:D5)
6	B	4	3	6	=AVERAGE(B6:D6)
7	C	3	2	7	=AVERAGE(B7:D7)
8	D	6	3	5	=AVERAGE(B8:D8)
9	E	3	3	3	=AVERAGE(B9:D9)
10	F	2	3	5	=AVERAGE(B10:D10)
11	G	4	4	5	=AVERAGE(B11:D11)
12	H	2	5	4	=AVERAGE(B12:D12)
13	I	2	1	5	=AVERAGE(B13:D13)
14	J	1	4	6	=AVERAGE(B14:D14)
15	K	3	2	6	=AVERAGE(B15:D15)
16	L	3	2	6	=AVERAGE(B16:D16)
17	M	3	4	5	=AVERAGE(B17:D17)
18	N	2	2	4	=AVERAGE(B18:D18)
19	O	3	3	5	=AVERAGE(B19:D19)
20					
21	*n*	=COUNT(B5:B19)	=COUNT(C5:C19)	=COUNT(D5:D19)	=COUNT(E5:E19)
22	Group means	=AVERAGE(B5:B19)	=AVERAGE(C5:C19)	=AVERAGE(D5:D19)	
23					
24				*k*	=COUNT(B21:D21)
25				*k*n*	=E24*E21
26				Grand mean	=AVERAGE(E5:E19)

(b)

	A	B	C	D	E
1		Rating of advertisements			
2					
3			Cues		
4	Person	No Cues	Generic Cues	Smoking-Related Cues	Person mean
5	A	2	4	7	4.33
6	B	4	3	6	4.33
7	C	3	2	7	4.00
8	D	6	3	5	4.67
9	E	3	3	3	3.00
10	F	2	3	5	3.33
11	G	4	4	5	4.33
12	H	2	5	4	3.67
13	I	2	1	5	2.67
14	J	1	4	6	3.67
15	K	3	2	6	3.67
16	L	3	2	6	3.67
17	M	3	4	5	4.00
18	N	2	2	4	2.67
19	O	3	3	5	3.67
20					
21	*n*	15	15	15	15
22	Group means	2.87	3.00	5.27	
23					
24				*k*	3
25				*k*n*	45
26				Grand mean	3.711

FIGURE 10.13 ● Calculating sum of squares and degrees of freedom between groups. (a) Formulas and functions. (b) Results of calculations.

(a)

	G	H	I
1	Subtract grand mean from group means,		
2	square the difference, multiply by n.		
3		Between-group variance: SS_{BG}	
4	No Cues	Generic Cues	Smoking-Related Cues
5	=(B22-$E$26)^2*B21	=(C22-$E$26)^2*C21	=(D22-$E$26)^2*D21
6			
7		SS_{BG}	df_{BG}
8		=SUM(G5:I5)	=E24-1

(b)

	G	H	I
1	Subtract grand mean from group means,		
2	square the difference, multiply by n.		
3		Between-group variance: SS_{BG}	
4	No Cues	Generic Cues	Smoking-Related Cues
5	10.696	7.585	36.296
6			
7		SS_{BG}	df_{BG}
8		54.578	2

We enclosed H7 through I8 in a box to highlight these as the first portion of the *F* table for Stage 6.

Stage 3. Calculating between-person variance: SS_{BP}. Between-person variance is one slice of the total error variance that will be subtracted from the within-group variance in the next section. To calculate between person variance,

- calculate the mean score for each participant across test conditions,

- subtract the grand mean from each person's mean,

- square the difference, and

- sum the squared differences and multiply by *k* to yield SS_{BP}.

To keep track of calculations, copy A4 through A19 to L4 through L19 and E4 to M4. In K3 through M3, label this section "Between-person variance: SS_{BP}". (Figure 10.14 includes in rows 1 and 2 a reminder of the calculation.) Type into cell M5 =(E5-E$26)^2*E$24, as shown in Figure 10.14a. Use the $ to anchor the reference to those cells. Select M5 and paste or fill down to M19. This yields the variances of each of the 15 participants, as shown in Figure 10.14b.

To keep track of the next calculations, label cells L21 and M21, respectively, "SS_{BP}" and "df_{BP}". Then we calculate those values, as shown in Figure 10.14a, yielding the results shown in Figure 10.14b:

L22: =SUM(M5:M19), yielding 15.244

M22: =E21-1, yielding 14

Stage 4. Calculating within-groups variance: SS_E. To calculate the total variance within groups (error),

- subtract the group mean from each score in the group,

- square the difference,

FIGURE 10.14 ● Calculating sum of squares and degrees of freedom between persons. (a) Formulas and functions. (b) Results of calculations.

(a)

	K	L	M
1	Subtract grand mean from participant		
2	means, square the difference, multiply by k.		
3		Between-person variance: SS$_{BP}$	
4		Person	Person mean
5		A	=(E5-E$26)^2*E$24
6		B	=(E6-E$26)^2*E$24
7		C	=(E7-E$26)^2*E$24
8		D	=(E8-E$26)^2*E$24
9		E	=(E9-E$26)^2*E$24
10		F	=(E10-E$26)^2*E$24
11		G	=(E11-E$26)^2*E$24
12		H	=(E12-E$26)^2*E$24
13		I	=(E13-E$26)^2*E$24
14		J	=(E14-E$26)^2*E$24
15		K	=(E15-E$26)^2*E$24
16		L	=(E16-E$26)^2*E$24
17		M	=(E17-E$26)^2*E$24
18		N	=(E18-E$26)^2*E$24
19		O	=(E19-E$26)^2*E$24
20			
21		*SS*$_{BP}$	*df*$_{BP}$
22		=SUM(M5:M19)	=E21-1

(b)

	K	L	M
1	Subtract grand mean from participant		
2	means, square the difference, multiply by k.		
3		Between-person variance: SS$_{BP}$	
4		Person	Person mean
5		A	1.16
6		B	1.16
7		C	0.25
8		D	2.74
9		E	1.52
10		F	0.43
11		G	1.16
12		H	0.01
13		I	3.27
14		J	0.01
15		K	0.01
16		L	0.01
17		M	0.25
18		N	3.27
19		O	0.01
20			
21		*SS*$_{BP}$	*df*$_{BP}$
22		15.244	14

- sum the squared differences to yield SS_{WG}, and

- from SS_{WG}, subtract SS_{BP} to yield SS_E.

To keep track of calculations, copy the "No Cues", "Generic Cues", and "Smoking-Related Cues" labels from B4 through D4 and paste them in O4 through Q4. In O3 through Q3, label this section "Within-group (error) variance: SS_E ". (Figure 10.15 includes in rows 1 and 2 a reminder of the calculation.) Subtract the No Cues group's mean from the first score in the group and square the difference by typing into cell O5: =(B5-B$22)^2, as shown in Figure 10.15a. Anchoring the cell address of the group mean, B22, as B$22 allows the formula in O5 to be pasted or filled down through O19. Selecting O5 through O19 allows pasting or filling right through Q5 to Q19. This yields for the 15 scores in each group the squared deviations from their group mean, as shown in Figure 10.15b.

To keep track of the next calculations, label cells P21 and Q21, respectively, "$SS_E = SS_{WG} - SS_{BP}$" and "df_E". Then calculate those values, as shown in Figure 10.15a, yielding the results shown in Figure 10.15b.

FIGURE 10.15 ● **Calculating sum of squares and degrees of freedom for error. (a) Formulas and functions. (b) Results of calculations.**

(a)

	O	P	Q
1	Subtract group mean from each score in the group,		
2	square the difference, sum differences, subtract SS_{BP}.		
3		Within-group (error) variance: SS_E	
4	**No Cues**	**Generic Cues**	**Smoking-Related Cues**
5	=(B5-B$22)^2	=(C5-C$22)^2	=(D5-D$22)^2
6	=(B6-B$22)^2	=(C6-C$22)^2	=(D6-D$22)^2
7	=(B7-B$22)^2	=(C7-C$22)^2	=(D7-D$22)^2
8	=(B8-B$22)^2	=(C8-C$22)^2	=(D8-D$22)^2
9	=(B9-B$22)^2	=(C9-C$22)^2	=(D9-D$22)^2
10	=(B10-B$22)^2	=(C10-C$22)^2	=(D10-D$22)^2
11	=(B11-B$22)^2	=(C11-C$22)^2	=(D11-D$22)^2
12	=(B12-B$22)^2	=(C12-C$22)^2	=(D12-D$22)^2
13	=(B13-B$22)^2	=(C13-C$22)^2	=(D13-D$22)^2
14	=(B14-B$22)^2	=(C14-C$22)^2	=(D14-D$22)^2
15	=(B15-B$22)^2	=(C15-C$22)^2	=(D15-D$22)^2
16	=(B16-B$22)^2	=(C16-C$22)^2	=(D16-D$22)^2
17	=(B17-B$22)^2	=(C17-C$22)^2	=(D17-D$22)^2
18	=(B18-B$22)^2	=(C18-C$22)^2	=(D18-D$22)^2
19	=(B19-B$22)^2	=(C19-C$22)^2	=(D19-D$22)^2
20			
21		$SS_E = SS_{WG} - SS_{BP}$	df_E
22		=SUM(O5:Q19)-L22	=(E24-1)*(E21-1)

(b)

	O	P	Q
1	Subtract group mean from each score in the group,		
2	square the difference, sum differences, subtract SS_{BP}.		
3		Within-group (error) variance: SS_E	
4	**No Cues**	**Generic Cues**	**Smoking-Related Cues**
5	0.75	1.00	3.00
6	1.28	0.00	0.54
7	0.02	1.00	3.00
8	9.82	0.00	0.07
9	0.02	0.00	5.14
10	0.75	0.00	0.07
11	1.28	1.00	0.07
12	0.75	4.00	1.60
13	0.75	4.00	0.07
14	3.48	1.00	0.54
15	0.02	1.00	0.54
16	0.02	1.00	0.54
17	0.02	1.00	0.07
18	0.75	1.00	1.60
19	0.02	0.00	0.07
20			
21		$SS_E = SS_{WG} - SS_{BP}$	df_E
22		37.422	28

P22: =SUM(O5:Q19)-L22, yielding 37.422

Q22: = (E24-1)*(E21-1), yielding 28

We enclosed P21 through Q22 in a box to highlight these as the third portion of the *F* table for Stage 6.

Stage 5. Calculating total variance: SS_T. To determine the total variance among all scores in the entire study, we

- subtract the grand mean from each of the scores,

- square each difference, and

- sum the squared differences to yield the SS_T.

To keep track of calculations, copy the "No Cues", "Generic Cues", and "Smoking-Related Cues" labels from B4 through D4 and paste them in S4 through U4. In S3 through U3, label this section "Total variance: SS_T". (Figure 10.16 includes in rows 1 and 2 a reminder of the calculation.) Subtract the grand mean from the first score in the No Cues group and square the difference by entering into cell S5 =(B5-$E$26)^2, as in Figure 10.16a. Anchoring the cell address of the group mean, E26, as $E$26 allows the formula in S5 to be pasted or filled down through S19. Select S5 to S19 and paste or fill right through U5 to U19. This yields for the 15 scores in a group the squared deviations from their grand mean, as shown in Figure 10.16b.

To keep track of the next calculations, label cells T21 and U21, respectively, "SS_T" and "df_T". Then we calculate those values, as shown in Figure 10.16a, yielding the results shown in Figure 10.16b.

T22: =SUM(S5:U19), yielding 107.244

U22: =E25-1, yielding 44

As mentioned at the end of Step 3, $SS_T = SS_{BG} + SS_{BP} + SS_{WG}$. We can now confirm that $107.244 = 54.578 + 15.224 + 37.442$.

Stage 6. Completing the F table. The *F* table lists the sum of squares (*SS*), degrees of freedom (*df*), mean squares (*MS*), and value of the test statistic (*F*). In cells W4 through AA4, type the following headings: "Source of Variation," "*SS*", "*df*", "*MS*", and "*F*", as in Figure 10.17. In cells W5 through W8, below "Source of Variation," list the sources that we have just calculated: "Between groups", "Between persons", "Within groups (error)", and "Total", as shown in Figure 10.17.

For the four values of *SS* and four values of *df*, we refer to the cells in which we have calculated those values in Stages 2, 3, 4, and 5, as shown in Figure 10.17.

Four values of *SS*:

X5: =H8 to display SS_{BG}

X6: =L22 to display SS_{BP}

X7: =P22 to display SS_E

X8: =T22 to display SS_T

FIGURE 10.16 ● **Calculating total sum of squares and degrees of freedom. (a) Formulas and functions. (b) Results of calculations.**

(a)

	S	T	U
1	Subtract grand mean		
2	from each score, square the difference.		
3		Total variance: SS$_T$	
4	No Cues	Generic Cues	Smoking-Related Cues
5	=(B5-$E$26)^2	=(C5-$E$26)^2	=(D5-$E$26)^2
6	=(B6-$E$26)^2	=(C6-$E$26)^2	=(D6-$E$26)^2
7	=(B7-$E$26)^2	=(C7-$E$26)^2	=(D7-$E$26)^2
8	=(B8-$E$26)^2	=(C8-$E$26)^2	=(D8-$E$26)^2
9	=(B9-$E$26)^2	=(C9-$E$26)^2	=(D9-$E$26)^2
10	=(B10-$E$26)^2	=(C10-$E$26)^2	=(D10-$E$26)^2
11	=(B11-$E$26)^2	=(C11-$E$26)^2	=(D11-$E$26)^2
12	=(B12-$E$26)^2	=(C12-$E$26)^2	=(D12-$E$26)^2
13	=(B13-$E$26)^2	=(C13-$E$26)^2	=(D13-$E$26)^2
14	=(B14-$E$26)^2	=(C14-$E$26)^2	=(D14-$E$26)^2
15	=(B15-$E$26)^2	=(C15-$E$26)^2	=(D15-$E$26)^2
16	=(B16-$E$26)^2	=(C16-$E$26)^2	=(D16-$E$26)^2
17	=(B17-$E$26)^2	=(C17-$E$26)^2	=(D17-$E$26)^2
18	=(B18-$E$26)^2	=(C18-$E$26)^2	=(D18-$E$26)^2
19	=(B19-$E$26)^2	=(C19-$E$26)^2	=(D19-$E$26)^2
20			
21		SS$_T$	df$_T$
22		=SUM(S5:U19)	=E25-1

(b)

	S	T	U
1	Subtract grand mean		
2	from each score, square the difference.		
3		Total variance: SS$_T$	
4	No Cues	Generic Cues	Smoking-Related Cues
5	2.93	0.08	10.82
6	0.08	0.51	5.24
7	0.51	2.93	10.82
8	5.24	0.51	1.66
9	0.51	0.51	0.51
10	2.93	0.51	1.66
11	0.08	0.08	1.66
12	2.93	1.66	0.08
13	2.93	7.35	1.66
14	7.35	0.08	5.24
15	0.51	2.93	5.24
16	0.51	2.93	5.24
17	0.51	0.08	1.66
18	2.93	2.93	0.08
19	0.51	0.51	1.66
20			
21		SS$_T$	df$_T$
22		107.244	44

Selecting X5 through X8 and filling right to Y5 through Y8 or copying and pasting to Y5 through Y8 yields the cells containing the values for *df*, as shown in Figure 10.17. Four values of *df*:

Y5: =I8 to display df_{BG}

Y6: =M22 to display df_{BP}

Y7: =Q22 to display df_{E}

Y8: =U22 to display df_{T}

We use the values for *SS* and for *df* to calculate MS_{BG}, MS_{BP}, and MS_{E}. The formula for variance is *SS* divided by *df*, so we divide across the row to compute each mean square.

To compute the variance or mean square between groups, we divide SS_{BG} by df_{BG}. In cell Z5, enter =X5/Y5, as shown in Figure 10.17a, to yield

$$MS_{BG} = \frac{54.578}{2} = 27.289$$

as shown in Figure 10.17b.

Likewise, to compute the variance or **mean square between persons** and within groups (error), we divide SS_{BP} by df_{BP} and also divide SS_E by df_E. Select Z5 and fill down to Z7, or copy Z5 and paste to Z6 through Z7, as shown in Figure 10.17a, which yields:

$$MS_{BP} = \frac{15.244}{14} = 1.089$$

in cell Z6, and

$$MS_E = \frac{37.422}{28} = 1.337$$

in cell Z7, as shown in Figure 10.17b.

The formula for the F statistic is the mean square between groups divided by the mean square error. In cell AA5, enter =Z5/Z7 , as shown in Figure 10.17a, which yields

$$F_{obt} = \frac{27.289}{1.337} = 20.418$$

as shown in Figure 10.17b.

Step 4: Make a decision. To make a decision, we compare the obtained value to the critical value. As shown in Figure 10.17b, the obtained value (20.418) is greater than the critical value (3.34); it falls well into the rejection region. The decision is to reject the null hypothesis.

FIGURE 10.17 ● Summary table for one-way within-subjects ANOVA and calculation of effect size. (a) Formulas and functions. (b) Results of calculations.

(a)

	W	X	Y	Z	AA
4	**Source of Variation**	*SS*	*df*	*MS*	*F*
5	**Between groups** =H8		=I8	=X5/Y5	=Z5/Z7
6	**Between persons** =L22		=M22	=X6/Y6	
7	**Within groups (error)** =P22		=Q22	=X7/Y7	
8	**Total** =T22		=U22		
9					
10	**Effect size**				
11	**partial η²** =X5/SUM(X5,X7)				

(b)

	W	X	Y	Z	AA
4	**Source of Variation**	*SS*	*df*	*MS*	*F*
5	**Between groups**	54.578	2	27.289	20.418
6	**Between persons**	15.244	14	1.089	
7	**Within groups (error)**	37.422	28	1.337	
8	**Total**	107.244	44		
9					
10	**Effect size**				
11	**partial η²**	.59			

Mean square between persons (MS_{BP}) is the variance attributed to differences in scores between persons.

Measuring Effect Size With Partial Eta Squared

In Example 10.2, we concluded that the group means significantly varied by group. We can also determine the size of the effect using the proportion of variance estimate with partial eta squared. A proportion of variance is used to measure how much variability in the dependent variable (ratings of effectiveness) can be accounted for by the levels of the factor (the different types of ads).

Using a partial proportion of variance, we remove or partial out the between-persons variation before calculating the proportion of variance. We do this because the between-persons variation was removed from the denominator of the test statistic for the one-way within-subjects ANOVA; thus it is also removed when calculating effect size.

Using partial eta squared, we remove the sum of squares between persons from the sum of squares total in the denominator. There are two ways we can remove the sum of squares between persons. We can subtract the sum of squares between persons from the sum of squares total:

$$\eta_P^2 = \frac{SS_{BG}}{SS_T - SS_{BP}}$$

or we can add the sum of squares between groups and the sum of squares error. This will leave the sum of squares between persons out of the denominator:

$$\eta_P^2 = \frac{SS_{BG}}{SS_{BG} + SS_E}$$

For Example 10.2, we'll use the second option. Type into cells W10 and W11, respectively, "Effect size" and "η_P^2". Using the values in Figure 10.17, enter into cell X11 =X5/SUM(X5,X7), yielding the calculation of partial eta squared:

$$\eta_P^2 = \frac{54.578}{54.578 + 37.422} = .593$$

We conclude the 59.3% of the variability in ratings can be explained by the type of ad being rated. Using the effect size conventions listed in the second column of Table 9.2 in Learning Unit 9 (p. 138), we determine that this is a large effect size. Here is how we might report partial eta squared with the significant result:

A one-way analysis of variance showed that ratings of effectiveness for the three advertisements significantly varied, $F(2, 28) = 72.286$, $p < .05$ ($\eta_P^2 = .593$).

Post Hoc Test Using Tukey's HSD

In Example 10.2, we decided to reject the null hypothesis: At least one pair of group means significantly differs. Because we have more than two groups, we need to make multiple pairwise comparisons using a post hoc test to determine which pair or pairs of group means significantly differ. The post hoc test analyzes differences for all possible pairs of group means or pairwise comparisons. Mean ratings in Example 10.2 are 2.87 (Group No Cue), 3.0 (Group Generic Cue), and 5.27 (Group Smoking-Related Cue). In Example 10.2, then, there are three possible pairwise comparisons:

Comparison 1: Smoking-Related Cue and No Cue: $5.27 - 2.87 = 2.4$

Comparison 2: Smoking-Related Cue and Generic Cue: $5.27 - 3.0 = 2.27$

Comparison 3: Generic Cue and No Cue: $3.0 - 2.87 = 0.13$

All post hoc tests ensure that no matter how many tests we compute, the overall likelihood of committing a Type I error is .05. In other words, all post hoc tests control for experimentwise alpha, which is the overall alpha level for multiple tests conducted on the same data. Here we can use the same post hoc test as we used in Example 10.1: Tukey's HSD. The calculations for this test are described for between-subjects ANOVA and shown in Figure 10.18a and 10.18b.

That being said, of the post hoc tests listed in Figure 10.9 (p. 182), the Bonferroni procedure is probably best adapted for use following a significant one-way within-subjects ANOVA. However, keep in mind that this procedure gets too conservative as k increases. With a larger number of comparisons, more specialized tests beyond the scope of this book, such as trend analysis, are recommended.

FIGURE 10.18 ● **Post hoc comparisons for the one-way within-subjects ANOVA. (a) Formulas and functions. (b) Results of calculations.**

(a)

	W	X
13	Post hoc comparison	difference
14	Smoking-related Cues and No Cues	=D22-B22
15	Smoking Related Cues and Generic Cues	=D22-C22
16	No Cues and Generic Cues	=C22-B22
17	q_α	3.5
18	critical value	=X17*(Z7/E21)^0.5

(b)

	W	X
13	Post hoc comparison	difference
14	Smoking-related Cues and No Cues	2.40
15	Smoking Related Cues and Generic Cues	2.27
16	No Cues and Generic Cues	0.13
17	q_α	3.50
18	critical value	1.04

Computing the One-Way Within-Subjects ANOVA Using the Analysis Toolpak

We can also calculate this ANOVA using the Analysis ToolPak available in Excel for easy and accurate calculation. Return to the workbook Antismoking_Advertisement .xlsx. Click on the Data tab, and then on the Data Analysis icon all the way to the right. Select "Anova: Two-Factor Without Replication," shown in Figure 10.19a, which yields the dialog box shown in Figure 10.19b. Our data are grouped so that each test condition is contained within a column, and each participant is contained on one row. Enter $A$4:$D$19 for Input Range. Notice that this range includes the labels we gave to each participant and each group. Check the box to the left of Labels so that the output will contain the labels of the participants and names of the groups that we used. The value for alpha we specify as .05. Select Output Range for the result to be displayed in the worksheet and click in the box to the right. Then click in cell AC1 of the spreadsheet.

Clicking "OK" on the dialog box returns the output table in Figure 10.20. Notice that the values in the table for *SS*, *df*, *MS*, and *F* are the same as the ones we

FIGURE 10.19 ● **Performing a one-way within-subjects ANOVA with Analysis ToolPak in Excel. (a) Selecting "Anova: Two-Factor Without Replication" to perform a one-way within-subjects ANOVA. (b) Specifying the location of the data and parameters for the ANOVA.**

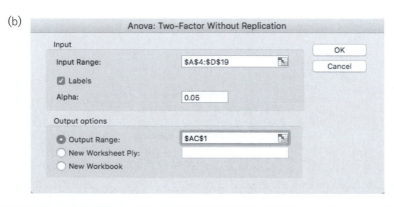

calculated. For this ANOVA, the terms in the summary table are not labeled as is customary. We could change the "Rows" label to "Between persons" and change the "Columns" label to "Between groups". Although the output table gives neither an estimate of effect size such as eta squared nor post hoc comparisons, it does provide the means for each group and all the components of the ANOVA summary table needed. Only the studentized range statistic, q, would need to be found in Appendix C4.

FIGURE 10.20 ● **Results of the one-way within-subjects ANOVA using the Analysis ToolPak.**

	AC	AD	AE	AF	AG	AH	AI
1	Anova: Two-Factor Without Replication						
2							
3	SUMMARY	Count	Sum	Average	Variance		
4	A	3	13	4.333	6.333		
5	B	3	13	4.333	2.333		
6	C	3	12	4.000	7.000		
7	D	3	14	4.667	2.333		
8	E	3	9	3.000	0.000		
9	F	3	10	3.333	2.333		
10	G	3	13	4.333	0.333		
11	H	3	11	3.667	2.333		
12	I	3	8	2.667	4.333		
13	J	3	11	3.667	6.333		
14	K	3	11	3.667	4.333		
15	L	3	11	3.667	4.333		
16	M	3	12	4.000	1.000		
17	N	3	8	2.667	1.333		
18	O	3	11	3.667	1.333		
19							
20	No Cues	15	43	2.867	1.410		
21	Generic Cues	15	45	3.000	1.143		
22	Smoking-Related Cues	15	79	5.267	1.210		
23							
24							
25	ANOVA						
26	Source of Variation	SS	df	MS	F	P-value	F crit
27	Rows	15.244	14	1.089	0.815	.648	2.064
28	Columns	54.578	2	27.289	20.418	.000	3.340
29	Error	37.422	28	1.337			
30							
31	Total	107.244	44				

Two-Way Analysis of Variance: Between-Subjects Factorial Design

Excel Toolbox

Mathematical operators

- *
- ^2 [square])
- –
- +
- /

Functions

- COUNT
- AVERAGE
- SUM

Other tools

- format cells
- freeze panes

(Continued)

(Continued)

- anchor cell reference
- fill down or paste
- Analysis ToolPak

In this learning unit, we explore the nature of hypothesis testing when observations are made across the levels of two or more factors, how to compute and interpret observed effects, and the informativeness of hypothesis testing for making such comparisons. We further explore other ways of adding information about the nature of observed effects and how to appropriately interpret them.

An Introduction to Factorial Design

For the *t* tests and one-way ANOVAs, the designs were varied either in how many levels of the factor were observed (one or two levels of one factor for the *t* tests, two or more levels of one factor for the one-way ANOVAs), and how participants were treated (between-subjects versus within-subjects). In all cases, however, we observed participants across the levels of a single factor.

In the **factorial design**, we describe a new way to change the complexity of a design—we add a second factor; that is, we observe participants across the levels of two factors at the same time. While we can add as many additional factors as needed to test a hypothesis using the factorial design, in this learning unit, we focus on factorial designs with two factors.

Adding a second factor is particularly useful because many factors likely contribute to the behaviors we observe, similar to how multiple ingredients contribute to the foods we eat. For example, certainly we can study whether apples are needed to bake a pie, and we will find they are! However, there are also other ingredients that contribute to making the pie, such as melted butter, white and brown sugar, cinnamon, and pie crust. Like the multitude of ingredients in an apple pie, a multitude of factors likely contribute to a given behavior, which makes the factorial design particularly useful for studying behavior.

In the behavioral sciences, there are two common reasons we observe two factors in a single study:

First, a hypothesis may require that we observe two factors. As an example of a hypothesis adapted from research on the utility of books in the classroom (Bell & Limber, 2010; Weiten, Halpern, & Bernstein, 2012), suppose we state that the higher the difficulty level of a book, the less students will comprehend when there is highlighting in the book. This hypothesis identifies two factors: the presence of highlighting (yes, no) and book difficulty (easy, difficult). To test this hypothesis, then, we must observe the levels of both factors at the same time.

The **factorial design** is a research design in which participants are observed across the combination of levels of two or more factors.

TABLE 11.1 ● The structure of a study that combines the levels of two factors.			
If the hypothesis is correct, then we expect this group to have the lowest test scores.			
		Highlighting	
		No	Yes
Book Difficulty	Easy	Group Easy, No	Group Easy, Yes
	Difficult	Group Difficult, No	Group Difficult, Yes

On the basis of the hypothesis, we expect that participants reading the difficult book with highlighting in it (Group Difficult, Yes) will have the lowest scores.

The structure of this design is illustrated in Table 11.1. If we measure comprehension as a test score, then on the basis of our hypothesis, we expect scores to be lowest in the group with a difficult book that has highlighting in it.

Second, adding a second factor allows us to control or account for threats to validity. Broadly defined, *validity* is the extent to which we demonstrate the effect we claim to be demonstrating. For example, suppose we state the hypothesis that the more positive a teacher is with his or her students, the more students will like their teacher. To test this hypothesis, we could randomly assign a sample of teachers to interact positively or negatively with students in a classroom setting, and then have students rate how much they like the teacher.

One possible threat to the validity of our hypothesis or claim is the subject being taught. Maybe ratings reflect the subject taught and not the teacher interactions. We could account for this possibility by adding the subject taught as a factor in the study. Suppose we tested this hypothesis using a sample that consisted of biology and psychology teachers. As illustrated in Table 11.2, we can include the subject taught as a second factor. On the basis of our hypothesis, we expect the type of interaction (positive, negative) and not the subject taught (biology, psychology) to be associated with differences in ratings. We included the subject taught as a factor only to account for it as a possible threat to the validity of our claim.

Structure and Notation for the Two-Way ANOVA

The research design for a study in which the levels of two or more factors are combined is called a *factorial design*. In a factorial design with two factors, we use the

TABLE 11.2 ● The structure of a study that combines the levels of two factors.			
If our hypothesis is correct, then we expect only the levels of this factor to show significant differences.			
		Teacher Interaction	
		Positive	Negative
Subject Taught	Biology	Group Pos., Biol.	Group Neg., Biol.
	Psychology	Group Pos., Psychol.	Group Neg., Psychol.

On the basis of the hypothesis, we expect the type of interaction (positive, negative) and not the subject taught (biology, psychology) to be associated with differences in ratings.

two-way ANOVA to analyze the data, and this also leads to new terminology. The new terminology and notation for the two-way ANOVA are described in this section.

The **two-way ANOVA** is a statistical procedure used to test hypotheses concerning the variance of groups created by combining the levels of two factors. This test is used when the variance in any one population is unknown.

A **cell** is the combination of one level from each factor, as represented in a cross tabulation. Each cell is a group in a research study.

A **complete factorial design** is a research design in which each level of one factor is combined or crossed with each level of the other factor, with participants observed in each cell or combination of levels.

A **between-subjects factor** is a type of factor in which different participants are observed at each level of the factor.

In a two-way ANOVA, each factor is identified with a letter in alphabetical order: Factor A, then Factor B. Separating the factors with a multiplication sign and listing only the letters can simplify this notation. For example, we can state a two-way ANOVA as an A × B ANOVA. The multiplication sign represents a "by" statement; we read this test as an "A by B" ANOVA.

More common is to identify the levels of each factor numerically. For example, if we measure how quickly (in seconds) subjects respond to a stimulus that varies in size (small, medium, large) and color (light, dark), we might designate Factor A as size and Factor B as color. Factor A has three levels (small, medium, large), and Factor B has two levels (light, dark). Using the levels of each factor, we can state this test as a 3 × 2 (read "3 by 2") ANOVA. Each number represents the levels of each factor. Table 11.3 shows the structure of this hypothetical study with two factors.

We often arrange the data for a two-way ANOVA in a table, and when we do, there is special notation to indicate each entry. The levels of Factor A are symbolized as p, and the levels of Factor B are symbolized as q. The combination of one level from each factor is represented in the table as a **cell**. To calculate the number of cells in a two-way ANOVA, we multiply the levels of each factor:

$$\text{Total number of cells} = pq.$$

The number of cells is the number of groups in a study. In other words, each combination of one level from each factor creates a new group. In the example for a 3 × 2 ANOVA shown in Table 11.3, the number of cells is $pq = 3 \times 2 = 6$; there are six groups in this study. In this learning unit, we introduce only **complete factorial designs**, where each level of each factor is combined. For example, if subjects were not observed in each cell shown in Table 11.3, then the ANOVA would not be a complete factorial design. In this book, we do not cover situations in which some cells are empty. These situations require statistical procedures beyond the scope of this book.

For a factorial design with two factors in which we use a two-way ANOVA to analyze the data, we can observe the same or different participants in each group or cell. When different participants are observed at each level of one factor, we call the factor a **between-subjects factor**. When the same participants are observed across the levels of one factor, we call the factor a **within-subjects factor**. In this learning unit, we evaluate a two-way ANOVA when both factors are between-subjects factors.

TABLE 11.3 ● The structure of a hypothetical study with two factors.

		Factor A (Size)		
		1 (Small)	2 (Medium)	3 (Large)
Factor B (Color)	1 (Light)	A_1B_1	A_2B_1	A_3B_1
	2 (Dark)	A_1B_2	A_2B_2	A_3B_2

Each cell is a combination of levels of each factor. For example, the combination of Factor A Level 2 (medium) with Factor B Level 1 (light) is A_2B_1.

Describing Variability: Main Effects and Interactions

In this learning unit, we introduce an analysis of variance using the 2-between or between-subjects factorial design called the **two-way between-subjects ANOVA**. When we combine the levels of two factors in which different participants are observed in each cell, four sources of variation can be measured: One source is error variation, and three sources are between-groups variation, which is variation associated with having different groups. We will conduct a hypothesis test for each between-groups variation. With a one-way ANOVA, we only have one source of between-groups variation, so we conduct only one hypothesis test. For the two-way between-subjects ANOVA, we have three sources of between-groups variation, so we will conduct three hypothesis tests. Each source of variation, the *F* statistic for each, and each hypothesis test are introduced in this section.

Sources of Variability

Figure 11.1 identifies four sources of variation that arise when we combine the levels of two factors and observe different participants in each cell or combination of levels. One source of variation is associated with differences attributed to error, which is variation that has nothing to do with differences associated with having different groups. The other three sources of variation are associated with differences between group means for each factor and for the combination of levels of each factor. Each source of variation for the two-way between-subjects ANOVA is described in this section.

One source of variation is associated with differences in participant scores within each group (located in the cells of a table summary). This variation, called *within-groups variation*, is also called *error* because it cannot be attributed to differences

---

FIGURE 11.1 ● The different sources of variation in the two-way between-subjects ANOVA.

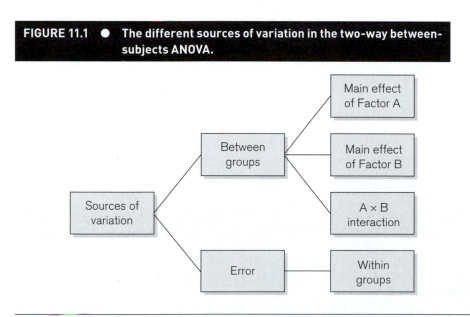

There are three sources of variation between groups and one source of error (within groups).

A **within-subjects factor** is a type of factor in which the same participants are observed across the levels of the factor.

The **two-way between-subjects ANOVA** is a statistical procedure used to test hypotheses concerning the combination of levels of two factors using the 2-between or between-subjects design.

between group means. This is the same error variation measured for the *t* tests and one-way ANOVAs. Table 11.4 shows that this source of variation is located in the cells of a table summary for a 2 × 2 between-subjects ANOVA with *n* = 5 participants in each group. Because participants in each cell experience the same treatment, differences in participant scores in each cell or group cannot be attributed to differences between group means. As it is for the *t* tests and one-way ANOVAs, this source of error is placed in the denominator of the test statistic. The test statistic for the two-way between-subjects ANOVA follows the same general form used for the one-way ANOVAs:

$$F_{obt} = \frac{\text{variance between groups}}{\text{error variance}}$$

Three between-groups sources of variation, or three ways that group means can be compared, are also shown in Table 11.4. Each set of group means is a source of variation that can be measured. We can measure the variation of group means across the levels of Factor A (the column means in Table 11.4) and across the levels of Factor B (the row means in Table 11.4). These sources of variation are called **main effects**, and each is a source of between-groups variation:

1. Main effect of Factor A

2. Main effect of Factor B

Notice also that we can compute the mean at each combination of levels for each factor or in each cell. The third between-groups variation is associated with the variance of group means in each cell (the cell means in Table 11.4). This source of variation is called an **interaction**, and this is the third source of between-groups variation:

3. The interaction of Factors A and B, called the A × B interaction

In an analysis of variance, we want to decide whether group means significantly vary. In the two-way between-subjects ANOVA, there are three ways that the group means can vary (in the rows, columns, and cells). Therefore, we must compute three hypothesis tests: one for each source of between-groups variation. We make two main effect tests (one for Factor A and one for Factor B) and one interaction test (one for the combination of levels for Factors A and B). The within-groups (or error) variation is the denominator for each test. The test statistic for each test is described here.

Testing Main Effects

The hypothesis test for each main effect (one for Factor A and one for Factor B) determines whether group means significantly vary across the levels of a single factor. In a table summary, such as that given in Table 11.4, we compare the variance of row and column means. To compute the test statistic for a main effect, we place the between-groups variance of one factor in the numerator and the error variance in the denominator. We again measure the variance as a mean square (*MS*), the same as we did for the one-way ANOVAs. The test statistic for the main effect of Factor A is

A **main effect** is a source of variation associated with mean differences across the levels of a single factor. In the two-way ANOVA, there are two factors and therefore two main effects: one for Factor A and one for Factor B.

An **interaction** is a source of variation associated with the variance of group means across the combination of levels of two factors. It is a measure of how cell means at each level of one factor change across the levels of a second factor.

$$F_A = \frac{\text{variance of group mean for Factor A}}{\text{variance attributed to error}} = \frac{MS_A}{MS_E}$$

The test statistic for the main effect of Factor B is

$$F_B = \frac{\text{variance of group means for Factor B}}{\text{variance attributed to error}} = \frac{MS_B}{MS_E}$$

TABLE 11.4 ● A cross-tabulation illustrating the sources of variability in the two-way between-subjects ANOVA.

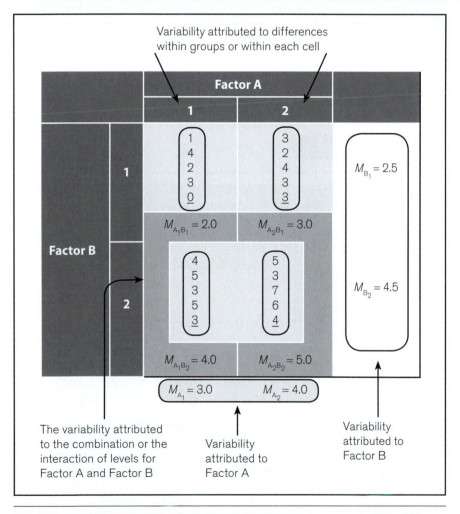

The within-groups (or error) variation is associated with differences in participant scores within each cell, which has nothing to do with differences attributed to having different groups. The other three sources of variation are associated with differences between group means: one for Factor A (main effect), one for Factor B (main effect), and one for the combination of levels for Factors A and B (interaction).

A significant main effect indicates that group means significantly vary across the levels of one factor, independent of the second factor. To illustrate, suppose the data in Table 11.4 are quiz scores, where Factor A is whether students studied for a quiz (no, yes) and Factor B is their class attendance (high, low). Table 11.5 identifies each main effect and shows how each would be interpreted, if significant. Notice that the interpretation of a significant main effect is similar to the interpretation of significant results using the one-way ANOVA.

Testing the Interaction

The hypothesis test for the combination of levels of two factors is called an A x B interaction test, where each letter refers to one factor (A or B). The interaction test determines whether group means at each level of one factor significantly change across the levels of a second factor. To put it another way, a significant interaction indicates that differences in group means across the levels of one factor depend on which level of the second factor you look at. In a table summary, such as that given in Table 11.4, we compare the variance of cell means.

TABLE 11.5 ● Main effects.

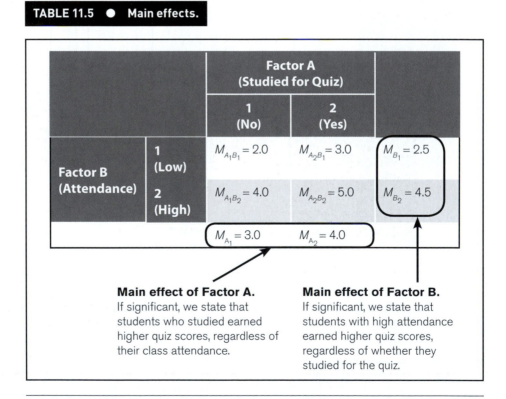

Main effect of Factor A.
If significant, we state that students who studied earned higher quiz scores, regardless of their class attendance.

Main effect of Factor B.
If significant, we state that students with high attendance earned higher quiz scores, regardless of whether they studied for the quiz.

The main effect for each factor reflects the difference between the row and column means in the table. There are two main effects (one for Factor A and one for Factor B) in a two-way ANOVA.

To compute the test statistic for an interaction, we place the between-groups variance for the combination of levels for two factors (the cell means) in the numerator and the error variance in the denominator. We again measure the variance as a mean square (*MS*). The test statistic for the A × B interaction test is

$$F_{A \times B} = \frac{\text{variance of cell means}}{\text{variance attributed to error}} = \frac{MS_{A \times B}}{MS_E}$$

A significant interaction indicates that group means across the levels for one factor significantly vary depending on which level of the second factor you look at. To illustrate this interpretation, let us go back again to the quiz scores study, where Factor A is whether students studied for a quiz (no, yes) and Factor B is class attendance (high,

TABLE 11.6 ● Interaction.

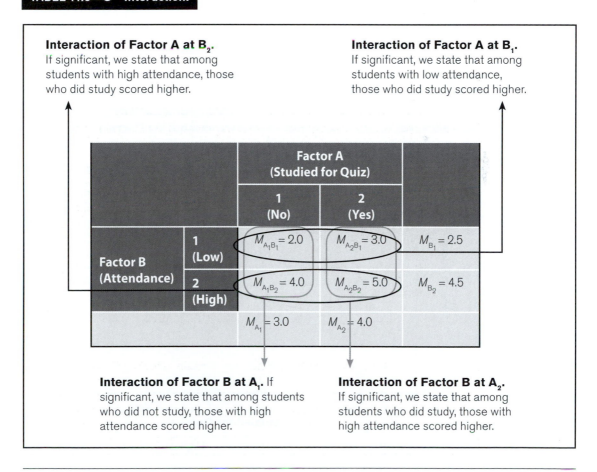

Interaction of Factor A at B_2. If significant, we state that among students with high attendance, those who did study scored higher.

Interaction of Factor A at B_1. If significant, we state that among students with low attendance, those who did study scored higher.

Interaction of Factor B at A_1. If significant, we state that among students who did not study, those with high attendance scored higher.

Interaction of Factor B at A_2. If significant, we state that among students who did study, those with high attendance scored higher.

A significant interaction indicates that group means at each level of one factor significantly change across the levels of a second factor. For the interaction in a two-way ANOVA, we analyze cell or group means inside the table.

low). Table 11.6 identifies four ways to interpret the A × B interaction. For each inter-pretation, we look across the levels of one factor at each level of the second factor. Which interpretation we use to describe the interaction depends largely on how we want to describe the data.

The pattern of an interaction can be obvious when it is graphed. To graph an inter-action, we plot the cell means for each combination of factors. Figure 11.2 shows a graph of the cell means for the studying and class attendance example. There are two ways to interpret this graph:

1. When the two lines are parallel, this indicates that a significant interaction is not likely.

2. When the two lines touch or cross, this indicates that there is a possible significant interaction.

The pattern in Figure 11.2 shows that an interaction between class attendance and studying is unlikely. Parallel lines indicate that changes across the levels of both fac-tors are constant. In other words, it does not matter which level of a second factor you look at; the differences between group means will be the same. When the lines are not parallel, this indicates that changes are not constant; thus, changes in group means across the levels of one factor vary across the levels of the second factor. We

FIGURE 11.2 ● The cell means from the study in tables 11.5 and 11.6.

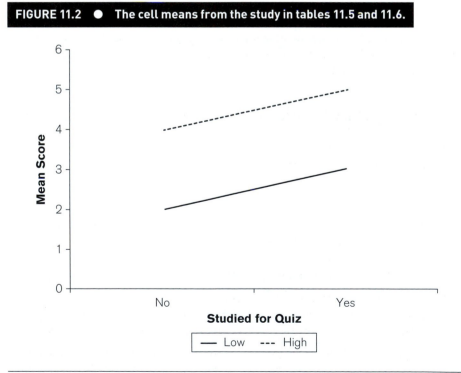

The graph indicates that an interaction is not likely because these lines are parallel.

compute the two-way between-subjects ANOVA to determine whether these changes are significant.

We compute three hypothesis tests using the two-way between-subjects ANOVA, and each hypothesis test is an independent test. Any combination of these three tests could be significant when we compute the two-way between-subjects ANOVA. In all, there are eight possible outcomes we could obtain:

1. All three hypothesis tests are not significant.

2. Significant main effect of Factor A only

3. Significant main effect of Factor B only

4. Significant main effect of Factor A and Factor B

5. Significant A × B interaction only

6. Significant main effect of Factor A and an A × B interaction

7. Significant main effect of Factor B and an A × B interaction

8. All three hypothesis tests are significant.

A significant main effect shows that group means vary across the levels of a single factor. A significant interaction is informative, because it indicates that mean differences cannot be readily explained by the levels of a single factor; it indicates that mean differences across the levels of one factor depend on which level of the second factor you look at. Therefore, we analyze a significant interaction before analyzing a significant main effect. Hence, if we obtain outcomes 6 to 8 from the list above, then we typically examine the interaction first.

Computing the Two-Way Between-Subjects ANOVA

In this section, we will compute the two-way between-subjects ANOVA. We use the two-way between-subjects ANOVA when we combine the levels of two factors using the 2-between or between-subjects design. We must make four assumptions to compute the two-way between-subjects ANOVA:

1. *Normality.* We assume that data in the population or populations being sampled from are normally distributed. This assumption is particularly important for small sample sizes. In larger samples, the overall variance is reduced, and this assumption becomes less critical as a result.

2. *Random sampling.* We assume that the data we measure were obtained from a sample that was selected using a random sampling procedure. It is generally considered inappropriate to conduct hypothesis tests with nonrandom samples.

3. *Independence.* We assume that the probabilities of each measured outcome in a study are independent or equal. Using random sampling usually satisfies this assumption.

4. *Homogeneity of variance.* We assume that the variance in each population is equal to that in the others. Violating this assumption can increase the likelihood of committing a Type I error (defined in Learning Unit 7, p. 108).

Keep in mind that satisfying the assumptions for the ANOVA is critically important. That said, for each example in this book, the data are intentionally constructed such that the assumptions for conducting the tests have been met. In Example 11.1 we follow the four steps to hypothesis testing introduced in Learning Unit 7 to compute a one-way between-subjects ANOVA at a two-tailed .05 level of significance using an example adapted from published research.

We now follow the four steps in hypothesis testing to compute a one-way between-subjects ANOVA.

Example 11.1. The more sugar people consume (increased exposure), the more they tend to like sugary foods (Di Lorenzo & Youngentob, 2013; Mennella & Bobowski, 2015; Privitera, 2016). As an example from this area of research, suppose a researcher hypothesizes that a person's level of sugar exposure can interfere or distract him or her during a computer task when food is present. To test this, the researcher uses the estimated daily intake scale for sugar (EDIS-S; Privitera & Wallace, 2011) to group participants by their level of exposure to sugars (low, moderate, high exposure). All participants then complete a computer task at a table with a buffet of sugary foods (buffet present) or a stack of papers (buffet absent) on the table. Slower times to complete the computer task indicate greater interference or distraction. We will compute the two-way between-subjects ANOVA to analyze the significance of these data using a .05 level of significance.

Step 1. State the hypotheses. The null hypothesis states that the group means for level of exposure to sugars (main effect), buffet presence or absence (main effect), and both factors combined (interaction) do not vary (variance = 0) in the population; the alternative hypothesis states that the group means do vary (variance > 0) in the population.

Mean times to complete the computer task do not vary by level of exposure to sugars, buffet presence or absence, and/or the combination of these two factors:

$$H_0: s^2_{\mu's} = 0$$

Mean times to complete the computer task do vary by level of exposure to sugars, buffet presence or absence, and/or the combination of these two factors:

$$H_1: \sigma^2_{\mu's} > 0$$

Step 2: Set the criteria for a decision. The level of significance for this test is .05. There are four sources of variation in the two-way between-subjects ANOVA, and we compute degrees of freedom for each source of variation—note that we will show these calculations in Excel when we get to Step 3.

The degrees of freedom for Factor A (exposure) are $p - 1$:

$$df_A = 3 - 1 = 2$$

The degrees of freedom for Factor B (buffet) are $q - 1$:

$$df_B = 2 - 1 = 1$$

To compute the degrees of freedom for the A × B interaction, we multiply the degrees of freedom for Factor A by the degrees of freedom for Factor B, or $(p - 1)(q - 1)$:

$$df_{A \times B} = 2(1) = 2$$

The degrees of freedom error are the total number of cells (pq) multiplied by the degrees of freedom for each cell $(n - 1)$, or $pq(n - 1)$:

$$df_E = (3)(1)(6 - 1) = 30$$

The total degrees of freedom are equal to the total number of participants, minus 1, which are the degrees of freedom for variance: $N - 1$, or $(npq) - 1$. We can add up the degrees of freedom we just computed, or we can calculate $(npq) - 1$, to find the total degrees of freedom:

> ### Appendix A12
>
> See **Appendix A12,** p. 298, for more on degrees of freedom for parametric tests.

$$df_E = 2 + 1 + 2 + 30 = 35$$

$$df_E = (6 \times 3 \times 2) - 1 = 35$$

We will compute three hypothesis tests: one for each main effect and one for the interaction. Each hypothesis test requires a different critical value. We will find critical values for each hypothesis test in Step 4, because it will be easier to see why the critical values are computed differently for each test if we wait until Step 4 to find the critical values.

Step 3: Compute the test statistic. To compute the test statistic, we follow six stages:

1. calculating, for each cell, the n and the means; and for each level of each factor, the n and the means, p, q, npq, and grand mean

2. calculating between-groups variance and sum of squares for Factor A and Factor B

3. calculating the A × B interaction variance and sum of squares

4. calculating within-groups (error) variance and sum of squares

5. calculating the total variance and sum of squares

6. completing the F table

For each hypothesis test, we compute the *F* statistic. The *F* statistic can be used to determine the total variance attributed to Factor A (exposure), Factor B (buffet), or the combination of factors A and B relative to the variance attributed to error. We compute the test statistic for each hypothesis test using a six-stage process, similar to that used for the one-way ANOVAs.

Download Sugary_Foods.xlsx from the student study site: http://study.sagepub .com/priviteraexcel1e. Columns C, D, and E contain the time in seconds that participants took to complete a computer task depending on whether their exposure to sugar was low (column C), moderate (column D), or high (column E). Within each of these three groups, participants were randomly assigned to either a sugar present or sugar absent condition. Some participants had a stack of papers on the table (Absent, rows 6 through 11) or a buffet of sugary snacks (Present, rows 15 through 20).

Stage 1. Calculating, for each cell, the n and the means; and for each level of each factor, the n and the means (referred to as the marginal n and the marginal mean), p, q, npq, and grand mean. As shown in Figure 11.3, start by labeling cells:

A12 and A21: Cell

A24 and F4: Marginal

B12, B21, B24, and F5: *n*

B13, B22, B25, and G5: mean

D27: *p*

D28: *q*

D29: Cell *n*

D30: *n*p*q*

D31: Grand mean

Next calculate the values as shown in Figure 11.3a:

In cell C12, enter =COUNT(C6:C11). Copy C12 and paste to D12, E12, C21, D21, and E21.

In cell C13, enter = AVERAGE(C6:C11). Copy C13 and paste to D13, E13, C22, D22 and E22.

In cell C24, enter =COUNT(C6:C11,C15:C20). In cell C25, enter =AVERAGE(C6:C11,C15:C20). Select C24 and C25 and fill to E24 and E25, or copy and paste from D24 to E25.

In cell F9, enter =COUNT(C6:E11). In cell G9, enter =AVERAGE(C6:E11). Select F9 and G9, copy, and paste to F18 and G18.

In cell E27, enter =COUNT(C25:E25).

In cell E28, enter =COUNT(G9:G18).

In cell E29, enter =C12.

In cell E30, enter =E27*E28*E29.

In cell E31, enter =AVERAGE(C6:E11,C15:E20).

These yield results for the *n*, cell means, level *n*, marginal means, *p*, *q*, *npq*, and grand mean, as shown in Figure 11.3b. These calculations provide the numbers for the next five stages: calculating sums of squares and degrees of freedom.

Stage 2. Calculating between-groups variance for factors A and B: SS_A and SS_B . For Factor A, exposure to sugars, we determine how much the groups differ from each other. (The difference among groups in Factor B is calculated separately.) To determine how much these groups of Factor A differ from each other, we

- subtract the grand mean from the marginal means for each level of Factor A,

- square each difference,

> **Appendix B**
>
> See **Appendix B2,** p. 301, for formatting cells.
>
> See **Appendix B3,** p. 303, for freezing panes.

FIGURE 11.3 ● Raw data with *n* and means for both cells and marginal, *p*, *q*, and grand mean. (a) Formulas and functions. (b) Results of calculations.

(a)

	A	B	C	D	E	F	G
2			Time (sec) to complete task				
3		Buffet of					
4		Sugary Food		Exposure to Sugars (Factor A)		Marginal	
5		(Factor B)	Low	Moderate	High	*n*	mean
6		Absent 8		10	13		
7		7		11	10		
8		9		12	11		
9		10		9	9	=COUNT(C6:E11)	=AVERAGE(C6:E11)
10		12		8	12		
11		8		10	11		
12	Cell	*n* =COUNT(C6:C11)		=COUNT(D6:D11)	=COUNT(E6:E11)		
13		mean =AVERAGE(C6:C11)		=AVERAGE(D6:D11)	=AVERAGE(E6:E11)		
14							
15		Present 6		13	15		
16		8		10	12		
17		4		9	14		
18		6		9	16	=COUNT(C15:E20)	=AVERAGE(C15:E20)
19		5		8	13		
20		7		11	14		
21	Cell	*n* =COUNT(C15:C20)		=COUNT(D15:D20)	=COUNT(E15:E20)		
22		mean =AVERAGE(C15:C20)		=AVERAGE(D15:D20)	=AVERAGE(E15:E20)		
23							
24	Marginal	*n* =COUNT(C6:C11,C15:C20)		=COUNT(D6:D11,D15:D20)	=COUNT(E6:E11,E15:E20)		
25		mean =AVERAGE(C6:C11,C15:C20)		=AVERAGE(D6:D11,D15:D20)	=AVERAGE(E6:E11,E15:E20)		
26							
27				*p* =COUNT(C25:E25)			
28				*q* =COUNT(G9:G18)			
29				Cell *n* =C12			
30				*n*p*q* =E27*E28*E29			
31				Grand mean =AVERAGE(C6:E11,C15:E20)			

(Continued)

FIGURE 11.3 ● (Continued)

(b)

	A	B	C	D	E	F	G
2			Time (sec) to complete task				
3		Buffet of					
4		Sugary Food	Exposure to Sugars (Factor A)			Marginal	
5		(Factor B)	Low	Moderate	High	n	mean
6		Absent	8	10	13		
7			7	11	10		
8			9	12	11		
9			10	9	9	18	10.0
10			12	8	12		
11			8	10	11		
12	Cell	n	6	6	6		
13		mean	9.0	10.0	11.0		
14							
15		Present	6	13	15		
16			8	10	12		
17			4	9	14		
18			6	9	16	18	10.0
19			5	8	13		
20			7	11	14		
21	Cell	n	6	6	6		
22		mean	6	10	14		
23							
24	Marginal	n	12	12	12		
25		mean	7.5	10.0	12.5		
26							
27				p	3		
28				q	2		
29				Cell n	6		
30				n*p*q	36		
31				Grand mean	10.0		

- sum the squared differences, and
- multiply by the marginal n to yield SS_A.

Appendix B

See **Appendix B4,** p. 304, for highlighting, pasting, and filling cells.

See **Appendix B6,** p. 306, for anchoring cell references.

To keep track of calculations, copy the labels in C4 through E5 (Exposure to Sugars, [Factor A]; Low; Moderate; and High) and paste them in I4 through K5. In I3, label this section "Between-groups variance: SS_A". (Figure 11.4 includes in rows 1 and 2 a reminder of the calculation.) Subtract the grand mean from each of the marginal means, square each of the differences, and multiply each difference by the sample size for the level of the factor (marginal n), as in Figure 11.4. Anchoring the cell address of the grand mean, E31, as $E$31 allows us to enter the formula into I6 and either fill or copy and paste to J6 and K6, as shown in Figure 11.4a, yielding the results show in Figure 11.4b.

I6: =(C25-$E$31)^2*C24

J6: =(D25-$E$31)^2*D24

K6: =(E25-$E$31)^2*E24

To keep track of the next calculations, label cells J8 and K8, respectively, SS_A and df_A. Then we calculate those values, as shown in Figure 11.4a, yielding the results shown in Figure 11.4b.

J9: =SUM(I6:K6)

K9: =E27-1

We enclosed J8 through K9 in a box to highlight these as the first portion of the F table for Stage 6.

Now we perform an analogous calculation for Factor B, sugary food absent or present. To keep track of calculations, copy B3 through B6 and paste in M3 through M6.

FIGURE 11.4 ● **Calculating sum of squares and degrees of freedom for Factor A. (a) Formulas and functions. (b) Results of calculations.**

(a)

	I	J	K
1	Subtract grand mean from marginal mean,		
2	square the difference, multiply by marginal n.		
3		Between-group variance: SS_A	
4		Exposure to Sugars (Factor A)	
5	Low	Moderate	High
6	=(C25-$E$31)^2*C24	=(D25-$E$31)^2*D24	=(E25-$E$31)^2*E24
7			
8		SS_A	df_A
9		=SUM(I6:K6)	=E27-1

(b)

	I	J	K
1	Subtract grand mean from marginal mean,		
2	square the difference, multiply by marginal n.		
3		Between-group variance: SS_A	
4		Exposure to Sugars (Factor A)	
5	Low	Moderate	High
6	75.0	0.0	75.0
7			
8		SS_A	df_A
9		150.0	2

Add "Present" in M7 for the second level of Factor B. Copy I3 to N5; change the label for the section to "Between-groups variance: SS_B". Subtract the grand mean from the marginal means of each level of Factor B, square each of the differences, and multiply each difference by the sample size for the level of the factor (marginal n), as in Figure 11.5. Enter the formula into N6 and N7, as shown in Figure 11.5a, yielding the results show in Figure 11.5b.

N6: =(G9-$E$31)^2*F9

N7: =(G18-$E$31)^2*F18

To keep track of the next calculations, label cells O9 and P9, respectively, SS_B and df_B. Then we calculate those values, as shown in Figure 11.5a, yielding the results shown in Figure 11.5b.

O10: =SUM(O6:P6)

P10: =E28-1

FIGURE 11.5 ● **Calculating sum of squares and degrees of freedom for Factor B. (a) Formulas and functions. (b) Results of calculations.**

(a)

	M	N	O	P
1	Subtract grand mean from group mean,			
2	square the difference, multiply by marginal n.			
3	Buffet of			
4	Sugary Food			
5	(Factor B)	Between-group variance: SS_B		
6	Absent	=(G9-$E$31)^2*F9		
7	Present	=(G18-$E$31)^2*F18		
8				
9			SS_B	df_B
10			=SUM(O6:P6)	=E28-1

(b)

	M	N	O	P
1	Subtract grand mean from group mean,			
2	square the difference, multiply by marginal n.			
3	Buffet of			
4	Sugary Food			
5	(Factor B)	Between-group variance: SS_B		
6	Absent	0.0		
7	Present	0.0		
8				
9			SS_B	df_B
10			0.0	1

We enclosed O9 through P10 in a box to highlight these as the second portion of the F table for Stage 6.

Stage 3. Calculating interaction variance: $SS_{A \times B}$. This calculation determines whether the effect of one factor depends on the level of the other factor with which it is combined. For each cell, which represents each unique combination of one level Factor A with one level of Factor B, we

- add the cell mean (for example, $M_{A_1 B_2}$) to the grand mean,

- subtract from that total each of the marginal means (for example, M_{A_1} and M_{B_2}),

- square each difference, and

- sum the squared differences to yield the $SS_{A \times B}$.

To keep track of calculations, copy M3 through M7 and paste to R3 through R7 to label Factor B and its levels. Copy I3 through K5 and paste to S3 through U5; in S3, change the SS_A to $SS_{A \times B}$. (Figure 11.6 includes in rows 1 and 2 a reminder of the calculation.) The cells in rows 4 and 5 provide the labels for Factor A. Anchoring the cells of the grand mean and the column or row, as appropriate, of the two marginal means allows us to enter the formula into S6 and S7 and either fill or copy and paste to T6 through U7, as shown in Figure 11.6a, yielding the results shown in Figure 11.6b.

S6: =(C13+\$E\$31-\$G9-C\$25)^2*C12, yielding 13.5

S7: =(C22+\$E\$31-\$G18-C\$25)^2*C21, yielding 13.5

T6: =(D13+\$E\$31-\$G9-D\$25)^2*D12, yielding 0.0

T7: =(D22+\$E\$31-\$G18-D\$25)^2*D21, yielding 0.0

U6: =(E13+\$E\$31-\$G9-E\$25)^2*E12, yielding 13.5

U7: =(E22+\$E\$31-\$G18-E\$25)^2*E21, yielding 13.5

To keep track of the next calculations, label cells T9 and U9, respectively, $SS_{A \times B}$ and $df_{A \times B}$. Then we calculate those values, as shown in Figure 11.6a, yielding the results shown in Figure 11.6b.

T10: =SUM(S6:U6,S7:U7), yielding 54.0

U9: =(E27-1)*(E28-1), yielding 2

We enclosed T9 through U10 in a box to highlight these as the third portion of the F table for Stage 6.

Stage 4. Calculating within-groups variance: SS_E. To calculate the total variance within groups,

- subtract the cell mean from each score in the cell,

- square the difference, and

- sum the squared differences to yield SS_E.

FIGURE 11.6 ● **Calculating sum of squares and degrees of freedom for A x B interaction. (a) Formulas and functions. (b) Results of calculations.**

(a)

	R	S	T	U
1	Sum cell and grand means, subtract both marginal			
2	means corresponding to cell, multiply by cell *n* .			
3	**Buffet of**		Interaction variance: SS $_{AxB}$	
4	**Sugary Food**		Exposure to Sugars (Factor A)	
5	**(Factor B)**	**Low**	**Moderate**	**High**
6	**Absent**	=(C13+$E$31-$G9-C$25)^2*C12	=(D13+$E$31-$G9-D$25)^2*D12	=(E13+$E$31-$G9-E$25)^2*E12
7	**Present**	=(C22+$E$31-$G18-C$25)^2*C21	=(D22+$E$31-$G18-D$25)^2*D21	=(E22+$E$31-$G18-E$25)^2*E21
8				
9			**SS** $_{AxB}$	**df** $_{AxB}$
10			=SUM(S6:U6,S7:U7)	=(E27-1)*(E28-1)

(b)

	R	S	T	U
1	Sum cell and grand means, subtract both marginal			
2	means corresponding to cell, multiply by cell *n* .			
3	**Buffet of**		Interaction variance: SS $_{AxB}$	
4	**Sugary Food**		Exposure to Sugars (Factor A)	
5	**(Factor B)**	**Low**	**Moderate**	**High**
6	**Absent**	13.5	0.0	13.5
7	**Present**	13.5	0.0	13.5
8				
9			**SS** $_{AxB}$	**df** $_{AxB}$
10			54.0	2

To keep track of calculations, copy R3 through U5 and paste them to W3 through Z5. In X3, change SS_{AxB} to SS_E . In cells W6 and W15, respectively, enter "Absent" and "Present" to identify the two levels of Factor B. (Figure 11.7 includes in rows 1 and 2 a reminder of the calculation.) Anchoring cells of the grand mean and the row of the cell mean allows us to enter =(C6–C$13)^2 into X6, fill right or copy and paste to Z6, and then fill down or copy and paste those three cells from X7 to Z11. We enter a similar formula, =(C15–C$22)^2, into cell X15 and perform the same manipulation to populate X15 through Z20 with the appropriate formulas. This is shown in Figure 11.7a; the results of the calculation are shown in Figure 11.7b.

To keep track of the next calculations, label cells Y22 and Z22, respectively, SS_E and df_E . Then we calculate those values, as shown in Figure 11.7a, yielding the results shown in Figure 11.7b.

Y23: =SUM(X6:Z20), yielding 72.0

Z23: =E27*E28*(E29–1), yielding 30

We enclosed Y22 through Z23 in a box to highlight these as the fourth portion of the *F* table for Stage 6.

FIGURE 11.7 ● Calculating sum of squares and degrees of freedom within groups (error). (a) Formulas and functions. (b) Results of calculations.

(a)

	W	X	Y	Z
1	Subtract group mean from each score			
2	in the group, square the difference.			
3	**Buffet of**	**Within-group (error) variance: SS $_E$**		
4	**Sugary Food**	**Exposure to Sugars (Factor A)**		
5	**(Factor B)**	**Low**	**Moderate**	**High**
6	**Absent** =(C6-C$13)^2	=(D6-D$13)^2	=(E6-E$13)^2	
7	=(C7-C$13)^2	=(D7-D$13)^2	=(E7-E$13)^2	
8	=(C8-C$13)^2	=(D8-D$13)^2	=(E8-E$13)^2	
9	=(C9-C$13)^2	=(D9-D$13)^2	=(E9-E$13)^2	
10	=(C10-C$13)^2	=(D10-D$13)^2	=(E10-E$13)^2	
11	=(C11-C$13)^2	=(D11-D$13)^2	=(E11-E$13)^2	
12				
13				
14				
15	**Present** =(C15-C$22)^2	=(D15-D$22)^2	=(E15-E$22)^2	
16	=(C16-C$22)^2	=(D16-D$22)^2	=(E16-E$22)^2	
17	=(C17-C$22)^2	=(D17-D$22)^2	=(E17-E$22)^2	
18	=(C18-C$22)^2	=(D18-D$22)^2	=(E18-E$22)^2	
19	=(C19-C$22)^2	=(D19-D$22)^2	=(E19-E$22)^2	
20	=(C20-C$22)^2	=(D20-D$22)^2	=(E20-E$22)^2	
21				
22			**SS $_E$**	**df $_E$**
23			=SUM(X6:Z20)	=E27*E28*(E29-1)

(b)

	W	X	Y	Z
1	Subtract group mean from each score			
2	in the group, square the difference.			
3	**Buffet of**	**Within-group (error) variance: SS $_E$**		
4	**Sugary Food**	**Exposure to Sugars (Factor A)**		
5	**(Factor B)**	**Low**	**Moderate**	**High**
6	**Absent**	1.0	0.0	4.0
7		4.0	1.0	1.0
8		0.0	4.0	0.0
9		1.0	1.0	4.0
10		9.0	4.0	1.0
11		1.0	0.0	0.0
12				
13				
14				
15	**Present**	0.0	9.0	1.0
16		4.0	0.0	4.0
17		4.0	1.0	0.0
18		0.0	1.0	4.0
19		1.0	4.0	1.0
20		1.0	1.0	0.0
21				
22			**SS $_E$**	**df $_E$**
23			72.0	30

Stage 5. Calculating total variance: SS_T. To determine the total variance among all scores in the entire study,

- subtract the grand mean from each score,

- square the difference, and

- sum the squared differences to yield SS_T.

To keep track of calculations, copy W3 through Z5 and paste them to AB3 through AE5. In AC3, change SS_E to SS_T. In cells AB6 and AB15, respectively, enter "Absent" and "Present" to identify the two levels of Factor B. (Figure 11.8 includes in rows 1 and 2 a reminder of the calculation.)

Subtract the grand mean from the first score in the "Low" group and square the difference by typing into cell AC6 =(C6-$E$31)^2, as in Figure 11.8a. Anchoring the cell address of the group mean as $E$31 allows the formula in AC6 to be filled right or copied and pasted through AE6. Selecting AC6 through AE6 allows filling down or copying and pasting from AC7 through AE11. Selecting AC6 through AE11 and copying allows pasting from AC15 to AE20. This yields for the 36 scores the squared deviations from their grand mean, as shown in Figure 11.8b.

To keep track of the next calculations, label cells AD22 and AE22, respectively, SS_T and df_T. Then we calculate those values, as shown in Figure 11.8a, yielding the results shown in Figure 11.8b.

AD23: =SUM(AC6:AE20), yielding 276.0

AE23: =E30-1, yielding 35

We enclosed AD22 through AE23 in a box to highlight these as the fifth portion of the F table for Stage 6.

Stage 6. Completing the F table. The F table lists the sum of squares (SS), degrees of freedom (df), mean squares (MS), and value of the test statistic (F). In cells AG5 through AK5, type the following headings: "Source of Variation", "SS", "df", "MS", and "F", as in Figure 11.9. In cells AG6 through AG10, below "Source of Variation," we list the sources that we have just calculated: "Factor A (exposure)", "Factor B (buffet)", "A x B (exposure × buffet)", "Error (within groups)", and "Total", as shown in Figure 11.9.

For the five values of SS and df, we refer to the cells in which we have calculated these values in Stages 2 through 5, as shown in Figure 11.9a.

FIGURE 11.8 ● **Calculating total sum of squares and degrees of freedom. (a) Formulas and functions. (b) Results of calculations.**

(a)

	AB	AC	AD	AE
1	Subtract grand mean			
2	from each score, square the difference.			
3	Buffet of	Total variance: SS_T		
4	Sugary Food	Exposure to Sugars (Factor A)		
5	(Factor B)	Low	Moderate	High
6	Absent	=(C6-$E$31)^2	=(D6-$E$31)^2	=(E6-$E$31)^2
7		=(C7-$E$31)^2	=(D7-$E$31)^2	=(E7-$E$31)^2
8		=(C8-$E$31)^2	=(D8-$E$31)^2	=(E8-$E$31)^2
9		=(C9-$E$31)^2	=(D9-$E$31)^2	=(E9-$E$31)^2
10		=(C10-$E$31)^2	=(D10-$E$31)^2	=(E10-$E$31)^2
11		=(C11-$E$31)^2	=(D11-$E$31)^2	=(E11-$E$31)^2
12				
13				
14				
15	Present	=(C15-$E$31)^2	=(D15-$E$31)^2	=(E15-$E$31)^2
16		=(C16-$E$31)^2	=(D16-$E$31)^2	=(E16-$E$31)^2
17		=(C17-$E$31)^2	=(D17-$E$31)^2	=(E17-$E$31)^2
18		=(C18-$E$31)^2	=(D18-$E$31)^2	=(E18-$E$31)^2
19		=(C19-$E$31)^2	=(D19-$E$31)^2	=(E19-$E$31)^2
20		=(C20-$E$31)^2	=(D20-$E$31)^2	=(E20-$E$31)^2
21				
22			SS_T	df_T
23			=SUM(AC6:AE20)	=E30-1

(b)

	AB	AC	AD	AE
1	Subtract grand mean			
2	from each score, square the difference.			
3	Buffet of	Total variance: SS_T		
4	Sugary Food	Exposure to Sugars (Factor A)		
5	(Factor B)	Low	Moderate	High
6	Absent	4.0	0.0	9.0
7		9.0	1.0	0.0
8		1.0	4.0	1.0
9		0.0	1.0	1.0
10		4.0	4.0	4.0
11		4.0	0.0	1.0
12				
13				
14				
15	Present	16.0	9.0	25.0
16		4.0	0.0	4.0
17		36.0	1.0	16.0
18		16.0	1.0	36.0
19		25.0	4.0	9.0
20		9.0	1.0	16.0
21				
22			SS_T	df_T
23			276.0	35

Five values of SS:

AH6: =J9 to display SS_A

AH7: =O10 to display SS_B

AH8: =T10 to display $SS_{A \times B}$

AH9: =Y23 to display SS_E

AH10: =AD23 to display SS_T

Selecting AH6 through AH10 and filling right or copying and pasting to AI6 through AI10 yields the cells containing the values for *df*, as shown in Figure 11.9.

To calculate *MS* we divide *SS* (column AH in Figure 11.9) by *df* (column AI in Figure 11.9) to calculate *MS*. The general formula for variance is

$$MS = \frac{SS}{df}$$

To calculate MS_A in cell AJ6, enter =AH6/AI6, as shown in Figure 11.9a. This yields

$$MS_A = \frac{150}{2} = 75$$

To calculate the remaining three values for variance or mean square (MS_E, $MS_{A \times B}$, MS_E) select cell AJ6 and fill down to AJ9, or copy and paste to AJ7 through AJ9. The resulting formulas and calculations for the values of *MS* are shown in Figure 11.9.

The two-way ANOVA test statistic, *F*, is basically the same as that for the one-way ANOVAs: It is the mean square between groups divided by the mean square error. For a two-way between-subjects ANOVA, we compute a different hypothesis test for each source of between-groups variation: one for each main effect and one for the interaction.

The test statistic for Factor A (exposure) is

$$F_A = \frac{MS_A}{MS_E}$$

In cell AK6, enter =AJ6/AJ$9 , as shown in Figure 11.9a. Anchoring the reference to MS_E in the denominator as AJ$9 allows us to select AK6 and fill down to AJ8, or copy and paste to AJ7 through AJ8. The resulting values are

$$F_A = \frac{75}{2.4} = 31.25$$

$$F_B = \frac{0.0}{2.4} = 0$$

$$F_{A \times B} \frac{27}{2.4} = 11.25$$

To find the critical value for each term, we need to know the degrees of freedom for Factor A, for Factor B, and for the A × B interaction. The degrees of freedom in the numerator for

Factor A is 2 (cell AI6 in Figure 11.9b),

Factor B is 1 (cell AI7 in Figure 11.9b), and

A × B interaction is 2 (cell AI8 in Figure 11.9b).

The degrees of freedom in the denominator for all three of these is the same: 30 (cell AI9 in Figure 11.9b).

FIGURE 11.9 ● **Summary table for two-way ANOVA. (a) Formulas and functions. (b) Results of calculations.**

(a)

	AG	AH	AI	AJ	AK
5	**Source of Variation**	*SS*	*df*	*MS*	*F*
6	Factor A (exposure)	=J9	=K9	=AH6/AI6	=AJ6/AJ$9
7	Factor B (buffet)	=O10	=P10	=AH7/AI7	=AJ7/AJ$9
8	A x B (exposure x buffet)	=T10	=U10	=AH8/AI8	=AJ8/AJ$9
9	Error (within groups)	=Y23	=Z23	=AH9/AI9	
10	Total	=AD23	=AE23		
11					
12	effect size, Factor A				
13	η^2 =AH6/AH10				
14					
15	effect size, A x B interaction				
16	η^2 =AH8/AH10				

(b)

	AG	AH	AI	AJ	AK
5	**Source of Variation**	*SS*	*df*	*MS*	*F*
6	Factor A (exposure)	150.0	2	75.0	31.25
7	Factor B (buffet)	0.0	1	0.0	0.00
8	A x B (exposure x buffet)	54.0	2	27.0	11.25
9	Error (within groups)	72.0	30	2.4	
10	Total	276.0	35		
11					
12	effect size, Factor A				
13	η^2 .54				
14					
15	effect size, A x B interaction				
16	η^2 .20				

At a .05 level of significance, the critical value associated with 2 and 30 degrees of freedom given in Table C.3 in Appendix C is 3.32, and the critical value associated with 1 and 30 degrees of freedom in that same table is 4.17.

Step 4: Make a decision. We will make a decision for each hypothesis test by comparing the value of the test statistic to the critical value.

Main effect of Factor A (exposure) is significant: $F_A = 31.25$ exceeds the critical value of 3.32; we reject the null hypothesis.

Main effect of Factor B (buffet) is not significant: $F_B = 0$ does not exceed the critical value of 4.17; we retain the null hypothesis.

The A × B interaction (exposure × buffet) is significant: $F_{A \times B} = 11.25$ exceeds the critical value of 3.32; we reject the null hypothesis.

If we were to report the result for Example 11.1 in a research journal, it would look something like this:

Using a two-way between-subjects ANOVA, a significant main effect of exposure, $F(2, 30) = 31.25$, $p < .05$, and a significant exposure × buffet interaction, $F(2, 30) = 11.25$, $p < .05$, were evident. A main effect of buffet (present, absent) was not evident ($F = 0$).

This study is an example of Outcome 6 in the list of eight possible outcomes given above under the subheading of Testing the Interaction. Now we have to determine which pairs of cell means differ. The interaction was significant, so analyzing this result is the next step.

Analyzing Main Effects and Interactions

If the decision is to retain the null hypothesis for all three hypothesis tests, then we stop: No pairs of group means significantly vary. However, when the decision is to reject the null hypothesis for even one of the three hypothesis tests, then we analyze the data further. If main effects are significant, then we conduct post hoc tests (as described in Learning Unit 10). If the interaction is significant, we analyze it using **simple main effect tests.**

Simple main effect tests are hypothesis tests used to analyze a significant interaction by comparing mean differences or simple main effects of one factor at each level of a second factor. After we compute simple main effect tests, we then compute post hoc tests for the significant simple main effects that we find. Figure 11.10 shows the steps for analyzing a significant two-way ANOVA. In this section, we describe how to compute and interpret simple main effect tests for a significant interaction.

Simple main effect tests are hypothesis tests used to analyze a significant interaction by comparing the mean differences or simple main effects of one factor at each level of a second factor.

The Interaction: Simple Main Effect Tests

A significant interaction indicates that at least one pair of group means for the A × B interaction (in the cells of a table summary) significantly differs. To analyze the interaction, we first need to know what question we want to answer. We follow three steps to analyze the interaction:

FIGURE 11.10 ● The steps following a two-way ANOVA.

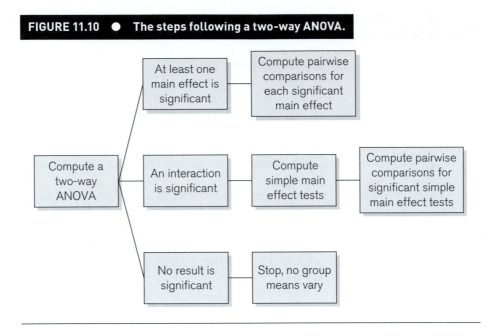

Step 1: Choose how to describe the data.
Step 2: Compute simple main effect tests.
Step 3: Compute pairwise comparisons.

Step 1: Choose how to describe the data. Table 11.7 shows two ways to interpret the interaction and five potential questions that can be asked. One way to interpret the interaction is to analyze the rows leading to Q1 and Q2 in the table; the second way is to analyze the columns leading to Q3, Q4, and Q5 in the table. We first choose which way we want to describe or interpret the data—typically determined by how to best answer the hypothesis being tested.

One way to interpret the interaction is to look in the table at how cell means for Factor A (exposure) change at each level of Factor B (buffet). This leads to two questions:

Q1: Does greater exposure to sugars interfere with completing a computer task when the buffet is absent?

Q2: Does greater exposure to sugars interfere with completing a computer task when the buffet is present?

By limiting our comparisons to one level of Factor B (buffet) at a time, we can compare the cell means for Factor A (exposure). In other words, we can compare the cell means at each level of exposure when the buffet was absent (top row of cells in Table 11.7) and make a separate comparison when the buffet was present (bottom row of cells in Table 11.7).

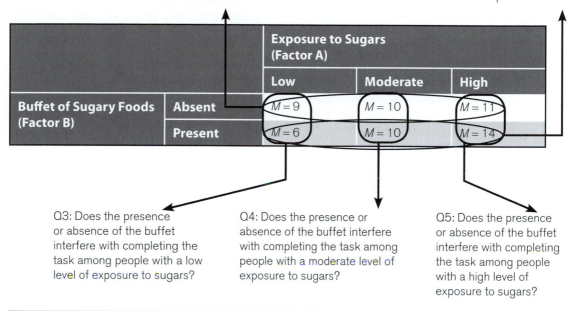

TABLE 11.7 ● Data for Example 11.1.

Q1: Does greater exposure to sugars interfere with completing a computer task when the buffet is absent?

Q2: Does greater exposure to sugars interfere with completing a computer task when the buffet is present?

		Exposure to Sugars (Factor A)		
		Low	Moderate	High
Buffet of Sugary Foods (Factor B)	Absent	$M = 9$	$M = 10$	$M = 11$
	Present	$M = 6$	$M = 10$	$M = 14$

Q3: Does the presence or absence of the buffet interfere with completing the task among people with a low level of exposure to sugars?

Q4: Does the presence or absence of the buffet interfere with completing the task among people with a moderate level of exposure to sugars?

Q5: Does the presence or absence of the buffet interfere with completing the task among people with a high level of exposure to sugars?

A significant interaction indicates that at least one pair of cell means is significantly different. There are two ways to analyze the A × B interaction. Analyzing across the rows addresses two questions (Q1 and Q2). Analyzing down the columns addresses three questions (Q3, Q4, and Q5) in this example.

A significant interaction indicates that at least one pair of cell means is significantly different. There are two ways to analyze the A × B interaction. Analyzing across the rows addresses two questions (Q1 and Q2). Analyzing down the columns addresses three questions (Q3, Q4, and Q5) in this example.

A second way to interpret the interaction is to look in the table at how the cell means for Factor B (buffet) change at each level of Factor A (exposure). This leads to three questions:

Q3: Does the presence or absence of the buffet interfere with completing the task among people with a low level of exposure to sugars?

Q4: Does the presence or absence of the buffet interfere with completing the task among people with a moderate level of exposure to sugars?

Q5: Does the presence or absence of the buffet interfere with completing the task among people with a high level of exposure to sugars?

By limiting our comparisons to one level of Factor A (exposure) at a time, we can compare the cell means for Factor B (buffet). In other words, we can compare the cell means at each level of buffet for persons with low exposure (left column of cells in Table 11.7), make a separate comparison for persons with moderate exposure (middle column of cells in Table 11.7), and make another separate comparison for persons with high exposure (right column of cells in Table 11.7).

To decide whether we want to answer Q1 and Q2; or Q3, Q4, and Q5; we need to determine which questions best address the hypothesis. In the exposure and buffet study, we want to determine whether a buffet of foods interferes with completing a computer task when the buffet is present (sugary foods are placed on the desk) versus absent (stacks of papers are placed on the desk). We can determine this by answering Q1 and Q2, so let us choose to answer these two questions.

Step 2: Compute simple main effect tests. To answer Q1, we will compare the top row of cell means in Table 11.7 for the buffet-absent group. To answer Q2, we will compare the bottom row of cell means in Table 11.7 for the buffet-present group. We will answer Q1 first.

To answer Q1, we compare the 18 participants from the three exposure groups (low, moderate, high) when the buffet of snacks was absent, data in cells C6 through E11 in Figure 11.3. Because different participants were assigned to each group or cell in this study, we can compute these data using a one-way between-subjects ANOVA (taught in Learning Unit 10)—this is the simple main effect test we will do with the Analysis ToolPak.

The top half of Figure 11.11 shows the summary statistics and the F table for the first simple main effect test. On the basis of the results shown in the F table, we decide to retain the null hypothesis. As expected, we conclude that a person's level of exposure to sugars does not interfere with the time it takes to complete a computer task when the buffet is absent.

To answer Q2, we compare the 18 participants from the three exposure groups (low, moderate, high) when the buffet of snacks was present, data in cells C15 through E20 in Figure 11.3. Because different participants were assigned to each group or cell in this study, we again compute these data using a one-way between-subjects ANOVA— this is the simple main effect test we will do with the Analysis ToolPak.

The bottom half of Figure 11.11 shows the summary statistics and the F table for the first simple main effect test. On the basis of the results shown in the F table, we decide to reject the null hypothesis. As expected, we conclude that a person's level of exposure to sugars interferes with the time it takes to complete a computer task when the buffet is present.

In this example, the researcher hypothesized that a person's level of sugar exposure can interfere with or distract him or her during a computer task when food is present. We had participants with different levels of exposure to sugars complete a computer task with and without the buffet present. We measured the time it took participants to complete the computer task and used a two-way between-subjects ANOVA to analyze the data. The simple effect tests we just computed confirmed this original hypothesis: The time it took to complete the computer task significantly varied when the buffet was present but not when it was absent.

Step 3: Compute pairwise comparisons. In this step, we compute post hoc tests to analyze only the significant simple main effect tests we computed in Step 2.

FIGURE 11.11 ● Analysis of simple main effects (one-way ANOVAs) using Analysis ToolPak.

	AM	AN	AO	AP	AQ	AR	AS
1	Anova: Single Factor Buffet Absent						
2							
3	SUMMARY						
4	Groups	Count	Sum	Average	Variance		
5	Low	6	54	9	3.2		
6	Moderate	6	60	10	2		
7	High	6	66	11	2		
8							
9							
10	ANOVA						
11	Source of Variation	SS	df	MS	F	P-value	F crit
12	Between Groups	12	2	6	2.50	0.116	3.682
13	Within Groups	36	15	2.4			
14							
15	Total	48	17				
16							
17							
18	Anova: Single Factor Buffet Present						
19							
20	SUMMARY						
21	Groups	Count	Sum	Average	Variance		
22	Column 1	6	36	6	2		
23	Column 2	6	60	10	3.2		
24	Column 3	6	84	14	2		
25							
26							
27	ANOVA						
28	Source of Variation	SS	df	MS	F	P-value	F crit
29	Between Groups	192	2	96	40.00	0.000	3.682
30	Within Groups	36	15	2.4			
31							
32	Total	228	17				

In this case, we will compare all possible pairs of cell means in the bottom row—to analyze the cell means for the significant simple main effect test for the buffet-present condition.

Step 3 is necessary only when we compare more than two cells. With two cells, only one pair of means can be compared; multiple pairwise comparisons are therefore unnecessary. In this example, multiple pairwise comparisons are necessary because we compared three cells or groups. The mean in each group in the bottom row of cells was $M = 6$ in the low-exposure group, $M = 10$ in the moderate-exposure group, and $M = 14$ in the high-exposure group.

In Learning Unit 10, we introduced Tukey's honestly significant difference (HSD) post hoc test, so let us use this test to compare each pair of cell means. For this post hoc test, the test statistic is the difference between each pair of group means. The critical value for each pairwise comparison is 3.05. (Refer to Learning Unit 10 for a description of how to find the critical value using this post hoc test.) The pairwise comparisons and the decision for each comparison are as follows:

Comparison 1: high exposure and low exposure: $14 - 6 = 8.00$ (Reject the null hypothesis; the test statistic value, 8.00, is greater than 3.05.)

Comparison 2: moderate exposure and low exposure: $10 - 6 = 4.00$ (Reject the null hypothesis; the test statistic value, 4.00, is greater than 3.05.)

Comparison 3: high exposure and moderate exposure: $14 - 10 = 4.00$ (Reject the null hypothesis; the test statistic value, 4.00, is greater than 3.05)

The results show that every pairwise comparison is significant. Hence, the more exposure participants had to sugars, the slower they were to complete a computer task when the buffet was present, but this effect did not occur when the buffet was absent. If we were to report the outcome of this analysis in a research journal, it would look something like this:

A two-way between-subjects ANOVA showed a significant main effect of exposure, $F(2, 30) = 31.25$, $p < .05$, and a significant exposure × buffet interaction, $F(2, 30) = 11.25$, $p < .05$. Simple main effect tests showed that times to complete the task were significantly different when the buffet was present, $F(2, 15) = 40.00$, $p < .001$, but not when it was absent ($p > .05$). The more exposure participants had to sugars, the slower their times were to complete the computer task when the buffet was present (Tukey's HSD, $p < .05$).

Main Effects: Pairwise Comparisons

If an interaction is significant, you should analyze the interaction. It may also be necessary to analyze significant main effects, particularly if such an outcome is predicted by the hypothesis being tested. To analyze a significant main effect, you skip straight to Step 3 and compute pairwise comparisons. Keep in mind that in a table summary, the main effects are located outside the table—we compare the row or column means for a single factor, independent of the second factor. The sample size at each level of a single factor will be larger than the sample size per cell. In this example, a significant main effect of exposure was evident. Note that $n = 12$ participants per group, because participants in the buffet-absent and buffet-present cells were combined at each level of the exposure factor. The mean values compared were as follows: low, 7.5 seconds; moderate, 10 seconds; high, 12.5 seconds; as shown in cells C25 through E25 of Figure 11.3.

Measuring Effect Size With Eta Squared

We can compute effect size using proportion of variance for each effect tested using the two-way between-subjects ANOVA. Proportion of variance estimates how much of the variability in the dependent variable (time it took to complete the computer task) can be explained by each group (the two main effects and the interaction). Two measures of proportion of variance are eta squared and omega squared. In this section, we measure effect size for the significant results obtained in this example.

Eta squared can be computed for each main effect and the interaction. It is the sum of squares of the main effect or interaction divided by the sum of squares total. Based on the results given in Figure 11.9, $SS_A = 150$ and $SS_T = 276$. The proportion of variance for Factor A is

$$\eta_A^2 = \frac{SS_A}{SS_T} = \frac{150}{276} = .54$$

We conclude that 54% of the variability in the time it took to complete the computer task can be explained by the participants' level of exposure to sugars. To find the proportion of variance for the significant A × B interaction, we substitute the sum of squares for the interaction, $SS_{A \times B} = 54$ in Figure 11.9, into the numerator of the formula:

$$\eta_{A \times B}^2 = \frac{SS_{A \times B}}{SS_T} = \frac{54}{276} = .20$$

We conclude that 20% of the variability in the time it took to complete the computer task can be explained by the combination of the two factors. The proportion of variance for the interaction is less informative than for the main effects, because a significant interaction must be analyzed further. For this reason, many researchers will analyze the interaction first and report an effect size only for the significant simple main effects.

Note that you can compute effect size in Excel using a simple formula. For example, for Factor A, you can label one cell "Eta squared" and in the adjacent cell create a formula from Figure 11.9: =AH6/AH10. Likewise, for the A × B interaction, you follow the same steps to compute the effect size from Figure 11.9 using the following calculation: =AH8/AH10.

Based on the effect size conventions listed in the second column of Table 9.2 in Learning Unit 9 (p. 138), this is a medium effect size. Here is how we might report eta squared with the significant result:

> A two-way between-subjects ANOVA showed a significant main effect of exposure, $F(2, 30) = 31.25$, $p < .05$ ($\eta^2 = .54$), and a significant exposure × buffet interaction, $F(2, 30) = 11.25$, $p < .05$ ($\eta^2 = .20$). Simple main effect tests showed that times to complete the task were significantly different when the buffet was present, $F(2, 15) = 40.00$, $p < .001$, but not when it was absent ($p > .05$). The more exposure participants had to sugars, the slower their times were to complete the computer task when the buffet was present (Tukey's HSD, $p < .05$).

FIGURE 11.12 ● Raw data in contiguous cells for use in Analysis ToolPak.

	AU	AV	AW	AX
4		**Exposure to Sugars (Factor A)**		
5	**(Factor B)**	**Low**	**Moderate**	**High**
6	**Absent**	8	10	13
7		7	11	10
8		9	12	11
9		10	9	9
10		12	8	12
11		8	10	11
12	**Present**	6	13	15
13		8	10	12
14		4	9	14
15		6	9	16
16		5	8	13
17		7	11	14

Computing the Two-Way Between-Subjects ANOVA Using the Analysis ToolPak

We can also calculate this ANOVA using the Analysis ToolPak available in Excel for easy and accurate calculation. Return to the workbook Sugary_Foods.xlsx. To perform this analysis, the data must be in contiguous cells. Copy B4 through E11 and paste from AU4 through AX11. Copy B15 through E20 and paste from AU12 through AX17. The raw data, including labels, should appear as shown in Figure 11.12. Our data are grouped so that each test condition of Factor A (exposure) is contained within a column. One level of the test condition of Factor B (buffet absent) is in the first six rows, and the other level of Factor B (buffet present) is in the next six rows.

Click on the Data tab, and then on the Data Analysis icon all the way to the right. Select "Anova: Two Factor With Replication," as shown in Figure 11.13a, which yields the dialog box shown in Figure 11.13b. Enter $AU\$5:\$AX\$17$ for Input Range. Note that this includes the labels for the levels of the two factors. The value for alpha we specify as .05. Select Output Range for the result to be displayed in the worksheet, and click in the box to the right. Then click in cell AZ2 of the spreadsheet.

Clicking "OK" on the dialog box returns the output table in Figure 11.14. Notice that the values in the table for summary statistics, *SS*, *df*, *MS*, *F*, and F_{crit} are the same as the ones described earlier. The output table labels the levels of the Factor A (low, moderate, high) and Factor B (absent, present), but it does not label the factors

FIGURE 11.13 ● **Performing a two-way ANOVA with Analysis ToolPak in Excel. (a) Selecting "Anova: Two-factor With Replication" to perform a two-way ANOVA. (b) Specifying the location of the data and parameters for the ANOVA.**

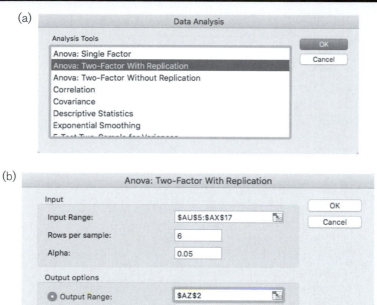

in the ANOVA summary table. In that table, Sample (cell AZ26) refers to Factor B (buffet) and Columns (cell AZ27) refers to Factor A. Interaction (cell AZ28) refers to the A × B interaction. We could change the default labels provided by Excel simply by editing the text in those cells. Although the output table gives neither an estimate of effect size such as eta squared nor post hoc comparisons, it does provide the means for each group and all the components of the ANOVA summary table needed. Only the studentized range statistic, q, would need to be found in Appendix C4.

FIGURE 11.14 ● Results of the two-way ANOVA using the Analysis ToolPak.

	AZ	BA	BB	BC	BD	BE	BF
2	Anova: Two-Factor With Replication						
3							
4	SUMMARY	Low	Moderate	High	Total		
5	*Absent*						
6	Count	6	6	6	18		
7	Sum	54	60	66	180		
8	Average	9	10	11	10		
9	Variance	3.2	2	2	2.82		
10							
11	*Present*						
12	Count	6	6	6	18		
13	Sum	36	60	84	180		
14	Average	6	10	14	10		
15	Variance	2	3.2	2	13.41		
16							
17	*Total*						
18	Count	12	12	12			
19	Sum	90	120	150			
20	Average	7.5	10	12.5			
21	Variance	4.82	2.36	4.27			
22							
23							
24	ANOVA						
25	*Source of Variation*	*SS*	*df*	*MS*	*F*	*P-value*	*F crit*
26	Sample	0	1	0	0	1.000	4.171
27	Columns	150	2	75	31.25	.000	3.316
28	Interaction	54	2	27	11.25	.000	3.316
29	Within	72	30	2.4			
30							
31	Total	276	35				

Identifying Patterns and Making Predictions

Testing relationships between variables can be quite informative, and these relationships are a natural type of association to evaluate. We can identify, for example, how constructs such as love, attachment, personality, motivation, and cognition are related to other factors or behaviors, such as tendencies toward depression, emotional well-being, and physical health. In everyday situations, you may notice relationships between exercise and health (e.g., people who are healthier tend to exercise more often) or between education and income (e.g., people who are more educated tend to earn a higher income). We can even ask questions about prediction, or the extent to which the relationships we observe can lead to a better understanding of what could happen in the future (i.e., our ability to predict behavior).

In hypothesis testing, there are often cases where we want to evaluate the relationship between two variables, or the extent to which we can predict behavior. In the basic structure of such a study, we measure two variables to test whether they change in a related or in an independent fashion, or to test whether values of one factor can predict changes in another. For example, suppose we record the SAT scores and the freshman grade point averages (GPAs) in a sample of college students. We can evaluate how they are related (e.g., in this example, we may observe that higher SAT scores are related to higher GPA). Many colleges, however, may want to know whether higher GPA scores among college applicants will predict higher GPA scores when the students enter college. Hence, in this example, understanding the relationship between these scores (correlation) and the ability of SAT scores to predict college freshman GPA (regression) is informative.

In this section, we explore the nature of hypothesis testing to evaluate the relationship between two variables and to evaluate predictive relationships. We further assess how to compute and interpret observed effects, and we explore other ways of adding information about the nature of observed effects and how to appropriately interpret them.

LEARNING UNIT 12

Correlation

Excel Toolbox

Mathematical operators

- –
- /
- *

Functions

- COUNT
- AVERAGE
- STDEV.S
- SUM
- PEARSON
- RANK.AVG

Other tools

- format cells
- freeze panes
- anchor cell reference

(Continued)

(Continued)

- fill down or paste
- create chart
- format chart
- Analysis ToolPak

The Structure of Data Used for Identifying Patterns

Hypothesis testing was introduced in Learning Unit 7, and in the intervening learning units, we have described a variety of ways to compare group means. For each hypothesis test, we observed the levels of one factor, and in Learning Unit 11, we observed the combination of levels for two factors. Each level or combination of levels was a group, and in each group, we measured a dependent variable and analyzed mean differences between groups. Using this approach, significance indicated that two or more groups were different. Another approach to testing for mean differences is to compare two dependent variables to determine the extent to which changes in values for each variable are related, or change in an identifiable pattern. This type of approach is called a **correlation** and is most often used to identify the linear pattern or relationship between two variables.

Throughout this learning unit, data for correlations are plotted in a graph called a **scatter plot**, which is used to illustrate the relationship between two variables, denoted (x, y). The x variable is plotted along the x-axis of the graph, and the y variable is plotted along the y-axis. Pairs of values for x and y are called **data points**. The data points are plotted along the x- and y-axes of a graph to see whether a pattern emerges. The pattern that emerges can be described by the value of a correlation, as described in this learning unit.

Fundamentals of the Correlation

Using a correlation, we compare two dependent variables to determine the extent to which changes in values for one variable are related to changes in values in the other variable. While the general structure of this analysis is much different from our previous approach, in which we compared mean differences between groups, it is also comparable to that approach. To illustrate, suppose we observe students texting or not texting in class and compare differences in class performance (as an exam grade out of 100 points). In this example, illustrated in Figure 12.1a, the factor is texting (yes, no), and the dependent variable is class performance (an exam grade). This type of analysis will require the use of the two-independent-sample t test, because we are comparing mean difference in exam scores between groups of students who did and did not text during class.

A **correlation** is a statistical procedure used to describe the strength and direction of the linear relationship between two factors.

A **scatter plot**, also called a **scatter gram**, is a graphical display of discrete data points (x, y) used to summarize the relationship between two variables.

Data points are the x- and y-coordinates for each plot in a scatter plot.

FIGURE 12.1 ● Comparing groups means versus the correlational methods.

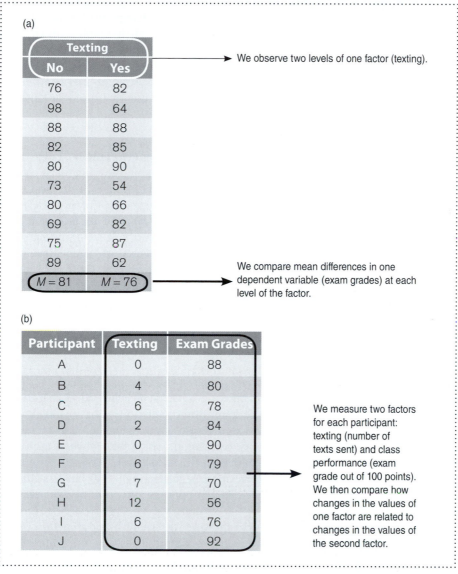

(a)

Texting	
No	Yes
76	82
98	64
88	88
82	85
80	90
73	54
80	66
69	82
75	87
89	62
$M = 81$	$M = 76$

We observe two levels of one factor (texting).

We compare mean differences in one dependent variable (exam grades) at each level of the factor.

(b)

Participant	Texting	Exam Grades
A	0	88
B	4	80
C	6	78
D	2	84
E	0	90
F	6	79
G	7	70
H	12	56
I	6	76
J	0	92

We measure two factors for each participant: texting (number of texts sent) and class performance (exam grade out of 100 points). We then compare how changes in the values of one factor are related to changes in the values of the second factor.

An alternative method using a correlation is to treat each factor like a dependent variable and measure the relationship between each pair of variables. For example, we could measure texting during class (number of texts sent) and class performance (an exam grade out of 100 points) for each student in a class. We could then test to see if there is a relationship between the pairs of scores for each participant. In this example, illustrated in Figure 12.1b, if the scores are related, then we would expect exam scores to decrease as the number of texts sent increases.

A correlation can be used to (1) describe the pattern of data points for the values of two factors and (2) determine whether the pattern observed in a sample is also present in the population from which the sample was selected. The pattern of data points is described by the direction and strength of the relationship between two factors. In behavioral research, we mostly describe the linear (or straight-line) relationship between two factors. For this reason, this learning unit focuses on linear relationships.

The Direction of a Correlation

The value of a correlation, measured by the **correlation coefficient (r)**, ranges from −1.0 to +1.0. Values closer to ±1.0 indicate stronger correlations, meaning that a correlation coefficient of $r = -1.0$ is as strong as a correlation coefficient of $r = +1.0$. The sign of the correlation coefficient (− or +) indicates only the direction or slope of the correlation.

A **positive correlation** ($0 < r \leq +1.0$) means that as the values of one factor increase, the values of the second factor also increase; as the values of one factor decrease, the values of the second factor also decrease. If two factors have values that change in the same direction, we can graph the correlation using a straight line. Figure 12.2 shows that values on the y-axis increase as values on the x-axis increase.

Figure 12.2a shows a *perfect* positive correlation, which occurs when each data point falls exactly on a straight line, although this is rare. More commonly, as shown in Figure 12.2b, a positive correlation is greater than 0 but less than +1.0, where the values of two factors change in the same direction but not all data points fall exactly on a straight line.

A **negative correlation** ($-1.0 \leq r < 0$) means that as the values of one factor increase, the values of the second factor decrease. If two factors have values that change in the opposite direction, we can also graph the correlation using a straight line. Figure 12.3 shows that values on the y-axis decrease as values on the x-axis increase.

Figure 12.3a shows a *perfect* negative correlation, which occurs when each data point falls exactly on a straight line, although this is also rare. More commonly, as shown in Figure 12.3b, a negative correlation is greater than −1.0 but less than 0, where the values of two factors change in the opposite direction but not all data points fall exactly on a straight line.

The *correlation coefficient (r)* is used to measure the strength and direction of the linear relationship, or correlation, between two factors. The value of r ranges from −1.0 to +1.0.

The Strength of a Correlation

A zero correlation ($r = 0$) means that there is no linear pattern or relationship between two factors. This outcome is rare because usually by mere chance, at least some values of one factor, X, will show some pattern or relationship with values of a second factor, Y. The closer a correlation coefficient is to $r = 0$, the weaker the correlation and the less likely that two factors are related; the closer a correlation coefficient is to $r = ±1.0$, the stronger the correlation and the more likely that two factors are related.

A **correlation coefficient (r)** is used to measure the strength and direction of the linear relationship, or correlation, between two factors. The value of r ranges from −1.0 to +1.0.

A **positive correlation** ($0 < r \leq +1.0$) is a positive value of r that indicates that the values of two factors change in the same direction: As the values of one factor increase, the values of the second factor also increase; as the values of one factor decrease, the values of the second factor also decrease.

A **negative correlation** ($-1.0 \leq r < 0$) is a negative value of r that indicates that the values of two factors change in different directions, meaning that as the values of one factor increase, the values of the second factor decrease.

FIGURE 12.2 ● A perfect positive (a) and a positive (b) linear correlation.

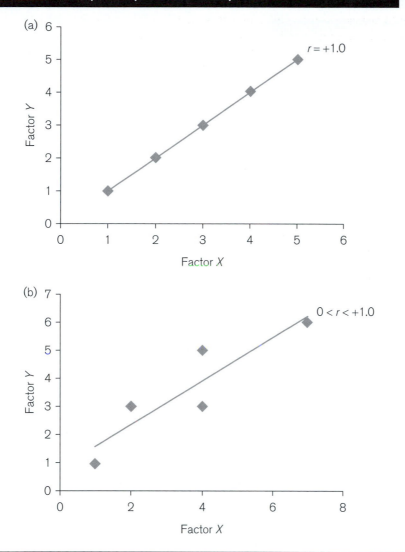

Both the table and the scatter plot show the same data for (a) and (b).

The strength of a correlation reflects how consistently scores for each factor change. When plotted in a scatter plot, scores are more consistent the closer they fall to a **regression line**, or the straight line that best fits a set of data points. The best-fitting straight line minimizes the total distance of all data points that fall from it. Figure 12.4 shows two positive correlations between exercise (Factor X) and body image satisfaction (Factor Y), and Figure 12.5 shows two negative correlations between number of class absences (Factor X) and grade on a quiz (Factor Y). In both figures, the closer a set of data points falls to the regression line, the stronger the correlation; hence, the closer a correlation coefficient is to $r = \pm1.0$.

Regression line the best-fitting straight line to a set of data points. A best-fitting line is the line that minimizes the distance that all data points fall from it.

FIGURE 12.3 ● A perfect negative (a) and a negative (b) linear correlation.

X	Y
1	5
2	4
3	3
4	2
5	1

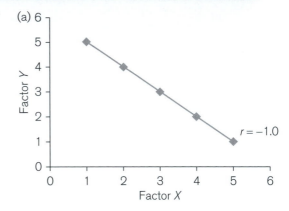

X	Y
1	5
2	3
2	3
4	3
6	1

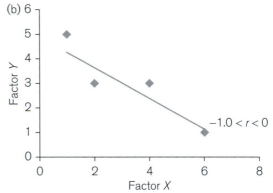

Both the table and the scatter plot show the same data for (a) and (b).

FIGURE 12.4 ● The consistency of scores for a positive correlation.

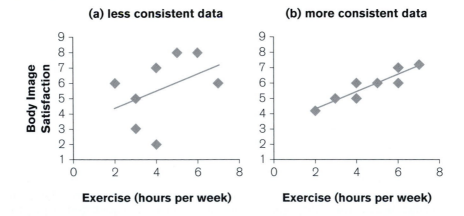

Both figures show approximately the same regression line, but the data points in (b) are more consistent, and thus show a stronger correlation, because they fall closer to the regression line than those in (a).

FIGURE 12.5 • **The consistency of scores for a negative correlation.**

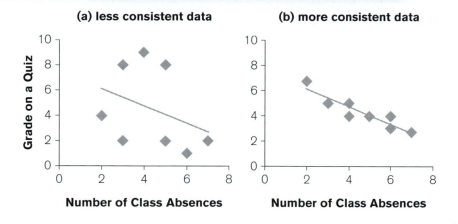

Both figures show approximately the same regression line, but the data points in (b) are more consistent, and thus show a stronger correlation, because they fall closer to the regression line than those in (a).

The Pearson Correlation Coefficient

The most commonly used formula for computing r is the **Pearson correlation coefficient**, also called the **Pearson product-moment correlation coefficient**. The Pearson correlation coefficient is used to determine the strength and direction of the relationship between two factors on an interval or ratio scale of measurement. Recall from Learning Unit 5 that we located z scores by computing a z transformation on a set of data. In the same way, we can locate a sample of data points by converting them to z scores and computing the following formula:

$$r = \frac{\sum(z_X z_Y)}{n-1}$$

Note that computing the z scores would be tedious by hand. However, using Excel, this is quite simple—we will therefore use this formula to compute the Pearson correlation in Excel. Notice that the general formula for the Pearson correlation coefficient is similar to that for computing variance. The correlation coefficient, r, measures the **covariance** of X and Y. The larger the covariance, the closer data points will fall to the regression line. When all data points for X and Y fall exactly on a regression line, the covariance equals the total variance, making the formula for r equal to +1.0 or –1.0, depending on the direction of the relationship. The farther that data points fall from the regression line, the smaller the covariance will be compared to the total variance in the denominator, resulting in a value of r closer to 0.

If we conceptualize covariance as circles, as illustrated in Figure 12.6, then the variance of each factor (X and Y) is contained within each circle. The two circles, then, contain the total measured variance. The covariance of X and Y reflects the extent to which the total variance or the two circles overlap. In terms of computing r, the overlap or covariance is placed in the numerator; the total variance contained within each

The **Pearson correlation coefficient (r)**, also called the **Pearson product-moment correlation coefficient**, is a measure of the direction and strength of the linear relationship of two factors in which the data for both factors are measured on an interval or ratio scale of measurement.

Covariance is the extent to which the values of two factors (*X* and *Y*) vary together. The closer data points fall to the regression line, the more the values of two factors vary together.

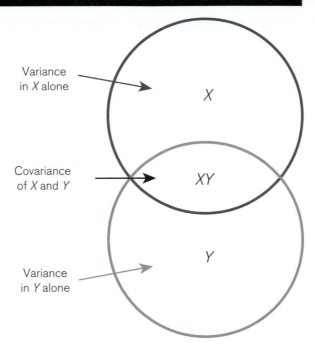

FIGURE 12.6 ● Each circle represents the variance of a factor.

Variance in *X* alone

Covariance of *X* and *Y*

Variance in *Y* alone

X

XY

Y

Two factors covary inasmuch as the two circles overlap. The more overlap or shared variance of two factors, *the more the two factors are related.*

circle is placed in the denominator. The more the two circles overlap, the more the covariance (in the numerator) will equal the independent variances contained within each circle (in the denominator)—and the closer *r* will be to ±1.0.

Computing the Pearson Correlation Coefficient

In this section we will compute the Pearson correlation coefficient. We make three assumptions to compute the correlation coefficient.

Homoscedasticity is the assumption that there is an equal ("homo") variance or scatter ("scedasticity") of data points dispersed along the regression line.

Linearity is the assumption that the best way to describe a pattern of data is using a straight line.

1. **Homoscedasticity** (pronounced "ho-mo-skee-das-ti-ci-ty") is the assumption of constant variance among data points. We assume that there is an equal ("homo") variance or scatter ("scedasticity") of data points dispersed along the regression line. When the variance of data points from the regression line is not equal, the Pearson correlation coefficient (*r*) tends to underestimate the strength of a correlation.

2. **Linearity** is the assumption that the best way to describe a pattern of data is using a straight line. In truth, we could fit just about any set of data points to a best-fitting straight line, but the data may actually conform better to other

shapes, such as curvilinear shapes. In these cases, a linear correlation should not be used to describe the data, because the assumption of linearity is violated.

3. To test for linear correlations, we must assume that the data points are *normally distributed*. This assumption is more complex than the assumptions of normality for the *t* tests and ANOVA tests. For a linear correlation between two factors, the assumption of normality requires that a population of *X* and *Y* scores for two factors forms a bivariate (two-variable) normal distribution, such that

   a. the population of *X* scores is normally distributed;

   b. the population of *Y* scores is normally distributed;

   c. for each *X* score, the distribution of *Y* scores is normal; and

   d. for each Y score, the distribution of X scores is normal.

Keep in mind that satisfying the assumptions for the correlations is critically important. That said, for each example in this book, the data are intentionally constructed such that the assumptions for conducting the tests have been met. In Example 12.1 we follow the four steps to hypothesis testing introduced in Learning Unit 7 to compute a Pearson correlation coefficient at a two-tailed .05 level of significance using an example adapted from published research.

Example 12.1. An area of research of particular interest is the relationship between mood and appetite (Baxter, 2016; Hammen & Keenan-Miller, 2013; Sander, DeBoth, & Ollendick, 2016). As an example of one such study from this area of research, suppose a health psychologist tests whether mood and eating are related by recording data for each variable in a sample of 8 participants. She measures mood using a 9-point rating scale in which higher ratings indicate better mood. She measures eating as the average number of calories per meal that each participant consumed in the previous week. Download the spreadsheet titled Mood_Eating.xlsx from the student study site: http://study.sagepub .com/priviteraexcel1e. We will compute the Pearson correlation coefficient using these data.

Step 1: Compute preliminary calculations. We begin by calculating *z* scores as we did in Learning Unit 5. As a reminder, the signs (+ and –) of the values we compute are essential to making accurate computations.

Label cells A13 through A15, respectively, *n*, *M*, and σ, as shown in Figure 12.7a.

Compute for *X* and for *Y* the sample size, mean, and standard deviation, as shown in Figure 12.7a:

B13: =COUNT(B4:B11)

B14: =AVERAGE(B4:B11)

B15: =STDEV.S(B4:B11)

> **Appendix B**
>
> See **Appendix B2,** p. 301, for formatting cells.
>
> See **Appendix B3,** p. 303, for freezing panes.

We assume that every participant has a score for both mood (*X*) and calories (*Y*), so there is no need to calculate *n* for both variables. Select B14 and B15 and fill to C14 through C15, or copy and paste to C14 through C15. We now have the number of pairs of scores and the means and standard deviations of each variable.

Recall that the formula for the Pearson correlation coefficient is

$$r = \frac{\sum (z_X z_Y)}{n-1}$$

With the mean and the standard deviation for each variable, we can now calculate the components of the numerator of the Pearson correlation coefficient, z_X and z_Y.

Step 2: Compute the z scores. Label cell E1 "z Scores". Copy B2 through C2 and paste them to E2 through F2. Label E3 and F3, respectively, "z_X" and "z_Y", as shown in Figure 12.7a.

From each X and each Y score, first subtract the mean for that variable, and then divide by the standard deviation for that variable. In cell E4, type =(B4-B\$14)/B\$15, using the \$ to anchor the cell references to the rows containing the mean and the

---

FIGURE 12.7 ● Calculating Pearson *r*. (a) Formulas and functions. (b) Results of the calculations of formulas and functions.

(a)

	A	B	C	D	E	F	G
1		Raw scores				z Scores	
2		Mood	Calories		Mood	Calories	
3		X	Y		z_X	z_Y	$z_X * z_Y$
4	6		480		=(B4-B\$14)/B\$15	=(C4-C\$14)/C\$15	=E4*F4
5	4		490		=(B5-B\$14)/B\$15	=(C5-C\$14)/C\$15	=E5*F5
6	7		500		=(B6-B\$14)/B\$15	=(C6-C\$14)/C\$15	=E6*F6
7	4		590		=(B7-B\$14)/B\$15	=(C7-C\$14)/C\$15	=E7*F7
8	2		600		=(B8-B\$14)/B\$15	=(C8-C\$14)/C\$15	=E8*F8
9	5		400		=(B9-B\$14)/B\$15	=(C9-C\$14)/C\$15	=E9*F9
10	3		545		=(B10-B\$14)/B\$15	=(C10-C\$14)/C\$15	=E10*F10
11	1		650		=(B11-B\$14)/B\$15	=(C11-C\$14)/C\$15	=E11*F11
12							
13	*n* =COUNT(B4:B11)					Sum =SUM(G4:G11)	
14	*M* =AVERAGE(B4:B11)		=AVERAGE(C4:C11)			*r* =G13/(B13-1)	
15	σ =STDEV.S(B4:B11)		=STDEV.S(C4:C11)			Pearson *r* =PEARSON(B4:B11,C4:C11)	

(b)

	A	B	C	D	E	F	G
1		Raw scores			z Scores		
2		Mood	Calories		Mood	Calories	
3		X	Y		z_X	z_Y	$z_X * z_Y$
4		6	480		1.00	-0.65	-0.65
5		4	490		0.00	-0.52	0.00
6		7	500		1.50	-0.40	-0.60
7		4	590		0.00	0.72	0.00
8		2	600		-1.00	0.85	-0.85
9		5	400		0.50	-1.64	-0.82
10		3	545		-0.50	0.16	-0.08
11		1	650		-1.50	1.47	-2.21
12							
13	*n*	8				Sum	-5.207
14	*M*	4	531.88			*r*	-.744
15	σ	2	80.18			Pearson *r*	-.744

standard deviation, as shown in Figure 12.7a. Select E4 and fill down through E11, or copy E4 and paste from E5 through E11.

The scatterplot in Figure 12.8 further illustrates the meaning of Pearson correlation coefficient. Participants with small (negative) z scores for mood score tend to have large (positive) z scores for calories consumed. Participants with large (positive) z scores for mood score tend to have small (negative) z scores for calories consumed.

Step 3: Compute the product of each pair's z scores. To complete the next step in the numerator, we compute $z_X z_Y$. Label cell G3 "$z_X * z_Y$", as shown in Figure 12.7. In cell G4, type =E4*F4, as shown in Figure 12.7a. Select G4 and fill down to G11, or copy G4 and paste from G5 to G11. G4 through G11 now contain the product of the z scores from each participant. When each participant's z score for mood is multiplied by his or her z score for calories consumed, most of those products are negative, as shown in cells G4 through G11 in Figure 12.7b.

Step 4: Compute the Pearson correlation coefficient (*r*). Label F13 "Sum" and F14 "*r*", as shown in Figure 12.7. The correlation coefficient is the sum of the products of the z scores $\Sigma(z_X z_Y)$ divided by the number of pairs minus 1 ($n-1$). In cell G13, type =SUM(G4:G11), as shown in Figure 12.7a. Not surprisingly, the sum of the mostly negative products of z scores is −5.207, as shown in Figure 12.7b. In cell G14, type =G13/(B13-1) to obtain the Pearson correlation coefficient, *r*, of −.744, also as shown in Figure 12.7b.

Appendix B

See **Appendix B4,** p. 304, for highlighting, pasting, and filling cells.

See **Appendix B6,** p. 306, for anchoring cell references.

Appendix B

See **Appendix B7**, p. 307, for how to create and format a chart.

FIGURE 12.8 ● Scatterplot of z_X (mood score) and z_Y (calories consumed). *X* and *Y* axes appear at 0, the mean for the *z* score of each variable.

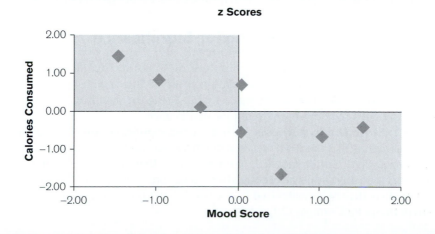

$$r = \frac{-5.207}{7} = -.744$$

Excel also offers a function to calculate a correlation coefficient. In cell G15, type =PEARSON(B4:B11,C4:C11), as shown in Figure 12.7a. The first argument in the function specifies the first array of data, and the second argument in the function specifies the second array of data. This function yields the same result as the previous calculation in cell G14. Although the Analysis ToolPak has an option to do a correlation, the output is limited to a Pearson correlation coefficient. Although there is no advantage to using it for a single bivariate correlation, it could be used to compute a series of bivariation correlations among pairs of variables when there are more than two variables.

Effect Size: The Coefficient of Determination

A correlation coefficient ranges from –1.0 to +1.0, so it can be negative. To compute proportion of variance as an estimate of effect size, we square the correlation coefficient r to make it positive. The value of r^2 or R^2 is called the **coefficient of determination**. The result of this calculation is a value between 0 and +1 that is mathematically equivalent to the value of eta squared (η^2), which we computed for the t tests and analyses of variance (ANOVAs).

In Example 12.1, we want to measure the proportion of variance in calories consumed (eating) that can be explained by ratings of mood. The coefficient of determination for the data in Example 12.1 is

$$r^2 = -(.744)^2 = .553$$

In terms of proportion of variance, we conclude that about 55% of the variability in calories consumed can be explained by participants' ratings of their mood.

The **coefficient of determination (r^2 or R^2)** is a formula that is mathematically equivalent to eta squared and is used to measure the proportion of variance of one factor (Y) that can be explained by known values of a second factor (X).

Hypothesis Testing: Testing for Significance

Coefficient of determination is a formula that is mathematically equivalent to eta squared and is used to measure the proportion of variance of one factor (Y) that can be explained by known values of a second factor (X).

We can also follow the steps to hypothesis testing to test for significance. By doing so, we can determine whether the correlation observed in a sample is present in the population from which the sample was selected. Using the data from Example 12.1, we will conduct a hypothesis test to test for significance.

Step 1: State the hypotheses. To test for the significance of a correlation, the null hypothesis is that there is no relationship between two factors (a zero correlation) in the population. The alternative hypothesis is that there is a relationship between two factors (a positive or negative correlation) in the population. For a population, the correlation coefficient is symbolized by the Greek letter rho, ρ. We can therefore state the hypotheses for Example 12.1 as follows:

H_0: $\rho = 0$ (Mood is not related to eating in the population.)

H_1: $\rho \neq 0$ (Mood is related to eating in the population.)

Step 2: Set the criteria for a decision. We will compute a two-tailed test at a .05 level of significance. The degrees of freedom are the number of scores that are free to vary for X and for Y. All X scores except one are free to vary, and all Y scores except one are free to vary. Hence, the degrees of freedom for a correlation are $n - 2$. In Example 12.1, $n = 8$; therefore, the degrees of freedom for this test are $8 - 2 = 6$.

To locate the critical values for this test, look in Table C.5 in Appendix C. Table 12.1 shows a portion of this table. The alpha levels for one-tailed and two-tailed tests are given in each column, and the degrees of freedom are in the rows. At a .05 level of significance, the critical values for this test are ±.707. The probability is less than 5% that we will obtain a correlation stronger than $r = \pm.707$ when $n = 8$. If r is stronger than or exceeds ±.707, then we reject the null hypothesis; otherwise, we retain the null hypothesis.

> **Appendix A12**
>
> See **Appendix A12,** p. 298, for more on degrees of freedom for parametric tests.

TABLE 12.1 ● A portion of the Pearson correlation table in Table C.5 in Appendix C.

Level of Significance for Two-Tailed Test				
$df = n - 2$	.10	.05	.02	.01
1	.988	.997	.9995	.9999
2	.900	.950	.980	.990
3	.805	.878	.934	.959
4	.729	.811	.882	.917
5	.669	.754	.833	.874
6	.622	.707	.789	.834
7	.582	.666	.750	.798
8	.549	.632	.716	.765
9	.521	.602	.685	.735
10	.497	.576	.658	.708

Source: Table III in Fisher, R. A., & Yates, F. (1974). *Statistical tables for biological, agricultural and medical research* (6th ed.). London, England: Longman Group Ltd. (previously published by Oliver and Boyd Ltd., Edinburgh). Adapted and reprinted with permission of Addison Wesley Longman.

Step 3: Compute the test statistic. The correlation coefficient r is the test statistic for the hypothesis test. We already measured this: $r = -.744$.

Step 4: Make a decision. To decide whether to retain or reject the null hypothesis, we compare the value of the test statistic to the critical values. Because $r = -.744$ exceeds the lower critical value, we reject the null hypothesis. We conclude that the correlation observed between mood and eating reflects a relationship between mood and eating in the population. If we were to report this result in a research journal, it would look something like this:

> Using the Pearson correlation coefficient, a significant relationship between mood and eating was evident, $r = -.744$, $p < .05$.

Although the Analysis ToolPak has an option to do a correlation, the output is limited to a Pearson correlation coefficient and does not yield a p value.

Limitations in Interpretation: Causality, Outliers, and Restriction of Range

Fundamental limitations using the correlational method require that a significant correlation be interpreted with caution. Among the many considerations for interpreting a significant correlation, in this section we consider causality, outliers, and restriction of range.

Causality

Using a correlational design, we do not manipulate an independent variable, and we certainly do not overtly control for other possible factors that may covary with the two variables we measured. For this reason, a significant correlation does not show that one factor causes changes in a second factor (causality). Instead, a significant correlation shows the direction and the strength of the relationship between two factors. To highlight limitations of causality for a correlation, let us look at four possible interpretations for the significant correlation measured in Example 12.1.

1. Decreases in how we feel (mood) can cause an increase in the amount we eat (eating). This possibility cannot be ruled out.

2. Increases in the amount we eat (eating) can cause a decrease in how we feel (mood). So the direction of causality can be in the opposite direction. Hence, instead of changes in mood causing changes in eating, maybe changes in eating cause changes in mood. This possibility, called **reverse causality**, cannot be ruled out either.

3. The two factors could be systematic, meaning that they work together to cause a change. If two factors are systematic, then Conclusions 1 and 2 could be correct. The worse we feel, the more we eat, and the more we eat, the worse we feel. This possibility, that each factor causes the other, cannot be ruled out either.

Reverse causality is a problem that arises when the causality between two factors can be in either direction.

4. Changes in both factors may be caused by a third unanticipated factor, called a **confound variable**. Perhaps biological factors, such as increased parasympathetic activity, make people feel worse and increase how much they want to eat. So, it is increased parasympathetic activity that could be causing changes in both mood and eating. This confound variable and any number of additional confound variables could be causing changes in mood and eating and cannot be ruled out either.

Figure 12.9 summarizes each possible explanation for an observed correlation between mood and eating. The correlational design cannot distinguish between these four possible explanations. Instead, a significant correlation shows that two factors are related. It does not provide an explanation for how or why they are related.

FIGURE 12.9 ● Four potential explanations for a significant correlation.

1. Changes in mood cause changes in eating:

2. Changes in eating cause changes in mood (reverse causality):

3. The two variables work together (systematically) to cause an effect:

4. Changes in both factors are caused by a third confound variable:

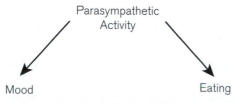

Because factors are measured, but not manipulated, using the correlational method, any one of these possibilities could explain a significant correlation.

A **confound variable**, or **third variable**, is an unanticipated variable not accounted for in a research study that could be causing or associated with observed changes in one or more measured variables.

Outliers

In addition, outliers can obscure the relationship between two factors by altering the direction and the strength of an observed correlation. An outlier is a score that falls substantially above or below most other scores in a data set. Figure 12.10a shows data for the relationship between income and education without an outlier in the data. Figure 12.10b shows how an outlier, such as the income earned by a child movie star, changes the relationship between two factors. Notice in Figure 12.10 that the outlier changed both the direction and the strength of the correlation.

Restriction of Range

When interpreting a correlation, it is also important to avoid making conclusions about relationships that fall beyond the range of data measured. The **restriction of range** problem occurs when the range of data measured in a sample is restricted or smaller than the range of data in the general population.

Figure 12.11 shows how the range of data measured in a sample can lead to erroneous conclusions about the relationship between two factors in a given population. In the figure, a positive correlation for a hypothetical population (top graph) and the correlations in three possible samples we could select from this population (smaller graphs at bottom) are shown. Notice that, depending on the range of data measured, we could identify a positive, a negative, or zero correlation from the same population, although the data in the population are actually positively correlated. To avoid the problem of restriction of range, the direction and the strength of a significant correlation should only be generalized to a population within the limited range of measurements observed in the sample.

Restriction of range is a problem that arises when the range of data for one or both correlated factors in a sample is limited or restricted, compared to the range of data in the population from which the sample was selected.

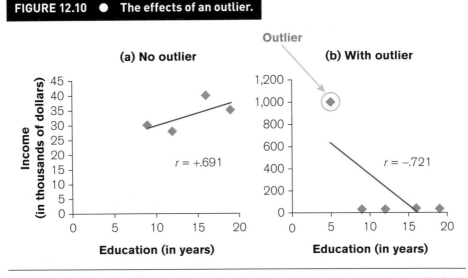

FIGURE 12.10 ● The effects of an outlier.

(a) displays a typical correlation between income and education, with more education being associated with higher income. (b) shows the same data with an additional outlier of a child movie star who earns $1 million. The inclusion of this outlier changed both the direction and the strength of the correlation.

FIGURE 12.11 ● The effects of restriction of range.

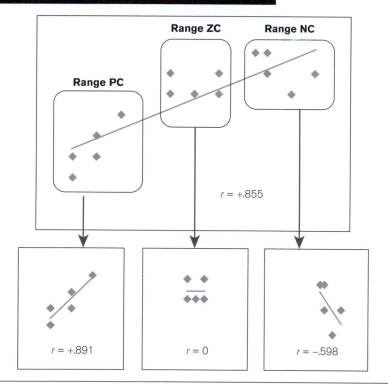

In this population, shown in the top graph, there is a positive correlation between two factors (r = +.855). Also depicted are three possible samples we could select from this population. Range PC shows a positive correlation (r = +.891), Range ZC shows a zero correlation (r = 0), and Range NC shows a negative correlation (r = -.598)—all within the same population. Because different ranges of data within the same population can show very different patterns, correlations should never be interpreted beyond the range of data measured in a sample.

An Alternative to Pearson for Ranked Data: Spearman

The Pearson correlation coefficient is used to describe the relationship between two factors on an interval or ratio scale. To analyze the correlation between factors on different scales of measurement requires new formulas. Each of these new formulas was derived from the Pearson correlation coefficient, and therefore, the Pearson formula can be used to conduct each of the additional tests introduced in this learning unit. In this section, we will compute the Spearman test. This test is appropriate for use with ranked or ordinal data, and it is particularly useful in situations when interval or ratio data contain an outlier, as demonstrated in Example 12.2.

In certain research situations, we want to determine the relationship between two ranked factors (ranks are an ordinal scale measurement). For example, we may want to identify the relationship between different polls in ranking college sports teams, or we may want to see how the order in which a series of tasks is completed is related from the first to the second trial. To measure the relationship between two ranked factors, we use the **Spearman rank-order correlation coefficient (r_s)**, or **Spearman's rho**. If scores for one or both variables are not ranked, then they must be transformed to ranks for this test.

There are several computational formulas for a correlation with ranked or ordinal data. They all produce a value between –1.0 and +1.0. The differences among them are beyond the scope of this text. We present in Example 12.2 one example with raw data converted to ranks.

Note that if one or more ranks are tied, or the same, those tied ranks must be averaged before computing the correlation coefficient. To average, we sum the ranked places that are tied, and divide by the number of ranks. For example, if we have ranks of 1, 2, 2, and 4, we sum the second and third ranks and divide by two: (2+3)/2 = 5/2 = 2.5. The new ranks would be 1, 2.5, 2.5, and 4. If there were more than two tied ranks, we would sum those ranked positions and divide by the number of rank places. Although a few tied ranks present little problem, many tied ranks may call for the use of a different formula that is beyond the scope of this text.

As mentioned above, the formulas for various correlation coefficients were derived from the Pearson formula. Therefore, we will use the Pearson correlation coefficient on ordinal or ranked data, because it yields the same result as a Spearman formula.

Example 12.2. Higher education institutions are concerned about retaining students from the end of the students' first year to the start of their second year. Many factors may influence whether a student stays or transfers. One of them may be whether students feel engaged (Bonet & Walters, 2015). Suppose education researchers examine whether universities with students who felt more engaged retained a higher percentage of students from the first to the second year. For 37 universities, they measure the average student engagement score, which can range from 0 to 60. They also measure student retention as the percentage of students who arrived initially as freshmen and returned as sophomores. Download the spreadsheet titled Engagement_Retention.xlsx from the student study site: http://study.sagepub.com/priviteraexcel1e. We will compute a correlation coefficient for these data using the PEARSON function in Excel.

We calculate the Pearson correlation coefficient in cell C42, as shown in Figure 12.12a, using the function resident in Excel, as we did in Example 12.1. The result is $r = .389$, as shown in Figure 12.12b. With $df = 35$, the critical value at $p = .05$ is .325. If the null hypothesis were that student engagement scores are not related to student retention rate, we would reject the null hypothesis.

The **Spearman rank-order correlation coefficient** (r_s), or **Spearman's rho**, is a measure of the direction and strength of the linear relationship of two ranked factors on an ordinal scale of measurement.

Visual inspection of a scatterplot suggests that data set may contain one outlier, as shown in Figure 12.13. If we simply delete the outlier, we obtain $r = .271$. Try it in your spreadsheet by deleting the value in either B39 or C39, the X and Y values for the apparent outlier.

Rather than delete the apparent outlier, we can minimize its effect by converting scores within each variable to ranks and then computing the correlation coefficient on the ranks. Copy B2 through C3 and paste to E2 through F3. In E1, type "Ranks of" to identify these columns of numbers. In cell E4, type =RANK.AVG(B4,B$4:B$40). This function returns the rank of a number (the first argument in the function) in the context of a range of numbers (the second argument in the function). The RANK.

AVG function will return the average rank when there are tied ranks, as we noted above was essential to do. Anchoring rows 4 through 40 with the $ allows us to easily paste or fill to other cells. Select E4 through E40 and fill down, or select E4 and copy and paste from E5 through E40. Notice that there are two pairs of tied ranks that have been appropriately averaged. Select E4 through F40 and fill right or copy E4 through E40 and paste from F4 to F40. Notice that there are three pairs of tied ranks.

We calculate the correlation coefficient in cell F42, as shown in Figure 12.12a, using the function resident in Excel. The result is $r_s = .270$, as shown in Figure 12.12b. The critical values for a Spearman correlation coefficient are given in Table C.6 in Appendix C. A portion of this table is shown in Table 12.2. Table C.6 is similar to the table for Pearson except that n (not df) is listed in the rows. Because $n = 37$ in Example 12.2, and 37 is not listed in the table, the most conservative next step is to choose the next smallest value for degrees of freedom, which is at 35 in the table. The critical value at a .05 level of significance is .335. Again, for this test the null hypothesis would have been that student engagement scores were not related to student retention rate; because the value of r_s (.270) now does not exceed the critical value (.335), we would retain the null hypothesis.

TABLE 12.2 ● A portion of the Spearman correlation table in Table C.6 in Appendix C.

Source of Variation	SS	df	MS	F_{obt}
Between groups	4.50	2	2.25	4.50
Between persons	8.25	3	2.75	
Within groups (error)	3.00	6	0.50	
Total	15.75	11		

Source: Reprinted with permission from the Journal of the American Statistical Association. Copyright 1972 by the American Statistical Association. All rights reserved.

FIGURE 12.12 ● Pearson and Spearman correlation coefficients for the same data set. (a) Functions for calculating the correlation coefficients. (b) Results of the functions for Pearson and Spearman.

(a)

	A	B	C	D	E	F
37	34	26.1	76.1		=RANK.AVG(B37,B$4:B$40)	=RANK.AVG(C37,C$4:C$40)
38	35	32.6	63.3		=RANK.AVG(B38,B$4:B$40)	=RANK.AVG(C38,C$4:C$40)
39	36	4.3	61.2		=RANK.AVG(B39,B$4:B$40)	=RANK.AVG(C39,C$4:C$40)
40	37	44.5	90.6		=RANK.AVG(B40,B$4:B$40)	=RANK.AVG(C40,C$4:C$40)
41						
42		Pearson *r*	=PEARSON(B4:B40,C4:C40)		Spearman (r_s)	=PEARSON(E4:E40,F4:F40)

(Continued)

FIGURE 12.12 ● (Continued)

(b)

	A	B	C	D	E	F
1					Ranks of	
2		Engagement	Retention		Engagement	Retention
3	Institution	Score	Rate		Score	Rate
37	34	26.1	76.1		34	26
38	35	32.6	63.3		30	34
39	36	4.3	61.2		37	37
40	37	44.5	90.6		12	6.5
41						
42		Pearson r	0.389		Spearman (r_s)	0.270

FIGURE 12.13 ● Retention rate as a function of student engagement scores. The data point circled in gray could be an outlier that unduly affects the correlation coefficient.

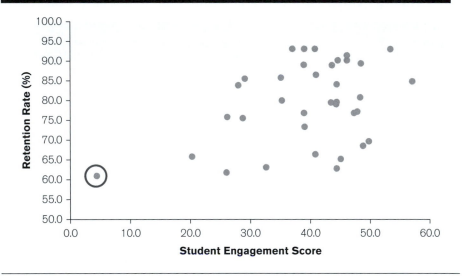

An Overview of Other Alternatives to Pearson

Each of the new formulas introduced in this learning unit was derived from the Pearson correlation coefficient, and therefore, the Pearson formula can be used to conduct each of the additional tests introduced in this unit. The decision about which test to use depends largely on the scale of measurement of the data being measured. Table 12.3 lists Pearson, Spearman, and two other common alternatives to Pearson with explanations for when each test is appropriate based on the scale of measurement for the data being measured.

Correlation Coefficient	Scale of Measurement for Correlated Variables
TABLE 12.3 ● The scales of measurement for factors tested using the Pearson, Spearman, point-biserial, and phi correlation coefficients.	
Pearson	Both factors are interval or ratio data.
Spearman	Both factors are ranked or ordinal data.
Point-Biserial	One factor is dichotomous (nominal data), and the other factor is continuous (interval or ratio data).
Phi	Both factors are dichotomous (nominal data).

LEARNING UNIT 13

Linear Regression

Excel Toolbox

Mathematical operators

- −
- *
- ^2 [square]
- +
- /
- ^.5 [square root]

Functions

- COUNT
- AVERAGE
- SUM
- SLOPE
- INTERCEPT
- PEARSON

Other tools

- format cells
- freeze panes

(Continued)

(Continued)

- anchor cell reference
- fill down or paste
- create chart
- format chart
- Analysis ToolPak

O ne of the basic goals of science is prediction. In mental health, for example, we often want to predict the occurrence of disorders, identify factors that predict such disorders, and understand behavioral measures that predict the prevention or treatment of such disorders. Prediction, introduced in this learning unit, is an extension of correlation. Indeed, we will use the correlation coefficient, introduced in Learning Unit 12, to help us make predictions.

In Learning Unit 12, we described procedures that used the correlation coefficient, r, to measure the extent to which two factors (X and Y) were related. The value of r indicates the direction and strength of a correlation. When r is negative, two factors change in opposite directions; when r is positive, two factors change in the same direction. The closer r is to ±1.0, the stronger the correlation, and the more closely two factors are related.

We can use the information provided by r to predict values of one factor, given known values of a second factor. The strength of a correlation reflects how closely a set of data points falls to a regression line (the straight line that most closely fits a set of data points). In this learning unit, we use the value of r to compute the equation of a regression line and then use this equation to predict values of one factor, given known values of a second factor in a population—this statistical procedure is called **linear regression**. We begin by introducing the fundamentals of linear regression in the next section.

Linear regression, also called **regression**, is a statistical procedure used to determine the equation of a regression line for a set of data points, and the extent to which the regression equation can be used to predict values of one factor given known values of a second factor in a population.

The **predictor variable** or **known variable** (X) is the variable with values that are known and can be used to predict values of another variable.

The **criterion variable** or **to–be– predicted variable** (Y) is the variable with unknown values that can be predicted or estimated, given known values of the predictor variable.

Fundamentals of Linear Regression

Linear regression, like analysis of variance, can be used to analyze any number of factors. In this learning unit, however, we use regression to describe the linear relationship between two factors (X and Y) because many of the behaviors measured by researchers are related in a linear or straight–line pattern.

To use linear regression, we identify two types of variables: the predictor variable and the criterion variable. The **predictor variable (X)** is the variable with values that are known and can be used to predict values of the criterion variable; the predictor variable is plotted on the x–axis of a graph. The **criterion variable (Y)** is the variable with unknown values that we are trying to predict, given known values of the predictor variable; the criterion variable is plotted on the y–axis of a graph.

We can use linear regression to answer the following questions about the pattern of data points and the significance of a linear equation:

1. Is a linear pattern evident in a set of data points?

2. Which equation of a straight line can best describe this pattern?

3. Are the predictions made from this equation significant?

The Regression Line

Once we have determined that there is a linear pattern in a set of data points, we want to find the regression line, or the straight line that has the best fit. The criterion we use to determine the equation of a regression line is the sum of squares (SS), or the sum of the squared distances of data points from a straight line. The line associated with the smallest total value for SS is the best–fitting straight line, which we call the regression line. The method of least squares is the statistical procedure used to square the distance that each data point falls from the regression line and to sum the squared distances.

To illustrate why each deviation is squared before summing, suppose we measure two factors, one predictor variable plotted on the x–axis and one criterion variable plotted on the y–axis. Figure 13.1 shows hypothetical data for these two factors.

The distance of each data point from the regression line is shown in the figure. Notice that data points A and D fall on the regression line. The distance of these data points from the regression line is 0. However, data points B and C in the scatter plot fall two units from the regression line. Data point B falls two units below the regression line (-2 units), and data point C falls two units above the regression line ($+2$ units). The sum of the distances of each data point from the regression line is $0 + 0 + 2 - 2 = 0$. A zero solution will always occur when we sum the distances of data points from a regression line—same as the outcome observed when we sum the deviations of scores from the mean (see Learning Unit 2).

To avoid a solution of 0, we compute SS by squaring the distance of each data point from the regression line, then summing—same as the solution used to find the variance of scores from the mean (see Learning Unit 2). When we square the distance of each data point and then sum, we obtain $SS = 0^2 + 0^2 + 2^2 + (-2)^2 = 8$. This is the smallest possible solution for SS. The method of least squares, then, is the method of determining the line associated with the least squares, or the smallest possible value of the sum of squares (SS).

Any line other than the regression line shown in Figure 13.1 will produce a value of SS that is larger than 8 in this example. To illustrate, we fit another straight line to the same data in Figure 13.2. The distance of each data point from this line is $+3$ units and $+4$ units above the line and -2 units and -3 units below the line. If we compute the SS for these distances, we obtain $SS = 3^2 + 4^2 + (-2)^2 + (-3)^2 = 38$. This result is much larger than $SS = 8$, which is the value we obtained for the least squares regression line. Different lines have different values of SS. The regression line, or line of best fit, is the line with the smallest or least value of the SS.

The Equation of the Regression Line

If we know the equation of the regression line, we can predict values of the criterion variable, Y, so long as we know values of the predictor variable, X. To make use of this equation, we need to know the equation of a straight line. The equation of a straight line is

$$Y = bX + a$$

FIGURE 13.1 ● A table and scatter plot of four hypothetical data points.

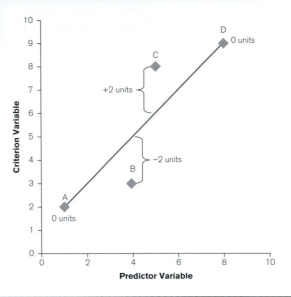

Predictor Variable	Criterion Variable
X	Y
1	2
4	3
5	8
8	9

The regression line and the distances, in units, between the data points and the regression line are shown. Both the table and the scatter plot show the same data.

FIGURE 13.2 ● A scatter plot of the same data shown in Figure 13.1.

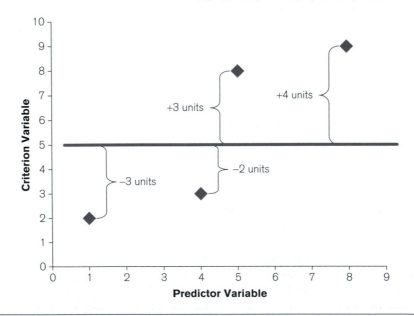

In this graph, a horizontal line is fit to the data, and the data points are now a farther total distance from the line compared to the best-fitting straight line for these data points, which is shown in Figure 13.1.

In this equation, Y is a value we plot for the criterion variable, X is a value we plot for the predictor variable, b is the slope of a straight line, and a is the y–intercept (where the line crosses the y–axis). To make use of this equation, we need to know the values of a and b in the equation. In this section, we explain what a and b measure, and in the next section, we use the method of least squares to find the values of a and b.

The **slope**, represented as b, is a measure of how much a regression line rises or declines along the y–axis as values on the x–axis increase. The slope indicates the direction of a relationship between two factors, X and Y. When values of Y increase as values of X increase, the slope is positive. When the values of Y decrease as values of X increase, the slope is negative.

Thus, the slope of a straight line is used to measure the change in Y relative to the change in X:

$$\text{slope } (b) = \frac{\text{change in } Y}{\text{change in } X}$$

The **y–intercept**, represented as a, is where a straight line crosses the y–axis on a graph. More specifically, the y–intercept is the value of Y when $X = 0$. The y–intercept is the value of the criterion variable (Y) when the predictor variable (X) is absent or equal to 0.

Using the Method of Least Squares to Find the Regression Line

We use the **method of least squares** to find the equation of the regression line, which is the best–fitting straight line to a set of data points. Using this method in Example 13.1, we measure SS for Factor X and Factor Y and then use these values to compute the slope (b) and y–intercept (a) of the regression line. To use the method of least squares, we complete three steps:

Step 1: Compute preliminary calculations.

Step 2: Calculate the slope (b).

Step 3: Calculate the y–intercept (a).

Example 13.1. Factors that can predict the effectiveness of behavioral therapies are of interest to clinicians and researchers (Cuijpers, Cristea, Weitz, Gentili, & Berking, 2016; Hans & Hiller, 2013). As an example of research for this area of study, suppose a psychologist wants to predict the effectiveness of a behavioral therapy (measured as the number of symptoms patients express) given the number of sessions a patient attends. She selects a sample of eight patients who expressed the same number of symptoms at the start of treatment. She then records the number of sessions attended (X) and the number of symptoms expressed (Y) by each patient. Download Behavioral_Therapy.xlsx from the student study site:

The **slope (b)** of a straight line is used to measure the change in Y relative to the change in X. When X and Y change in the same direction, the slope is positive. When X and Y change in opposite directions, the slope is negative.

The **y–intercept (a)** of a straight line is the value of the criterion variable (Y) when the predictor variable (X) equals 0.

The **method of least squares** is a statistical procedure used to compute the slope (b) and y–intercept (a) of the best–fitting straight line to a set of data points.

http://study.sagepub.com/priviteraexcel1e. Column A contains an identifier for each participant. Column B contains each participant's number of sessions. Column C contains each participant's number of symptoms by the end of therapy.

Step 1: Compute preliminary calculations. We begin by making preliminary calculations. The signs (+ and –) of the values we measure for each factor are essential to making accurate computations. The goal of this step is to compute the sum of squares needed to calculate the slope (*b*) and *y*–intercept (*a*). We will describe each calculation in Figure 13.3 working from left to right. Refer to that Figure to see each of the cell references for the four stages described below.

Appendix B

See **Appendix B2,** p. 301, for formatting cells.

See **Appendix B3,** p. 303, for freezing panes.

Stage 1. Compute the average X and Y score. In this example, the number of sessions attended is the predictor variable, *X*, and the number of symptoms expressed is the criterion variable, *Y*. Calculate the mean number of sessions by typing into cell B14 =AVERAGE(B4:B11). Select B14 and fill right to C14, or copy and paste into C14. These yield the means for the two variables: $M_X = 5.25$ and $M_Y = 2.75$.

Appendix B

See **Appendix B4**, p. 304, for highlighting, pasting, and filling cells.

See **Appendix B6**, p. 306, for anchoring cell references.

Stage 2. Subtract from each score its respective group's mean. In cell E4 enter =B4-B$14, using the $ to anchor the cell reference for the mean in row 14. Select E4 and fill down to E11, or copy E4 and paste from E5 to E11. Select E4 through E11 and fill right to F4 through F11, or copy E4 through E11 and paste from F4 to F11.

Stage 3. Multiply deviation scores for X and Y, and square the deviation scores for X and for Y. We computed deviation scores by subtracting from each score its group's mean. Now,

The **sum of products (SP)** is the sum of squares for two factors, *X* and *Y*, which are also represented as SS_{XY}. SP is the numerator for the Pearson correlation formula. To compute SP, we multiply the deviation of each *X* value by the deviation of each *Y* value.

- Multiply across the rows in columns E and F: In cell G4 enter =E4*F4.

- Square the values in column E: In cell H4 enter =E4^2.

- Square the values in column F: In cell I4 enter =F4^2.

- Select G4 through I4 and fill down to G11 through H11, or copy G4 through I4 and paste from G5 through I11.

Stage 4. Calculating SS_{XY}, SS_X, and SS_Y. Label cells G13 through I13, respectively, "SS_{XY}," "SS_X," and "SS_Y". In cell G14 enter =SUM(G4:G11), which yields the sum of squares for *XY*, also called the **sum of products (SP):** SP = SS_{XY} = –22.50. Select G14 and fill right to I14, or copy G14 and paste from H14 to I14. H14 now contains the sum of squares for *X*: $SS_X = 39.50$, and I14 now contains the sum of squares for *Y*: $SS_Y = 15.50$.

FIGURE 13.3 ● Calculating the regression line equation. (a) Formulas and functions. (b) Results of the formulas and functions.

(a)

	A	B	C	D	E	F	G	H	I
1			Number of						
2		Sessions	Symptoms		Sessions	Symptoms			
3	Patient	X	Y		X-M_X	Y-M_Y	$(X$-$M_X)*(Y$-$M_Y)$	$(X$-$M_X)^2$	$(Y$-$M_Y)^2$
4	A	9	0		=B4-B$14	=C4-C$14	=E4*F4	=E4^2	=F4^2
5	B	5	3		=B5-B$14	=C5-C$14	=E5*F5	=E5^2	=F5^2
6	C	8	2		=B6-B$14	=C6-C$14	=E6*F6	=E6^2	=F6^2
7	D	2	5		=B7-B$14	=C7-C$14	=E7*F7	=E7^2	=F7^2
8	E	6	3		=B8-B$14	=C8-C$14	=E8*F8	=E8^2	=F8^2
9	F	3	4		=B9-B$14	=C9-C$14	=E9*F9	=E9^2	=F9^2
10	G	5	2		=B10-B$14	=C10-C$14	=E10*F10	=E10^2	=F10^2
11	H	4	3		=B11-B$14	=C11-C$14	=E11*F11	=E11^2	=F11^2
12									
13	*n*	=COUNT(B4:B11)					SS_{XY}	SS_X	SS_Y
14	*M*	=AVERAGE(B4:B11)	=AVERAGE(C4:C11)			=SUM(G4:G11)		=SUM(H4:H11)	=SUM(I4:I11)
15									
16						Terms in regression line equation			
17						*a* (*y*-intercept)	=C14-(H18*B14)		=INTERCEPT(C4:C11,B4:B11)
18						*b* (slope)	=G14/H14		=SLOPE(C4:C11,B4:B11)
19									
20						Prediction equation: Ŷ=-0.57(X)+5.74			
21						if X = 7			
22						then Ŷ = =H18*H21+H17			

(b)

	F	G	H	I
1				
2	Symptoms			
3	Y-M_Y	$(X$-$M_X)*(Y$-$M_Y)$	$(X$-$M_X)^2$	$(Y$-$M_Y)^2$
4	-2.75	-10.31	14.06	7.56
5	0.25	-0.06	0.06	0.06
6	-0.75	-2.06	7.56	0.56
7	2.25	-7.31	10.56	5.06
8	0.25	0.19	0.56	0.06
9	1.25	-2.81	5.06	1.56
10	-0.75	0.19	0.06	0.56
11	0.25	-0.31	1.56	0.06
12				
13		SS_{XY}	SS_X	SS_Y
14		-22.50	39.50	15.50
15				
16		Terms in regression line equation		
17		*a* (*y*-intercept)	5.74	5.74
18		*b* (slope)	-0.57	-0.57
19				
20		Prediction equation: Ŷ=-0.57(X)+5.74		
21		if X =	7	
22		then Ŷ =	1.75	

Step 2: Calculate the slope (*b*). The slope of a straight line indicates the change in Y relative to the change in X. Because the value of SP, which is the same as SS_{XY}, can be negative or positive, this value indicates the direction that Y changes as X increases. We will use SP to estimate changes in Y, and we will use SS_X to estimate changes in X. The formula for computing the slope (*b*) is

$$b = \frac{\text{change in } Y}{\text{change in } X} = \frac{SS_{XY}}{SS_X} \text{ or } \frac{SP}{SS_X}$$

Label cells G16, G17, and G18, respectively, "Terms in regression line equation", "*a* (*y*–intercept)", and "*b* (slope)", as shown in Figure 13.3. We already computed SS_{XY} = –22.50 and SS_X = 39.50. In cell H18 enter =G14/H14, which yields the slope of the best–fitting straight line, as shown in Figure 13.3:

$$b = \frac{-22.50}{39.50} = -0.57$$

Understanding now the meaning of the slope from seeing these calculations, we could also use the Excel function called SLOPE. In cell I18, enter =SLOPE(C4:C11,B4:B11), as shown in Figure 13.3. Note that in contrast to the order of arguments for PEARSON, this function requires values for Y, the consequent, first. The values for X, the antecedent, are in the second argument. That is why the values in column C appear before the values in column B. Cell I18 displays the result of the function, which is identical to our calculation in H18.

Step 3: Calculate the *y*–intercept (*a*). The *y*–intercept is the value of Y when $X = 0$. To find this value, we need to know the mean of Y (M_Y), the mean of X (M_X), and the slope we just computed. The formula for determining the *y*–intercept (*a*) is

$$a = M_Y - bM_X$$

We already computed M_Y = 2.75, M_X = 5.25, and b = –0.57. In cell H17 enter =C14-(H18*B14), as shown in Figure 13.3, which yields the *y*–intercept of the regression line:

$$a = 2.75 - [(-0.57)(5.25)] = 5.74$$

Understanding now the meaning of the *y*–intercept from seeing these calculations, we could also use the Excel function called INTERCEPT. In cell I17, enter =INTERCEPT(C4:C11,B4:B11), as shown in Figure 13.3. Note again that the values for Y are specified in the first argument and the values for X in the second argument. Cell I17 displays the result of the functions, which is identical to our calculation in H17.

Because we computed the slope, $b = -0.57$, and the *y*–intercept, $a = 5.74$, we can now state the equation of the least squares regression line as

$$\hat{Y} = -0.57X + 5.74$$

In this equation, $\hat{Y}$ is the predicted value of Y, given values of X. For example, we can set up cells in the spreadsheet to calculate $\hat{Y}$ for a given X. Label cell G20 "Prediction equation: $\hat{Y} = -0.57(X) + 5.74$". Then label G21 and G22, respectively, "if $X =$" and "then $\hat{Y} =$". Suppose we want to predict the number of symptoms for a patient who has attended seven therapy sessions ($X = 7$). In cell H21 enter 7. In cell H22, type =H18*H21+H17, as shown in Figure 13.3. This formula references the slope in H18, the value of X of 7 therapy sessions in H21, and the y–intercept in H17. It yields the value:

$$\hat{Y} = -0.57(7) + 5.74 = 1.75$$

In this example, we expect or predict that a patient will express 1.75, or between 1 and 2, symptoms following four therapy sessions. In this way, we use the equation to show how many symptoms we expect a patient to exhibit after a particular number of therapy sessions.

We have calculated the regression equation that describes the relationship between sessions of behavior therapy and symptoms. We will now create a graph with the trend line plotted to visualize the relationship. Highlighting B3 through C11 allows us to select a chart from the ribbon of the Insert tab. Select a scatter plot. Select the chart just created, and from the Chart Design ribbon, select Trendline from Add Chart Element. Your chart should resemble the one in Figure 13.4.

Appendix B

See **Appendix B7**, p. 307, for more on creating and formatting a chart.

FIGURE 13.4 ● Scatter plot and trend line for session of therapy and symptoms displayed.

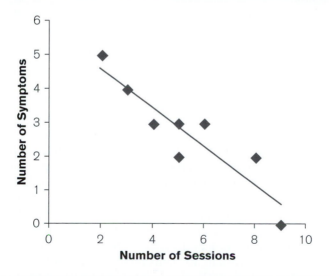

Note the correspondence between the regression equation we calculate and the graph created. Two aspects are worth mentioning.

1. If we were to extend the trendline in the graph to the y–axis, it would intersect the axis close to but below the value of 6. This corresponds to the y–intercept calculated of 5.74.

2. For every decrease in symptoms by 1, number of sessions increases by about 2. This corresponds to the slope calculated of -0.57.

Using Regression to Determine Significance

Analysis of regression, or **regression analysis**, is a statistical procedure used to test hypotheses for one or more predictor variables to determine whether the regression equation for a sample of data points can be used to predict values of the criterion variable (Y) given values of the predictor variable (X) in the population.

In Example 13.1, we used the method of least squares to determine the equation of the regression line for a sample of data. However, we did not determine the significance of this regression line. In other words, we did not determine whether this equation could be used to predict values of Y (criterion variable), given values of X (predictor variable) in the population.

To determine whether the regression equation for a sample of data can be used to make predictions of Y in the population, we use **analysis of regression**. An analysis of regression is similar to an ANOVA. In an analysis of regression, we measure the variation in Y and split the variation into two sources; these are comparable to the two sources of variation used in the one–way between–subjects ANOVA in Learning Unit 10. In this section, we follow the four steps to hypothesis testing to perform an analysis of regression using the data in Example 13.1.

Step 1: State the hypotheses. The null hypothesis is that the variance in Y is not related to changes in X. The alternative hypothesis is that the variance in Y is related to changes in X. The hypotheses in Example 13.1 are as follows:

H_0: The variance in the number of symptoms expressed (Y) is not related to changes in the number of therapy sessions attended (X).

H_1: The variance in the number of symptoms expressed (Y) is related to changes in the number of therapy sessions attended (X).

Regression variation is the variance in Y that is related to or associated with changes in X. The closer data points fall to the regression line, the larger the value of regression variation.

Residual variation is the variance in Y that is not related to changes in X. This is the variance in Y that is left over or remaining. The farther data points fall from the regression line, the larger the value of residual variation.

To evaluate these hypotheses, we measure the variance in Y that is and is not related to changes in X. The variance in Y that is related to changes in X is called **regression variation**. The closer data points fall to the regression line, the larger the regression variation will be. The variance in Y that is not related to changes in X is called **residual variation**. This is the variance in Y that is residual, left over, or remaining. The farther data points fall from the regression line, the larger the residual variation will be.

An analysis of regression measures only the variance in Y, the criterion variable, because it is the value we want to predict. The total variance measured, then, equals the variance in Y. As shown in Figure 13.5, we attribute some of the variance in Y to changes in X (regression variation); the remaining variance in Y is not attributed to changes in X (residual variation). The more variance in Y that we attribute to changes

FIGURE 13.5 ● An analysis of regression measures the variance in Y.

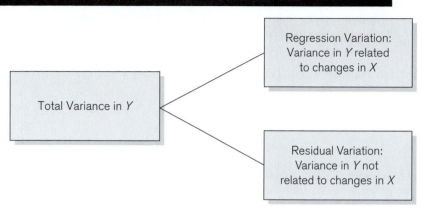

Some of the variance is attributed to changes in X; the remaining variance is not attributed to changes in X.

in X (regression variation), the more likely we are to decide to reject the null hypothesis and conclude that values of X significantly predict values of Y.

Step 2: Set the criteria for a decision. We will use a .05 level of significance, as we have for all hypothesis tests. We compute degrees of freedom (*df*) for each source of variation. The degrees of freedom for regression variation, or degrees of freedom numerator, are equal to the number of predictor variables. Because we have one predictor variable (X) in Example 13.1, *df* for regression variation is 1.

The degrees of freedom for residual variation, or degrees of freedom denominator, are equal to the sample size minus 2. We subtract 2 from n because we plot two scores for each data point (one X score and one Y score). In Example 13.1, $n = 8$, so *df* for residual variation is $(8 - 2) = 6$.

> **Appendix A12**
>
> See **Appendix A12,** p. 298, for more on degrees of freedom for parametric tests.

The critical value for this test is listed in Table C.3 in Appendix C. The critical value for a test with 1 (*df* numerator) and 6 (*df* denominator) degrees of freedom at a .05 level of significance is 5.99.

Step 3: Compute the test statistic. To compute the test statistic, we measure variance as a mean square, the same as we did using the ANOVA tests. We place the variance or mean square (*MS*) attributed to regression variation in the numerator, and the variance or mean square attributed to residual variation in the denominator:

$$F_{obt} = \frac{\text{variance of } Y \text{ related to changes in } X}{\text{variance of } Y \text{ not related to changes in } X} = \frac{MS_{regression}}{MS_{residual}}$$

To compute the test statistic, we need to calculate r^2, which is the coefficient of determination and is needed to calculate values in the F table. The F table is set up just as it was for the ANOVA tests in Learning Unit 10. We will do this in five stages. As shown in Figure 13.6, we prepare for the calculations by labeling K3 through K5, respectively, "Regression Statistics", "r", and "r^2". Next, as shown in Figure 13.7, we label K11 through K14, respectively, "Source of Variation", "Regression", "Residual (error)", and "Total". Finally, also as shown in Figure 13.7, we label L11 through O11, respectively, "SS", "df", "MS", and "F_{obt}".

Stage 1. Calculate r^2. Using the data given in Figure 13.3, we can calculate the value of r:

$$r = \frac{SS_{XY}}{\sqrt{SS_X SS_Y}}$$

In cell L4 enter =G14/(H14*I14)^0.5, as shown in Figure 13.6a. This formula references the cells containing SS_{XY}, SS_X, and SS_Y, which yields –.91, as shown in Figure 13.6b. The value in L4 is the same correlation coefficient obtained when using the PEARSON function, as shown in cell M4 in Figure 13.6.

$$r = \frac{-22.50}{\sqrt{39.50 \times 15.50}} = -.91$$

Typing into cell L5 =L4^2, as shown in Figure 13.6a, yields r^2, the coefficient of determination, which is .83, as shown in Figure 13.6b.

Stage 2. Calculate sums of squares. In our computations of the test statistic, we first compute the SS for each source of variation and then complete the F table. Multiplying the coefficient of determination by the variability in Y (SS_y) will give us the proportion of variance in Y (number of symptoms) that is predicted by or related to changes in X (the number of sessions attended):

$$SS_{regression} = r^2 SS_Y$$

FIGURE 13.6 ● Correlation coefficient and coefficient of determination. (a) Formulas and functions. (b) Results of the formulas and functions.

(a)

	K	L	M
3	**Regression Statistics**		
4	*r*	=G14/(H14*I14)^0.5	=PEARSON(B4:B11,C4:C11)
5	*r²*	=L4^2	

(b)

	K	L	M
3	**Regression Statistics**		
4	*r*	-.91	-.91
5	*r²*	.83	

In cell L12 type =L5*I14, as shown in Figure 13.7, which yields:

$$SS_{\text{regression}} = .83 \times 15.50 = 12.82$$

The total variability of Y is 15.50 ($SS_Y = 15.50$), of which we attribute 12.83 units of variability to changes in X. The remaining sum of squares, or sum of squares residual, is computed by multiplying SS_Y by the remaining proportion of variance $(1 - r^2)$:

$$SS_{\text{residual}} = (1 - r^2)\, SS_Y$$

The residual variation formula will give us the proportion of variance in Y (number of symptoms) that is not predicted by or related to changes in X (the number of sessions attended). If we substitute the values of r^2 and SS_Y, we obtain the remaining variation in Y measured as the sum of squares residual. In cell L13 type =(1–L5)*I14, as shown in Figure 13.7a, which yields

$$SS_{\text{residual}} = (1 - .83) \times 15.50 = 2.68$$

as shown in Figure 13.7b.

These two sources of variation, regression and residual (error), equal total variation in Y. When we add the values for $SS_{\text{regression}}$ and SS_{residual}, this will sum to the total variability in Y. Thus, typing into cell L14 =SUM(L12:L13), as shown in Figure 13.7a, will yield the same result as in cell I14: 15.50, as shown in Figure 13.3b.

$$SS_Y = SS_{\text{regression}} + SS_{\text{residual}} = 12.83 + 2.67 = 15.50$$

FIGURE 13.7 ● Summary table for regression analysis. (a) Formulas. (b) Results of the calculations of the formulas.

(a)

	K	L	M	N	O
11	*Source of Variation*	*SS*	*df*	*MS*	*F*obt
12	Regression	=L5*I14	1	=L12/M12	=N12/N13
13	Residual (error)	=(1-L5)*I14	=B13-2	=L13/M13	
14	Total	=SUM(L12:L13)	=SUM(M12:M13)		
15					
16		s_e =N13^0.5			

(b)

	K	L	M	N	O
11	*Source of Variation*	*SS*	*df*	*MS*	*F*obt
12	Regression	12.82	1	12.82	28.66
13	Residual (error)	2.68	6	0.45	
14	Total	15.50	7		
15					
16	s_e	0.67			

Stage 3. Calculate degrees of freedom. As described in Step 2, the degrees of freedom for the regression is 1, because we have one predictor variable. Enter 1 into cell M12, as shown in Figure 13.7. The degrees of freedom for the residual (error) is the number of pairs minus two ($n - 2$). Enter into cell M13 =B13-2, as shown in Figure 13.7a, which yields $n - 2 = 6$, as shown in Figure 13.7b. The total degrees of freedom is the sum of the degrees of freedom for regression and residual. Enter into cell M14 =SUM(M12:M13), as shown in Figure 13.7a, which yields $1 + 6 = 7$, as shown in Figure 13.7b.

Stage 4. Calculate mean squares. As with ANOVA, covered in Learning Units 10 and 11, the mean square is the sum of squares divided by the degrees of freedom:

$$MS = \frac{SS}{df}$$

Divide $SS_{regression}$ by $df_{regression}$ by typing into cell N12 =L12/M12, as shown in Figure 13.7a. This yields $MS_{regression}$:

$$MS_{regression} = \frac{12.82}{1} = 12.82$$

as shown in Figure 13.7b.

Divide $SS_{residual}$ by $df_{residual}$ by typing into cell N13 =L13/M13, as shown in Figure 13.7a. This yields $MS_{residual}$:

$$MS_{residual} = \frac{2.68}{6} = 0.45$$

as shown in Figure 13.7b.

Stage 5. Calculate F. The test statistic for Example 13.1 is the $MS_{regression}$ divided by the $MS_{residual}$, as stated at the outset of Step 3. In cell O12 type =N12/N13, as shown in Figure 13.7a, which yields

$$F_{obt} = \frac{12.82}{0.45} = 28.66$$

as shown in Figure 13.7b.

Step 4. Make a decision. To decide whether to retain or reject the null hypothesis, we compare the value of the test statistic to the critical value. Because $F_{obt} = 28.66$ exceeds the critical value (5.99), we reject the null hypothesis. We conclude that the number of symptoms expressed (Y) is related to changes in the number of therapy sessions attended (X). That is, we can predict values of Y, given values of X in the population, using the equation we computed using the method of least squares: $\hat{Y} = -0.57X + 5.74$. If we were to report this result in a research journal, it would look something like this:

An analysis of regression showed that the number of therapy sessions attended can significantly predict the number of symptoms expressed, $F(1, 6) = 28.83$, $p < .05$, $R^2 = .83$, using the following equation: $\hat{Y} = -0.57X + 5.74$.

In Example 13.1, we concluded that the equation $\hat{Y} = -0.57X + 5.74$ can predict values of Y given values of X in the population. Of course, not all the data points in our sample fell exactly on this line. Many data points fell some distance from the regression line. Whenever even a single data point fails to fall exactly on the regression line, there is error in how accurately the line will predict an outcome. This error can be measured using the **standard error of estimate (s_e)**.

The standard error of estimate, s_e, measures the standard deviation or distance that data points in a sample fall from the regression line. It is computed as the square root of the mean square residual:

$$s_e = \sqrt{MS_{\text{residual}}}$$

In Example 13.1, the mean square residual was 0.45 (cell N13 in Figure 13.7). Hence, the standard error of estimate is

$$s_e = \sqrt{0.45} = 0.67$$

The standard error of estimate indicates the accuracy of predictions made using the equation of a regression line, with smaller values of s_e associated with better or more accurate predictions. The standard error of estimate is quite literally a standard deviation (or the square root of the variance) for the residual variation. So it is a measure of the error or deviation of data points from the regression line.

Computing the Analysis of Regression With the Analysis ToolPak

We can also calculate the regression and the ANOVA using the Analysis ToolPak available in Excel for easy and accurate calculation. Click on the Data tab, and then on the Data Analysis icon all the way to the right. Select "Regression," shown in Figure 13.8a, which yields the dialog box shown in Figure 13.8b. Enter $C$3:$C$11 for Input Y Range and $B$3:$B$11 for Input X Range. Note that this includes the labels for the levels of the two variables. Check the Labels box so that the output contains the labels from B3 and C3. Select Output Range for the result to be

The **standard error of estimate (s_e)** is an estimate of the standard deviation or distance that a set of data points falls from the regression line. The standard error of estimate equals the square root of the mean square residual.

FIGURE 13.8 ●   Performing a regression analysis with Analysis ToolPak in Excel. (a) Selecting "Regression" to perform a regression analysis. (b) Specifying the location of the data and output for the regression analysis.

(a)

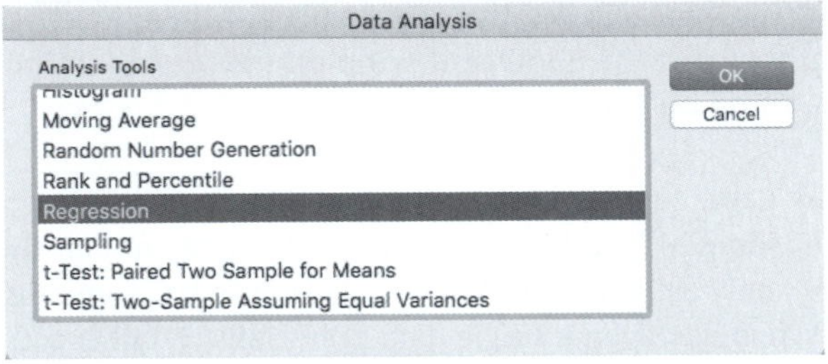

(b)

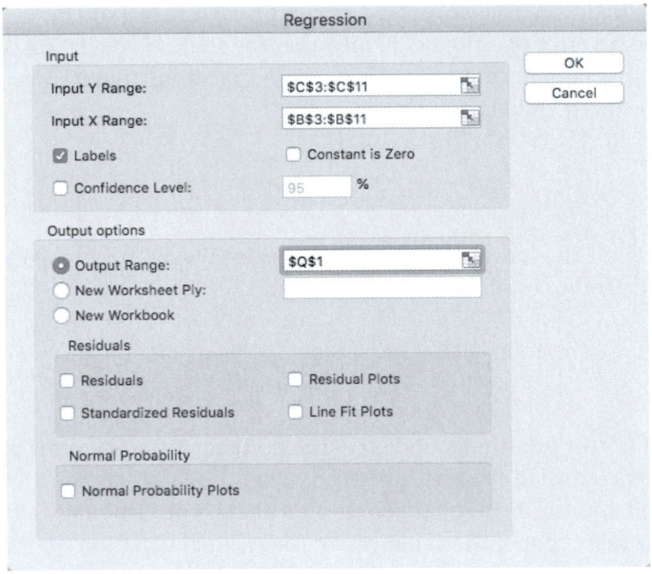

displayed in the worksheet and click in the box to the right. Then click in cell Q1 of the spreadsheet. We will be able to compare the output from the Analysis ToolPak with the numbers that we calculated.

Clicking "OK" on the dialog box returns the output table in Figure 13.9. Notice that the values for

Multiple R and R Square (rows 4 and 5)

Regression, Residual, and Total (rows 12 through 14), and

Intercept and (the slope) X (rows 17 and 18)

are the same as the values that we calculated to the left on those same rows.

FIGURE 13.9 ● Results of the regression analysis using the Analysis ToolPak.

	Q	R	S	T	U	V	W	X	Y
1	SUMMARY OUTPUT								
2									
3	*Regression Statistics*								
4	Multiple R	.91							
5	R Square	.83							
6	Adjusted R Square	.80							
7	Standard Error	.67							
8	Observations	8							
9									
10	ANOVA								
11		*df*	*SS*	*MS*	*F*	*Significance F*			
12	Regression	1	12.82	12.82	28.66	.002			
13	Residual	6	2.68	0.45					
14	Total	7	15.50						
15									
16		*Coefficients*	*Standard Error*	*t Stat*	*P-value*	*Lower 95%*	*Upper 95%*	*Lower 95.0%*	*Upper 95.0%*
17	Intercept	5.74	0.61	9.46	.00008	4.26	7.22	4.26	7.22
18	X	-0.57	0.11	-5.35	.00174	-0.83	-0.31	-0.83	-0.31

• Appendix A •

Core Statistical Concepts

This appendix provides an overview of core statistical concepts that relate to many areas of analysis. Concepts such as shapes of distributions and scales of measurement, for example, are important for many aspects of inferential statistics and for understanding data across learning units. For this reason, we provide these core concepts in an easy to search appendix to help you find and refer to these concepts as you progress through the learning units in this book. This eliminates the need to search the book for where these concepts were first introduced. In each learning unit, marginal notes are provided to tell you where in this appendix core concepts are needed to guide your learning.

A1: Normal and Skewed Distributions

The **normal distribution** is a symmetrical distribution in which scores are similarly distributed above and below the mean, the median, and the mode at the center of the distribution. In 1733, Abraham de Moivre introduced the normal distribution as a mathematical approximation to the binomial distribution, although de Moivre's 1733 work was not widely recognized until the accomplished statistician Karl Pearson rediscovered it in 1924. The shape of the curve in a normal distribution can drop suddenly at the tails, or the tails can be stretched out. Figure A1.1 shows three examples of normal distributions—notice in the figure that a normal distribution can vary in appearance.

A normal distribution has many characteristics that make it *normally* distributed. Here we highlight six core characteristics of a normal distribution:

1. The mean, the median, and the mode are all located at the 50th percentile. In a normal distribution, the mean, the median, and the mode are the same value at the center of the distribution. Thus, half the data (50%) in a normal distribution fall above the mean, the median, and the mode, and half the data (50%) fall below these measures.

2. The normal distribution is symmetrical. The normal distribution is symmetrical, in that the distribution of data above the mean is the same as the distribution of data below the mean. If you were to fold a normal curve in half, both sides of the curve would exactly overlap.

3. The mean can equal any value. The normal distribution can be defined by its mean and standard deviation. The mean of a normal distribution can equal any number from positive infinity ($+\infty$) to negative infinity ($-\infty$).

> The **normal distribution** is a theoretical distribution in which scores are symmetrically distributed above and below the mean, the median, and the mode at the center of the distribution.

279

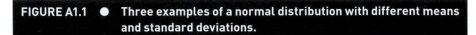

FIGURE A1.1 ● **Three examples of a normal distribution with different means and standard deviations.**

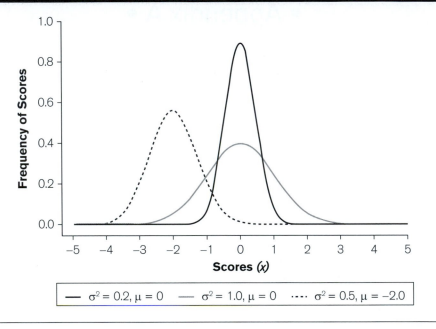

4. The standard deviation can equal any positive value. The standard deviation (*SD*) is a measure of variability. Data can vary (*SD* > 0) or not vary (*SD* = 0). A negative standard deviation is meaningless. In the normal distribution, then, the standard deviation can be any positive value greater than 0.

5. The total area under the curve of a normal distribution is equal to 1.0. The area under the normal curve has the same characteristics as probability: Portions of it vary between 0 and 1 and can never be negative. In this way, the area under the normal curve can be used to determine the probabilities at different points along the distribution. In Characteristic 1, we stated that 50% of all data fall above and 50% fall below the mean. This is the same as saying that half (.50) of the area under the normal curve falls above and half of the area (.50) falls below the mean. The total area, then, is equal to 1.0. Figure A1.2 shows the proportions of area under the normal curve 3 *SD* above and below the mean (±3 *SD*).

6. The tails of a normal distribution are asymptotic. In a normal distribution, the tails are asymptotic, meaning that as you travel away from the mean the tails of the distribution are always approaching the *x*-axis but never touch it. Because the tails of the normal distribution go out to infinity, this characteristic allows for the possibility of outliers (or scores far from the mean) in a data set.

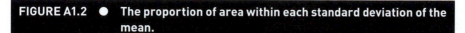

FIGURE A1.2 ● The proportion of area within each standard deviation of the mean.

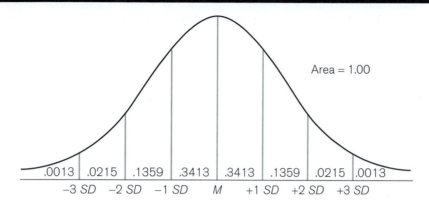

Area = 1.00

.0013 | .0215 | .1359 | .3413 | .3413 | .1359 | .0215 | .0013
−3 SD −2 SD −1 SD M +1 SD +2 SD +3 SD

For distributions that are not normal, but instead skewed: Some data sets can have scores that are unusually high or low that skew (or distort) the data set. A **skewed distribution** occurs whenever a data set includes a score or group of scores that fall substantially above (**positively skewed distribution**) or substantially below (**negatively skewed distribution**) most other scores in a distribution. Figure A1.3

FIGURE A1.3 ● The position of the mean and mode for positively skewed and negatively skewed distributions, relative to the normal distribution.

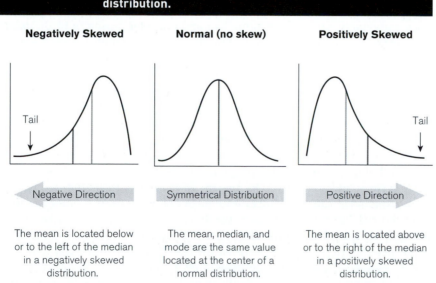

Negatively Skewed

Tail

Negative Direction

The mean is located below or to the left of the median in a negatively skewed distribution.

Normal (no skew)

Symmetrical Distribution

The mean, median, and mode are the same value located at the center of a normal distribution.

Positively Skewed

Tail

Positive Direction

The mean is located above or to the right of the median in a positively skewed distribution.

Notice that in each distribution shown here, the mode does not change, but the mean is pulled in the direction of the tail of a skewed distribution.

A **skewed distribution** is a distribution of scores that includes scores that fall substantially above or below most other scores in a data set.

A **positively skewed distribution** is a distribution of scores that includes scores that are substantially larger (toward the right tail in a graph) than most other scores.

A **negatively skewed distribution** is a distribution of scores that includes scores that are substantially smaller (toward the left tail in a graph) than most other scores.

illustrates how a skewed distribution shifts the value of the mean. In a normal distribution, the mean and mode are equal (they are both at the center of the distribution). Notice in Figure A1.3 that the value of the mean in a skewed distribution is pulled toward the skewed data points. In a positively skewed distribution, the mean is greater than the mode; in a negatively skewed distribution, the mean is less than the mode. The location of the median is actually unpredictable, and it can fall on any side of the mode, depending on how the scores are distributed (Ottenbacher, 1993; Sinacore, Chang, & Falconer, 1992).

Scores that fall substantially above or below most other scores in a distribution will distort the value of the mean, making it a less meaningful measure for describing all data in a distribution. The value of the median, on the other hand, is not influenced by the value of these unusually high or low scores. For this reason, the median is more representative of all data in a skewed distribution and is therefore the most appropriate measure of central tendency to describe these types of distributions.

A2: Scales of Measurement

In the early 1940s, Harvard psychologist S. S. Stevens coined the terms *nominal*, *ordinal*, *interval*, and *ratio* to classify **scales of measurement** (Stevens, 1946). Scales of measurement are rules that describe the properties of numbers. These rules imply that the extent to which a number is informative depends on how it was used or measured.

Numbers on a **nominal scale** identify something or someone; they provide no additional information. Common examples of nominal numbers include ZIP codes, license plate numbers, credit card numbers, country codes, telephone numbers, and Social Security numbers. In research settings, common examples include a person's race, sex, nationality, sexual orientation, hair and eye color, season of birth, marital status, or other demographic or personal information. These numbers simply identify locations, vehicles, or individuals and nothing more. One credit card number, for example, is not greater than another; it is simply different.

An **ordinal scale** of measurement is one that conveys only that some value is greater or less than another value (i.e., order). Examples of ordinal scales include finishing order in a competition, education level, and rankings. These scales only indicate that one value is greater than or less than another, so differences between ranks do not have meaning. Consider, for example, the *U.S. News & World Report* rankings for the top psychology graduate school programs in the United States. Table A2.1 shows the rank, college, and actual score for the top 25 programs, including ties, in 2017. Based on ranks alone, can we say that the difference between the psychology graduate programs ranked 3 and 7 is the same as the difference between those ranked 13 and 17? No. In both cases, 7 ranks separate the schools. However, if you look at the actual scores for determining rank, you find that the difference between ranks 3 and 7 is 0.2 points, whereas the difference between ranks 13 and 17 is 0.1 point. Hence, the difference in points is not the same. Ranks alone do not convey this difference. They simply indicate that one rank is greater than or less than another rank.

Scales of measurement identify how the properties of numbers can change with different uses. Four scales of measurement are nominal, ordinal, interval, and ratio.

Nominal scales are measurements in which a number is assigned to represent something or someone.

Ordinal scales are measurements that convey order or rank alone.

TABLE A2.1 ● Rankings are ordinal scale data.		
Rank	**College Name**	**Actual Score**
1	Stanford University	4.8
1	University of California, Berkeley	4.8
3	Harvard University	4.7
3	University of California, Los Angeles	4.7
3	University of Michigan, Ann Arbor	4.7
3	Yale University	4.7
7	University of Illinois at Urbana-Champaign	4.5
8	Massachusetts Institute of Technology	4.4
8	Princeton University	4.4
8	University of Minnesota, Twin Cities	4.4
8	University of Pennsylvania	4.4
8	University of Texas at Austin	4.4
13	University of California, San Diego	4.3
13	University of North Carolina at Chapel Hill	4.3
13	University of Wisconsin–Madison	4.3
13	Washington University in St. Louis	4.3
17	Carnegie Mellon University	4.2
17	Columbia University	4.2
17	Duke University	4.2
17	Indiana University Bloomington	4.2
17	Northwestern University	4.2
17	University of Chicago	4.2
17	University of Virginia	4.2
24	Cornell University	4.1
24	The Ohio State University	4.1

A list of the *U.S. News & World Report* rankings for the top 25 psychology graduate school programs in the United States in 2017, including ties (left column) and the actual points used to determine their rank (right column).

Source: https://www.usnews.com/best-graduate-schools/top-humanities-schools/psychology-rankings.

An **interval scale** of measurement can be understood readily by two defining principles: equidistant scales and no true zero. An equidistant scale is a scale with intervals or values distributed in equal units. Many behavioral scientists assume that scores on a rating scale are distributed in equal units. For example, if you are asked to rate your satisfaction with a spouse or job on a 7-point scale from 1 (*completely unsatisfied*) to 7 (*completely satisfied*), then you are using an interval scale, if you make this assumption. By assuming that the distance between each point (1 to 7) is the same or equal, a statement such as "The difference in job satisfaction among men and women was 2 points" is appropriate.

An interval scale does not, however, have a *true zero*. A common example of a scale without a true zero is temperature. A temperature equal to zero for most measures of temperature does not mean that there is no temperature; it is just an arbitrary zero point. Values on a rating scale also have no true zero. For the example we used, a rating of 1 indicated the absence of satisfaction. Each value (including 0) is arbitrary. That is, we could use any number to represent none of something. Measurements of latitude and longitude also fit this criterion. The implication is that without a true zero, there is no outright value to indicate the absence of the phenomenon you are observing (so a zero proportion is not meaningful). For this reason, stating a ratio such as "Satisfaction ratings were three times greater among men compared to women" is not appropriate with interval scale measurements.

Ratio scales are similar to interval scales in that scores are distributed in equal units. Yet, unlike interval scales, a distribution of scores on a ratio scale has a true zero. Common examples of ratio scales include counts and measures of length, height, weight, and time. For scores on a ratio scale, order is informative. For example, a person who is 30 years old is older than another who is 20. Differences are also informative. For example, the difference between 70 and 60 seconds is the same as the difference between 30 and 20 seconds (the difference is 10 seconds). Ratios are also informative on this scale because a true zero is defined—it truly means nothing. Hence, it is meaningful to state that 60 pounds is twice as heavy as 30 pounds. This is an ideal scale in behavioral research, because any mathematical operation can be performed on the values that are measured.

A3: Outliers

Interval scales are measurements that have no true zero and are distributed in equal units.

Ratio scales are measurements that have a true zero and are distributed in equal units.

Outliers are extreme scores that fall substantially above or below most of the scores in a particular data set.

For any type of data distribution, the distribution can include **outliers** in a set of data. An outlier is an extreme score that falls substantially above or below most other scores in a distribution of data. Outliers are typically scores that are not representative of most of the remaining data. These atypical scores can exist in almost any type of distribution, and graphically, outliers can be found in the "tails" of the distribution.

In a normal distribution, for example, if an outlier exists on one side of the distribution, then an outlier will also be at approximately the same distance from the mean on the other side of the distribution—because each "tail" of a normal distribution is similar. For example, suppose a final exam had a normal distribution of scores with a mean of 70. All students, except for two, scored between a 60 and an 80, with one outlier student scoring a 100 and another outlier student scoring a 40. One score is 20 points higher than the next best grade; the other score is 20 points lower than the next worst grade. In this example, an outlier is in each tail (one below and one above the mean) in this normal distribution.

In a skewed distribution, if an outlier exists, it exists on only one side of the distribution, or in only one tail. For a positively skewed distribution, the outlier would be located in the upper tail; in a negatively skewed distribution, the outlier would be located in the lower tail. For example, annual household income in the United States is positively skewed, with most citizens earning a modest income and a few outliers (in the upper tail of the distribution of income) earning millions or even billions annually. On the other hand, times to run one mile would be negatively skewed, with a few outliers (e.g., Olympic athletes) in the lower tail of the distribution able to complete it in less than 4 minutes, and most others needing much longer to run one mile. In each case, an outlier, or outliers, exists in one tail.

The types of distributions that can have outliers have implications for choosing an appropriate measure of central tendency to describe a data set. In Learning Unit 1 (p. 3), we discuss the various distributions for choosing an appropriate measure of central tendency. It can be useful to review this to understand how outliers can affect how we describe data.

A4: The Empirical Rule for Normal Distributions

For various shapes of distributions, the question often arises regarding the informativeness of the standard deviation to describe how scores vary in a given distribution. For data that are normally distributed, the standard deviation is quite informative. For normal distributions with any mean and any variance, we can make the following three statements:

1. At least 68% of all scores lie within one standard deviation of the mean.

2. At least 95% of all scores lie within two standard deviations of the mean.

3. At least 99.7% of all scores lie within three standard deviations of the mean.

These statements are often called the **empirical rule**. Empiricism is *to observe*. The name of this rule arises because many of the behaviors that researchers *observe* are approximately normally distributed. The empirical rule, then, is an approximation—the percentages are correct, give or take a few fractions of a standard deviation. Nevertheless, this rule is critical because of how specific it is for describing normally distributed behavior.

To illustrate how useful the empirical rule is, consider how we can apply it to a sample data set and can come to some immediate conclusions about the distribution of scores. Suppose that a researcher selects a sample of 5,000 full-time employees and records the time (in hours per week) that they spend thinking about work when they are not working. These data are normally distributed with a mean equal to 12 ($M = 12$) and a standard deviation equal to 4 ($SD = 4$). Without knowing the time for each employee, we still know a lot about this sample. In fact, because the data are normally distributed, we can distribute at least 99.7% of the data simply by plotting three standard deviations above and below the mean, as shown in Figure A4.1. We add the SD

The **empirical rule** states that for data that are normally distributed, at least 99.7% of data lie within three standard deviations of the mean, at least 95% of data lie within two standard deviations of the mean, and at least 68% of data lie within one standard deviation of the mean.

FIGURE A4.1 ● The empirical rule.

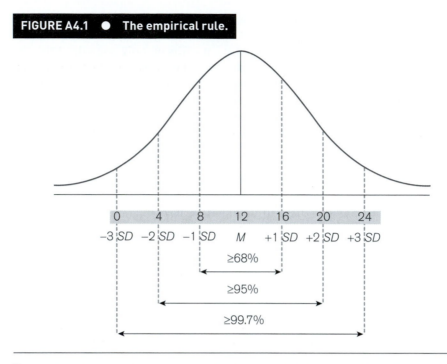

The proportion of scores under a normal curve at each standard deviation above and below the mean. The data are distributed as 12 ± 4 (*M* ± *SD*).

value to *M* to plot standard deviations above the mean; to plot standard deviations below the mean, we subtract the *SD* value from *M*.

Although the researcher did not report the time (in hours) recorded for each individual employee in this sample, we know a lot about these data because we know the mean and the standard deviation. For example, we know that at least 68% of employees spent between 8 and 16 hours thinking about work when they were not working (per week), and we know that any time (in hours) beyond three standard deviations from the mean is unlikely. This makes the empirical rule very informative for determining the likelihood of outcomes for data that are normally distributed.

A5: Chebyshev's Theorem for Any Type of Distribution

For various shapes of distributions, the question often arises regarding the informativeness of the standard deviation to describe how scores vary in a given distribution. For data with any type of distribution (normal, skewed, or any other shape) the standard deviation is still quite informative. The Russian mathematician Pafnuty Chebyshev devised the theorem that explains the standard deviation for any distribution.

Chebyshev's theorem defines the percentage of data from any distribution that will be contained within any number of standard deviations (where *SD* > 1).

Chebyshev explained that the proportion of all data for any distribution (sample or population; normal or not) must lie within *k* standard deviations above and below the mean, where *k* is greater than 1. **Chebyshev's theorem** is defined as follows:

$$1 - \frac{1}{k^2}, \text{where } k \text{ is greater than } 1$$

Notice that if k were 1 standard deviation (1 SD), the solution would be 0%. So this theorem can describe only the proportion of data falling within *greater* than 1 SD of the mean. Let us see how this theorem compares to the empirical rule. Recall that 95% of all data fall within 2 SD of the mean for normal distributions. Chebyshev's theorem explains that for any distribution *at least* 75% of the data fall within 2 SD of the mean:

$$1 - \frac{1}{k^2} = 1 - \frac{1}{2^2} = 0.75 \text{ or } 75\%$$

Recall that 99.7% of all data fall within 3 SD of the mean for normal distributions. Chebyshev's theorem explains that for any distribution *at least* 89% of the data fall within 3 SD of the mean:

$$1 - \frac{1}{k^2} = 1 - \frac{1}{3^2} = 0.89 \text{ or } 89\%$$

In fact, it would take 10 standard deviations (10 SD) from the mean to account for *at least* 99% of the data for nonnormal distributions according to Chebyshev's theorem:

$$1 - \frac{1}{k^2} = 1 - \frac{1}{10^2} = 0.99 \text{ or } 99\%$$

While the standard deviation is most precise for normal distributions, because most data fall within 3 SD of the mean, it is also informative for any other distribution. We can still define the percentage of scores that will fall within each standard deviation from the mean for any distribution using this theorem. The informativeness of the standard deviation for any type of distribution, thus, makes it one of the most complete and meaningful measures for determining the variability of scores from their mean.

A6: Expected Value as a Long-Term Mean

In addition to using probability distributions to identify the probabilities for each outcome of a random variable, we can use them to predict the outcome (or value of the outcome) of a random variable that we can expect to occur, on average. For example, you may read an article reporting that one murder is expected to occur in the United States every 32.6 minutes, or that we can expect the average mother to have 3.14 children in her lifetime. Of course, murders do not occur exactly every 32.6 minutes, and it is not even possible for a mother to have 3.14 children. Instead, you should interpret these statistics as averages.

The use of probability to predict the expected mean value of a random variable is called **mathematical expectation**, or **expected value**. To compute the mean value, μ, of a random variable, we (1) multiply each possible outcome, x, by the probability of its occurrence, p, and (2) sum all the products:

A **mathematical expectation**, or **expected value**, is the mean, or average expected outcome, of a given random variable. The expected outcome of a random variable is the sum of the products for each random outcome multiplied by the probability of its occurrence.

$$\mu = \Sigma(xp)$$

By definition, to determine the expected value of a random variable, we compute the mean of a probability distribution of that random variable. The mean of a probability distribution, then, is the value we predict will occur on average.

We can think of expected value as a long-term mean. To illustrate, suppose we flip two fair coins three times and observe two heads face up on each flip. The random variable is the number of heads per coin flip. The possible outcomes of the random variable are 0, 1, and 2 flips of heads. In three flips, we observed two heads face up on each flip. On the basis of these observations, can we say that we should expect to observe two heads on every flip? No, because we only flipped the coins three times. On average, we did observe two heads on each flip, but with a finite number of flips, the mean is a short-term mean—it is the mean for a finite number of observations of a random variable.

Expected value, on the other hand, is an estimate of the mean outcome for a random variable assuming that the random variable was observed an infinite number of times. An expected value is not based on making three observations; instead, the expected value is based on the assumption that the two fair coins were flipped an infinite number of times—it is a long-term mean.

To find the expected value, we multiply the value of each outcome of the random variable by its corresponding probability and then sum the products:

$$\mu = (0 \times .25) + (1 \times .50) + (2 \times .25) = 1.00.$$

Table A6.1 shows the probability distribution for flipping heads with two fair coins.

On average, we expect one to land heads up each time we flip two fair coins. Of course, in three flips, we may not observe this outcome, but if we flipped the two coins an infinite number of times, we would expect one to land heads up per flip. So expected value is really a long-term mean—it is the average expected outcome for a random variable, assuming that the random variable is observed an infinite number of times.

TABLE A6.1 ● The probability distribution for flipping heads with two fair coins.			
Number of Heads	**0**	**1**	**2**
$p(x)$	.25	.50	.25

A7: The Informativeness of the Mean and Standard Deviation for Finding Probabilities

Finding probabilities for scores in a sample or population requires knowledge of the type of distribution for the data, and knowing the mean and standard deviation. Here, let's assume that a set of data are normally distributed to illustrate how the mean and standard deviation are informative for finding probabilities.

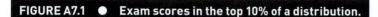

FIGURE A7.1 ● Exam scores in the top 10% of a distribution.

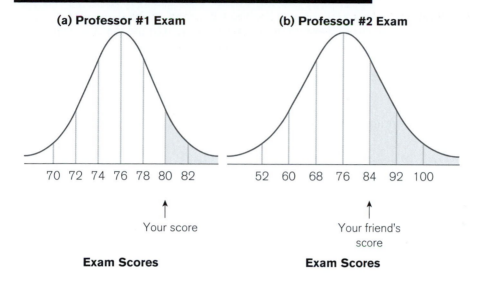

A distribution of exam scores with your grade on Professor 1's exam (a) and your friend's grade on Professor 2's exam (b). M = 76 in both distributions, but the standard deviations are different.

Keep in mind that the standard deviation is very informative, particularly for normally distributed data, which is why we will use this distribution in our example. To illustrate, consider that when students get an exam grade back, they often compare their grades to the grades of others in the class. Suppose, for example, that two professors give an exam, where the top 10% of scores receive an A grade. You take the exam given by Professor 1 and receive an 80 on the exam. Figure A7.1(a) shows that grades for that exam were 76 ± 2.0 ($M \pm SD$). You then ask your friend how he did on Professor 2's exam and find that he scored an 84 on the same exam. Figure A7.1(b) shows that grades for that exam were 76 ± 8.0 ($M \pm SD$). Thus the mean grade for each exam was a 76.

Because the mean grade is the same in both distributions, you might conclude that your friend performed better on the exam than you did, but you would be wrong. To see why, we can follow the steps to locate the cutoff score for earning an A on the exam, which is the top 10% of scores in each distribution.

The lowest score you can get and still receive an A on Professor 1's exam can be computed as follows:

Step 1: The top 10% of scores is $p = .1000$ toward the tail located in Column C in the unit normal table in Table C.1 in Appendix C. The z score associated with $p = .1000$ is $z = 1.28$.

Step 2: Substitute 1.28 for z in the z transformation formula and solve for x:

$$1.28 = \frac{x - 76}{2}$$

$$x - 76 = 2.56 \text{ (multiply both sides by 2)}$$
$$x = 78.56 \text{ (solve for } x\text{).}$$

Your score on Professor 1's exam was an 80. Your score is in the top 10%; you earned an A on the exam.

The lowest score you can get and still receive an A on Professor 2's exam can be computed as follows:

Step 1: We already located this z score. The z score associated with the top 10% is $z = 1.28$.

Step 2: Substitute 1.28 for z in the z transformation equation and solve for x:

$$1.28 = \frac{x - 76}{8}$$

$$x - 76 = 10.24 \text{ (multiply both sides by 8)}$$
$$x = 86.24 \text{ (solve for } x\text{).}$$

Your friend's score on Professor 2's exam was an 84. This score is outside the top 10%; your friend did not earn an A on the exam. Therefore, your 80 is an A, and your friend's 84 is not, even though the mean was the same in both classes. The mean tells you only the average outcome—the standard deviation tells you the distribution of all other outcomes. Your score was lower than your friend's score, but you outperformed a larger percentage of your classmates than your friend did. The standard deviation is important because it gives you information about how your score compares relative to all other scores.

A8: Comparing Differences Between Two Groups

When data are grouped, a visual inspection of the data by groups can often be quite informative. Using an example with just two groups, we use the test statistic to evaluate whether two groups are different (i.e., the difference is statistically significant, and we decide to reject the null hypothesis) or are the same (i.e., the difference is not statistically significant, and we decide to retain the null hypothesis). In terms of evaluating the difference between two groups, we are really determining the extent to which scores between the groups are overlapping. The less that scores in two groups overlap, the more likely we are to decide that two groups are different.

To illustrate how we identify whether two groups are different, Figure A8.1 shows data for two hypothetical experiments in which there is a 3-point treatment effect between two groups in both experiments; that is, the mean difference between the two groups is 3.0. When scores do not overlap, as shown in Figure A8.1a (left figure), all scores for the group receiving Treatment A are smaller than scores for the group receiving Treatment B. This result indicates that the groups are likely different—Treatment A likely produced the 3-point effect, because individuals at each level, or in each group, are behaving differently.

FIGURE A8.1 ● **A hypothetical example of two experiments in which there is no overlap (a) in one experiment and there is overlap (b) in scores between groups in the second experiment.**

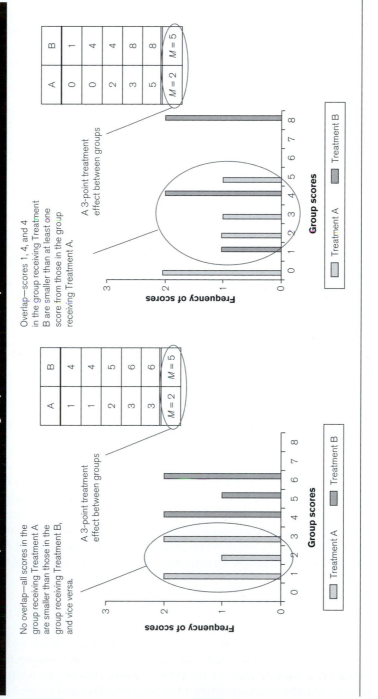

When scores do overlap, as shown in Figure A8.1b (right figure), then any observed difference between two or more groups in an experiment is likely due to random variability, or error. Although the same 3-point treatment effect was observed in Figure A8.1b, some participants receiving Treatment B behaved as if they received Treatment A; that is, their scores overlap with the scores of those receiving Treatment A. When scores overlap with those for other groups, it indicates that the 3-point treatment effect between groups is likely not significant—greater overlap increases the amount of error measured. Hence, the two groups are less likely to be different when participant response substantially overlaps from one group to the next.

To think of this another way, we can ask the following two questions as we work through the same data given in Figure A8.1:

1. Are groups different? If yes, then the manipulation is causing the effect.

2. Are people different? If yes, then individual differences are causing an effect.

When viewing a graph of data, we identify all data for one group and look to see how many scores from the other group fall within the range of scores for the group we identified. As illustrated in Figure A8.1, when scores in each group do not overlap (left figure), we can determine that the groups are different, because we can clearly divide the scores by group. When the scores from each group do overlap (right figure), we can determine that people are different, because we cannot clearly divide the scores by group. Using this strategy to interpret data presented graphically can help you decipher how to recognize whether groups are different or people are different.

Keep in mind that the strategy introduced here can only be used to get an idea of whether people are different or groups are different. To determine the actual likelihood that people are different or groups are different, we use inferential statistical analysis.

A9: Calculation and Interpretation of the Pooled Sample Variance

The pooled sample variance is the mean sample variance of two samples. When the sample size is unequal, the variance in each group or sample is weighted by its respective degrees of freedom. A pooled sample variance is the mean sample variance for two samples. When the sample size is unequal, the variance is a weighted mean so that the pooled sample variance is weighted toward the sample mean computed from the larger sample size—the larger n is, the better the estimate of sample variance will be. The formula for computing pooled sample variance when the sample size is different in each group is

$$s_p^2 = \frac{s_1^2 (df_1) + s_2^2 (df_2)}{df_1 + df_2}$$

The degrees of freedom are the weights in the formula. When we have equal sample sizes, we do not have to weight each sample variance by its respective degrees of freedom. Thus, we can compute the pooled sample variance by adding the two sample variances and dividing by 2 when the sample size is equal or the same in each group:

$$s_p^2 = \frac{s_1^2 + s_2^2}{2}$$

When we have equal sample sizes, we do not have to weight the sample variances by their degrees of freedom. We compute a straightforward arithmetic mean of the two sample variances.

TABLE A9.1 ● The sample sizes and variances for two hypothetical samples.		
Sample:	**1**	**2**
Sample Size	$n_1 = 20$	$n_2 = 20$
Sample Variance	$S_1^2 = 12$	$S_2^2 = 18$

To illustrate, suppose we have two samples with the sizes and variances listed in Table A9.1. Notice both samples are the same size and therefore have the same degrees of freedom: Both samples have 19 degrees of freedom. If we substitute the values of s^2 and df into the formula for the pooled sample variance with unequal sample sizes, we obtain

$$s_p^2 = \frac{s_1^2(df_1) + s_2^2(df_2)}{df_1 + df_2} = \frac{12(19) + 18(19)}{19 + 19} = 15$$

Notice that the value for the pooled sample variance is the middle value between the two sample variances (12 and 18) when the sample sizes are equal. If we substitute the values of s^2 and df into the formula for the pooled sample variance with equal sample sizes, we obtain the same value for the pooled sample variance:

$$s_p^2 = \frac{s_1^2 + s_2^2}{2} = \frac{12 + 18}{2} = 15$$

Both formulas for pooled sample variance produce the same result when $n_1 = n_2$. Only when the sample sizes are unequal is it necessary to weight each sample variance by its respective degrees of freedom.

A10: Reducing Standard Error by Computing Difference Scores

The related-samples t test is different from the two-independent-sample t test in that first we subtract one score in each pair from the other to obtain the *difference score* for each participant; then we compute the test statistic.

There is a good reason for finding the difference between scores in each pair before computing the test statistic using a related-samples t test: It eliminates the source of error associated with observing different participants in each group or treatment. When we select related samples, we observe the same, or matched, participants in each group, not different participants. So we can eliminate this source of error.

Consider the hypothetical data shown in Table A10.1 for four participants (A, B, C, and D) observed in two groups (Q and Z). Table A10.1 identifies three places where differences can occur with two groups. The null hypothesis makes a statement about the mean difference between groups, which is the difference we are testing. Any other difference is called *error*, because these other differences cannot be attributed to having different groups.

As shown in Table A10.2, when we reduce pairs of scores to a single column of difference scores, we eliminate the between-persons error that was illustrated in Table A10.1. Between-persons error is associated with differences associated with observing different participants in each group or treatment. However, using the related-samples design, we observe the same (or matched) participants in each group, not different participants, so we can eliminate this source of error before computing the test statistic.

Error in a study is measured by the estimate of standard error. Eliminating between-persons error makes the total value of error smaller, thereby reducing standard error. This is a key advantage of computing difference scores prior to computing the test statistic: It reduces standard error, thereby increasing the power to detect an effect.

TABLE A10.1 ● A hypothetical set of data for four participants.

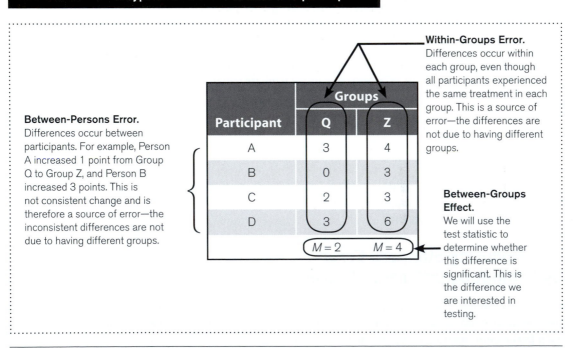

There are three places where differences can occur. Mean differences (the between-groups effect) are the differences we are testing. The other two places where differences occur are regarded as errors in that they have nothing to do with having different groups.

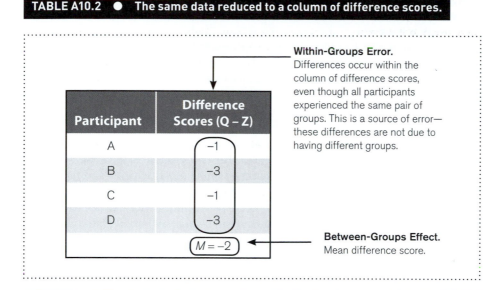

Participant	Difference Scores (Q – Z)
A	−1
B	−3
C	−1
D	−3
	M = −2

TABLE A10.2 ● The same data reduced to a column of difference scores.

Within-Groups Error. Differences occur within the column of difference scores, even though all participants experienced the same pair of groups. This is a source of error—these differences are not due to having different groups.

Between-Groups Effect. Mean difference score.

Notice that when we find the difference between paired scores, only one source of error remains (within-groups error). The between-persons error is eliminated when the same or matched participants are observed in each group.

A11: Categories of Related-Samples Designs

Related samples are samples in which the participants are observed in more than one group or matched on common characteristics. There are two types of research designs commonly used to select related samples: the repeated-measures design and the matched-pairs design. Both research designs are briefly described in this appendix.

The most common related-samples design is the *repeated-measures design,* in which each participant is observed repeatedly, meaning that the same participants are observed in each group. Table A11.1 shows a situation with two groups. In a

TABLE A11.1 ● In a repeated-measures design with two treatments, *n* participants are observed two times.

Group 1	Group 2
n_1	n_1
n_2	n_2
n_3	n_3
n_4	n_4
n_5	n_5

repeated-measures design, each participant (n_1, n_2, etc.) is observed twice (once in each group). We can create repeated measures by using a pre-post design or a within-subjects design.

Using the *pre-post design*, we measure a dependent variable for participants observed before (pre) and after (post) a treatment. For example, we can measure athletic performance (the dependent variable) in a sample of athletes before and after a training camp. We can compare the difference in athletic performance before and after the camp. This type of repeated-measures design is limited to observing participants two times (i.e., before and after a treatment).

Using the *within-subjects design*, we observe participants across many groups but not necessarily before and after a treatment. For two groups, suppose we study the effects of exercise on memory. We can select a sample of participants and have them take a memory test after completing an anaerobic exercise, and again after completing an aerobic exercise. In this example, we observe participants twice, but not necessarily before and after a treatment. Thus, this design can be used with more than two groups as well. Any time the same participants are observed in each group, either pre-post or within-subjects, we are using the repeated-measures design to observe related samples.

The *matched-pairs design* is also used to study related samples. In the matched-pairs design, participants are selected and then matched, experimentally or naturally, based on common characteristics or traits. The matched-pairs design is limited to observing two groups, where pairs of participants are matched. Using this design, Table A11.2 shows a situation with two groups. In a matched-pairs design, different, yet matched, participants (n_1, n_2, etc.) are observed in each treatment, and scores from each matched pair of participants are compared.

We can obtain matched pairs in one of two ways: experimental manipulation or natural occurrence. Matching through experimental manipulation is typical for research studies in which the researcher manipulates the traits or characteristics upon which participants are matched. We can match pairs of participants on any number of variables, including their level of intelligence, their personality type, their eating habits, their level of education, and their sleep patterns. We could measure these characteristics and then match participants. For example, we could measure intelligence

TABLE A11.2 ● In a matched-pairs design, n pairs are matched and observed one time.

Treatment 1	Treatment 2
n_1	n_2
n_3	n_4
n_5	n_6
n_7	n_8
n_9	n_{10}

and then match the two participants scoring the highest, the two participants scoring the next highest, and so on. Matching through experimental manipulation requires that we measure some trait or characteristic before we match participants into pairs.

Matching through natural occurrence is typical for quasi-experiments in which participants are matched based on preexisting traits. The preexisting traits are typically biological or physiological in nature. For example, we could match participants based on genetics (e.g., biological twins) or family affiliation (e.g., brothers, sisters, or cousins). Each trait or characteristic is inherent to the participant. There is no need to measure this in order to pair participants. Instead, the participants are already matched naturally. Pairs of identical twins or brothers, for example, are paired together naturally. One member of each pair is assigned to a group or a treatment, and differences between pairs of scores are observed. Any time participants are matched on common traits, either experimentally or through natural occurrence, we are using the matched-pairs design to select related samples. Figure A11.1 summarizes the types of designs used with related samples.

FIGURE A11.1 ● Two designs associated with selecting related samples: the repeated-measures design and the matched-pairs design.

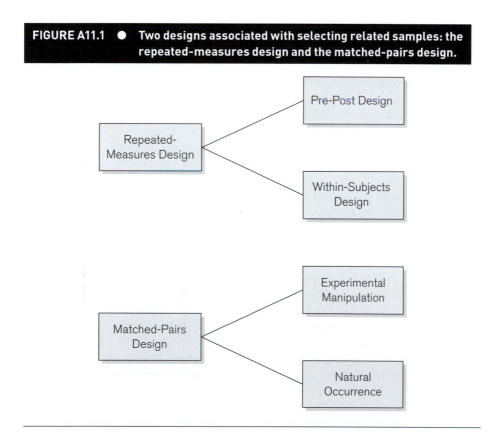

Repeated measures can be selected by observing participants before and after a treatment (pre-post design) or across treatments (within-subjects design). Matched pairs can be selected through experimental manipulation or natural occurrence.

A12: Degrees of Freedom for Parametric Tests

Parametric tests—specifically, the *t* tests, ANOVAs, regression, and correlation—are associated with a certain number of degrees of freedom. Degrees of freedom are first introduced in Learning Unit 2 for sample variance—and again for each parametric test taught in this book (in Section IV and Section V). The degrees of freedom for sample variance are $n - 1$.

Note that the sample variance (s^2) estimates the population variance (σ^2). The numerator for sample variance is the sum of squares (*SS*). However, if we divide *SS* by n, then the sample variance is biased. Specifically, if we compute SS/n, then on average the sample variance will underestimate the population variance. In other words, the sample variance will be a *biased estimator* of the population variance. The following statement describes this rule:

$$\text{The sample variance is biased: If } s^2 = \frac{SS}{n-1}, \text{ then } s^2 < \sigma^2 \text{ on average.}$$

That said, if we make a simple correction and subtract 1 in the denominator ($n - 1$), then the sample variance will be unbiased. Specifically, if we compute $SS/(n - 1)$, then on average the sample variance will equal the population variance. In other words, the sample variance will be an un*biased estimator* of the population variance. The following statement describes this rule:

$$\text{The sample variance is unbiased: If } s^2 = \frac{SS}{n-1}, \text{ then } s^2 = \sigma^2 \text{ on average.}$$

For the *t* tests, ANOVAs, regression, and correlation—all are parametric tests—we use the sample variance to estimate the population variance in each respective test statistic. For this reason, each test is associated with $n - 1$ degrees of freedom, with one (sort of) exception for correlation. In this appendix, we identify the commonality of degrees of freedom across these parametric tests.

***t* tests.** For the *t* tests, each sample or group is associated with a value for degrees of freedom. Thus, the degrees of freedom for the *t* test conform to $n - 1$.

For one sample—the one-sample *t* test—the degrees of freedom are simply $n - 1$. For example, if 50 participants are observed, then the degrees of freedom are $50 - 1 = 49$.

For two samples with different participants observed in each group—the two-independent-sample *t* test—the degrees of freedom are $n - 1$ for each sample or group. We sum the degrees of freedom. For example, if 25 participants are observed in each of two groups, then the degrees of freedom for each group are $25 - 1 = 24$. The sum is the total degrees of freedom for the test: $24 + 24 = 48$ total degrees of freedom.

For two samples with the same participants observed in each group—the related-samples *t* test—we first compute difference scores, then compute the test statistic. Therefore, the degrees of freedom are the number of difference scores minus one: $n_D - 1$. For example, if 50 participants are observed two times, then we will compute 50 difference scores; the degrees of freedom are $50 - 1 = 49$.

ANOVAs. For the ANOVAs, we assign degrees of freedom to each factor or "effect" and error variation. However, the total degrees of freedom are always $n - 1$. Thus, we begin with $n - 1$ degrees of freedom and then divvy up those degrees of freedom to each factor and error variation.

For the one-way ANOVAs, for example, suppose we observe 45 total participants. The total degrees of freedom are $45 - 1 = 44$. For each one-way ANOVA design, we divvy up those degrees of freedom, but in each case, when we add up the degrees of freedom, they will total 44 ($n - 1$). Likewise for the factorial ANOVAs, the total degrees of freedom are $n - 1$, and we divvy up those degrees of freedom to each factor or "effect" and error. Regardless, when we add up the degrees of freedom, they will total $n - 1$.

Regression. For regression, we assign degrees of freedom to the predictor variable (called regression variation) and to error variation (called residual variation). However, again, the total degrees of freedom are always $n - 1$. Thus we begin with $n - 1$ degrees of freedom and then divvy up those degrees of freedom to the regression and to the residual variation. The degrees of freedom for regression variation are always equal to the number of predictor variables in the model; the degrees of freedom for residual variation are always equal to whatever allows for the total degrees of freedom to equal $n - 1$.

Pearson correlation. For correlation, the degrees of freedom ($n - 1$) are associated with each X and Y variable. For this case, since each column of scores is analyzed in the test statistic, each X and Y column is associated with $n - 1$ degrees of freedom. However, the exception for correlation is that instead of adding the degrees of freedom for each column, we simply compute degrees of freedom as $n - 2$. For example, if we record the age (X) and life satisfaction score (Y) for 25 participants, then we have two columns of data for each participant. The degrees of freedom for the correlation are $25 - 2 = 23$. For correlation, the subtraction of 2 is to remove one degree of freedom for each variable (X and Y).

Whether you are computing a t test, ANOVA, regression, or correlation, the computation and inclusion of degrees of freedom are aligned. In each case, these tests are associated with $n - 1$ degrees of freedom—either total, or for each variable in the case of correlation. The reason is that sample variance is associated with $n - 1$ degrees of freedom, and each of these tests must compute sample variance in the test statistic to estimate the population variance. Seeing firsthand the commonality of degrees of freedom across these tests can help to make sense of degrees of freedom for parametric testing.

• Appendix B •

Global Excel Skills

This appendix describes how to use some key features in Excel in Microsoft Office. Where the procedures differ for Windows and for Mac, we provide that description as well. In each learning unit, marginal notes are provided to tell you where in this appendix global Excel skills are needed to guide your learning.

When you open an Excel spreadsheet, you should see at the top of each page a ribbon filled with tabs. As described in Orientation to Excel at the start of this book (p. xxi), clicking different tabs (Home, Insert, Page Layout. . .) reveals different icons in that ribbon. The icons in the ribbon allow you to manipulate different aspects of your spreadsheet. In this appendix, we will utilize these icons often. If you are unable to find an icon or a caption, be sure to open the spreadsheet's window as wide as possible.

B1: Viewing in Cells the Functions or Formulas Versus the Results of Those Functions or Formulas

Excel offers the option of viewing the function or formula in a cell or viewing the result of the calculation. You can switch between the two views in two different ways.

Click on the Formulas tab, and then click from the ribbon this icon ⬚, which is accompanied by the caption Show Formulas. Doing so toggles between the two views.

Another way to toggle between the two views is by pressing simultaneously two keys, Control and ` (grave accent).

B2: Formatting Cells: Decimals, Alignment, Merge Cells, Fonts, Bold, Borders, Superscripts, Subscripts

The appearance of the cell and the text within a cell can be modified. Modifications can be made by selecting from the Home tab the Format icon, as shown in Figure B2.1a. Either option presents the drop-down menu shown in Figure B2.1b. Select Format Cells to get the dialog box shown in Figure B2.1c.

Some aspects of formatting can also be done through icons on the ribbon without opening the Format Cells dialog box. Such cases will be noted below.

FIGURE B2.1 ● Formatting cells and their contents.

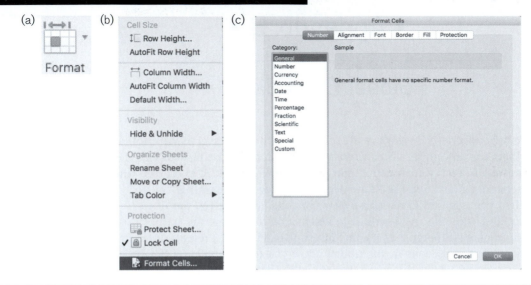

Digits Left and Right of the Decimal. We use the following rules of thumb for decimals:

1. When displaying a number whose value does not usually exceed 1, do not display the 0 to the left of the decimal.

2. When calculating means and standard deviations, keep at least one if not two more decimal places than were in the level of precision in our original measurement.

To adjust the decimals in a cell, click on the cell or highlight the range of cells that you want to adjust. In the Format Cells dialog box, select the Number tab, which gives you many options for formatting. Custom is an easy shortcut to getting the format that you want if it is not predefined in another category. For example, displaying three digits to the left or the right of the decimal, even when they are zeros (not significant digits), is easily accomplished by selecting Custom and entering your desired format.

Additionally, in the ribbon of the Home tab, find this icon 🔲 Merge & Center ▾ to adjust the number of digits to the right of the decimal. Click on the left side to increase the number of decimal places; click on the right side to decrease the number of decimal places. Excel rounds the decimals as appropriate.

Alignment, Merge Cells. In many figures in this book, we change the default alignment and even merge cells. In the Format Cells dialog box, select the Alignment tab to find controls for changing the horizontal alignment of cell content and for merging cells, which essentially converts two or more cells into one cell.

Additionally, from the ribbon of the Home tab, clicking any of the three icons shown in the lower left of Figure B2.2 changes alignment to left, center, or right, respectively. Also in the ribbon of the Home tab, clicking Merge & Center, shown in

FIGURE B2.2 ● Icons in the ribbon of the Home tab that allow changing of alignment and merging of cells.

FIGURE B2.3 ● Features in the ribbon of the Home tab that allow changing the font and its appearance.

the lower right of Figure B2.2, easily employs this often-used feature. Notice that the arrow to the right of Merge & Center will display other formatting options.

Fonts: Style, Size, Bold, Italic, Superscript, Subscript. In many figures in this book, we change the appearance of the font. In the Format Cells dialog box, select the Font tab to find controls for changing various aspects of the contents, including font style, font size, bold, italics, superscript, and subscript.

Additionally, from the ribbon of the Home tab, there are drop-down menus for changing the font style and the font size, as shown in the top half of Figure B2.3. Also in the ribbon of the Home tab are icons for changing the appearance of the font, such as bold or italics, as shown in the lower left of Figure B2.3.

Borders. In many figures in this book, we change the border around a cell. In the Format Cells dialog box, select the Border tab to find controls to add a border to one or more sides of the cell and to adjust the appearance of that border.

Additionally, from the ribbon of the Home tab, there is a drop-down menu for changing the border of a cell, as shown in the center of the lower half of Figure B2.2.

B3: Freezing the Display of Some Rows and Columns

When using a spreadsheet for calculations, columns and rows of data should labeled. Those labels typically appear to the left of a row and at the top a column. The cells containing data in columns and rows of a spreadsheet will often be bigger than can be displayed on a computer screen at one time. Thus, we must scroll to the right or scroll down to see data or to see the calculations that we have Excel perform on those data. To keep informative labels displayed at the top and to the left of the spreadsheet, we can freeze the information in one or more rows or columns that contain those labels.

The View tab displays three icons for freezing a portion of the display of our spreadsheet (Figure B3.1a). In the simplest scenario, we may have a single row that we want

FIGURE B3.1 ● Freezing the display of rows and columns.

(a)

Freeze
Panes

Freeze
Top Row

Freeze First
Column

(b)

Unfreeze
Panes

to preserve at the top our data; that row may be row 1 or some other row. Clicking the Freeze Top Row icon preserves at the top of your spreadsheet the single row that is currently displayed, which may or may not be row 1. Alternatively, if we want to freeze a single column, clicking the Freeze First Column icon will preserve the first column shown in your spreadsheet, which may or may not be column A.

In a slightly more complex scenario, we may want to freeze one or more rows and one or more columns. In this case, adjust the display of your spreadsheet with the rows and columns that you want to preserve at the top and the left, respectively. Then select the cell at the upper left of the data range that is below the last row you want to preserve and to the right of the last column that you want to preserve. In the view tab, click Freeze Panes to preserve both the rows and the columns above and to the left of the cell that you have selected. This can also be accomplished from the Window drop-down menu.

Once a portion of the spreadsheet is frozen, the leftmost icon will read Unfreeze Panes as shown in Figure B3.1b Clicking the Unfreeze Panes icon removes any rows or columns that you preserved in the display. This can also be accomplished from the Window drop-down menu.

B4: Highlighting Portions of Spreadsheet, Pasting, or Filling

Most people are probably familiar with highlighting portions of a computer file by clicking and dragging. For our purposes in Excel, you can also use the arrow keys to move to the start of the range and hold the Shift key as you arrow down (or up, left, or right) to the end of the range. You can also use the arrow keys from the first cell in the range: Hold down Shift, hold down Control, arrow down. You will now see highlighted all the contiguous cells with numbers in them. On a Mac computer, both the combinations of Shift + Control and Shift + Command will accomplish this.

One circumstance in which we highlight a portion of a spreadsheet is to copy and paste that portion of a spreadsheet elsewhere. When pasting functions or formulas to adjacent cells, we can use the fill feature. The fill feature can be employed in at least two ways.

- Highlight the cell containing the source of the content and the cells that are the destination of the content. Click the Fill icon in the ribbon of the Home tab, and choose the appropriate option of filling Down, Right, Up, or Left.

FIGURE B4.1 ● The fill handle at the bottom right of a cell.

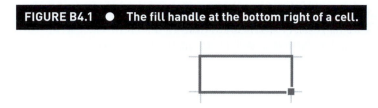

- Click the source cell or highlight the source cells. Drag the fill handle at the bottom right to cover the destination of the content. The fill handle is the small, solid-colored square at the bottom right of a cell or of a set of highlighted cells, as shown in Figure B4.1.

B5: Sorting Data in a Spreadsheet

Highlight the cell range that you want to sort. These cells could be all within a column, or in a block across several columns.

FIGURE B5.1 ● Icons for sorting. (a) Icon in ribbon of Home tab. (b) Drop-down menu from ribbon in Home tab. (c) Icon in ribbon of Data tab.

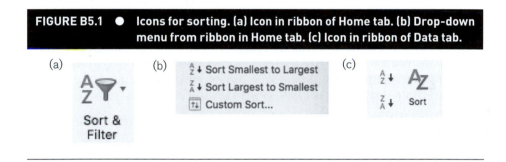

FIGURE B5.2 ● Dialog box for advanced sorting options, such as sorting by two criteria simultaneously.

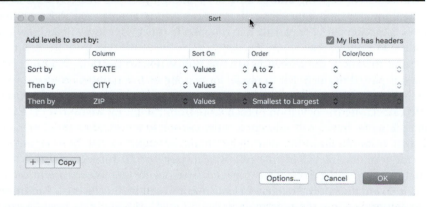

If your cells are all within one column, find the Sort and Filter icon in the Home ribbon, as shown in Figure B5.1a. It reveals the options in Figure B5.1b. Choose whether you want to sort from small to large or from large to small. This can also be done from the Data tab, as shown in Figure B5.1c.

In many situations, you want to reorder rows of information while preserving the information within a row. In such a scenario, a block of cells across rows and columns is highlighted. To sort, choose Custom Sort from the drop-down menu in Figure B5.1b, or choose Sort from the Data tab. Either choice opens the dialog box in Figure B5.2. From this box, choose the column containing the data by which you want to reorder the rows. Select also whether you want the smallest or the largest values to appear at the top. This will preserve all the cells with a row but reorder the entire row according the values in the column that you select.

There are several other features available when sorting from the dialog box.

- If columns have labels and you highlight them, then click "My list has headers," and those titles appear as choices when sorting.

- You can sort based on the information in more than one row. Click the + in the lower left to add a new sort criterion. Each subsequent sort criterion will be nested within each value of the previous sort criterion. For example, if you had rows of information with the states, cities, and zip codes in which people reside, you could sort first alphabetizing in forward or reverse alphabetical order by state; and then, within state, by city; and then, within city, by zip code from small to large or from large to small.

- A less-often used feature is sorting columns rather than rows. To do this, click Options and then choose Sort left to right.

B6: Anchoring Cell References

One advantage of copying and pasting or of filling functions and formulas is that Excel will automatically adjust the cell references. A function may add all the numbers in a row. Simply copying or pasting that function to the rows below will automatically adjust the row references.

In some instances, the references to a row should remain the same as a function or formula is pasted or filled. For example, for a group of five numbers comprising our raw scores, we may calculate a mean score, as shown in cell B8 in Figure B6.1. On the way to calculating the deviation of each score from the mean, we subtract the mean from each score. In the cell adjacent to each raw score, we calculate the deviation of that score from the mean by entering a formula, as shown in cell C2 in Figure B6.1. With the formula entered in that cell, we can paste or fill through cell C6. To get accurate results, we let Excel adjust the cell reference for each raw score in cells B2 through B6 but anchor the reference to the mean in cell B8 by placing a $ in front of the row number. Thus, if the formula in cell C2 reads =B2-B$8, this formula can be

FIGURE B6.1 ● To calculate a deviation score, the formula in cell C2 can be pasted or filled through cell C6, because the reference row of the raw scores in cells B2 through B6 will be increased by one, but the reference to the mean score in cell B8 is anchored by the $ between the B and the 8.

	A	B	C
1		Raw Scores	Deviation Score
2		1	=B2-B$8
3		2	=B3-B$8
4		3	=B4-B$8
5		4	=B5-B$8
6		5	=B6-B$8
7			
8	Mean	=AVERAGE(B2:B6)	

pasted or filled through C6. The result is that the reference to the formulas will correctly increase the row number by one in reference to each raw score but will hold the reference to the mean in the same cell.

Each cell address in a formula or function can anchor

- the column with a $ in front of the first letter specifying the column: $A1,

- the row with a $ in front of the first number specifying the row: A$1, or

- both the column and row with the $ in both places: $A$1.

B7: Inserting (Creating) and Formatting a Chart (Graph of Data)

Highlight the data that are to be represented in a chart. For the examples in this section, the data would be contained in a column of labels and a column of numbers (Column Chart) or two columns of numbers (XY Scatter Chart). The columns may have labels at the top describing the variable in that column. That label can be included in the highlighting. In the ribbon of the Insert tab, select the desired type of chart from Recommended Charts. Clicking on Recommended Charts gives a preview of how your selected data will appear in a graph. Alternatively, click on the icon of the desired type of chart, such as Column or Scatter Chart. Reposition and resize the chart too your liking by clicking and dragging.

Excel uses a default format for each chart. The format can be changed by double clicking on an element of the chart, such as the chart title, the vertical axis,

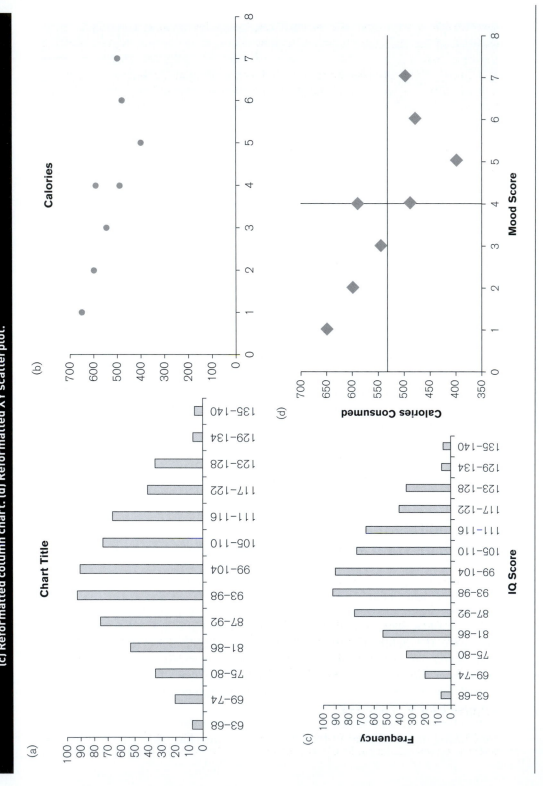

FIGURE B7.1 ● Default and reformatted charts, which can be saved as templates. (a) Default column chart. (b) Default XY scatterplot. (c) Reformatted column chart. (d) Reformatted XY scatterplot.

the horizontal axis, plot area, or gridlines. This allows you to edit any existing elements of the chart simply by typing new text or deleting existing text boxes or chart elements.

Figure B7.1 shows the default column and scatter charts and both chart types reformatted to be consistent with guidelines in the *Publication Manual for the American Psychological Association.*

Deleting or Changing Chart Features

Here are some pointers on how to transform the default charts in Figure B7.1a and B7.1b to charts formatted according to guidelines such as those in the *Publication Manual of the American Psychological Association* (2010) in Figures B7.1c and B7.1d.

- Select the chart title and delete it.

- Select the horizontal and vertical gridlines and delete.

- Double click the horizontal (category) or vertical (value) axis. This opens a side bar, shown in Figure B7.2a. From here you can explore changes to several aspects of the axis. There are options nested within the four icons across the top of the side bar. For example:

  o Insert an axis line by clicking the paint can icon (Fill & Line), selecting Line, selecting solid line, and selecting a line color of black.

  o Change the upper and lower bounds of an axis by double clicking on the axis (if necessary), clicking the column chart icon (Axis Options), and typing in new values in Bounds.

  o Change the placement of the horizontal axis line by double clicking the vertical axis, clicking the column chart icon, and typing into the Horizontal axis crosses box a new value of the vertical axis at which you want the horizontal axis to be placed. Follow a similar procedure for placement of the vertical axis at a particular value of the horizontal axis.

- Click on one of the columns in a column chart, which will select all columns and open a different side bar, shown in Figure B7.2b. Select the paint can icon. For the simplest appearance, select Solid fill and the color gray.

- Click on one of the points in an XY scatterplot, which will select all points and open a side bar, shown in Figure B7.2b. Select the paint can icon. Select the Marker tab, which presents the Marker Options menu. This menu allows you to change the appearance of the marker.

Adding Chart Features

Alternatively, you may want to add to your chart something that does not exist. Select the chart. Select Add Chart Element from the Chart Design tab, and then

FIGURE B7.2 ● Tools for formatting. (a) Chart axes and text. (b) Columns and symbols used to plot data.

FIGURE B7.3 ● Adding chart elements. (a) Icon on the Chart Design ribbon. (b) Menu of elements that can be added. (c) Selecting Axis Titles, two primary axis titles can be added: Primary Horizontal and Primary Vertical.

select from the drop-down menu the element of the chart to be added. For example,

- From Add Chart Element in the Chart Design (Design in Windows) ribbon, as shown in Figure B7.3a, select Axis Titles from the drop-down menu, and then select Primary Vertical Axis. Click in the vertical axis text box, and name the axis "Frequency" in the case of the column chart or "Calories Consumed" in the case of the XY scatterplot.

- From Add Chart Element in the Chart Design tab, select Axis Titles from the drop-down menu, and then select Primary Horizontal Axis. Click in the vertical axis text box, and name the axis "IQ Score" in the case of the column chart or "Mood Score" in the case of the XY scatterplot.

With a chart formatted as needed, it can be saved as a template. Select the chart. Select Change Chart Type from the Chart Design ribbon, as shown in Figure B7.4a. Then

FIGURE B7.4 ● Selecting Change Chart Type also allows you to save a current chart as a template and apply saved templates to a current chart.

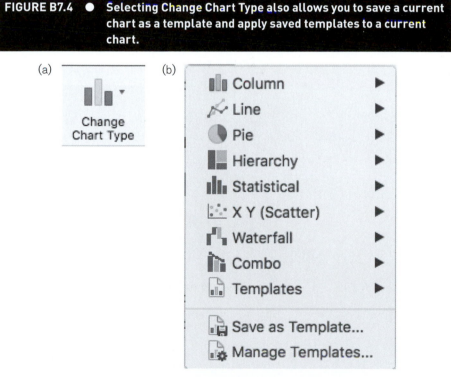

select Save as Template. . ., as shown in Figure B7.4b. Give the template a name. For future charts, highlight the data you wish to put in a chart. From the Chart Design ribbon, select Change Chart Type, and from that menu select Templates. You will find the template that you saved. Select it to apply the format that you created to a chart of new data.

B8: Inserting Equations

Text within cells can be formatted to represent Greek letters, superscripts and subscripts, and mathematical operators. We use these in this text to label some calculations. When needed, more complex mathematical expressions can also be represented by selecting the Equation icon from the Insert tab. Rather than the equation being text in a cell, the equation will be in a text box that can be placed anywhere on the spreadsheet by selecting and dragging the box. These equations are simply text characters and do not perform calculations as do the functions and formulas entered into cells.

• Appendix C •

Statistical Tables

TABLE C.1 ● The Unit Normal Table

Column (A) lists *z*-score values. Column (B) lists the proportion of the area between the mean and the *z*-score value. Column (C) lists the proportion of the area beyond the *z* score in the tail of the distribution. (*Note:* Because the normal distribution is symmetrical, areas for negative *z* scores are the same as those for positive *z* scores.)

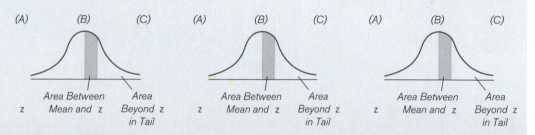

(A) z	(B) Area Between Mean and z	(C) Area Beyond z in Tail	(A) z	(B) Area Between Mean and z	(C) Area Beyond z in Tail	(A) z	(B) Area Between Mean and z	(C) Area Beyond z in Tail
0.00	.0000	.5000	0.15	.0596	.4404	0.30	.1179	.3821
0.01	.0040	.4960	0.16	.0636	.4364	0.31	.1217	.3783
0.02	.0080	.4920	0.17	.0675	.4325	0.32	.1255	.3745
0.03	.0120	.4880	0.18	.0714	.4286	0.33	.1293	.3707
0.04	.0160	.4840	0.19	.0753	.4247	0.34	.1331	.3669
0.05	.0199	.4801	0.20	.0793	.4207	0.35	.1368	.3632
0.06	.0239	.4761	0.21	.0832	.4168	0.36	.1406	.3594
0.07	.0279	.4721	0.22	.0871	.4129	0.37	.1443	.3557
0.08	.0319	.4681	0.23	.0910	.4090	0.38	.1480	.3520
0.09	.0359	.4641	0.24	.0948	.4052	0.39	.1517	.3483
0.10	.0398	.4602	0.25	.0987	.4013	0.40	.1554	.3446
0.11	.0438	.4562	0.26	.1026	.3974	0.41	.1591	.3409
0.12	.0478	.4522	0.27	.1064	.3936	0.42	.1628	.3372
0.13	.0517	.4483	0.28	.1103	.3897	0.43	.1664	.3336
0.14	.0557	.4443	0.29	.1141	.3859	0.44	.1700	.3300

(Continued)

TABLE C.1 ● (Continued)

(A) z	(B) Area Between Mean and z	(C) Area Beyond z in Tail	(A) z	(B) Area Between Mean and z	(C) Area Beyond z in Tail	(A) z	(B) Area Between Mean and z	(C) Area Beyond z in Tail
0.45	.1736	.3264	0.78	.2823	.2177	1.11	.3665	.1335
0.46	.1772	.3228	0.79	.2852	.2148	1.12	.3686	.1314
0.47	.1808	.3192	0.80	.2881	.2119	1.13	.3708	.1292
0.48	.1844	.3156	0.81	.2910	.2090	1.14	.3729	.1271
0.49	.1879	.3121	0.82	.2939	.2061	1.15	.3749	.1251
0.50	.1915	.3085	0.83	.2967	.2033	1.16	.3770	.1230
0.51	.1950	.3050	0.84	.2995	.2005	1.17	.3790	.1210
0.52	.1985	.3015	0.85	.3023	.1977	1.18	.3810	.1190
0.53	.2019	.2981	0.86	.3051	.1949	1.19	.3830	.1170
0.54	.2054	.2946	0.87	.3078	.1922	1.20	.3849	.1151
0.55	.2088	.2912	0.88	.3106	.1894	1.21	.3869	.1131
0.56	.2123	.2877	0.89	.3133	.1867	1.22	.3888	.1112
0.57	.2157	.2843	0.90	.3159	.1841	1.23	.3907	.1093
0.58	.2190	.2810	0.91	.3186	.1814	1.24	.3925	.1075
0.59	.2224	.2776	0.92	.3212	.1788	1.25	.3944	.1056
0.60	.2257	.2743	0.93	.3238	.1762	1.26	.3962	.1038
0.61	.2391	.2709	0.94	.3264	.1736	1.27	.3980	.1020
0.62	.2324	.2676	0.95	.3289	.17 11	1.28	.3997	.1003
0.63	.2357	.2643	0.96	.3315	.1685	1.29	.4015	.0985
0.64	.2389	.2611	0.97	.3340	.1660	1.30	.4032	.0968
0.65	.2422	.2578	0.98	.3365	.1635	1.31	.4049	.0951
0.66	.2454	.2546	0.99	.3389	.1611	1.32	.4066	.0934
0.67	.2486	.2514	1.00	.3413	.1587	1.33	.4082	.0918
0.68	.2517	.2483	1.01	.3438	.1562	1.34	.4099	.0901
0.69	.2549	.2451	1.02	.3461	.1539	1.35	.4115	.0885
0.70	.2580	.2420	1.03	.3485	.1515	1.36	.4131	.0869
0.71	.2611	.2389	1.04	.3508	.1492	1.37	.4147	.0853
0.72	.2642	.2358	1.05	.3531	.1469	1.38	.4162	.0838
0.73	.2673	.2327	1.06	.3554	.1446	1.39	.4177	.0823
0.74	.2704	.2296	1.07	.3577	.1423	1.40	.4192	.0808
0.75	.2734	.2266	1.08	.3599	.1401	1.41	.4207	.0793
0.76	.2764	.2236	1.09	.3621	.1379	1.42	.4222	.0778
0.77	.2794	.2206	1.10	.3643	.1357	1.43	.4236	.0764

(A) z	(B) Area Between Mean and z	(C) Area Beyond z in Tail	(A) z	(B) Area Between Mean and z	(C) Area Beyond z in Tail	(A) z	(B) Area Between Mean and z	(C) Area Beyond z in Tail
1.44	.4251	.0749	1.77	.4616	.0384	2.10	.4821	.0179
1.45	.4265	.0735	1.78	.4625	.0375	2.11	.4826	.0174
1.46	.4279	.0721	1.79	.4633	.0367	2.12	.4830	.0170
1.47	.4292	.0708	1.80	.4641	.0359	2.13	.4834	.0166
1.48	.4306	.0694	1.81	.4649	.0351	2.14	.4838	.0162
1.49	.4319	.0681	1.82	.4656	.0344	2.15	.4842	.0158
1.50	.4332	.0668	1.83	.4664	.0336	2.16	.4846	.0154
1.51	.4345	.0655	1.84	.4671	.0329	2.17	.4850	.0150
1.52	.4357	.0643	1.85	.4678	.0322	2.18	.4854	.0146
1.53	.4370	.0630	1.86	.4686	.0314	2.19	.4857	.0143
1.54	.4382	.0618	1.87	.4693	.0307	2.20	.4861	.0139
1.55	.4394	.0606	1.88	.4699	.0301	2.21	.4864	.0136
1.56	.4406	.0594	1.89	.4706	.0294	2.22	.4868	.0132
1.57	.4418	.0582	1.90	.4713	.0287	2.23	.4871	.0129
1.58	.4429	.0571	1.91	.4719	.0281	2.24	.4875	.0125
1.59	.4441	.0559	1.92	.4726	.0274	2.25	.4878	.0122
1.60	.4452	.0548	1.93	.4732	.0268	2.26	.4881	.0119
1.61	.4463	.0537	1.94	.4738	.0262	2.27	.4884	.0116
1.62	.4474	.0526	1.95	.4744	.0256	2.28	.4887	.0113
1.63	.4484	.0516	1.96	.4750	.0250	2.29	.4890	.0110
1.64	.4495	.0505	1.97	.4756	.0244	2.30	.4893	.0107
1.65	.4505	.0495	1.98	.4761	.0239	2.31	.4896	.0104
1.66	.4515	.0485	1.99	.4767	.0233	2.32	.4898	.0102
1.67	.4525	.0475	2.00	.4772	.0228	2.33	.4901	.0099
1.68	.4535	.0465	2.01	.4778	.0222	2.34	.4904	.0096
1.69	.4545	.0455	2.02	.4783	.0217	2.35	.4906	.0094
1.70	.4554	.0446	2.03	.4788	.0212	2.36	.4909	.0091
1.71	.4564	.0436	2.04	.4793	.0207	2.37	.4911	.0089
1.72	.4573	.0427	2.05	.4798	.0202	2.38	.4913	.0087
1.73	.4582	.0418	2.06	.4803	.0197	2.39	.4916	.0084
1.74	.4591	.0409	2.07	.4808	.0192	2.40	.4918	.0082
1.75	.4599	.0401	2.08	.4812	.0188	2.41	.4920	.0080
1.76	.4608	.0392	2.09	.4817	.0183	2.42	.4922	.0078

(Continued)

TABLE C.1 ● (Continued)

(A) z	(B) Area Between Mean and z	(C) Area Beyond z in Tail	(A) z	(B) Area Between Mean and z	(C) Area Beyond z in Tail	(A) z	(B) Area Between Mean and z	(C) Area Beyond z in Tail
2.43	.4925	.0075	2.74	.4969	.0031	3.05	.4989	.0011
2.44	.4927	.0073	2.75	.4970	.0030	3.06	.4989	.0011
2.45	.4929	.0071	2.76	.4971	.0029	3.07	.4989	.0011
2.46	.4931	.0069	2.77	.4972	.0028	3.08	.4990	.0010
2.47	.4932	.0068	2.78	.4973	.0027	3.09	.4990	.0010
2.48	.4934	.0066	2.79	.4974	.0026	3.10	.4990	.0010
2.49	.4936	.0064	2.80	.4974	.0026	3.11	.4991	.0009
2.50	.4938	.0062	2.81	.4975	.0025	3.12	.4991	.0009
2.51	.4940	.0060	2.82	.4976	.0024	3.13	.4991	.0009
2.52	.4941	.0059	2.83	.4977	.0023	3.14	.4992	.0008
2.53	.4943	.0057	2.84	.4977	.0023	3.15	.4992	.0008
2.54	.4945	.0055	2.85	.4978	.0022	3.16	.4992	.0008
2.55	.4946	.0054	2.86	.4979	.0021	3.17	.4992	.0008
2.56	.4948	.0052	2.87	.4979	.0021	3.18	.4993	.0007
2.57	.4949	.0051	2.88	.4980	.0020	3.19	.4993	.0007
2.58	.4951	.0049	2.89	.4981	.0019	3.20	.4993	.0007
2.59	.4952	.0048	2.90	.4981	.0019	3.21	.4993	.0007
2.60	.4953	.0047	2.91	.4982	.0018	3.22	.4994	.0006
2.61	.4955	.0045	2.92	.4982	.0018	3.23	.4994	.0006
2.62	.4956	.0044	2.93	.4983	.0017	3.24	.4994	.0006
2.63	.4957	.0043	2.94	.4984	.0016	3.25	.4994	.0006
2.64	.4959	.0041	2.95	.4984	.0016	3.30	.4995	.0005
2.65	.4960	.0040	2.96	.4985	.0015	3.35	.4996	.0004
2.66	.4961	.0039	2.97	.4985	.0015	3.40	.4997	.0003
2.67	.4962	.0038	2.98	.4986	.0014	3.45	.4997	.0003
2.68	.4963	.0037	2.99	.4986	.0014	3.50	.4998	.0002
2.69	.4964	.0036	3.00	.4987	.0013	3.60	.4998	.0002
2.70	.4965	.0035	3.01	.4987	.0013	3.70	.4999	.0001
2.71	.4966	.0034	3.02	.4987	.0013	3.80	.4999	.0001
2.72	.4967	.0033	3.03	.4988	.0012	3.90	.49995	.00005
2.73	.4968	.0032	3.04	.4988	.0012	4.00	.49997	.00003

Source: Based on Freund, J. E. (2004). *Modern elementary statistics* (11th ed.). Upper Saddle River, NJ: Pearson Prentice Hall.

TABLE C.2 ● Critical Values for the *t* Distribution

Table entries are values of *t* corresponding to proportions in one tail or in two tails combined.

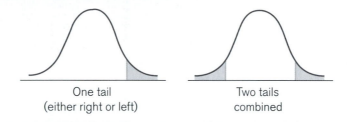

One tail
(either right or left)

Two tails
combined

	Proportion in One Tail					
	.25	.10	.05	.025	.01	.005
	Proportion in Two Tails Combined					
df	.50	.20	.10	.05	.02	.01
1	1.000	3.078	6.314	12.706	31.821	63.657
2	0.816	1.886	2.920	4.303	6.965	9.925
3	0.765	1.638	2.353	3.182	4.541	5.841
4	0.741	1.533	2.132	2.776	3.747	4.604
5	0.727	1.476	2.015	2.571	3.365	4.032
6	0.718	1.440	1.943	2.447	3.143	3.707
7	0.711	1.415	1.895	2.365	2.998	3.499
8	0.706	1.397	1.860	2.306	2.896	3.355
9	0.703	1.383	1.833	2.282	2.821	3.250
10	0.700	1.372	1.812	2.228	2.764	3.169
11	0.697	1.363	1.796	2.201	2.718	3.106
12	0.695	1.356	1.782	2.179	2.681	3.055
13	0.694	1.350	1.771	2.160	2.650	3.012
14	0.692	1.345	1.761	2.145	2.624	2.977
15	0.691	1.341	1.753	2.131	2.602	2.947
16	0.690	1.337	1.746	2.120	2.583	2.921
17	0.689	1.333	1.740	2.110	2.567	2.898
18	0.688	1.330	1.734	2.101	2.552	2.878
19	0.688	1.328	1.729	2.093	2.539	2.861

(Continued)

TABLE C.2 ● (Continued)

df	Proportion in One Tail					
	.25	**.10**	**.05**	**.025**	**.01**	**.005**
	Proportion in Two Tails Combined					
	.50	**.20**	**.10**	**.05**	**.02**	**.01**
20	0.687	1.325	1.725	2.086	2.528	2.845
21	0.686	1.323	1.721	2.080	2.518	2.831
22	0.686	1.321	1.717	2.074	2.508	2.819
23	0.685	1.319	1.714	2.069	2.500	2.807
24	0.685	1.318	1.711	2.064	2.492	2.797
25	0.684	1.316	1.708	2.060	2.485	2.787
26	0.684	1.315	1.706	2.056	2.479	2.779
27	0.684	1.314	1.703	2.052	2.473	2.771
28	0.683	1.313	1.701	2.048	2.467	2.763
29	0.683	1.311	1.699	2.045	2.462	2.756
30	0.683	1.310	1.697	2.042	2.457	2.750
40	0.681	1.303	1.684	2.021	2.423	2.704
60	0.679	1.296	1.671	2.000	2.390	2.660
120	0.677	1.289	1.658	1.980	2.358	2.617
∞	0.674	1.282	1.645	1.960	2.326	2.576

Source: Table III of Fisher, R. A., & Yates, F. (1974). *Statistical tables for biological, agricultural and medical research* (6th ed.). London, England: Longman Group Ltd. (previously published by Oliver and Boyd Ltd., Edinburgh). Adapted and reprinted with permission of Addison Wesley Longman.

TABLE C.3 ● Critical Values for the *F* Distribution

Critical values at a .05 level of significance are given in lightface type.

Critical values at a .01 level of significance are given in boldface type.

Degrees of Freedom Denominator	Degrees of Freedom Numerator: 1	2	3	4	5	6	7	8	9	10	20	∞
1	161 **4052**	200 **5000**	216 **5403**	225 **5625**	230 **5764**	234 **5859**	237 **5928**	239 **5928**	241 **6023**	242 **6056**	248 **6209**	254 **6366**
2	18.51 **98.49**	19.00 **99.00**	19.16 **99.17**	19.25 **99.25**	19.30 **99.30**	19.33 **99.33**	19.36 **99.34**	19.37 **99.36**	19.38 **99.38**	19.39 **99.40**	19.44 **99.45**	19.5 **99.5**
3	10.13 **34.12**	9.55 **30.92**	9.28 **29.46**	9.12 **28.71**	9.01 **28.24**	8.94 **27.91**	8.88 **27.67**	8.84 **27.49**	8.81 **27.34**	8.78 **27.23**	8.66 **26.69**	8.5 **26.1**
4	7.71 **21.20**	6.94 **18.00**	6.59 **16.69**	6.39 **15.98**	6.26 **15.52**	6.16 **15.21**	6.09 **14.98**	6.04 **14.80**	6.00 **14.66**	5.96 **14.54**	5.80 **14.02**	5.6 **13.5**
5	6.61 **16.26**	5.79 **13.27**	5.41 **12.06**	5.19 **11.39**	5.05 **10.97**	4.95 **10.67**	4.88 **10.45**	4.82 **10.27**	4.78 **10.15**	4.74 **10.05**	4.56 **9.55**	4.37 **9.02**
6	5.99 **13.74**	5.14 **10.92**	4.76 **9.78**	4.53 **9.15**	4.39 **8.75**	4.28 **8.47**	4.21 **8.26**	4.15 **8.10**	4.10 **7.98**	4.06 **7.87**	3.87 **7.39**	3.67 **6.88**
7	5.59 **13.74**	4.74 **9.55**	4.35 **8.45**	4.12 **7.85**	3.97 **7.46**	3.87 **7.19**	3.79 **7.00**	3.73 **6.84**	3.68 **6.71**	3.63 **6.62**	3.44 **6.15**	3.23 **5.65**
8	5.32 **11.26**	4.46 **8.65**	4.07 **7.59**	3.84 **7.01**	3.69 **6.63**	3.58 **6.37**	3.50 **6.19**	3.44 **6.03**	3.39 **5.91**	3.34 **5.82**	3.15 **5.36**	2.93 **4.86**
9	5.12 **10.56**	4.26 **8.02**	3.86 **6.99**	3.63 **6.42**	3.48 **6.06**	3.37 **5.80**	3.29 **5.62**	3.23 **5.47**	3.18 **5.35**	3.13 **5.26**	2.93 **4.80**	2.71 **4.31**
10	4.96 **10.04**	4.10 **7.56**	3.71 **6.55**	3.48 **5.99**	3.33 **5.64**	3.22 **5.39**	3.14 **5.21**	3.07 **5.06**	3.02 **4.95**	2.97 **4.85**	2.77 **4.41**	2.54 **3.91**
11	4.84 **9.65**	3.98 **7.20**	3.59 **6.22**	3.36 **5.67**	3.20 **5.32**	3.09 **5.07**	3.01 **4.88**	2.95 **4.74**	2.90 **4.63**	2.86 **4.54**	2.65 **4.10**	2.40 **3.60**
12	4.75 **9.33**	3.89 **6.93**	3.49 **5.95**	3.26 **5.41**	3.11 **5.06**	3.00 **4.82**	2.92 **4.65**	2.85 **4.50**	2.80 **4.39**	2.76 **4.30**	2.54 **3.86**	2.30 **3.36**
13	4.67 **9.07**	3.80 **6.70**	3.41 **5.74**	3.18 **5.20**	3.02 **4.86**	2.92 **4.62**	2.84 **4.44**	2.77 **4.30**	2.72 **4.19**	2.67 **4.10**	2.46 **3.67**	2.21 **3.17**
14	4.60 **8.86**	3.74 **6.51**	3.34 **5.56**	3.11 **5.03**	2.96 **4.69**	2.85 **4.46**	2.77 **4.28**	2.70 **4.14**	2.65 **4.03**	2.60 **3.94**	2.39 **3.51**	2.13 **3.00**

(Continued)

TABLE C.3 ● (Continued)

		Degrees of Freedom Numerator										
		1	2	3	4	5	6	7	8	9	10	20	∞
15	4.54	3.68	3.29	3.06	2.90	2.79	2.70	2.64	2.59	2.55	2.33	2.07
	8.68	**6.36**	**5.42**	**4.89**	**4.56**	**4.32**	**4.14**	**4.00**	**3.89**	**3.80**	**3.36**	**2.87**
16	4.49	3.63	3.24	3.01	2.85	2.74	2.66	2.59	2.54	2.49	2.28	2.01
	8.53	**6.23**	**5.29**	**4.77**	**4.44**	**4.20**	**4.03**	**3.89**	**3.78**	**3.69**	**3.25**	**2.75**
17	4.45	3.59	3.20	2.96	2.81	2.70	2.62	2.55	2.50	2.45	2.23	1.96
	8.40	**6.11**	**5.18**	**4.67**	**4.34**	**4.10**	**3.93**	**3.79**	**3.68**	**3.59**	**3.16**	**2.65**
18	4.41	3.55	3.16	2.93	2.77	2.66	2.58	2.51	2.46	2.41	2.19	1.92
	8.28	**6.01**	**5.09**	**4.58**	**4.25**	**4.01**	**3.85**	**3.71**	**3.60**	**3.51**	**3.07**	**2.57**
19	4.38	3.52	3.13	2.90	2.74	2.63	2.55	2.48	2.43	2.38	2.15	1.88
	8.18	**5.93**	**5.01**	**4.50**	**4.17**	**3.94**	**3.77**	**3.63**	**3.52**	**3.43**	**3.00**	**2.49**
20	4.35	3.49	3.10	2.87	2.71	2.60	2.52	2.45	2.40	2.35	2.12	1.84
	8.10	**5.85**	**4.94**	**4.43**	**4.10**	**3.87**	**3.71**	**3.56**	**3.45**	**3.37**	**2.94**	**2.42**
21	4.32	3.47	3.07	2.84	2.68	2.57	2.49	2.42	2.37	2.32	2.09	1.81
	8.02	**5.78**	**4.87**	**4.37**	**4.04**	**3.81**	**3.65**	**3.51**	**3.40**	**3.31**	**2.88**	**2.36**
22	4.30	3.44	3.05	2.82	2.66	2.55	2.47	2.40	2.35	2.30	2.07	1.78
	7.94	**5.72**	**4.82**	**4.31**	**3.99**	**3.76**	**3.59**	**3.45**	**3.35**	**3.26**	**2.83**	**2.31**
23	4.28	3.42	3.03	2.80	2.64	2.53	2.45	2.38	2.32	2.28	2.04	1.76
	7.88	**5.66**	**4.76**	**4.26**	**3.94**	**3.71**	**3.54**	**3.41**	**3.30**	**3.21**	**2.78**	**2.26**
24	4.26	3.40	3.01	2.78	2.62	2.51	2.43	2.36	2.30	2.26	2.02	1.73
	7.82	**5.61**	**4.72**	**4.22**	**3.90**	**3.67**	**3.50**	**3.36**	**3.25**	**3.17**	**2.74**	**2.21**
25	4.24	3.38	2.99	2.76	2.60	2.49	2.41	2.34	2.28	2.24	2.00	1.71
	7.77	**5.57**	**4.68**	**4.18**	**3.86**	**3.63**	**3.46**	**3.32**	**3.21**	**3.13**	**2.70**	**2.17**
26	4.22	3.37	2.98	2.74	2.59	2.47	2.39	2.32	2.27	2.22	1.99	1.69
	7.72	**5.53**	**4.64**	**4.14**	**3.82**	**3.59**	**3.42**	**3.29**	**3.17**	**3.09**	**2.66**	**2.13**
27	4.21	3.35	2.96	2.73	2.57	2.46	2.37	2.30	2.25	2.20	1.97	1.67
	7.68	**5.49**	**4.60**	**4.11**	**3.79**	**3.56**	**3.39**	**3.26**	**3.14**	**3.06**	**2.63**	**2.10**
28	4.20	3.34	2.95	2.71	2.56	2.44	2.36	2.29	2.24	2.19	1.96	1.65
	7.64	**5.45**	**4.57**	**4.07**	**3.76**	**3.53**	**3.36**	**3.23**	**3.11**	**3.03**	**2.60**	**2.07**
29	4.18	3.33	2.93	2.70	2.54	2.43	2.35	2.28	2.22	2.18	1.94	1.63
	7.60	**5.42**	**4.54**	**4.04**	**3.73**	**3.50**	**3.33**	**3.20**	**3.08**	**3.00**	**2.57**	**2.04**

Degrees of Freedom Denominator

					Degrees of Freedom Numerator							
		1	2	3	4	5	6	7	8	9	10	20	∞

Degrees of Freedom Denominator	1	2	3	4	5	6	7	8	9	10	20	∞
30	4.17	3.32	2.92	2.69	2.53	2.42	2.34	2.27	2.21	2.16	1.93	1.61
	7.56	**5.39**	**4.51**	**4.02**	**3.70**	**3.47**	**3.30**	**3.17**	**3.06**	**2.98**	**2.55**	**2.01**
31	4.16	3.30	2.91	2.68	2.52	2.41	2.32	2.25	2.20	2.15	1.92	1.60
	7.53	**5.36**	**4.48**	**3.99**	**3.67**	**3.45**	**3.28**	**3.15**	**3.04**	**2.96**	**2.53**	**1.89**
32	4.15	3.29	2.90	2.67	2.51	2.40	2.31	2.24	2.19	2.14	1.91	1.59
	7.50	**5.34**	**4.46**	**3.97**	**3.65**	**3.43**	**3.26**	**3.13**	**3.02**	**2.93**	**2.51**	**1.88**
33	4.14	3.28	2.89	2.66	2.50	2.39	2.30	2.23	2.18	2.13	1.90	1.58
	7.47	**5.31**	**4.44**	**3.95**	**3.63**	**3.41**	**3.24**	**3.11**	**3.00**	**2.91**	**2.49**	**1.87**
34	4.13	3.28	2.88	2.65	2.49	2.38	2.29	2.23	2.17	2.12	1.89	1.57
	7.44	**5.29**	**4.42**	**3.93**	**3.61**	**3.39**	**3.22**	**3.09**	**2.98**	**2.89**	**2.47**	**1.86**
35	4.12	3.27	2.87	2.64	2.49	2.37	2.29	2.22	2.16	2.11	1.88	1.56
	7.42	**5.27**	**4.40**	**3.91**	**3.59**	**3.37**	**3.20**	**3.07**	**2.96**	**2.88**	**2.45**	**1.85**
36	4.11	3.26	2.87	2.63	2.48	2.36	2.28	2.21	2.15	2.11	1.87	1.55
	7.40	**5.25**	**4.38**	**3.89**	**3.57**	**3.35**	**3.18**	**3.05**	**2.95**	**2.86**	**2.43**	**1.84**
37	4.11	3.25	2.86	2.63	2.47	2.36	2.27	2.20	2.14	2.10	1.86	1.54
	7.37	**5.23**	**4.36**	**3.87**	**3.56**	**3.33**	**3.17**	**3.04**	**2.93**	**2.84**	**2.42**	**1.83**
38	4.10	3.24	2.85	2.62	2.46	2.35	2.26	2.19	2.14	2.09	1.85	1.53
	7.35	**5.21**	**4.34**	**3.86**	**3.54**	**3.32**	**3.15**	**3.02**	**2.92**	**2.83**	**2.40**	**1.82**
39	4.09	3.24	2.85	2.61	2.46	2.34	2.26	2.19	2.13	2.08	1.84	1.52
	7.33	**5.19**	**4.33**	**3.84**	**3.53**	**3.30**	**3.14**	**3.01**	**2.90**	**2.81**	**2.39**	**1.81**
40	4.08	3.23	2.84	2.61	2.45	2.34	2.25	2.18	2.12	2.07	1.84	1.51
	7.31	**5.18**	**4.31**	**3.83**	**3.51**	**3.29**	**3.12**	**2.99**	**2.88**	**2.80**	**2.37**	**1.80**
42	4.07	3.22	2.83	2.59	2.44	2.32	2.24	2.17	2.11	2.06	1.82	1.50
	7.27	**5.15**	**4.29**	**3.80**	**3.49**	**3.26**	**3.10**	**2.96**	**2.86**	**2.77**	**2.35**	**1.78**
44	4.06	3.21	2.82	2.58	2.43	2.31	2.23	2.16	2.10	2.05	1.81	1.49
	7.24	**5.12**	**4.26**	**3.78**	**3.46**	**3.24**	**3.07**	**2.94**	**2.84**	**2.75**	**2.32**	**1.76**
60	4.00	3.15	2.76	2.53	2.37	2.25	2.17	2.10	2.04	1.99	1.75	1.39
	7.08	**4.98**	**4.13**	**3.65**	**3.34**	**3.12**	**2.95**	**2.82**	**2.72**	**2.63**	**2.20**	**1.60**
120	3.92	3.07	2.68	2.45	2.29	2.18	2.09	2.02	1.96	1.91	1.66	1.25
	6.85	**4.79**	**3.95**	**3.48**	**3.17**	**2.96**	**2.79**	**2.66**	**2.56**	**2.47**	**2.03**	**1.38**
∞	3.84	3.00	2.60	2.37	2.21	2.10	2.01	1.94	1.88	1.83	1.57	1.00
	6.63	**4.61**	**3.78**	**3.32**	**3.02**	**2.80**	**2.64**	**2.51**	**2.41**	**2.32**	**1.88**	**1.00**

Source: The entries in this table were computed by the author.

TABLE C.4 ● ´ The Studentized Range Statistic (q)

The critical values for q correspond to alpha = .05 (lightface type) and alpha = .01 (boldface type).

df_E	Range								
	2	**3**	**4**	**5**	**6**	**7**	**8**	**9**	**10**
6	3.46	4.34	4.90	5.30	5.63	5.91	6.13	6.32	6.50
	5.24	**6.32**	**7.02**	**7.55**	**7.98**	**8.33**	**8.62**	**8.87**	**9.10**
7	3.34	4.17	4.68	5.06	5.36	5.60	5.82	5.99	6.15
	4.95	**5.91**	**6.54**	**7.00**	**7.38**	**7.69**	**7.94**	**8.17**	**8.38**
8	3.26	4.05	4.53	4.89	5.17	5.41	5.60	5.78	5.93
	4.75	**5.64**	**6.21**	**6.63**	**6.97**	**7.26**	**7.47**	**7.70**	**7.89**
9	3.20	3.95	4.42	4.76	5.03	5.24	5.43	5.60	5.74
	4.60	**5.43**	**5.95**	**6.34**	**6.67**	**6.91**	**7.13**	**7.33**	**7.50**
10	3.15	3.88	4.33	4.66	4.92	5.12	5.30	5.46	5.60
	4.48	**5.27**	**5.77**	**6.14**	**6.43**	**6.67**	**6.89**	**7.06**	**7.22**
11	3.11	3.82	4.27	4.59	4.83	5.03	5.21	5.36	5.49
	4.38	**5.16**	**5.63**	**5.98**	**6.25**	**6.48**	**6.69**	**6.85**	**7.01**
12	3.08	3.78	4.20	4.51	4.75	4.96	5.12	5.26	5.39
	4.32	**5.05**	**5.50**	**5.84**	**6.10**	**6.32**	**6.52**	**6.67**	**6.82**
13	3.05	3.73	4.15	4.47	4.69	4.88	5.06	5.21	5.33
	4.26	**4.97**	**5.41**	**5.74**	**5.98**	**6.19**	**6.39**	**6.53**	**6.68**
14	3.03	3.70	4.11	4.41	4.64	4.83	4.99	5.13	5.25
	4.21	**4.90**	**5.33**	**5.64**	**5.88**	**6.10**	**6.28**	**6.41**	**6.56**
15	3.01	3.68	4.09	4.38	4.59	4.79	4.95	5.09	5.21
	4.17	**4.84**	**5.26**	**5.56**	**5.80**	**6.01**	**6.18**	**6.31**	**6.46**
16	2.99	3.65	4.05	4.33	4.56	4.74	4.89	5.03	5.15
	4.13	**4.79**	**5.19**	**5.50**	**5.72**	**5.94**	**6.10**	**6.23**	**6.37**
17	2.98	3.63	4.02	4.30	4.52	4.70	4.85	4.99	5.11
	4.10	**4.75**	**5.15**	**5.44**	**5.66**	**5.86**	**6.02**	**6.14**	**6.28**
18	2.97	3.62	4.01	4.29	4.49	4.68	4.84	4.97	5.08
	4.07	**4.71**	**5.10**	**5.39**	**5.60**	**5.80**	**5.95**	**6.08**	**6.21**
19	2.96	3.59	3.98	4.26	4.47	4.65	4.80	4.93	5.04
	4.05	**4.68**	**5.05**	**5.35**	**5.56**	**5.75**	**5.91**	**6.03**	**6.15**

df_E	Range								
	2	3	4	5	6	7	8	9	10
20	2.95	3.58	3.96	4.24	4.45	4.63	4.78	4.91	5.01
	4.02	**4.64**	**5.02**	**5.31**	**5.51**	**5.71**	**5.86**	**5.98**	**6.09**
22	2.94	3.55	3.93	4.20	4.41	4.58	4.72	4.85	4.96
	3.99	**4.59**	**4.96**	**5.27**	**5.44**	**5.62**	**5.76**	**5.87**	**6.00**
24	2.92	3.53	3.91	4.17	4.37	4.54	4.69	4.81	4.92
	3.96	**4.55**	**4.92**	**5.17**	**5.37**	**5.55**	**5.70**	**5.81**	**5.93**
26	2.91	3.52	3.89	4.15	4.36	4.53	4.67	4.79	4.90
	3.94	**4.51**	**4.87**	**5.13**	**5.33**	**5.49**	**5.63**	**5.74**	**5.86**
28	2.90	3.50	3.87	4.12	4.33	4.49	4.63	4.75	4.86
	3.91	**4.48**	**4.83**	**5.09**	**5.28**	**5.45**	**5.58**	**5.69**	**5.81**
30	2.89	3.49	3.85	4.10	4.30	4.47	0.60	4.73	4.84
	3.89	**4.45**	**4.80**	**5.05**	**5.24**	**5.40**	**5.54**	**5.64**	**5.76**
40	2.86	3.45	3.79	4.05	4.23	4.39	4.52	4.65	4.73
	3.82	**4.37**	**4.70**	**4.93**	**5.11**	**5.26**	**5.39**	**5.49**	**5.60**
60	2.83	3.41	3.75	3.98	4.16	4.31	4.44	4.56	4.65
	3.76	**4.28**	**4.60**	**4.82**	**4.99**	**5.13**	**5.25**	**5.36**	**5.45**
100	2.81	3.36	3.70	3.93	4.11	4.26	4.39	4.50	4.59
	3.72	**4.22**	**4.52**	**4.74**	**4.90**	**5.04**	**5.15**	**5.23**	**5.34**
∞	2.77	3.31	3.63	3.86	4.03	4.17	4.28	4.39	4.47
	3.64	**4.12**	**4.40**	**4.60**	**4.76**	**4.88**	**4.99**	**5.08**	**5.16**

Source: The entries in this table were computed by the author.

TABLE C.5 ● Critical Values for the Pearson Correlation*

*To be significant, the sample correlation, r, must be greater than or equal to the critical value in the table.

	Level of Significance for One-Tailed Test			
	.05	.025	.01	.005
	Level of Significance for Two-Tailed Test			
$df = n - 2$	.10	.05	.02	.01
1	.988	.997	.9995	.99999
2	.900	.950	.980	.990
3	.805	.878	.934	.959
4	.729	.811	.882	.917
5	.669	.754	.833	.874
6	.622	.707	.789	.834
7	.582	.666	.750	.798
8	.549	.632	.716	.765
9	.521	.602	.685	.735
10	.497	.576	.658	.708
11	.476	.553	.634	.684
12	.458	.532	.612	.661
13	.441	.514	.592	.641
14	.426	.497	.574	.623
15	.412	.482	.558	.606
16	.400	.468	.542	.590
17	.389	.456	.528	.575
18	.378	.444	.516	.561
19	.369	.433	.503	.549
20	.360	.423	.492	.537
21	.352	.413	.482	.526
22	.344	.404	.472	.515
23	.337	.396	.462	.505

df = n − 2	Level of Significance for One-Tailed Test			
	.05	.025	.01	.005
	Level of Significance for Two-Tailed Test			
	.10	.05	.02	.01
24	.330	.388	.453	.496
25	.323	.381	.445	.487
26	.317	.374	.437	.479
27	.311	.367	.430	.471
28	.306	.361	.423	.463
29	.301	.355	.416	.456
30	.296	.349	.409	.449
35	.275	.325	.381	.418
40	.257	.304	.358	.393
45	.243	.288	.338	.372
50	.231	.273	.322	.354
60	.211	.250	.295	.325
70	.195	.232	.274	.302
80	.183	.217	.256	.283
90	.173	.205	.242	.267
100	.164	.195	.230	.254

Source: Table VI of Fisher, R. A., & Yates, F. (1974). *Statistical tables for biological, agricultural and medical research* (6th ed.). London, England: Longman Group Ltd., 1974 (previously published by Oliver and Boyd Ltd., Edinburgh). Adapted and reprinted with permission of Addison Wesley Longman.

TABLE C.6 ● Critical Values for the Spearman Correlation*

*To be significant, the sample correlation, r, must be greater than or equal to the critical value in the table.

	Level of Significance for One-Tailed Test			
	.05	.025	.01	.005
	Level of Significance for Two-Tailed Test			
n	.10	.05	.02	.01
4	1.000			
5	.900	1.000	1.000	
6	.829	.886	.943	1.000
7	.714	.786	.893	.929
8	.643	.738	.833	.881
9	.600	.700	.783	.833
10	.564	.648	.745	.794
11	.536	.618	.709	.755
12	.503	.587	.671	.727
13	.484	.560	.648	.703
14	.464	.538	.622	.675
15	.443	.521	.604	.654
16	.429	.503	.582	.635
17	.414	.485	.566	.615
18	.401	.472	.550	.600
19	.391	.460	.535	.584
20	.380	.447	.520	.570
21	.370	.435	.508	.556
22	.361	.425	.496	.544
23	.353	.415	.486	.532
24	.344	.406	.476	.521
25	.337	.398	.466	.511
26	.331	.390	.457	.501

	Level of Significance for One-Tailed Test			
	.05	.025	.01	.005
	Level of Significance for Two-Tailed Test			
n	.10	.05	.02	.01
27	.324	.382	.448	.491
28	.317	.375	.440	.483
29	.312	.368	.433	.475
30	.306	.362	.425	.467
35	.283	.335	.394	.433
40	.264	.313	.368	.405
45	.248	.294	.347	.382
50	.235	.279	.329	.363
60	.214	.255	.300	.331
70	.190	.235	.278	.307
80	.185	.220	.260	.287
90	.174	.207	.245	.271
100	.165	.197	.233	.257

Sources: Reprinted with permission from the *Journal of the American Statistical Association.* Copyright 1972 by the American Statistical Association. All rights reserved. Zar, J. H. (1972). Significance testing of the Spearman rank correlation coefficient. *Journal of the American Statistical Association, 67,* 578.

• Glossary •

This glossary includes all of the key terms that were defined in each learning unit. The number in parentheses following each definition indicates the learning unit or appendix where the term was defined.

Alpha level (α): the level of significance or criterion for a hypothesis test. It is the largest probability of committing a Type I error that researchers will allow and still decide to reject the null hypothesis (7).

Alternative hypothesis (H₁): a statement that directly contradicts a null hypothesis by stating that the actual value of a population parameter, such as the mean, is less than, greater than, or not equal to the value stated in the null hypothesis (7).

Analysis of regression: a statistical procedure used to test hypotheses for one or more predictor variables to determine whether the regression equation for a sample of data points can be used to predict values of the criterion variable (Y) given values of the predictor variable (X) in the population; also called *regression analysis* (13).

Analysis of variance (ANOVA): a statistical procedure used to test hypotheses for one or more factors concerning the variance among two or more group means ($k \geq 2$), where the variance in one or more populations is unknown (10).

Arithmetic mean: see *mean* (1).

Array function: an Excel function that performs complex calculations based on information from a range of cells (3).

Average: see *mean* (1).

Bell-shaped distribution: see *normal distribution* (4).

Beta (β) error: see *Type II error* (7).

Between-groups variation: the variation attributed to mean differences between groups (10).

Between-persons variation: the variation attributed to differences between person means averaged across groups. Because the same participants are observed across groups using a within-subjects design, this source of variation is removed or omitted from the error term in the denominator of the test statistic for within-subjects designs ANOVA (10).

Between-subjects factor: a type of factor in which different participants are observed at each level of the factor (11).

Bin: a term in the Excel array function FREQUENCY that is equivalent to interval width (3).

Binomial distribution: see *binomial probability distribution* (4).

Binomial probability distribution: the distribution of probabilities for each outcome of a bivariate random variable (4).

Bivariate random variable: any random variable with only two possible outcomes; also called a *dichotomous variable* (4).

Cell: the combination of one level from each factor, as represented in a cross tabulation. Each cell is a group in a research study (11).

Central limit theorem: a theorem that stats that regardless of the distribution of scores in a population, the sampling distribution of sample means selected at random from that population will approach the shape of a normal distribution, as the number of samples in the sampling distribution increases; note that as sample size increases, the number of samples in a sampling distribution also increases.

Central tendency: statistical measures for locating a single score that is most representative or descriptive of scores near the center of a distribution. Examples include the mean, the median, and the mode (1).

Chebyshev's theorem: defines the percentage of data from *any* distribution that will be contained within any number of standard deviations from the mean, where $SD > 1$ (A5).

Coefficient of determination: a formula that is mathematically equivalent to eta squared and is used to measure the proportion of variance of one factor (Y)

that can be explained by known values of a second factor (*X*) (12).

Complete factorial design: a research design in which each level of one factor is combined or crossed with each level of the other factor, with participants observed in each cell or combination of levels (11).

Confidence interval: the interval or range of possible values within which an unknown population parameter is likely to be contained (7).

Confound variable: an unanticipated variable not accounted for in a research study that could be causing or associated with observed changes in one or more measured variables; also called a *third variable* (12).

Correlation: a statistical procedure used to describe the strength and direction of the linear relationship between two factors (12).

Correlation coefficient (r): used to measure the strength and direction of the linear relationship, or correlation, between two factors. The value of *r* ranges from –1.0 to +1.0 (12).

Covariance: a measure for the extent to which the values of two factors (*X* and *Y*) vary together. The closer data points fall to the regression line, the more that values of two factors vary together (12).

Criterion variable: the variable with unknown values that can be predicted or estimated, given known values of the predictor variable; also called the *to-be-predicted variable* (13).

Data points: the *x*- and *y*-coordinates for each plot in a scatter plot (12).

Deciles: measures that divide a set of data into 10 equal parts (2).

Degrees of freedom: the number of scores in a sample that are free to vary. All scores except one are free to vary in a sample: (*n* – 1) (2, 9).

Degrees of freedom between groups: the degrees of freedom associated with the variance for the group means in the numerator of the test statistic. They are equal to the number of groups (*k*) minus 1; also called *degrees of freedom numerator* (10).

Degrees of freedom between persons: the degrees of freedom associated with the variance of person means averaged across groups. They are equal to the number of participants (*n*) minus 1 (10).

Degrees of freedom denominator: see *degrees of freedom error* (10).

Degrees of freedom error: the degrees of freedom associated with the error variance in the denominator. They are equal to the total sample size (*N*) minus the number of groups; also called *degrees of freedom denominator* or *degrees of freedom within groups* (10).

Degrees of freedom numerator: see *degrees of freedom between groups* (10).

Degrees of freedom within groups: see *degrees of freedom error* (10).

Dichotomous variable: see *bivariate random variable* (4).

Difference score: a score or value obtained by subtracting one score from another (9).

Directional tests: hypothesis tests where the alternative hypothesis is stated as "greater than" (>) or "less than" (<) a value stated in the null hypothesis. Hence, the researcher is interested in a specific alternative to the null hypothesis; also called *one-tailed tests* (7).

Effect: a difference or disparity between what is thought to be true in a population and what is observed in a sample. In hypothesis testing, an effect is not significant when we retain the null hypothesis; an effect is significant when we reject the null hypothesis (7, 8).

Effect size: a statistical measure of the size of an observed effect in a population, which allows researchers to describe how far scores shifted in the population, or the percentage of variance that can be explained by a given variable (7, 8).

Empirical rule: states that for data that are normally distributed, at least 99.7% of data lie within 3 *SD* of the mean, at least 95% of data lie within 2 *SD* of the mean, and at least 68% of data lie within 1 *SD* of the mean (4, A4).

Error variation: see *within-groups variation* (10).

Estimated Cohen's d: a measure for effect size in terms of the number of standard deviations that mean scores have shifted above or below the population mean stated by the null hypothesis. The larger the value for *d*, the larger the effect in the population (9).

Estimated standard error: an estimate of the standard deviation of a sampling distribution of sample means selected from a population with an unknown variance. It is an estimate of the standard error or the standard distance that sample means can be expected to deviate from the value of the population mean stated in the null hypothesis (9).

Estimated standard error for the difference: an estimate of the standard deviation of a sampling distribution of mean differences between two sample means. It is an estimate of the standard error or the standard distance that mean differences can be expected to deviate from the mean difference stated in the null hypothesis (9).

Estimated standard error for the difference scores: an estimate of the standard deviation of a sampling distribution of mean difference scores. It is an estimate of the standard error or standard distance that mean difference scores can be expected to deviate from the mean difference score stated in the null hypothesis (9).

Estimation: a statistical procedure in which a sample statistic is used to estimate the value of an unknown population parameter. Two types of estimation are point estimation and interval estimation (7).

Expected value: see *mathematical expectation* (A6).

Experimentwise alpha: the aggregated alpha level, or probability of committing a Type I error for all tests, when multiple tests are conducted on the same data (10).

F distribution: a positively skewed distribution derived from a sampling distribution of F ratios (10).

Factorial design: a research design in which participants are observed across the combination of levels of two or more factors (11).

Fixed event: any event in which the outcome observed is always the same (4).

Fractiles: measures that divide a set of data into two or more equal parts; examples include the median, deciles, quartiles, and percentiles (2).

Gaussian distribution: see *normal distribution* (4).

Grouped data: counts of frequencies in defined groups of scores or intervals of scores (3).

Homoscedasticity: the assumption that there is an equal ("homo") variance or scatter ("scedasticity") of data points dispersed along the regression line (12).

Hypothesis: a statement or proposed explanation for an observation, a phenomenon, or a scientific problem that can be tested using the research method. A hypothesis is often a statement about the value for a parameter in a population (7).

Hypothesis testing: a method for testing a claim or hypothesis about a parameter in a population, using data measured in a sample. In this method, we test a hypothesis by determining the likelihood that a sample statistic would be selected if the hypothesis regarding the population parameter were true. Also called *significance testing* (7).

Interaction: a source of variation associated with the variance of group means across the combination of levels of two factors. It is a measure of how cell means at each level of one factor change across the levels of a second factor (11).

Interquartile range (IQR): the range of values between the upper (Q_3) and lower (Q_1) quartiles of a data set (2).

Interval: a discrete range of values within which the frequency of a subset of scores is contained (3).

Interval estimate: a statistical procedure in which a sample of data is used to find the interval or range of possible values within which a population parameter is likely to be contained (7).

Interval scales: measurements that have no true zero and are distributed in equal units. Examples include Likert scores, temperature, latitude, and longitude (A2).

Interval width: the range of values contained in each interval of a grouped frequency distribution; also called *class width* (3).

Known variable: see *predictor variable* (13).

Kurtosis: describes the frequency of scores that fall in the tails of a distribution; distributions with large kurtosis include data well beyond 3 SD in a normal distribution (4).

Law of large numbers: a theorem or a rule that increasing the number of observations or the sample size in a study will decrease the standard error. Hence, larger samples are associated with closer estimates of the population mean on average (6).

Leptokurtic distribution: a distribution that has very few extreme scores in both tails (4).

Level of confidence: the probability or likelihood that an interval estimate will contain an unknown population parameter (7).

Level of significance: refers to criterion of judgment upon which a decision is made regarding the value stated in a null hypothesis. The criterion is based on the probability of obtaining a statistic measured in a sample if the value stated in the null hypothesis were true. Also called *significance level* (7).

Levels of the factor: symbolized as *k,* the number of groups or different ways in which an independent or quasi-independent variable is observed; also called the *levels of the independent variable* for groups in experimental research designs (10).

Linear regression: a statistical procedure used to determine the equation of a regression line to a set of data points and the extent to which the regression equation can be used to predict values of one factor, given known values of a second factor in a population; also called *regression* (13).

Linearity: the assumption that the best way to describe a pattern of data is using a straight line (12).

Lower quartile: the median value of the lower half of a data set at the 25th percentile of a distribution (2).

Main effect: a source of variation associated with mean differences across the levels of a single factor (11).

Mathematical expectation: the mean, or average expected outcome, for a given random variable. The expected outcome for a random variable is the sum of the products of each random outcome multiplied by the probability of its occurrence; also called an *expected value* (A6).

Mean: the sum of a set of scores in a distribution, divided by the total number of scores summed; also called an *arithmetic mean* or *average* (1).

Mean square between groups: the variance attributed to differences between group means. It is the numerator of the test statistic for an ANOVA (10).

Mean square between persons: the variance attributed to mean differences in scores between persons (10).

Mean square error: the variance attributed to differences within each group. It is the denominator of the test statistic for an ANOVA; also called *mean square within groups* (10).

Mean square within groups: see *mean square error* (10).

Median: the middle value in a distribution of data listed in numeric order (1,2).

Median quartile: the median value of a data set at the 50th percentile of a distribution (2).

Method of least squares: a statistical procedure used to compute the slope (*b*) and *y*-intercept (*a*) of the best-fitting straight line to a set of data points (13).

Mode: the value in a data set that occurs most often or most frequently (1).

Negative correlation: a negative value for *r*, which indicates that the values of two factors change in different directions, meaning that as the values of one factor increase, the values of the second factor decrease; a correlation is negative when $-1.0 \leq r < 0$ (12).

Negatively skewed distribution: a distribution of scores that includes scores that are substantially smaller (toward the left tail in a graph) than most other scores (4, A1).

Nominal scales: measurements in which a number is assigned to represent something or someone (A2).

Nondirectional tests: hypothesis tests in which the alternative hypothesis is stated as *not equal to* (≠) a value stated in the null hypothesis. Hence, the researcher is interested in any alternative to the null hypothesis; also called *two-tailed tests* (7).

Normal distribution: a theoretical distribution with data that are symmetrically distributed around the mean, median, and mode; also called a *symmetrical, Gaussian,* or *bell-shaped distribution* (4, A1).

Null hypothesis (H$_0$): a statement about a population parameter, such as the population mean, that is assumed to be true (7).

One-sample *t* test: a statistical procedure used to compare a mean value measured in a sample to a known value in the population. It is specifically used to test hypotheses concerning the mean in a single population with an unknown variance (9).

One-tailed tests: see *directional tests* (7).

One-way between-subjects ANOVA: a statistical procedure used to test hypotheses for one factor with two or more levels concerning the variance among the group means. This test is used when different participants are observed at each level of a factor and the variance in any one population is unknown (10).

One-way repeated-measures ANOVA: see *one-way within-subjects ANOVA* (10).

One-way within-subjects ANOVA: a statistical procedure used to test hypotheses for one factor with two or more levels concerning the variance among the group means. This test is used when the same participants are observed at each level of a factor and the variance in any one population is unknown (10).

Ordinal scales: measurements where values convey order or rank alone (A2).

Outcome space: see *sample space* (4).

Outliers: extreme scores that fall substantially above or below most of the scores in a particular data set (A3).

***p* value:** the probability of obtaining a sample outcome, given that the value stated in the null hypothesis is true. The *p* value for obtaining a sample outcome is compared to the level of significance or criterion for making a decision (7).

Pairwise comparison: a statistical comparison for the difference between two group means. A post hoc test evaluates all possible pairwise comparisons for an ANOVA with any number of groups (10).

Pearson correlation coefficient (*r*): a measure of the direction and strength of the linear relationship of two factors in which the data for both factors are measured on an interval or ratio scale of measurement; also called the *Pearson product-moment correlation coefficient* (12).

Pearson product-moment correlation coefficient: see *Pearson correlation coefficient (r)* (12).

Percentiles: measures that divide a set of data into 100 equal parts (2).

Platykurtic distribution: a distribution that has many extreme scores in both tails (4).

Point estimate: a statistical procedure that involves the use of a sample statistic to estimate a population parameter (7).

Pooled sample standard deviation: the combined sample standard deviation of two samples. It is computed by taking the square root of the pooled sample variance. This measure estimates the standard deviation for the difference between two population means (9).

Pooled sample variance: the mean sample variance of two samples. When the sample size is unequal, the variance in each group or sample is weighted by its respective degrees of freedom (9).

Population mean: the sum of a set of scores in a population, divided by the total number of scores summed (1).

Population standard deviation: a measure of variability for the average distance that scores in a population deviate from their mean. It is calculated by taking the square root of the population variance (2).

Population variance: a measure of variability for the average squared distance that scores in a population deviate from the mean. It is computed only when all scores in a given population are recorded (2).

Positive correlation: a positive value of *r* that indicates that the values of two factors change in the same direction: As the values of one factor increase, the values of the second factor also increase; as the values of one factor decrease, the values of the second factor also decrease; a correlation is positive when $0 < r \leq 1.0$ (12).

Positively skewed distribution: a distribution of scores that includes scores that are substantially larger (toward the right tail in a graph) than most other scores (4, A1).

Post hoc test: a statistical procedure computed following a significant ANOVA to determine which pair or pairs of group means significantly differ. These tests are necessary when $k > 2$ because multiple comparisons are needed. When $k = 2$, only one comparison is made because only one pair of group means can be compared (10).

Power: the probability of rejecting a false null hypothesis. Specifically, it is the probability that a randomly selected sample will show that the null hypothesis is false when the null hypothesis is in fact false (7, 8).

Predictor variable: the variable with values that are known and can be used to predict values of another variable; also called the *known variable* (13).

Probability: the frequency of times an outcome occurs divided by the total number of possible outcomes (4).

Proportion of variance: is a measure of effect size in terms of the proportion or percentage of variability in a dependent variable that can be explained or accounted for by a treatment (9).

Quartile deviation: see *semi-interquartile range* (2).

Quartiles: divide data evenly into four equal parts (2).

Random event: any event in which the outcomes observed can vary (4).

Range: the difference between the largest value (*L*) and smallest value (*S*) in a data set (2).

Ratio scales: measurements that have a true zero and are distributed in equal units (A2).

Real range: one more than the difference between the largest value and the smallest value in a data set (3).

Regression: see *linear regression* (13).

Regression analysis: see *analysis of regression* (13).

Regression line: the best-fitting straight line to a set of data points. A best-fitting line is the line that minimizes the distance that all data points fall from it (12).

Regression variation: the variance in *Y* that is related to or associated with changes in *X*. The closer that data points fall to the regression line, the larger the value of regression variation (13).

Related-samples *t* test: an inferential statistic used to test hypotheses concerning two related samples selected from populations in which the variance in one or both populations is unknown (9).

Relative frequency: a proportion from 0 to 1.0 that describes the portion of data in each interval (4).

Residual variation: the variance in *Y* that is not related to changes in *X*. This is the variance in *Y* that is left over or remaining. The farther that data points fall from the regression line, the larger the value of residual variation (13).

Restriction of range: a problem that arises when the range of data for one or both correlated factors in a sample is limited or restricted, compared to the range of data in the population from which the sample was selected (12).

Reverse causality: a problem that arises when the direction of causality between two factors can be in either direction (12).

Standard deviation, also called the **root mean square deviation:** is a measure of variability for the average distance that scores deviate from their mean. It is calculated by taking the square root of the variance.

Sample design: a specific plan or protocol for how individuals will be selected or sampled from a population of interest (6).

Sample mean: the sum of a set of scores in a sample, divided by the total number of scores summed (1).

Sample space: the total number of possible outcomes that can occur in a given random event; also called *outcome space* (4).

Sample standard deviation: a measure of variability for the average distance that scores in a sample deviate from their mean. It is calculated by taking the square root of the sample variance (2).

Sample variance: a measure of variability for the average squared distance that scores in a sample deviate from the mean. It is computed when only a portion or sample of data is measured in a population (2).

Sampling distribution: a distribution of all sample means or sample variances that could be obtained in samples of a given size from the same population (6).

Sampling error: the extent to which sample means selected from the same population differ from one another. This difference, which occurs by chance, is measured by the standard error of the mean (6).

Scales of measurement: identify how the properties of numbers can change with different uses. Four scales of measurement are nominal, ordinal, interval, and ratio (A2).

Scatter gram: see *scatter plot* (12).

Scatter plot: a graphical display of discrete data points (*x*, *y*) used to summarize the relationship between two variables; also called a *scatter gram* (12).

Semi-interquartile range (SIQR): a measure of half the distance between the upper quartile (Q_3) and lower quartile (Q_1) of a data set, and is computed by dividing the IQR in half; also called a *quartile deviation* (2).

Significance: a decision made concerning a value stated in the null hypothesis. When the null hypothesis is rejected, we reach significance. When the null hypothesis is retained, we fail to reach significance. Also called *statistical significance* (7).

Significance level: see *level of significance* (7).

Significance testing: see *hypothesis testing* (7).

Simple frequency distribution: a summary display for (i) the frequency of each individual score or category (ungrouped data) in a distribution or (ii) the frequency of scores falling within defined groups or intervals (grouped data) in a distribution (3).

Simple main effect tests: hypothesis tests used to analyze a significant interaction by comparing the mean differences or simple main effects of one factor at each level of a second factor (11).

Skewed distribution: a distribution of scores that includes scores that fall substantially above or below most other scores in a data set (4, A1).

Slope (b): a measure of the change in Y relative to the change in X. When X and Y change in the same direction, the slope is positive. When X and Y change in opposite directions, the slope is negative (13).

Source of variation: any variation that can be measured in a study (10).

Spearman rank-order correlation coefficient: a measure of the direction and strength of the linear relationship of two ranked factors on an ordinal scale of measurement; also called *Spearman's rho* (12).

Spearman's rho: see *Spearman rank-order correlation coefficient* (12).

Standard deviation: a measure of variability for the average distance that scores deviate from their mean. It is calculated by taking the square root of the variance; also called the *root mean square deviation* (2).

Standard error: see *standard error of the mean* (6).

Standard error of estimate: an estimate of the standard deviation or distance that a set of data points falls from the regression line. The standard error of estimate equals the square root of the mean square residual (13).

Standard error of the mean: the standard deviation of a sampling distribution of sample means. It is the standard error or distance that sample mean values deviate from the value of the population mean; also stated as *standard error* (6).

Standard normal distribution: a normal distribution with a mean equal to 0 and a standard deviation equal to 1. It is distributed in z score units along the x-axis; also called a z *distribution* (5).

Standard normal transformation: a formula that converts any normal distribution with any mean and any variance to a standard normal distribution with a mean equal to 0 and a standard deviation equal to 1; also called a z *transformation* (5).

Statistical significance: see *significance* (7).

Student's t: see t *distribution* (9).

Studentized range statistic: a statistic used to determine critical values for comparing pairs of means at a given range. This statistic is used in the formula to find the critical value for the Tukey's honestly significant difference (HSD) post hoc test (10).

Sum of products: the sum of squares for two factors, X and Y; also represented as SS_{XY}. SP is the numerator for the Pearson correlation formula. To compute SP, multiply the deviation of each X value by the deviation of each Y value (13).

Sum of squares: the sum of the squared deviations of scores from their mean. *SS* is the numerator in the variance formula (2).

Symmetrical distribution: see *normal distribution* (4).

t distribution: a normal-like distribution with greater variability in the tails than a normal distribution because the sample variance is substituted for the population variance to estimate the standard error in this distribution; also called *Student's t* (9).

t observed: see t *statistic* (9).

t obtained: see t *statistic* (9).

t statistic: an inferential statistic used to determine the number of standard deviations in a t distribution that a sample mean deviates from the mean value or mean difference stated in the null hypothesis. Also referred to as t *observed* or t *obtained* (9).

Test statistic: a mathematical formula that identifies how far or how many standard deviations a sample outcome is from the value stated in a null hypothesis. It allows researchers to determine the likelihood or probability of obtaining sample outcomes if the null hypothesis were true. The value of the test statistic is used to make a decision regarding a null hypothesis (7).

Testwise alpha: the alpha level, or probability of committing a Type I error, for each test or pairwise comparison made on the same data (10).

Third variable: see *confound variable* (12).

To-be-predicted variable: see *criterion variable* (13).

Treatment: any unique characteristic of a sample or any unique way that a researcher treats a sample in hypothesis testing (9).

Two-independent-sample t test: a statistical procedure used to compare the mean difference between two independent groups. This test is specifically used to test hypotheses concerning the difference between two population means, where the variance in one or both populations is unknown (9).

Two-tailed tests: see *nondirectional tests* (7).

Two-way ANOVA: a statistical procedure used to test hypotheses concerning the variance of groups created by combining the levels of two factors. This test is used when the variance in any one population is unknown (11).

Two-way between-subjects ANOVA: a statistical procedure used to test hypotheses concerning the combination of levels of two factors using the 2-between or between-subjects design (11).

Type I error: the probability of rejecting a null hypothesis that is actually true. Researchers directly control for the probability of committing this type of error by stating an alpha level (7).

Type II error: the probability of retaining a null hypothesis that is actually false. Also called *beta* (β) *error* (7).

Type III error: a type of error possible with one-tailed tests in which a decision would have been to reject the null hypothesis, but the researcher decides to retain the null hypothesis because the rejection region was located in the wrong tail. The "wrong tail" refers to the opposite tail from where a difference was observed and would have otherwise been significant (7).

Unbiased estimator: any sample statistic, such as a sample variance when we divide SS by $n - 1$, obtained from a randomly selected sample that equals the value of its respective population parameter, such as a population variance, on average (2, 6).

Ungrouped data: a set of scores or categories distributed individually, where the frequency for each individual score or category is counted (3).

Unit normal table: a type of probability distribution table displaying a list of z scores and the

corresponding probabilities (or proportions of area) associated with each z score listed (5).

Upper quartile: the median value of the upper half of a data set at the 75th percentile of a distribution (2).

Variability: a measure of the dispersion or spread of scores in a distribution. It ranges from 0 to +∞. Examples include the range, the variance, and the standard deviation (2).

Variance: the averaged squared distance that scores deviate from their mean (2).

Within-groups variation: the variation attributed to mean differences within each group. This source of variation cannot be attributed to or caused by having different groups and is therefore called error variation (10).

Within-subjects factor: a type of factor in which the same participants are observed across the levels of the factor (11).

y-intercept (a): the value of the criterion variable (Y) when the predictor variable (X) equals 0 (13).

z distribution: *see standard normal distribution* (5).

z score: a unit of measurement distributed along the x-axis of a standard normal distribution. The numerical value of a z score specifies the distance or the number of standard deviations that a value is above or below the mean (5).

z table: see *unit normal table* (5).

z transformation: *see standard normal transformation* (5).

• References •

American Psychological Association. (2010). *Publication Manual of the American Psychological Association* (6th ed). Washington, DC: American Psychological Association.

Baxter, L. C. (2016). Appetite changes in depression. *The American Journal of Psychiatry, 173*, 317–318. doi:10.1176/appi.ajp.2016.16010010

Bell, K. E., & Limber, J. E. (2010). Reading skill, textbook marking, and course performance. *Literacy Research and Instruction, 49*, 56–67. doi:10.1080/19388070802695879

Bonet, G., & Walters, B. R. (2015). High impact practices: Student engagement and retention. *The College Student, 15*, 224–235.

Cohen, J. (1988). *Statistical power analysis for the behavioral sciences*. Hillsdale, NJ: Erlbaum.

Cuijpers, P., Cristea, I. A., Weitz, E., Gentili, C., & Berking, M. (2016). The effects of cognitive and behavioural therapies for anxiety disorders on depression: A meta-analysis. *Psychological Medicine, 46*(16), 3451–3462. doi:10.1017/S0033291716002348

de Moivre, A. (1733, November 12). *Approximatio ad summam terminorum binomii (a+b)^n in seriem expansi*. London, UK: Author.

DeTienne, K. B., Agle, B. R., Phillips, J. C., & Ingerson, M.-C. (2012). The impact of moral stress compared to other stressors on employee fatigue, job satisfaction, and turnover: An empirical investigation. *Journal of Business Ethics, 110*, 377–391. doi:10.1007/s10551-011-1197-y

Di Lorenzo, P. M., & Youngentob, S. L. (2013). Taste and olfaction. In R. J. Nelson, S. J. Y. Mizumori, & I. B. Weiner (Eds.), *Handbook of psychology: Behavioral neuroscience* (Vol. 3, 2nd ed., pp. 272–305). New York, NY: Wiley.

Farrelly, M. C., Duke, J. C., Davis, K. C., Nonnemaker, J. M., Kamyab, K., Willett, J. G., & Juster, H. R. (2012). Promotion of smoking cessation with emotional and/or graphic antismoking advertising. *American Journal of Preventative Medicine, 43*, 475–482. doi:10.1016/j.amepre.2012.07.023

Fisher, R. A., & Yates, F. (1974). *Statistical tables for biological, agricultural and medical research* (6th ed.). London, UK: Longman.

Fisher-Thompson, D. (2017). Contributions of look duration and gaze shift patterns to infants' novelty preferences. *Infancy, 22*, 190-222. DOI: 10.1111/infa.12154

Freund, J. E. (2004). *Modern elementary statistics* (11th ed.). Upper Saddle River, NJ: Pearson Prentice-Hall.

Hagen, T., & Laeng, B. (2016). The change detection advantage for animals: An effect of ancestral priorities or progeny of experimental design? *i-Perception, 7*, 1–17. doi:10.1177/2041669516651366

Hammen, C., & Keenan-Miller, D. (2013). Mood disorders. In G. Stricker, T. A. Widiger, & I. B. Irving (Eds.), *Handbook of psychology: Clinical psychology* (Vol. 8, 2nd ed., pp.121–146). Hoboken, NJ: Wiley.

Hans, E., & Hiller, W. (2013). Effectiveness of and dropout from outpatient cognitive behavioral therapy for adult unipolar disorder: A meta-analysis of nonrandomized effectiveness studies. *Journal of Consulting and Clinical Psychology, 81*, 75–88. doi:10.1037/a0031080

Institute of Medicine (IOM). (2015). *Public health implications of raising the minimum age of legal access to tobacco products*. Washington, DC: National Academies Press.

Kruger, J., & Savitsky, K. (2006). *The persuasiveness of one- vs. two-tailed tests of significance: When weak results are preferred over strong* [Abstract]. Retrieved from http://ssrn.com/abstract=946199

Lee, S., Cappella, J. N., Lerman, C., & Strasser, A. A. (2013). Effects of smoking cues and argument strength of antismoking advertisements on former smokers' self-efficacy, attitude, and intention to refrain from smoking. *Nicotine & Tobacco Research, 15*, 527–533. doi:10.1093/ntr/nts171

Mediakix. (2016). *How much time do we spend on social media?* Retrieved from http://mediakix.com/2016/12/how-much-time-is-spent-on-social-media-lifetime/#gs.DImqxE4

Mennella, J. A., & Bobowski, N. K. (2015). The sweetness and bitterness of childhood: Insights from basic research on taste preferences. *Physiology & Behavior, 152* (Part B), 502–507. doi:10.1016/j.physbeh.2015.05.015

Morrell, K. (2016). Understanding and measuring employee turnover. In G. Saridakis & C. L. Cooper (Eds.), *Research handbook on employee turnover* (pp. 26–58). Northampton, MA: Edward Elgar.

New, J., Cosmides, L., & Tooby, J. (2007). Category-specific attention for animals reflects ancestral priorities, not expertise. *Proceedings of the National Academy of Sciences of the United States of America, 104,* 1598–1660. doi:10.1073/pnas.0703913104

New York State Department of Health. (2018, August). *Vital Statistics of New York State 2015.* Retrieved from https://www.health.ny.gov/statistics/vital_statistics/2015/

Ottenbacher, K. J. (1993). The interpretation of averages in health professions research. *Evaluation & the Health Professions, 16,* 333–341.

Pearson, K. (1924). Historical note on the origin of the normal curve of errors. *Biometrika, 16,* 402–404. doi:10.1093/biomet/16.3-4.402

Pew Research Center. (2018, March 1). *Social media use in 2018.* Retrieved from http://www.pewinternet.org/2018/03/01/social-media-use-in-2018/

Privitera, G. J. (2016). Health psychology. In C. McCarthy, M. DeLisi, A. Getzfeld, G. J. Privitera, C. Spence, J. Walker, . . . & C. Youssef (Eds.), *Introduction to applied behavioral science* (pp. 32–54). San Diego, CA: Bridgepoint Education.

Privitera, G. J., Mayeaux, D., Schey, R. L., & Lapp, H. E. (2013). Conditioned place preference deficits in adulthood following high fat and high sugar diet intake during pre- and periadolescence: A test of the specificity hypothesis. *Journal of Behavioral and Brain Science, 3,* 556–563. doi:10.4236/jbbs.2013.37057

Privitera, G. J., & Wallace, M. (2011). An assessment of liking for sugars using the estimated daily intake scale. *Appetite, 56,* 713–718. doi:10.1016/j.appet.2011.02.008

Sander, J. B., DeBoth, K., & Ollendick, T. H. (2016). Internalizing behaviors. In M. K. Holt & A. E. Grills (Eds.), *Critical issues in school-based mental health: Evidence-based research, practice, and interventions* (pp. 18–28). New York, NY: Routledge/Taylor & Francis.

Saridakis, G., & Cooper, C. L. (2016). *Research handbook on employee turnover.* Northampton, MA: Edward Elgar. doi:10.4337/978-1-78471-115-3

Sinacore, J. M., Chang, R. W., & Falconer, J. (1992). Seeing the forest despite the trees: The benefit of exploratory data analysis to program evaluation research. *Evaluation & The Health Professions, 15,* 131–146.

Stevens, S. S. (1946). On the theory of scales of measurement. *Science, 103,* 677–680.

Student. (1908). The probable error of a mean. *Biometrika, 6,* 1–25.

United States Census Bureau. (2016, September). *Income and Poverty in the United States: 2015.* Retrieved from https://www.census.gov/library/publications/2016/demo/p60-256.html

Weiten, W., Halpern, D. F., & Bernstein, D. A. (2012). A textbook case of textbook ethics. In E. R. Landrum & M. A. McCarthy (Eds.), *Teaching ethically: Challenges and opportunities* (pp. 43–54). Washington, DC: American Psychological Association.

• Index •

in normal distributions, 56 (figure), 57, 57 (figure)
pooled sample standard, 150
Standard error, 84
of the mean, 118
minimizing, 85–86, 86 (figure), 293–294, 294–295 (table)
reduced by computing difference scores, 293–294, 294–295 (table)
Standard error of the mean, 84
Standard normal distribution, 66–68 (figure), 66–69
Standard normal transformation, 67–68, 68 (figure)
Statistical tables
critical values for the *t* distribution, 317–318 (table)
unit normal table, 313–316 (table)
Statistics, every day role of, 4
Strength of correlations, 242–243, 244–245 (figure)
Student-Newman-Keuls (SNK) test, 183
Studentized range statistic, 322–323 (table)
Student's *t*, 129
Sum of squares (SS), 25–28

T distribution, 129
critical values for, 317–318 (table)
degrees of freedom and, 129–131, 130 (table)
Test statistic, 105–106
Testwise alpha, 182
Theoretical sampling, 79
Treatment, 137–138
True zero, 284
T statistic, 128
T tests
degrees of freedom for, 298
one-sample, 131–142, 143 (figure)
origins of, 128–131, 129 (figure), 130 (table)
related-samples, 155–163, 158 (figure), 163–164 (figure)
two-independent-sample, 143–154, 145 (table), 149 (figure), 153–155 (figure)
Tukey's HSD
one-way between-subjects ANOVA and, 181–185, 182 (figure)
one-way within-subjects ANOVA and, 198–199, 199 (figure)
Two-independent-sample *t* test
assumptions in, 143–144
Cohen's *d* for, 150
computed using Analysis TookPak, 153–154, 153–155 (figure)
confidence intervals for, 151–153

effect size for, 148–151, 149 (figure)
proportion of variance, 150–151
steps in, 144–148, 145 (table)
Two-tailed test, 109–110
Two-way ANOVA
introduction to factorial design in, 204–206, 205–206 (table)
structure and notation for, 205–206, 205–206 (table)
Two-way between-subjects ANOVA
assumptions in, 213–214
computed using the Analysis TookPak, 234–235, 235–236 (figure)
main effects and interactions in, 227–232, 228 (figure), 229 (table), 231 (figure)
measuring effect size in, with eta squared, 233, 234 (figure)
sources of variability and, 207–208, 207 (figure)
steps in, 214–227, 217–220 (figure), 222–224 (figure), 226 (figure)
testing interaction in, 210–213, 211–212 (figure)
testing main effects using, 209–210, 209–210 (table)
Type I error, 108
Type II error, 108
Type III error, 109–110

Unbiased estimator, 28, 81–82, 82 (table)
sample variance as, 94–95
Ungrouped data, 32
Unit normal table, 69–74, 70 (figure), 71 (table), 72–73 (figure), 313–316 (table)
Upper quartile, 19

Variability, 16–17
quartiles and interquartiles, 19–24, 22–23 (figure)
range, 17–19, 18 (figure)
sources of, 207–208, 207 (figure)
standard deviation, 28–30
two-way between-subjects ANOVA for describing, 207–213, 207 (figure), 209–212 (figure)
variance, 24–28, 24 (table), 27 (figure)
Variables
confound, 253
linear regression, 262–263
Variance, 24–28, 24 (table), 27 (figure)
minimum, sample mean, 84–85
pooled sample, 147, 292–293, 293 (table)